Keeping the People's Liberties

Keeping the People's Liberties

Legislators, Citizens, and Judges as Guardians of Rights

John J. Dinan

 University Press of Kansas

Published by the University Press of Kansas (Lawrence, Kansas 66049), which was organized by the Kansas Board of Regents and is operated and funded by Emporia State University, Fort Hays State University, Kansas State University, Pittsburg State University, the
University of Kansas, and Wichita State University.

Library of Congress Cataloging-in-Publication Data

Dinan, John J.
    Keeping the people's liberties : legislators, citizens, and judges
as guardians of rights / John Dinan.
       p.   cm.
    Includes bibliographical references and index.
    ISBN 0-7006-0905-9 (cloth : alk. paper)
    1. Civil rights—United States. 2. Civil rights—United States—
States. 3. Judicial power—United States—States. 4. Legislative
power—United States—States. 5. Constituent power—United States—
States. 6. United States—Politics and government. I. Title.
KF4749.D55   1998
342.73'085—dc21   98-13639

British Library Cataloguing in Publication Data is available.

Printed in the United States of America

10 9 8 7 6 5 4 3 2 1

The paper used in this publication meets the minimum requirements of the American
National Standard for Permanence of Paper for Printed Library Materials Z39.48-1984.

For my parents

Contents

Preface

Of all the tasks entrusted to American political institutions, none is more fundamental than securing individual rights. The individuals who founded American state and national governments were concerned above all with ensuring that these institutions would safeguard the people's liberties. The first step that several states took in 1776, prior even to separating from Great Britain, was to draft documents that enumerated the rights to which all individuals were entitled. When it came time to announce a formal separation, the signers of the Declaration of Independence made it clear that governments are instituted to secure rights and that they are legitimate only insofar as they do so effectively. Similarly, those who drafted the U.S. Constitution stated in the preamble that one of the primary purposes of establishing a national government was to secure the blessings of liberty. Even after these institutions had begun operating, the founding generation continued to reflect on a question posed most explicitly by James Madison in an essay entitled "Who Are the Best Keepers of the People's Liberties?"[1]

One might therefore expect that the centrality of rights in the American regime would inspire ongoing studies of the institutional arrangements under which rights are best protected. In fact, this question is rarely raised or addressed in an empirical and systematic manner. Although historians have been concerned with determining the original understanding of particular rights, and law professors continue to analyze judicial interpretations of these rights, political scientists have given remarkably little attention to the question of which institutions are the best keepers of the people's liberties.

The conventional understanding is that this question has already been answered. It is considered to have been addressed at the time of the founding, when the creation of an independent judiciary, the ratification of a bill of rights, and the establishment of judicial review demonstrated that rights were intended to be secured through judicial interpretation of bills of rights. It is thought to have been settled, furthermore, by the practice of the last forty years, during which time a number of important liberties have been secured through these institutions. It is thought to have been resolved, finally, by recent discussions among the nation's leading law faculty, who are nearly unanimous in holding that rights are best secured in this manner.

In fact, in the current era, as Robert Nagel has written, it is "difficult for many, whether in or out of the academy, even to imagine any alternative" to judicial review as a means of securing rights, much less to evaluate the effectiveness of any other institutional arrangements.[2] It has even come to the point that this view has become an orthodoxy that is accepted as an article of faith rather than as the product of systematic study. Ronald Dworkin, for instance, argues in *Law's Empire* that "The United States is a more just society than it would have been had its constitutional rights been left to the conscience of majoritarian institutions." He then admits, "I offer no argument for this flat claim; a further book would be necessary to do so."[3] Likewise, in his book *Judicial Review and the National Political Process,* Jesse Choper concludes that "the experience of history strongly suggests that vesting the majority with the ultimate power of judgment, although far from being calamitous, would not sufficiently protect minority rights." But then he acknowledges: "In advancing this conclusion, it must be admitted that the data have not been scientifically tested in that the American experience has not been compared to what would have occurred in the absence of judicial review. In the nature of things, there is no way to conduct such a controlled inquiry."[4]

It is my contention, however, that there is indeed a way to conduct such an inquiry, and that this might consist of a historical investigation into the manner in which rights have been protected in the American polity. The fundamental questions to be answered are the following. First, how have rights been protected at various times in American history? Which institutions have been viewed as most capable of protecting rights at any given time; what have been the role and behavior of legislators, judges, and citizens; and what have been the various mechanisms by which rights have been secured? Second, to what extent have each of these institutions been effective in securing rights? How well have the various institutions prevented violations of rights, how well have they provided for the extension of rights in response to changing circumstances, and how well have they provided for the recognition of rights that were only discovered in the course of American history?

Keeping the People's Liberties is an account of this inquiry. I have chosen to examine the extent to which rights have been protected in state institutions. The states, after all, were primarily responsible for securing rights for the greater part of American history, and they continue to be the site of deliberations over many rights. They also permit a consideration of a variety of institutional arrangements, in that they have an extensive tradition of constitutional amendment and revision, as well as the only experience with direct democratic institutions.

Because it is neither feasible nor desirable to analyze the records of all fifty states, and because it would be inappropriate to generalize from the experience of one case, I have chosen to examine four states: Massachusetts, Michigan, Oregon, and Virginia. These states are sufficiently representative of the American polity, in that each has served as a beacon in legislative, popular, judicial, or constitutional matters. They are also sufficiently diverse—on the basis of geography, political culture, and institutional design—to permit distinctions to be drawn when appropriate.

This inquiry into these states' legislative statutes, judicial decisions, convention debates, and initiative records between 1776 and 1990 has led me to identify three principal regimes of rights protection and to conclude that in two of these regimes, which encompass the greater part of American history, rights were not protected primarily through judicial enforcement of bills of rights.[5] During a republican regime, which had its origins in the initial state constitutions and predominated throughout the nineteenth century, rights were secured primarily through representative institutions and the political process, particularly through the passage of legislative statutes. In the first two decades of the twentieth century, a populist regime was introduced through a series of constitutional amendments and revisions. The ideal institutions of rights protection during this period were the initiative and the referendum, which were thought to provide the best expression of the views of the collective citizenry. Not until the middle of the twentieth century can we identify the emergence of a judicialist regime, which was instituted primarily through changes in the realm of thought and which holds that rights are best protected through judicial enforcement of bills of rights.

The overriding purpose of this investigation is not merely to identify these various institutional arrangements but to evaluate their capacity to secure rights. That is, by examining particular eras in which certain institutions were primarily responsible for protecting rights, we can gain some empirical knowledge about the general tendencies of these institutions. Contrary to the conventional understanding that courts are the sole institutions capable of keeping the people's liberties, it turns out that legislators, citizens, and judges are each capable of securing particular rights in certain situations. The challenge is to identify these rights and to define these circumstances and, in the process, to further our knowledge of who are the best keepers of the people's liberties.

This book began as a dissertation that was completed at the University of Virginia under the supervision of Martha Derthick and James Ceaser. I am grateful for their support and guidance both during this project and throughout the course of my studies. I have learned a great deal from each of them. I would also like to express my thanks to Henry Abraham and A. E. Dick Howard for serving as readers of the dissertation and to Steven Rhoads, Larry Sabato, and Kenneth Thompson for their support during my time in Charlottesville.

This book could not have been completed without financial assistance from a number of institutions. The Lynde and Harry Bradley Foundation, the Department of Government and Foreign Affairs at the University of Virginia, the Dexter Whitehead Fellowship, and the Shari Gayle Richman Fellowship provided support during the course of my research. The Wake Forest Graduate School and the White Burkett Miller Center of Public Affairs graciously supported the revision of the manuscript.

I am also indebted to Robert Nagel and Eben Moglen for reading the manuscript and suggesting ways that it could be strengthened. Fred Woodward and his colleagues at the University Press of Kansas were supportive throughout the publication process and a pleasure to work with.

Finally, I would like to thank my mother, who was always encouraging; my father, who read and commented on this project, as he did so many others throughout my school years; my brothers and sisters, who were confident that I would one day finish; and Lori, who was unfailing in her support.

1

The Theory and Design
of Republican Institutions

The delegates to the federal constitutional convention took a number of steps to safeguard individual liberties. In the belief that rights would be most secure when powers were exercised by separate institutions, they created an energetic executive and an independent judiciary and then furnished each with the means to maintain its independence against legislative encroachments. To prevent the passage of legislation that would be injurious to rights, they divided the lawmaking power and created a bicameral congress. In order to provide multiple sources of security for individual rights, they established a federal system. Finally, in an effort to prevent factious majorities from working their ill effects, they created a government that extended over a large territory.

As important as these decisions were, the delegates were fully conscious that security for individual rights in the new republic would depend primarily on the design of the state governments. Connecticut delegate—and future U.S. Supreme Court Chief Justice—Oliver Ellsworth therefore "turn[ed] his eyes to the states for the preservation of his rights. It was from these alone that he could derive the greatest happiness he expects in life."[1] All told, eleven states drafted constitutions between 1776 and 1787, additional states ratified constitutions prior to their admission to the Union, and all these states revised their constitutions at regular intervals throughout the eighteenth and nineteenth centuries. It was in these conventions, and in particular through the drafting of declarations of rights and frames of government, that citizens resolved the most important questions about how rights would be protected.

It turns out that the understanding of rights protection that emerges from these conventions differs dramatically from our current understanding. In particular, these documents do not conform to the understanding—which was first expressed by U.S. Supreme Court Justice Robert Jackson and has come to represent the common view of the matter—that the "purpose of a Bill of Rights was to withdraw certain subjects from the vicissitudes of political controversy, to place them beyond the reach of majorities and officials, and to establish them as legal principles to be applied by the courts."[2] In fact, delegates to eighteenth- and nineteenth-century conventions were not convinced that their liberties were secured primarily through bills of rights. Rather, they were principally concerned with designing proper frames of government. Nor did they believe that the principal purpose of these documents was to empower courts of justice to place rights beyond the reach of representative institutions. Rather, their common aim in drafting bills of rights and frames of government was to ensure that rights would be secured by elected officials acting through representative institutions.

DECLARATIONS OF RIGHTS

The citizens of all but three states eventually ratified the first ten amendments to the federal constitution,[3] and a majority of the states prefaced their own constitutions with bills of rights.[4] Significantly, though, bills of rights were rarely viewed as an important, much less a primary, source of protection for liberties. Moreover, even when bills of rights were drafted and ratified, they were prized more for their capacity to educate citizens and public officials than for their ability to serve as legal principles to be enforced through judicial decisions.

This was certainly the case at the national level. The prospect of adding a bill of rights to the federal constitution did not even surface until late in the convention proceedings, and then the motion was easily dismissed. Nor did the absence of a bill of rights figure prominently in the explication and defense of the constitution that appeared in the *Federalist Papers*. It was not until the penultimate paper that Alexander Hamilton took up the question of whether to add a bill of rights, only to reject the idea on several grounds. Hamilton's objections, although they differed in several respects from those of other convention delegates such as James Madison and James Wilson, served to express the general mind-set of the founding generation toward bills of rights.[5] Hamilton argued that "The Constitution is itself, in every rational sense, and to every useful purpose, A BILL OF RIGHTS." Rights were primarily secured, he contended, through provisions that outlined the "political privileges of the citizens in the structure and administration of the government," as well as through "certain immunities and modes of proceeding." The ultimate security for rights, then, "whatever fine declarations may be inserted in any constitution respecting it, must altogether depend on the general spirit of the people and of the government."[6]

Even when a consensus emerged in favor of adopting a federal bill of rights, this came about not so much because these theoretical objections were overcome but because political and prudential concerns dictated its passage. The individuals who drafted and secured the ratification of the first ten constitutional amendments were guided primarily by an effort to blunt the pressure for a second convention, which they feared would revise the structure of the new government, as well as a desire to make good on promises made in the course of constitutional and congressional campaigns.[7] Neither the supporters nor the opponents of the Bill of Rights thought that its provisions would be of much practical utility in protecting liberty.[8] Rather, as Jack Rakove has argued, the federal Bill of Rights was thought to establish a set of standards that would either "enable the people to judge the behavior of their governors" or "enable republican citizens to govern themselves—to resist the impulses of interest and passion that were the root of factious behavior."[9]

Bills of rights were viewed in a similar manner by state constitutional conventions. A number of the delegates to these conventions shared Hamilton's view that such documents were unnecessary. John Biddle argued, during the course of the Michigan Convention of 1835, that declarations of rights were "mere lumber in the constitution. All the world acknowledge the principles, and they are familiar to all."[10] Similarly, several speakers at the Oregon Convention of 1857 pleaded with the assembled delegates to dispense with the traditional declaration of rights. Stephen Chadwick "denounced the whole bill of rights as a humbug,"[11] and George Williams thought that a bill of rights "was merely a Fourth of July oration" and "entirely unnecessary."[12]

Some state convention delegates went so far as to argue that bills of rights could actually prove harmful to the protection of liberty. They feared that citizens would be led, mistakenly, to think that their rights were primarily protected through written declarations, thereby distracting them from the work of designing governing institutions and obtaining popular support for rights, which provided the real source of security for liberty. Borrowing liberally from *The Federalist,* Thomas Church pleaded with the Michigan Convention of 1850 not to load down the document by adding a bill of rights:

> I submit to the Convention, as a mere matter of taste, whether a constitution, commencing with the simple announcement that "we, the people of the state of Michigan, in convention assembled, to secure the blessings of liberty to ourselves and posterity, have ordained and do ordain this constitution of government;"—proceeding then to a division of the powers of government; then to an article establishing, for instance, the legislative department, setting out its construction, its operation, its limits and restrictions; then an article establishing the judiciary . . . ; describing with simplicity and clearness, each part of our government, its powers, and closing in each by the necessary checks and balances—would not present to the world a better document, one in better taste, and of more manifest utility, than one lumbered with a bill of rights, confused, miscellaneous, and calculated only to mislead the inquirer, by its unfortunate location of those principles.[13]

Even when these arguments proved unpersuasive and states chose to approve bills of rights, as nearly all of them did by the mid-nineteenth century,[14] these declarations served purposes that are quite distinct from the current understanding.[15]

To be sure, these documents made clear that certain spheres of liberty could not be transgressed by any legitimate government. Thus the Virginia Declaration of Rights, which was drafted less than a month prior to the Declaration of Independence, proclaimed: "That all men are by nature equally free and independent, and have certain inherent rights, of which, when they enter into a state of society, they cannot, by any compact, deprive or divest their posterity; namely, the enjoyment of life and liberty, with the means of acquiring and possessing property, and pursuing and obtaining happiness and safety."[16]

It is true, also, that these documents secured explicit protection for a variety of rights. Religious liberty enjoyed pride of place in many of these declarations. Thus the Oregon Bill of Rights held, in typical fashion, that: "All men shall be secured in their natural right to worship Almighty God according to the dictates of their own consciences."[17] Freedom of expression was featured prominently as well. The Michigan Bill of Rights declared, for instance, that "Every person may freely speak, write, and publish his sentiments on all subjects, being responsible for the abuse of that right." Also universally esteemed were the various guarantees of a fair trial. The Michigan Bill of Rights therefore stated: "In all criminal prosecutions, the accused shall have the right to a speedy and public trial by an impartial jury of the vicinage; to be confronted with the witnesses against him; to have compulsory process for obtaining witnesses in his favor; to have the assistance of counsel for his defence." Furthermore: "No person should be held to answer for a criminal offence, unless on the presentment or indictment of a grand jury." In addition: "No person for the same offence shall be twice put in jeopardy of punishment."[18] Other guarantees included the right of individuals to be secure from arbitrary searches and seizures, to bear arms in the defense of themselves or the state, and to be compensated adequately for land taken for public use.

It is significant, however, that no single institution was considered to be more likely than another to violate these guarantees. Rather, these documents were directed equally to all governing officials. As Mr. Williams argued in the Oregon Convention of 1857:

> I am in favor of distributing what is usually contained in a bill of rights throughout the constitution, and not have it all contained in one separate article. The people of this country are sovereigns; they make the government, and this bill of rights is intended to contain restrictions upon that government. Now, these restrictions must be either of the legislative, the executive, or the judicial departments of the government. I propose that so much of any bill of rights as restricts the legislative department shall be put under that head, and so with the rest.[19]

It is true that some of the clauses in these state bills of rights were intended, according to Thomas Cooley, author of the most prominent late-nineteenth-century constitutional treatise, "for the express purpose of operating as a restriction upon legislative power."[20] The Michigan Bill of Rights held, for instance, that "No bill of attainder, *ex post facto* law, or law impairing the obligation of contracts, shall be passed."[21] Similarly, the Massachusetts Declaration of Rights stated that "the Legislature shall not make any law that shall subject any person to a capital or infamous punishment, excepting for the government of the army and navy, without trial by jury."[22]

For the most part, though, these documents contained principles that were "declared rather as guides to the legislative judgment than as marking an absolute limitation of power."[23] As Cooley argued, many of the provisions took the form of an "admonition addressed to the judgment and the conscience of all persons in authority, as well as of the people themselves."[24] Thus the Virginia Declaration of Rights held "That the freedom of the press is one of the great bulwarks of liberty, and can never be restrained but by despotic governments,"[25] and the Oregon Bill of Rights urged that "Laws for the punishment of crime shall be founded on the principles of reformation, and not of vindictive justice."[26]

To the extent, finally, that there was any expectation that particular individuals or institutions would be responsible for remedying violations of these principles, this role was entrusted primarily to the people and to their representatives.

To be sure, judges were expected to abide by and to uphold these declarations, but they were given no more responsibility in this area than were other citizens and public officials. Delaxon Smith's defense of a bill of rights in the Oregon Convention of 1857 came perhaps the closest to expressing the consensus view of eighteenth- and nineteenth-century constitution makers in this regard. Smith did not believe that a bill of rights contributed significantly to the protection of individual liberties. He argued: "It is manifest that it is not absolutely necessary, certainly for any purposes connected with the constitution, that its main provisions shall be preceded by a declaration of rights, and should we omit it we should but follow the example of several of the states." But, he concluded:

> Believing, as I do, that these declarations, thus solemnly made by a convention and ratified by the people, will always not only command universal respect, but the attention of courts, I desire that such a bill may precede or become a part of our constitution. It is a sort of manual—a sort of textbook of weighty matters, placed there *multum in parvo*, and the reference of the most common mind to the constitution . . . teaches that mind its rights under our government. They are there in monosyllables; and although individuals of common capacity, or of ordinary pursuits, may not be regarded as expounders of the constitutional law, yet the doctrine is contained, the declarations embodied in that bill of rights, and the meanest capacity can understand them.[27]

Thus the Massachusetts Declaration of Rights acknowledged the right of citizens "to assemble to consult upon the common good; give instructions to their representatives, and to request of the legislative body, by the way of addresses, petitions, or remonstrances, redress of the wrongs done them, and of the grievances they suffer."[28] Moreover, it held that "[t]he legislature ought frequently to assemble for the redress of grievances."[29] Likewise, the Oregon Bill of Rights stipulated that no law be passed, "the taking effect of which shall be made to depend upon any authority except as provided in this constitution."[30] It further provided that "[t]he operation of the laws shall never be suspended except by the authority of the legislative assembly."[31] The view underlying these and similarly framed provisions was that rights were most secure in representative institutions, and therefore it was important to ensure that these institutions were accessible and responsible to the public.

Citizens were expected to play a role in protecting rights in several ways. They were exhorted to maintain the virtues that were essential to sustaining republican institutions and to remain vigilant for violations of liberty. The Massachusetts Declaration of Rights, for instance, urged the people to recur frequently to "the fundamental principles of the constitution" and in their selection of officers to pay particular attention to "piety, justice, moderation, temperance, industry, and frugality."[32] Through these provisions, constitution makers communicated the view that the ultimate security for liberty lay to a certain extent outside the operation of formal institutions and rather with the people's virtue. The founders prized virtue in the sense of sacrifice for the sake of the public interest, as when the Massachusetts Declaration of Rights announced that "[g]overnment is instituted for the common good," and "not for the profit, honor, or private interest of any one man, family, or class of men."[33] They also counseled virtue in the sense of moral uprightness, as when the Virginia Declaration of Rights admonished the people that "it is the mutual duty of all to practice Christian forbearance, love, and charity towards each other."[34] The Massachusetts Declaration of Rights even went on to exhort the citizens to retain their virtue in a religious sense, noting that it was "the right as well as the duty of all men in society, publicly and at stated seasons, to worship the Supreme Being."[35]

It is apparent, then, that the principal utility of declarations of rights did not lie in their ability to serve as judicially enforced limitations on the legislature. Bills of rights were intended, rather, to impress upon governing officials the importance of upholding certain standards and guarantees and thereby prevent them from being violated. In the event that infringements of rights did occur, these declarations would provide the citizens with a principled basis on which they could seek to persuade their elected representatives to reestablish their rights on a proper foundation.

FRAMES OF GOVERNMENT

According to Chancellor James Kent, author of the most prominent early-nineteenth-century constitutional treatise, security for rights consisted "not so much in bills of rights, as in the skillful organization of the government, and its aptitude, by means of its structure and genius, and the spirit of the people which pervades it, to produce wise laws, and a just, firm, and intelligent administration of justice."[36] Accordingly, constitution makers were principally concerned with designing a proper frame of government, one that would separate the various governing powers and ensure their proper exercise.

The first challenge was to prevent governing institutions from infringing on rights, as when public officials might act without benefit of adequate reflection and discussion or under the influence of a temporary passion or delusion. Constitution makers were concerned, therefore, with allocating power to the appropriate public officials and ensuring that that power was exercised in a responsible manner.

It was thought that there existed, by nature, a legislative, executive, and judicial power, and that rights were most secure when each of these powers was placed in a suitable institution. In order to guarantee this functional division, each institution was endowed with the means to prevent encroachments on its central functions. The executive veto, which would eventually come to serve as a means by which the executive could promote reasonable deliberation, was originally intended to provide executives with the capacity to resist encroachments on their office, thereby safeguarding the executive power.[37] Likewise, judicial review, which would soon become a vehicle for superintending legislation, was initially viewed as a means by which judges could maintain their jurisdiction, tenure, or salary against any encroachment, and thereby retain the ability to perform their judging function.[38]

The next step was to ensure that these powers were exercised responsibly. The most important means of preventing abuses of power was to permit citizens to hold public officials accountable for their actions. Effective exercise of popular control required, at a minimum, that the people have an opportunity to select their representatives and to pass judgment on their performance at frequent intervals.

A popularly elected assembly could still betray the public trust in a variety of ways, however, and, especially as the nineteenth century progressed, constitution makers approved a number of provisions to guard against this possibility. For one thing, legislators might shield their deliberations from the public in such a way that it would be difficult for the people to hold them accountable for their actions. Therefore, it was provided that "[t]he doors of each house shall be open unless the public welfare requires secrecy."[39] Legislators who were intent on enacting oppressive statutes might also propose, debate, and enact bills with such haste that citizens would not have a chance to register their disagreement. As a result, constitutional provisions were also enacted to require that each bill be read on three separate days before it could be approved.

Publicity was not a sufficient requirement for the protection of rights, however, because legislators might still evade popular scrutiny by disguising the contents of offensive bills. One way of doing so was to enact omnibus bills that contained numerous provisions, many of which were unrelated to one another and some of which were not even described in the title. The idea was that even the most vigilant citizens would be unable to detect offensive provisions that were hidden in such bills. Accordingly, it was stipulated that "[e]very act shall embrace but one subject, and matters properly connected therewith, which subject shall be expressed in the title."[40] Some states went even further and held that "[n]o act shall ever be revised or amended by mere reference to its title; but the act revised or section amended shall be set forth and published at full length."[41] A final danger was that popular control could be frustrated by the use of technical language that could mask the actual intent and implications of statutes. Accordingly, bills were required to be "plainly worded, avoiding, as far as practicable, the use of technical terms."[42]

The theory underlying these procedural requirements was that, "Prevented from doing harm, [the legislature] might then be trusted with power to do good."[43] Constitution makers believed that if elected representatives exercised only those powers for which they were best suited, if they could be held accountable for their actions at regular intervals, and if their deliberations were sufficiently public, then they could be counted on to provide appropriate redress for popular grievances.

Finally, in the event that representative institutions failed to prevent violations of rights, the founders also provided opportunities for periodic constitutional amendment and revision. The Virginia Constitution followed the proposal of Thomas Jefferson, who recommended that conventions be held every nineteen years in order to correct institutional imbalances. Virginia therefore mandated that "each twentieth year," the legislature would submit to the people the question of whether to hold a constitutional convention.[44] Other states required that referendums be held at even more frequent intervals. Massachusetts provided for a referendum every fifteen years, "[i]n order the more effectually to adhere to the principles of the constitution, and to correct those violations which by any means may be made therein, as well as to form such alterations as from experience shall be found necessary."[45] Michigan directed that the question of constitutional revision should be put to the people in "each sixteenth year."[46]

The general view underlying these provisions was that all constitutions, even the most skillfully designed, were susceptible to corruption over time.[47] But these clauses were also informed by the particular concern that legislators seeking to perpetuate their careers could fail to redraw district boundaries at regular intervals. Accordingly, constitution makers mandated a decennial census and, in some cases, reapportionment and redistricting by a body other than the legislature.[48] The Virginia Constitution, for instance, established a particularly elaborate mechanism for guaranteeing the right to an equal vote. In case the legislature could not agree on a redistricting plan, each house was directed to forward its preferred principle of representation to the governor, who would then submit these proposals for popular review. It was possible, though, that the assembly could still evade its responsibility by declining to submit any proposals to the governor. The constitution made provisions against this eventuality as well, providing that in case of a failure to forward any principles of representation, the governor would be ordered to hold a popular referendum at which time the people would select from among four possible principles of representation, and the most popular principle would be implemented at the next assembly session.[49]

In general, then, the republican regime relied on institutional arrangements to prevent violations of rights. To the extent that grievances did arise, the political process would provide appropriate opportunities for redress. In case both of these avenues proved fruitless, the citizens could amend or revise the constitution.

CONCLUSION

There is a tendency today to view frames of government and bills of rights as serving distinct purposes, with the former understood primarily as granting powers to governmental institutions and the latter thought to secure rights by limiting the exercise of those powers. This is not the view, however, that informed constitution making in the eighteenth and nineteenth centuries. In fact, bills of rights served several functions that we now ascribe to constitutions, and constitutions performed some roles that we now attribute to bills of rights.[50] Constitutions, or frames of government, specified the institutional arrangements by which citizens could exercise effective representation; bills of rights protected these channels of representation and exhorted the people to make wise and prudent use of their votes and petitions. In addition, frames of government specified the institutional arrangements that fostered deliberation; bills of rights affirmed these principles and encouraged the people's representatives to be faithful to their trust. Furthermore, both frames of government and bills of rights identified principles that all public officials were bound to uphold.

Far from serving a distinct purpose, therefore, bills of rights and frames of government were animated by a common understanding of how rights were best protected. Representative institutions were thought to be most capable of representing the considered judgment of the public. Elected representatives were sufficiently responsive to public opinion, but also far enough removed from popular passions, to be able to distinguish momentary ill humors from the public interest. Deliberation would take place through the political process, particularly through and among representative institutions, where competing claims of justice could be advanced, alternative means of securing justice could be discussed, and the consequences of these arrangements could be debated. Compliance with legal guarantees would obtain when decisions about rights protection were made by institutions that were governed by the representative principle. It was essential that the people have some agency in making the laws under which they were governed, but it was sufficient that this participation be indirect.

2

Republican Institutions and the Protection of Rights

Constitutions establish a general framework within which rights are protected, but in order to fully appreciate the way in which rights are secured at any given time, we should look beyond the formal institutional arrangements and study the actual behavior of public officials. It is important, in particular, to identify the norms that govern legislative, judicial, and citizen behavior, as well as the manner in which these individuals actually behave in the course of securing rights.

From the founding period until the close of the nineteenth century, legislators understood that they were primarily responsible for the protection of rights and that statutes were the principal means by which rights were secured. Judges generally refrained from removing questions from the political process. Their role consisted largely of superintending the forms of government and legislation and of rendering decisions that rested on statutory or common-law rules. Finally, the collective citizenry was prevented from deliberating over rights. Although a number of motions were entertained during this period to permit issues to be resolved directly by the people or their representatives assembled in constitutional conventions, these proposals were, more often than not, rejected on the ground that they improperly removed issues from the political process.

THE ROLE AND BEHAVIOR OF LEGISLATORS

The design and powers of the legislature underwent significant changes in the course of the eighteenth and nineteenth centuries. The earliest constitutions reflected legislative supremacy in their formation and content. In many states, legislatures drafted and ratified the constitution, retained responsibility for selecting the members of the executive and judicial branches, and encountered few limitations on their lawmaking power. It was not until well into the nineteenth century that many legislatures ceded the power to revise their constitutions, that legislators were stripped of their power to select the members of what were now seen as coordinate branches, and that significant procedural and substantive restrictions were imposed on the legislative process.[1]

What remained unchanged throughout this period, however, was a view—shared by legislators, judges, and citizens—that legislatures were best positioned to secure individual rights. Of the various public officials who might be charged with this responsibility, legislators were thought to be most capable of representing the popular understanding of rights; legislative assemblies were considered the proper forum for deliberating about the content of rights; and statutes were seen as providing the most effective means of securing their protection.

It was thought, in the first place, that legislators represented the reflective, rather than the reflexive, judgment of the public with respect to securing rights. More importantly, legislators were considered superior to others who might be charged with this task. It may have been true, as numerous pamphlets proclaimed during this period, that the people were the best governors, but the general public was not considered capable of providing adequate security for individual rights. As Delaware Supreme Court Chief Justice James Booth argued, in an 1848 opinion that was quoted widely throughout the country:

> Wherever the power of making laws, which is the supreme power in a State, has been exercised directly by the people under any system of polity, and not by representation, civil liberty has been overthrown. Popular rights and universal suffrage, the favorite theme of every demagogue, afford, without constitutional control or a restraining power, no security to the rights of individuals, or to the permanent peace and safety of society. In every government founded on popular will, the people, although intending to do right, are the subject of impulse and passion; and have been betrayed into acts of folly, rashness and enormity, by the flattery, deception, and influence of demagogues.[2]

Similarly, although judges were qualified by their education and training to interpret the law, they were too distant from popular opinion to be charged with sole responsibility for determining the rights to which individuals were entitled. In contrast, legislators provided a proper mix of responsiveness and reflection. Representative elections ensured that legislators could be held accountable to popular opinion, and therefore that they would be sufficiently responsive, but the rules and requirements of the legislative process ensured that their actions would be informed by a certain degree of reflection.

Furthermore, legislatures were thought to be well positioned to respond to changing conditions. The general understanding was that popular views of rights would evolve over time, and certain methods for securing rights would undoubtedly prove more effective than others. Neither constitutional conventions nor courts possessed the requisite flexibility to implement these changes. Conventions met too infrequently to take account of changing circumstances, and their decisions could be overturned only by a subsequent constitutional amendment or convention. In the words of Alfred Hanscom, a delegate to the Michigan Convention of 1850: "If the Legislature make mistakes they are easily corrected; if we [the convention delegates] make them the mischief is incalculable."[3] Judges, it is true, assembled more frequently than constitutional conventions, but judicial decisions suffered from the same inflexibility as constitutional provisions. Insofar as they rested on constitutional grounds, they could be overturned only by a subsequent constitutional decision or amendment. As Michigan Justice Sanford Manning noted in an 1858 opinion: "When the power in the legislature to pass a law is called in question, and there is a reasonable doubt as to the power, it is better the court should err in favor of the power than against it; as the error in that case may be more readily corrected by the people, through their representatives, than in the other, which would require an amendment of the constitution."[4] Legislators, because they met frequently, and because they could modify their previous decisions rather easily, were thought to possess a decided advantage over these other institutions.

Legislatures were also thought to be uniquely qualified to provide security for rights. To be sure, rights secured through constitutional provisions or judicial decisions were endowed with a certain degree of permanence, because these acts were so difficult to overturn. But insofar as public officials were concerned not merely with obtaining legal protection for rights but with guaranteeing their actual security, they believed that legislative statutes possessed an advantage over these other methods. The view was that citizens were particularly inclined to respect rights that were secured through statutes because they had an indirect role in making them and therefore felt a certain pride in preserving and upholding their guarantees. Of the two most prominent nineteenth-century foreign analysts, Alexis de Tocqueville was the first to take note of the particular capacity of statutes to generate popular compliance, commenting in the 1830s that "however annoying a law may be, the American will submit to it, not only as the work of the majority but also as his own doing; he regards it as a contract to which he is one of the parties."[5] James Bryce remarked later in the century that "It is the best result that can be ascribed to the direct participation of the people in their government that they have the love of the maker for his work, that every citizen looks upon a statute as a regulation made by himself for his own guidance no less than for that of others."[6] As a result, legislative assemblies could assume with some confidence that their efforts to secure rights would be no less permanent than actions taken by constitutional or judicial institutions, and in fact that they were more likely to be effective in providing practical security for these rights. As the Virginia General Assembly noted in the closing section of the 1786 Statute on Religious Freedom:

> [T]hough we all know that this Assembly elected by the people for the ordinary purposes of legislation only, have no power to restrain the Acts of

succeeding Assemblies, constituted with powers equal to our own, and that therefore to declare this Act to be irrevocable would be of no effect in law; yet we are free to declare, and do declare, that the rights hereby asserted are of the natural rights of mankind, and that if any act shall be hereafter passed to repeal the present, or to narrow its operation, such act will be an infringement of natural right.[7]

Legislatures, then, were thought to be responsive to popular opinion, adept at taking account of changing circumstances, and capable of providing security for legal guarantees. Moreover, they possessed these qualities in their proper measure. As a result, they were charged with taking appropriate action to secure individual rights, which meant in practice that they were responsible for translating general principles into particular legal guarantees and for remedying violations of these guarantees.

Legislators assumed responsibility, in the first place, for giving practical meaning to the general principles that were expressed in declarations of rights. It was one thing for constitution makers to stipulate that "the freedom of the press is one of the great bulwarks of liberty, and can never be restrained but by despotic governments," or that "excessive bail ought not to be required, nor excessive fines imposed, nor cruel and unusual punishments inflicted." But in order for these exhortations to have any practical effect, legislatures had to enact statutes that defined these terms and applied them to particular situations. As the Virginia Court of Appeals explained in an 1851 decision that required the judges to interpret a series of laws: "If we trace our legislation on this subject from the revolution down to the present day, it will be apparent . . . that its whole purpose was and is to carry into practical operation the 8th section of the bill of rights which guaranties to every one accused of crime a speedy trial, and thereby secures him against protracted imprisonment."[8]

More importantly, legislatures were responsible for remedying violations of these legal guarantees, which meant that they either repealed old statutes or enacted new statutes, depending on the circumstances. In some cases, these guarantees were breached by legislatures themselves, which enacted statutes inadvertently, with no knowledge that they would have the effect of depriving certain individuals of their rights. To secure rights in these cases simply required the legislature to acknowledge its error and rewrite the statute. For instance, in 1783, when the Virginia General Assembly became aware that it had mistakenly stripped Quakers and Mennonites of their citizenship, it promptly repealed the offending provisions.[9]

In other cases, statutes were enacted in haste, without the benefit of adequate consideration of their consequences. To secure rights in these cases required legislatures to undertake the requisite amount of deliberation and to repeal the offensive law. Thus, in 1855 in the midst of a heavy influx of Catholic immigrants, the members of the Massachusetts General Court enacted a law that had the effect of forcing Catholic schoolchildren to read from a version of the Bible with which they were not comfortable. But in 1862, after a number of Catholics called attention to the injustice of the law, and after legislators had an opportunity to reflect on these petitions, the General Court amended the act so that it would be more acceptable to members of all religious faiths.[10]

Still other statutes had the effect of violating rights by virtue of the fact that they were inconsistent with evolving standards of justice. In these cases, legislatures secured rights by rewriting statutes so that they conformed to the popular understanding. In 1799, for instance, the Virginia General Assembly noted that the Virginia Declaration of Rights declared religion to be a matter of conscience, yet previous legislatures had enacted laws that "admit the church established under the regal government, . . . have bestowed property upon that church; have asserted a legislative right to establish any religious sect; and have incorporated religious sects, all of which is inconsistent with the principles of the constitution, and of religious freedom." Consequently, the legislature enacted a statute to "repeal certain acts, and to declare the construction of the bill of rights and constitution concerning religion."[11]

In some instances, rights were violated by judicial decisions that failed to conform to evolving standards of justice. In an 1808 case, for instance, the Massachusetts Supreme Court ruled that defendants in libel cases could not present evidence that would attest to the truth of their statements. Then, in 1825, it reaffirmed this holding. Chief Justice Isaac Parker wrote that "this is certainly the common law doctrine, and it never has been repealed by any statute of this commonwealth, nor overruled by any decision of this Court."[12] Yet one year later, the Massachusetts General Court accepted the invitation to alter the common-law rule, and it enacted a statute that recognized the right of individuals to demonstrate the truth of their statements that were charged as libelous.[13]

It is important, therefore, to distinguish between the belief that legislatures are incapable of violating rights and the belief that legislatures are best capable of remedying violations of rights. Few public officials in the eighteenth and nineteenth centuries would have subscribed to the first statement. They were fully aware that legislatures were prone, though no more nor no less than any other institution, to disregard the guarantees contained in declarations of rights. But when these officials reflected upon the institution that was best suited to remedy these violations, they turned to the legislature.

THE ROLE AND BEHAVIOR OF JUDGES

The power of state supreme courts to invalidate legislative statutes was established early in the history of the Republic. State judges were reviewing the constitutionality of legislation well before U.S. Supreme Court Chief Justice John Marshall defended the power of judicial review in the 1803 case *Marbury v.*

Madison.[14] In fact, "the first case in the United States, where the question relative to the nullity of an unconstitutional law was ever discussed before a judicial tribunal" was the 1782 case *Commonwealth v. Caton,* in which the Virginia Court of Appeals invalidated a legislative act that had passed the house of delegates but had not been approved by the senate.[15] The Massachusetts Supreme Judicial Court also announced early in its history that it possessed the power to review legislation, and in 1814 the court made use of this power for the first time in overturning a statute that affected only one person.[16] By the middle of the nineteenth century, when the supreme courts of Michigan and Oregon began operation, judicial review was well entrenched. As Henry St. George Tucker, president of the Virginia Court of Appeals, proclaimed in 1837: "The power of the judiciary to decide on the constitutionality of a law is too firmly settled to be now questioned."[17]

The fact that state courts could declare legislation unconstitutional tells us little, however, about the manner in which courts actually secured rights. In addition to looking at the powers that courts formally possessed, it is important to understand the way in which judges conceived of their role in the political system.[18] When judges in the nineteenth century reflected on the way that rights were best secured, they were apt to conclude that this task was best performed by legislatures, and that, save for exceptional cases, judges should refrain from removing questions from the political process.[19]

This judicial posture is best illustrated by a series of opinions delivered by the justices of the Michigan Supreme Court in an 1856 case, *The People v. Gallagher,* where, in the course of sustaining a law that restricted the sale of alcohol, the justices engaged in a spirited debate over which institution was best suited to secure rights. The dissenting justices in this case contended not only that this particular legislative act violated "the natural rights of citizens" but also that legislatures were, in general, unfit to secure individual rights. In their view, any government that permitted legislatures to define rights could no longer "be justly deemed republican or free."

> Nor can those composing the minority be any longer certain of protection by government, or have the least security for the enjoyment of any rights which they may respectively possess; on the contrary, they must stand in no better attitude, irrespective of the fundamental principles and maxims of free government, than that of the most abject slaves to the majority, and at all times entirely dependent on the will, whim or caprice of the senators and representatives whom they may elect, for every right and for every privilege, political, civil or religious, they may enjoy.[20]

A majority of the justices, however, rejected the view that this particular act violated the rights of any individual, and they went on to contest the claim that legislatures were incompetent to secure rights. There was, to begin with, "the great practical difficulty of defining, with any degree of certainty, what these rights are." But over and above this question was another matter: "How, and by whom, are they to be settled and defined? In the distribution of power, this duty belongs to some department; if to the legislature, then the question is settled against the defendant; if to the judiciary, then there is this practical difficulty, that the legislature has no criterion by which they can test the validity of their own acts, until the judicial will shall have been expressed."[21]

When these justices compared the capabilities of these departments to secure rights, they concluded that legislatures were at least as competent as courts, if not more so.

> It would be pretty difficult to assign any reason why they are not as safe in the hands of one department as another. It may be true that legislative bodies, acting from temporary impulses, without sufficient time for discussion and deliberation, are more likely to be influenced by the highly excited condition of the public mind than courts of law. But the elements of the two bodies are the same—their motives the same: both are acting for themselves and their immediate constituents, to whom they are accountable; besides, over half a century's experience has demonstrated beyond cavil that the apprehension of evil upon *this ground*, if any apprehension ever existed, is utterly unfounded. Great wrongs may undoubtedly be perpetrated by legislative bodies, but this is only an argument against the exercise of discretionary power. It weighs nothing, for no government can exist without the existence of that power somewhere.[22]

The majority opinion was the view that predominated throughout the nineteenth century.[23] Although judges occasionally deviated from this position and argued that rights could be secured only through judicial enforcement,[24] these were exceptions to a dominant norm that discounted any judicial superiority in protecting rights.

It did not necessarily follow that judges played an insignificant role in the protection of rights. Although judges were not inclined to substitute their understandings of rights for those of the legislature, this did not exhaust the possible judicial contributions to rights protection. Judges might protect rights indirectly by superintending the forms of republican government and of legislation. They could also protect rights directly by deciding cases on the basis of statutory or common-law rules. Only in rare cases, however, did they secure rights by striking down laws that ran afoul of provisions of bills of rights.

Judges superintended the forms of republican government in several ways. One of their chief responsibilities was to safeguard the separation of powers. The view was that rights were most secure when each governing institution exercised only those powers for which it was best suited. Threats to the separation of powers, and thus to the security of individual rights, could take a variety of forms. Occasionally, legislatures tried to reduce judicial duties or salaries, or they attempted to assume judicial powers, for instance, when the Virginia General Assembly "proposed to reopen and annul in whole or in part a judgment rendered by a court of competent jurisdiction." The Virginia Court of Appeals ruled in 1878 that this was "an attempted exercise of judicial power" and that "[i]t is now too well settled to admit of serious dispute that the legislative department can no more exercise judicial power than that the judicial department can exercise legislative power." Justice Joseph Christian concluded: "That system which best preserves the independence of each department approaches nearest to the perfection of civil government and the security of civil liberty."[25]

Equally offensive were legislative efforts to give powers to the judiciary that properly belonged to the legislative or executive departments. Accordingly, when the Massachusetts General Court enacted a law that directed the judges on the Massachusetts Supreme Judicial Court to appoint election supervisors, Chief Justice Horace Gray reasoned that these positions were "strictly executive," and as a result: "We are unanimously of the opinion that the power of appointing such officers cannot be conferred upon the justices of this court without violating the Constitution of the Commonwealth."[26]

Judges were also concerned with superintending the forms of legislation.[27] The general understanding was that rights were secure insofar as laws were the product of adequate deliberation and publicity and insofar as they were generally applicable. Laws that did not benefit from proper deliberation were thought to be more likely to have unintended and harmful consequences for individual rights. Likewise, when laws were not debated in a public forum, there was a greater chance that they could infringe on liberties. Finally, laws that were directed at particular individuals or groups were also suspect, on the ground that they were more likely to sacrifice the public interest for special and local interests.

As a result, judges struck down laws that were introduced at such a late date in the legislative session that they could not have been accorded adequate consideration. The purpose of these decisions, according to Thomas Cooley's *Treatise on Constitutional Limitations*, was "[t]o prevent hasty and improvident legislation, and to compel, so far as any previous law can accomplish that result, the careful examination of proposed laws, or, at least, the affording of opportunity for that purpose."[28] But another object was to enable the people to better secure their rights, by providing them with "an opportunity to be heard upon proposed legislation affecting their interests." Michigan Justice Allen Morse argued:

> The legislative journals, referring as they do to the titles of all bills introduced, give some warning to the people of measures introduced. The right of petition and protest has ever been recognized as one of the established privileges of the people in a free country; and they have a right to notice of proposed legislation, and an opportunity to express their assent or dissent. If there was no constitutional inhibition against such practice, bills might be introduced upon the last days of the session, and rushed at once through both houses, without any chance for the people to be heard before their passage, or to rectify the action until another biennial session of the Legislature.[29]

Judges also enforced constitutional provisions that required that each law contain only one subject that was accurately described in its title.[30] These provisions were designed, in part, to prevent logrolling, but they were also intended to ensure that individuals had adequate opportunity to prevent the passage of legislation that was injurious to their rights. In particular, these provisions were designed "to prevent imposition being practiced upon unsuspecting members, by procuring their votes for bills with fair titles, which contain objectionable matters unconnected with the subject expressed in the title."[31] The purpose was "to put an end to legislation of the vicious character referred to, which was little less than a fraud upon the public, and to require that in every case the proposed measure should stand upon its own merits."[32] When "clauses were inserted in bills of which the titles gave no intimation, and their passage secured through legislative bodies whose members were not generally aware of their intention and effect,"[33] the inevitable result was that the people's representatives were rendered incapable of deliberating about the consequences and preventing the passage of offensive laws.

Judicial enforcement of these subject-title provisions also served to protect rights in a more direct manner. At times, individuals appealed their convictions on the ground that the laws they were accused of violating were hidden in the statute books in such a way that they were not even aware that their behavior was illegal. In what could be described as a rejection of the adage that ignorance of the law is no excuse, courts occasionally overturned these convictions and struck down the offensive laws. In 1881, for instance, a Michigan man who had been drinking in public was convicted of violating a particular provision of a liquor regulation act. He argued, however, that he had no way of knowing from the title of the act that what he had done was illegal. The Michigan Supreme Court agreed: "By no reasonable construction can the purpose of this section be said to be embraced within the title of the act. The punishment of a person for being drunk, without reference to where he obtained the means of intoxication, can have no possible connection with the object of the act as set forth in its title." The court concluded: "It is nothing more nor less than the insertion, in the body of the act, of a clause creating and punishing a misdemeanor entirely foreign to the ostensible purpose of the statute as entitled. No person reading the title would dream of any such provision being contained in the act."[34] In another case, a Michigan man who was accused of taking indecent liberties with a minor was charged under a statute entitled "An act to provide for the punishment of crimes in certain cases." The Michigan Supreme Court ruled that this title gave "no hint as to the character of the act to be punished," and it discharged the defendant.[35]

Judges were also concerned, particularly toward the end of the nineteenth century, with enforcing constitutional provisions prohibiting the passage of special or class legislation.[36] These rules, which were originally introduced to protect legislatures from being overrun by petitions for divorces, name changes, and incorporations, also came to be seen as an indirect guarantee of individual rights.

The dominant view of bans on special legislation, according to Michigan Justice Samuel Douglass, was that they were intended to deprive the legislature of a discretion that was "likely to be capriciously, improvidently, and sometimes unjustly exercised, and to leave only the power to enact general laws."[37] In the course of overturning a law that required meat peddlers (but not other similarly situated merchants) to buy licenses, the Michigan Supreme Court took the opportunity to discuss the purpose of bans on class legislation. The court explained: "This class legislation, when indulged in, seldom benefits the general public, but nearly always aids the few for whose benefit it is enacted, not only at the expense of the few against whom it is ostensibly directed, but also at the expense and to the detriment of the many, for whose benefit all legislation should be, in a republican form of government, framed and devised."[38]

The vast majority of judicial decisions, it should be emphasized, did not require any form of constitutional interpretation at all. In fact, many volumes of the nineteenth-century state court reports do not contain a single constitutional decision. Rather, judges decided cases on the basis of interpretations of statutes or common-law rules. As Judith Kaye has argued: "In state courts, the grand tradition has been not of constitutional but of common law decisionmaking."[39] What distinguished common-law and statutory judging from constitutional decision making was that these rulings did not remove questions from the political process. Rather, they preserved the opportunity for legislatures to enact new statutes, which could either clarify the legislative intent on a particular matter or modify a common-law rule that proved unworkable.

In a significant number of cases, therefore, judges secured rights simply by applying statutory guarantees in particular circumstances. Thus, in one case, the Massachusetts Supreme Court ruled that a religious dissenter who had been prevented from serving on a grand jury was entitled by statute to be empaneled and to be permitted to take an alternative oath.[40] In several other cases, the Massachusetts Supreme Court ruled that a statute permitted defendants in a criminal case to remain silent at trial and not be tainted by that choice.[41] Similarly, the Michigan Supreme Court overturned the conviction of one man, whose friends had been excluded from his trial, on the ground that this practice violated a statute that stipulated that "every court shall be public."[42] To provide one final example, the Michigan Supreme Court relied on a statute in one case to prevent a witness from being questioned about her religious beliefs. The court noted that Michigan had a constitutional provision directing that no person shall be rendered "*incompetent* to be a witness on account of his opinions on matters of religious belief," but that the statute "goes much farther" and states that no witness shall be "*questioned* in relation to his opinions thereon." Accordingly, "it was clearly incompetent to question the witness in this case, in reference to her belief in a God."[43]

When legislators had not yet addressed an area of the law, courts frequently relied on common-law rules to sort out the rights to which individuals were entitled. In 1867, for instance, the Virginia Court of Appeals turned to the common law to determine the admissibility of one man's confession. After learning that a constable, shortly after arresting the defendant, had urged him that he "had better tell all about it," Justice William Joynes determined that under common-law rules, the subsequent confession should be considered to have been "induced" and therefore inadmissible.[44]

On occasion, judges also relied on statutes and common-law principles to introduce new understandings of rights. Thus, in one case, it was unclear to the Virginia Court of Appeals whether the General Assembly had intended to provide a particular fair-trial guarantee. Acknowledging that the statute books were unclear, the court opted to construe the law to require this procedure. President Richard Moncure wrote: "If I am wrong, the Legislature, now in session, can correct the error."[45]

To be sure, in the course of their deliberations nineteenth-century judges had frequent occasion to interpret bills of rights. In general, though, they treated these provisions in a manner that is quite distinct from the modern understanding. Although the state court reports yield several cases in which judges interpreted bills of rights as legal principles that served to restrict legislative deliberations, the prevailing view was that bills of rights contained maxims that could be interpreted by legislators and citizens, as well as judges. Their chief value lay in their ability to guide and inform deliberations over rights, rather than to provide a rule of law for resolving particular questions.

Massachusetts Chief Justice Lemuel Shaw had occasion, in an 1837 opinion, to advert to the purpose of frames of government and bills of rights. He argued: "In construing this constitution, it must never be forgotten, that it was not intended to contain a detailed system of practical rules, for the regulation of the government or people in after times; but that it was rather intended, after an organization of the government, and distributing the executive, legislative and judicial powers, amongst its several departments, to declare a few broad, general, fundamental principles, for their guidance and general direction."[46] It was important, therefore, that those who sought to interpret bills of rights appreciate the spirit in which they were drafted. They should be viewed "as the annunciation of great and fundamental principles, to be always held in regard," rather than as "precise and positive directions and rules of action."[47] They were "not first prepared and drawn up by and for a people who were then, for the first time, establishing political and civil institutions," and as a result, each provision should "be expounded under the broad light thrown upon it by this constant reference, tacit or express, to established laws and institutions."[48]

The prevailing view, then, was that bills of rights did not admit of precise judicial interpretation and enforcement and therefore could not serve as a rule of constitutional law that could restrain legislative deliberations. The Massachusetts Supreme Court explained, in an 1859 case in which it was called upon to interpret a provision of the federal Bill of Rights: "This, like similar provisions in our own Declaration of Rights, declares a great general right, leaving it for other more specific constitutional provision or to legislation to provide for the preservation and practical security of such right, and for influencing and governing the judgment and conscience of all legislators and magistrates, who are thus required to recognize and respect such rights."[49]

As the Virginia Court of Appeals noted in an opinion handed down in 1871: "[W]hile these declarations of general principles must be recognized and followed, both in legislation and in the administration and execution of laws, we must give to each one of them a reasonable rather than a literal construction; certainly such a construction as will make each consistent with the others, and carry out most effectually the object and design of the whole instrument."[50]

It was not uncommon, therefore, to find judicial opinions that were informed by provisions in bills of rights but that ultimately rested on statutory or common-law grounds.[51] Thus, when Judge Paul Carrington of the Virginia Court of Appeals determined in 1799 that a district court could not order a group of defendants to pay a joint fine, he drew upon a variety of supporting evidence. He concluded: "Therefore, whether I consider the case upon principle, the doctrines of the common law, or the spirit of the Bill of Rights and the act of Assembly, I am equally clear in my opinion . . . that their judgment is erroneous, and must be reversed."[52]

Although the reluctance to rely on bills of rights to overturn legislative judgments was the norm during this period, it coexisted alongside important exceptions. In several circumstances, especially in the latter half of the nineteenth century, judges determined that rights could be better protected through constitutional decisions than through statutory or common-law rulings, and in these cases deference to legislative determinations was suspended.

For one thing, legislatures were occasionally deemed incapable of deliberating responsibly about rights during periods of social or political agitation. A prime example of this kind of legislative failure occurred in the 1850s, when, in their haste to restrict the production and sale of alcohol, legislators occasionally disregarded the guarantee against improper searches and seizures. Both Massachusetts and Michigan enacted Prohibition laws in the early 1850s that empowered magistrates to issue warrants and seize liquor solely upon the complaint of ordinary citizens. Both state supreme courts ruled, however, that these laws constituted an impermissible violation of individual liberty. Chief Justice Shaw identified a number of defects in the Massachusetts law. The question he faced was whether "the measures, directed and authorized by the statute in question, are so far inconsistent with the principles of justice, and the established maxims of jurisprudence, intended for the security of public and private rights, and so repugnant to the provisions of the Declaration of Rights and constitution of the Commonwealth, that it was not within the power of the legislature to give them the force of law, and that they must therefore be held unconstitutional and void."[53] He concluded that "The Court are all of opinion that they are." Michigan Justice Sandford Green identified similar problems with his state's Prohibition law, and the Michigan Supreme Court arrived at a similar verdict.[54]

Similarly, in the 1870s, in their haste to root out political corruption and dueling, several legislatures failed to provide adequate safeguards for the privilege against self-incrimination. In particular, the supreme courts of Massachusetts and Virginia held, in a pair of similar cases, that the legislatures had failed to properly secure the right. The question in Massachusetts was whether a senate committee could compel an individual to testify about corruption in the state police force.[55] At issue in Virginia was whether a grand jury could force someone to furnish evidence about a duel he had witnessed.[56] Although both legislatures maintained that these practices did not violate the privilege against self-incrimination because the witnesses' testimony could not be used against them, neither court accepted this argument. The Massachusetts Supreme Court concluded: "The terms of the provision in the Constitution of Massachusetts require a much broader interpretation."[57] It was not enough to provide that testimony could not be used to prosecute someone; the bill of rights stipulated that individuals could not be forced to provide this testimony in the first place.

In addition, state courts delivered a number of opinions that rested on constitutional grounds but did not fit neatly into any particular category. The Massachusetts Supreme Court overturned several statutes, for instance, that ran afoul of the bill of rights by permitting prosecutors to try defendants without first obtaining a grand jury indictment,[58] as well as a statute that sought to prohibit naturalized citizens from voting within the first thirty days after becoming a citizen.[59] The Michigan Supreme Court struck down a law that permitted the state attorney general to prosecute defendants in any county throughout the entire state, in what Judge Cooley noted was "a remarkable case on the law and on the facts."[60] One case, which was decided by the Virginia Court of Appeals in 1884, represents the only instance in which one of these courts invalidated a law on the ground that it violated the right to free speech. The General Assembly had enacted a law that sought to "prohibit the active participation in politics of certain officers of government," and a county school superintendent had been fired for attending a political rally, but the court held that the law violated the free-speech clause of the bill of rights, and it overturned the conviction.[61]

In general, though, cases such as these represented exceptions to a general norm that encouraged legislatures to assume responsibility for deliberating over rights and discouraged judges from taking actions that would prevent legislatures from exercising this responsibility. The dominant understanding of the judicial role was expressed by Judge Cooley, who in his casebook counseled judges not to "run a race of opinions upon points of right, reason and expediency with the law-making power." He argued: "The courts are not the guardians of the rights of the people of the State, unless those rights are secured by some constitutional provision which comes within the judicial cognizance. The remedy for unwise or oppressive legislation, within constitutional bounds, is by an appeal to the justice and patriotism of the representatives of the people. If this fail, the people in their sovereign capacity can correct the evil; but courts cannot assume their rights."[62]

THE ROLE AND BEHAVIOR OF CITIZENS

Republicanism admitted of a variety of meanings in the nineteenth century. It could refer to a polity that fostered a concern for the public good rather than self-interest. It could also refer to the qualifications for voting, in which case a state would be considered more or less republican depending on the extent of its suffrage. At the most fundamental level, however, republicanism referred to a regime that was governed by indirect rather than direct representation, or, as James Madison argued, by "the total exclusion of the people, in their collective capacity, from any share" in the administration of the government.[63]

Eighteenth- and nineteenth-century state governments qualified as republican in this final sense, in that they lodged primary responsibility for rights protection in the legislature rather than in the collective citizenry. Citizen participation was confined to representative elections, and the people were precluded from voting directly on legislation. As a result, legislatures could not refer bills to the people for their approval, nor could the people initiate and vote on laws independently of the legislature. Such devices were repeatedly deemed, by judges and constitutional convention delegates alike, to be incompatible with a republican form of government, to provide inadequate deliberation, and to afford insufficient security for individual rights.

The legitimacy of the popular referendum inspired a significant amount of debate in the constitutional conventions held during this period. A number of conventions chose to permit citizens of local governments to vote on where to locate a county seat, whether to set up a public school system, or whether to license or prohibit the sale of alcohol. Several conventions also voted to permit statewide referendums for limited purposes, such as where to locate the state capital, as in Oregon, or whether to permit certain banking regulations, as in Michigan. But convention delegates overwhelmingly rejected the use of the statewide referendum for general purposes. The dominant attitude toward legislative referendums was best expressed by Delaxon Smith, a delegate to the Oregon Convention of 1857. Smith argued: "[W]e might as well include all general and political subjects; we might as well abolish the legislature, and appoint a committee to frame laws for submission to the people; if the legislative power was to be exercised by the people en masse, why incur the expense of a legislative assembly."[64]

The issue was debated more often in the courts, where two cases are particularly useful for demonstrating the prevailing view of direct democracy. In 1855, the Michigan Supreme Court considered the validity of a Prohibition law that had been submitted for popular approval and, when the judges divided evenly, overturned the law.[65] Then, in 1894 the Massachusetts Supreme Court confronted the same question in the context of a proposed women's suffrage referendum, and five of the seven justices ruled that such a referendum would be unconstitutional.[66]

The dissenting justices in both cases, that is, those who voted to uphold the legislative referendums, advanced several arguments. Several of these justices contended that there was no difference between allowing the people to ratify constitutional amendments and permitting them to vote directly on legislation. Because citizens were permitted to pass direct judgment on constitutional matters, they argued, it made little sense to exclude them from voting directly on legislative matters.

Other dissenters, including Massachusetts Justice Oliver Wendell Holmes, voted to uphold the legislative referendum because they objected to a theory of representation that precluded the people from exercising direct sovereignty. The notion that the people could exercise only an indirect influence over public affairs seemed to Holmes, for one, to be "an echo of Hobbes's theory that the surrender of sovereignty by the people was final. I notice that the case from which most of the reasoning against the power of the Legislature has been taken by later decisions states that theory in language which almost is borrowed from the Leviathan. . . . Hobbes urged his notion in the interest of the absolute power of King Charles I, and one of the objects of the Constitution of Massachusetts was to deny it."[67]

But these arguments represented the minority view. The dominant understanding was that the legislative referendum was incompatible with the principles of republican government. In the first place, referendums were thought to be "a most flagrant violation of the constitution and our representative system of government." According to Justice Samuel Douglass of Michigan: "*[T]he power of enacting general laws cannot be delegated—not even to the people.* There is nothing in the constitution which authorizes or contemplates it; nothing in the nature of the power which requires it; nothing in the usages of our American government which sanctions it; no single adjudication of a court of last resort, in any state, which affirms it; and such delegation would be contrary to the intent manifested by the very structure of the legislative department of the government."[68]

The majority also argued that there was a crucial difference, which the dissenters conspicuously failed to grasp, between the expression of popular opinion through representative elections and the ratification of constitutional amendments, and its expression through direct review of legislation. As Massachusetts Justice Waldridge Field argued, the founders provided a number of opportunities for citizens to express their opinions. "They apparently relied upon frequent elections, when the officers were elective; upon the right of meeting and consulting upon the common good; upon the right of petition and of instructing their representatives; upon impeachment; and upon the right of reforming, altering, and totally changing the form of government when the protection, safety, prosperity, and happiness of the people required it."[69] However, the people "reserved to themselves no direct power of supervision."[70] In similar fashion, Justice Douglass argued:

[B]efore any proposed measure can become a law it must first struggle for ascendancy at the ballot box, amid the numerous issues involved in all political contests. It must pass through the ordeal of public and deliberate discussion in the legislature. It must receive the sanction of the concurrent vote of a majority, or, having been returned with the governor's veto, of two-thirds of the members of the two houses of which the legislature is composed—votes cast by men who are not the mere deputies of their immediate constituents, but the representatives of the whole people, and bound to act for the general good; who are responsible to the people for their action, and may be held to that responsibility. Public opinion will prevail, and pass into public law; but it will be *enlightened, deliberate, permanent and organically expressed public opinion*. It is this opinion alone which the constitution designed should govern. Such a government secures deliberation and responsibility in legislation, and affords protection against the despotism of official rulers on the one hand, and of irresponsible, numerical majorities on the other.[71]

The purpose of restricting public opinion to institutional channels was, therefore, not to limit the rule of the majority, as Holmes and the dissenters suggested, but rather to ensure that the majority will was expressed in such a way as to secure rights most effectively. Referendums threatened the security of rights, in the first place, because they deviated from the principle that rights were best protected by allocating powers to the institution best suited for exercising them. As Michigan Justice Abner Pratt argued: "It is, beyond all question, well for the stability and safety of the government, as well as for those "rights, privileges, and institutions which have been established under it, that this *law-making* power . . . cannot be delegated by a legislature at will, or whenever a majority of the members of that body may be disposed corruptly, or for want of moral courage, to avoid legislative responsibility."[72] Additionally, as Justice Douglass argued, referendums removed the protection for individual rights that was afforded by institutional deliberation. "[I]f the legislature may transfer this power and this responsibility to the people, where are the checks which the constitution intended to provide against hasty and inconsiderate legislation? Where are the securities against arbitrary and irresponsible power? We may be subjected to the dominion of the popular majority of the hour—a majority whose opinion *must* be formed without legislative discussion or deliberation—a majority responsible to no one, because it has no superior."[73] The inevitable result of such a system would be, Justice Pratt argued, that "our boasted system of representative government is to be perverted, and a *collective democracy,* the most uncertain and dangerous of governments, to be arbitrarily subjected in its stead." No American citizen, "out of a mad house," could be desirous of instituting such a system.[74] In general, then, judges and convention delegates believed that statewide referendums departed from republican principles, and they prohibited their use.

The people had one other opportunity to take part in securing rights, through their participation in the constitutional amendment and revision process. Citizens had the opportunity to call constitutional conventions, to select convention delegates, and to pass judgment on the proposed revisions. Significantly, though, the people consistently refrained from making use of the constitutional revision process to substitute popular conceptions of rights for legislative determinations. This is not to say that there were no temptations to remove issues from the legislature, nor that there were no instances of constitutional legislating. What is remarkable is the number of occasions on which these proposals were rejected, either by the convention delegates or by the people, on the ground that this practice departed from republican principles. Constitutional legislating was frowned upon, and those who sought to break with this norm did so hesitantly and were required to justify their behavior.

Practically every nineteenth-century constitutional convention addressed the question, with respect to some issue or another, of whether convention delegates or legislators were better positioned to determine the rights to which individuals were entitled. But several issues—the questions of whether to regulate the sale of alcohol, abolish the death penalty, or eliminate the grand jury—inspired these debates with particular frequency. These matters were debated constantly in representative elections and in legislative assemblies, and they were inevitably introduced into constitutional conventions as well. It is significant, however, that proposals to constitutionalize these issues were consistently rejected, on the view that they were best resolved by legislatures rather than in constitutional conventions.

A number of delegates were guided by prudential concerns. They supported these amendments on their merits but feared that their inclusion in the constitution would reduce the likelihood of securing ratification. Thus Earl Gardiner argued in the Michigan Convention of 1850: "I yield to no one in zeal or fervor in the cause of temperance; but I must say I do not consider this the proper place for any provision this Convention may think proper to adopt on the subject." He feared that the inclusion of a Prohibition plank would lead many citizens to vote against the whole document, and he did not wish "that the constitution, which has cost us much labor and expense to perfect, shall be risked on any such propositions."[75]

Other delegates supported the policies contained in these amendments but thought that it was improper to reconsider issues that had already been given an extensive hearing in the legislature. Convention delegates had no premium on honesty or wisdom, they argued, and therefore were in no better position than legislators to address these issues. Thus Edward Moore urged the Michigan Convention of 1850 to defeat a capital punishment plank. "I do not believe it is necessary to place it in the constitution. I hope that it will be left to the legislature." Henry Fralick agreed: "[I]t belonged primarily to the Legislature. We have a law upon this subject. The question has been fully discussed by the people, and I am perfectly willing that it shall be left to them to act in the matter as their best judgment may direct."[76]

Still other delegates argued that constitutional amendments lacked the flexibility of legislative statutes. James Kingsley voted against a constitutonal amendment that sought to abolish the grand jury on the ground that it was "too violent a method" and "looks too much like legislation." He argued: "It will probably be best to leave it to the legislature, and not abolish it. Before another legislature sits here, public opinion may be formed, and the legislature can then decide. They can dispense with the powers of the grand jury in part, and if that works well, they can go further; if it does not, they can reinstate them in the same position they occupy now."[77] Volney Hascall expressed similar concerns: "[H]is individual opinion was, that very serious objections might be urged against the institution of the grand jury. . . . He was not, however, ready to say that this institution should be absolutely abolished by a positive provision of the constitution. He would rather leave it open to the legislature to abolish it or not." According to Hascall, the legislature could easily restore the grand jury if the experiment did not work, but if it was abolished by constitutional action, "it could only be restored by an amendment, after much time and great inconvenience."[78]

Similarly, Robert McClelland favored the abolition of the death penalty, but he preferred to retain the current legislative ban rather than to adopt a constitutional amendment on the subject. He argued: "I would submit whether cases may not arise in which it would be absolutely necessary to take human life. The contingency may never occur; but we may have insurrections or war, rendering it absolutely necessary to be taken away. It is better to leave this to legislative action."[79] Other delegates were opposed to capital punishment but feared that a constitutional ban would have the unfortunate effect of preventing legislative efforts to reform its abuses. John Botts argued in the Virginia Convention of 1850–1851, for instance, that he was "very much inclined to the belief that capital punishment ought to be abolished." But he would "greatly prefer" that "the matter should be left entirely to the decision of the legislative department of the government." In this way, the legislature might undertake to abolish the practice, but "if the experiment did not answer a good purpose, they might return to capital punishment again, if necessary."[80]

It was one thing for convention delegates to reject proposals to constitutionalize matters such as the prohibition of alcohol, the abolition of capital punishment, or the elimination of the grand jury. These were sufficiently controversial, it could be argued, that they should not be resolved in a constitutional convention but rather should be addressed through the political process. It was quite another matter to contend that guarantees such as the right to a fair trial and the right to worship according to one's conscience should be defined by legislators rather than by constitutional conventions. In fact, these arguments were not only advanced in these conventions but were frequently influential in preventing the enactment of proposed amendments.

The Massachusetts Convention of 1820, in particular, featured a number of illuminating debates on this question. The convention considered a variety of measures, including proposals to regulate the privilege against self-incrimination, free speech, and religious liberty, all of which were rejected, either by the people's assembled representatives or by the people themselves. When a motion was made, for instance, to amend the constitution to permit defendants to testify in their own behalf, Delegate Charles Jackson responded that "this was a case for legislative provision. If an instance of injustice should occur, the Legislature would make the provision, and if found inconvenient, it could be repealed."[81] When another motion was made to constitutionalize the common-law rule with respect to libel, Jackson again objected: "The resolution therefore does not go far enough in one particular, and goes too far in another. Besides, the present law is on a proper footing, and if the decision should be overruled, it is in the power of the Legislature, by statute, to regulate it at pleasure."[82] Likewise, the convention decided that the legislature was well equipped to exempt religious dissenters from service in the militia. The dominant view was that "the Legislature would make such exceptions from time to time as they should think proper," and that it was not "expedient by a constitutional act to deprive the Legislature of the power to make such regulation as experience should show to be necessary."[83]

The prevailing attitude toward these sorts of amendments was perhaps most clearly expressed in the course of a debate over the best means of securing the guarantee against religious establishment. The Massachusetts General Court had enacted a statute in 1811 that exempted dissenters from paying taxes to support the established church, and the question before the convention delegates in 1820 was whether to elevate this law to constitutional status. Although several delegates evinced a distrust of the legislature—Heman Lincoln, for one, criticized those who would "leave our dearest rights, the rights of conscience, in the power of the Legislature"[84]— and although the delegates eventually recommended an amendment on the subject, the convention debates featured a series of spirited defenses of the capacity of representative institutions to secure rights, and the proposed amendment was defeated at the polls by a significant margin.

William Prescott argued, for instance, that there was no need for a constitutional amendment on the subject, because the principle of bicameralism would prevent the existing statutory guarantee from being overturned. "[H]e asked, why was not the legislature to be trusted? A proposition for the repeal of the law of 1811 must go through both branches—both branches must feel the evil of it before it could be repealed."[85] Likewise, Isaac Parker relied on the principle of representation to maintain these rights. "It was said that that law [of 1811] might be repealed. But there was no instance of a law of this kind, which extended an indulgence to a numerous class of people, being repealed. If it was repealed, it would produce a popular excitement that would require its reenactment. He considered it as permanent."[86] Moreover, Samuel Wilde argued, the right would actually be secured more effectively through legislation than through a constitutional provision, because the General Assembly was better positioned to respond to changing circumstances. "The reason why it should stand on the footing of a law, was, that if incorporated into the constitution, so that it could not be altered or modified, it would lead to abuses. . . . Was it right to restrain the Legislature for all future ages from making such modifications of the law as abuses under it might show to be proper?"[87] After comparing the benefits of legislative versus constitutional protection, Walter Dutton concluded in similar fashion:

[T]hese resolutions now propose to engraft into the constitution the second section of the Law of 1811. He was wholly opposed to this, not because he was opposed to the law, but because he was opposed to making it a part of the constitution. The whole difference in his opinion lay between having these provisions in a law, and having them in a constitution. So long as they remained a law, they were subject to revision and modification. Abuses might hereafter exist, which would require to be corrected. The law had been in operation only ten years; a much longer time was necessary to ascertain its bearing and influence. He did not know that any great abuses now existed, but he was not wise enough to foresee that none would exist fifty years hence, nor foolish enough to say that the Legislature should not have the power to correct them when they did exist. It was not wise to attempt to bind by an unchanging law, the ever changing interests and opinions of men; fix forever in one place that which is in its nature mutable and progressive. Laws can always be accommodated to the existing state of things. . . . On the other hand, the constitution is and always ought to be a body of general rules.[88]

To be sure, nineteenth-century conventions did not always reject constitutional amendments that sought to better secure rights. In some cases, public opinion had advanced to such a point that it was appropriate to place a matter on a constitutional footing or it was necessary to remove constitutional provisions that no longer reflected popular opinion. It should be emphasized, however, that the people were not seeking in these instances to limit the legislature or to substitute a popular view of rights for that of the elected representatives. According to James Willard Hurst, "In most cases such specific enactments of policy did not direct, but merely recorded, the currents of social change."[89]

In regard to one issue, however, convention delegates believed that they possessed a decided advantage over legislators, and they had few qualms about removing such matters from the political process. Although legislators were thought to be ordinarily competent to deliberate responsibly, their particular interest in maintaining their offices occasionally prevailed over the public interest in extending the suffrage or drawing district lines in an equitable manner. As a result, convention delegates spent a significant amount of time debating and resolving these issues.[90] As Delaxon Smith argued in the Oregon Convention of 1857:

I am satisfied from my experience in this country that the legislative assembly can never—will never—justly and equitably apportion the representation of the several counties of the state if left to them. . . . That is the only paramount reason why I desire to have the constitution settle that matter for the government of legislative bodies. And why will not legislative bodies do it as well as the convention of the people or delegates? Simply because where one man is elected to the legislature by a small constituency, if they have an advantage they want to maintain it. They are unwilling to part with it. And there is always enough to create a majority of that kind, especially in a new country like this.[91]

With this exception, convention delegates were guided by a general hostility toward constitutional legislating, especially in the first half of the nineteenth century. To be sure, this reluctance declined as the century progressed, and in a series of constitutional conventions held after the 1840s, delegates became slightly more active in placing procedural restrictions on the legislative process. Then, in the postbellum era, some state conventions began not only to restrict legislative deliberations but also to enact substantive provisions to resolve controversial issues.[92] Even after convention delegates began to yield more frequently to proposals to engage in constitutional legislation, however, there was still a stigma attached to such behavior. Delegates who proposed such amendments had to justify their behavior, and they were criticized for deviating from the institutional norm.

Philip Doddridge came perhaps the closest of any of the nineteenth-century convention delegates to expressing this regime norm. He argued in the course of the Virginia Convention of 1829–1830 that some matters "should be unalterably laid deep in the foundations of the Constitution." For instance, "at no time should an *ex post facto* law, or law impairing the obligation of contracts be passed, nor any provision for suspending the writ of *habeas corpus* in time of peace, or taking away the trial by jury, in criminal cases." But on other matters, he argued, the convention should remain silent: "[T]o place them on Constitutional foundations, is to suppose that at *no future time* and under no *possible* circumstances, will it be wise to change them for some other establishments more suited to the times," which was a supposition that Doddridge and his contemporaries were, for the most part, unwilling to make.[93]

CONCLUSION

It becomes possible, in the end, to identify a set of regime norms that governed institutional behavior in the eighteenth and nineteenth centuries. To be sure, public officials occasionally acted in ways that departed from these norms. It is true, also, that institutional behavior was not uniform throughout the era or across the states. Nevertheless, there was a shared understanding that certain constitutional provisions served as the principal guarantors of rights, that certain institutions were primarily responsible for securing rights, and that rights would ordinarily be protected in a particular manner.

The republican regime is distinguished, in the first place, by its reliance on constitutional provisions that established the frame of government. The most effective way to protect rights, according to this view, was to prevent them from being violated. This was achieved by allocating powers to separate institutions, ensuring that each institution performed its proper function, and giving each institution the means to prevent encroachments. Thus institutional principles, such as separation of powers and bicameralism, as well as restrictions on the legislative process, such as subject-title requirements and bans on special and local legislation, were the chief means of promoting effective deliberation and preventing the violation of rights.

Although a number of institutions contributed to the protection of rights, the legislature was entrusted with primary responsibility. Legislatures were thought to be sufficiently representative of the popular will and therefore were viewed as the appropriate forum for resolving claims of rights. Accordingly, judges and constitutional convention delegates generally deferred to the people's elected representatives for the protection of their most important rights.

Finally, statutes were the ideal vehicle for securing rights. On the one hand, statutes were preferable to constitutional amendments and judicial decisions, because these measures were too unwieldy and could be changed only by enacting a constitutional amendment. On the other hand, statutes were preferable to legislative referendums, because these measures failed to provide adequate opportunity for institutional deliberation.

3

Republican Institutions as Keepers of the People's Liberties

One searches in vain for systematic evaluations of rights protection in the nineteenth century. So accustomed are we to equating the protection of rights with decisions of the U.S. Supreme Court that conventional accounts usually begin no earlier than the second quarter of the twentieth century, when the U.S. Supreme Court began to apply the federal Bill of Rights to the states. As a result, scholars are apt to conclude, along with Robert Rutland, that:

> Not until the Fourteenth Amendment spread its broad umbrella did the Bill of Rights assume the guardianship role its authors intended. The 140 years between ratification of the First Amendment and *Near v. Minnesota* span a period when almost all the civil liberties of individuals were denied to citizens who were also abolitionists, religious zealots, suspected Confederate sympathizers, foreign-born members of the Industrial Workers of the World (or even obstreperous native IWWers), pacifists, conscientious objectors, supporters of the newborn Soviet Union, labor leaders, or suffragettes.[1]

Even among the relatively modest number of scholars who have turned their gaze to the state courts, the view still predominates "that courts did not actively protect these rights in any substantive sense,"[2] and that they were "supine" with respect to the guarantee of a fair trial, among other rights.[3]

This conventional narrative is unsatisfying for several reasons. Most importantly, as we have seen, it looks in the wrong place for evidence of rights protection. According to Suzanna Sherry: "In the modern world, the search for state protections of liberty generally conjures up an image of state courts using state constitutions to prevent infringement of such core civil liberties as freedom of the press and security from unreasonable searches and seizures." But "the absence of modern civil liberties cases in those reports does not mean that the past is barren, only that we are looking for the wrong thing."[4] Connecticut Supreme Court Justice

Ellen Peters argued, similarly, that "we should cast a wider net to discover the variety of ways in which substantive rights were protected in state courts in our early years," other than through constitutional decision making.[5] Although Sherry and Peters are concerned primarily with the way in which state courts protected rights in nonconstitutional ways, the next step is to investigate the record of state legislatures in protecting rights, which was the dominant method during this period. It is important, therefore, in determining how well rights were protected in the eighteenth and nineteenth centuries, to take account of the full range of ways in which institutions can secure rights. This includes occasions when legislatures enacted statutes that secured rights, as well as instances when structural arrangements prevented the passage of statutes that would have violated rights.

The conventional account is also deficient in that it does not take account of the various ways in which rights can be violated. As a result, it fails to distinguish between violations of rights that are attributable to the existing institutional arrangement and violations that are a product of an immature popular conception of rights. As Lawrence Friedman argued: "We tend, of course, to look at the past through the lenses of today. It is natural, then, to ask why this or that was missing in the nineteenth century. The nineteenth century had its own viewpoint. To understand the period, we have to look at civil rights and civil liberties as contemporaries saw them."[6] Because nineteenth-century attitudes and expectations "were considerably more limited than twentieth-century expectations,"[7] it would be improper to hold institutions responsible for the inability to provide a level of protection for rights that would match current expectations.

It is important, in particular, to acknowledge that there are several categories of rights. Certain rights are of a constant character, in that they were recognized throughout the era; others are of an evolving character, in that they were only recognized in the course of the era; and others, finally, are of a variable character, in that their status shifted constantly throughout the period. To distinguish between rights in this manner, it should be emphasized, is to place no less importance on the failure to protect rights of any kind. Rather, this enables us to separate the relative contributions of popular understanding of rights, on the one hand, from the role of institutional arrangements, on the other hand.

We are led, therefore, to raise different analytical questions, depending on the type of right at issue. The relevant question with regard to constant rights is: To what extent did legislatures prevent them from being violated and provide for their extension as circumstances dictated? The important question with respect to evolving rights is somewhat different: To what extent did legislatures succeed in recognizing these rights in a suitable fashion? Finally, with respect to variable rights, the relevant question becomes: To what extent did legislatures provide a forum for registering and deliberating about various changes in public opinion?

Clearly there is room for debate over which rights should be placed in which categories. One would also expect some disagreement over the proper standard for judging the level of protection of these rights. Because it would be unwise to demand more precision than a subject permits, it is appropriate to acknowledge the force of these objections and proceed by advancing the most reasonable judgments that the evidence will support.

FREEDOM TO WORSHIP

None of the four states permitted actual violations of the freedom to worship during this period. The principal issue with which legislatures were concerned was the proper way to extend this right to provide exemptions from ministerial taxes, militia service, Sabbatarian laws, and religious oaths, as well as to give practical meaning to the general guarantee of religious liberty in the context of various public institutions.

Freedom from Ministerial Taxes

The aspect of religious liberty that sparked the most intense and sustained controversy during this era was the right to be exempt from paying taxes to support an established church. Michigan and Oregon were spared these discussions, because by the time they drafted their constitutions, religious liberty was thought to preclude state support of religion. Both the Virginia and Massachusetts constitutions initially interpreted religious liberty in a more narrow fashion, however, and popular opinion in those states only gradually evolved to a broader understanding. In both states, legislation served as the primary vehicle for recording this evolving interpretation.

Virginia was the first of these states to disestablish. The Virginia General Assembly took a significant step in the direction of securing religious liberty in 1776 at the very first session held under its new constitution. At the urging of memorials from a number of churches,[8] and with the support of Thomas Jefferson, the legislature repealed all acts that made "criminal the maintaining any opinions in matters of religion . . . or the exercising any mode of worship whatsoever," and it suspended for one year all laws that required taxes for the support of the clergy.[9] As a result, "no taxes for religious purposes were ever paid in Virginia after January 1, 1777."[10] Subsequent memorials led to a series of temporary suspensions of the tax, and finally, in 1779, the legislature "confirmed what the acts of 1776, 1777, and 1778 had practically perpetuated," by enacting a permanent repeal of the assessment tax.[11]

The right remained insecure, however, because according to Jefferson, "although the majority of our citizens were dissenters, . . . a majority of the Legislature were churchmen."[12] Therefore, when Episcopalian, as well as some Presbyterian, churches supported a bill in 1784 to renew the old ministerial tax, and the bill actually proceeded as far as a second reading in the House of Delegates, James Madison, one of the leading opponents of the measure, sought to enlist the support of the citizens of Virginia. Madison succeeded in postponing a third reading of the bill until the November 1785 session, and in the meantime, he secured the passage of a resolution directing that the proposed bill, along with a list of its legislative supporters and opponents, be distributed throughout the state. The wisdom of Madison's strategy soon became apparent. He wrote to James Monroe in May 1785:

> The printed bill has excited great discussion, and is likely to prove the sense of the community to be in favor of the liberty now enjoyed. I have heard of several counties where the representatives have been laid aside for voting for the bill, and not a single one where the reverse has happened. The Presbyterian clergy, too, who were in general friends of the scheme, are already in another tone, either compelled by the laity of that sect or alarmed at the probability of farther interference of the Legislature, if they begin to dictate in matters of religion.[13]

As a result of the flood of ensuing petitions and memorials, as well as the shift in the attitude of Presbyterian leaders, the assessment bill was defeated. In the wake of the defeat, Madison took the opportunity to introduce what is now referred to as Jefferson's Statute for Religious Freedom, which passed both houses by a significant margin. It declared: "That no man shall be compelled to frequent or support any religious worship, place, or ministry whatsoever, nor shall be enforced, restrained, molested, or burthened in his body or goods, nor shall otherwise suffer on account of his religious opinions or beliefs."[14]

Several vestiges of establishment remained, however, most notably the continued Episcopal ownership of the glebe lands that supported the parish ministers. Accordingly, after a series of further memorials, the General Assembly in 1799 proceeded to declare that the continued possession of these lands was no longer consistent with the prevailing interpretation of the religious liberty clause in the declaration of rights.[15] But although this act invalidated all Episcopal Church claims to the properties, it did not call for the sale of any particular glebe lands,[16] and it was not until 1802 that the General Assembly ordered all the glebe lands to be sold, thereby completing the process of disestablishment.[17]

At this point, one of the parish wardens sought to prevent the sale of his lands, and he pleaded his case before the Virginia Court of Appeals. If not for what has been called "a marked intervention of providence," the previous extensions of the right to religious liberty would have been overturned.[18] The president of the court, Justice Edmund Pendleton, had prepared an opinion that would have voided the 1802 law as an improper encroachment on the churches' right to the land. But "the opinion was not delivered, as he died the night before it was to have been pronounced."[19] The ensuing appointment of Justice St. George Tucker produced a reconfigured court that reversed itself and left undisturbed the disestablishment legislation.[20]

The road to disestablishment in Massachusetts was much longer, and the right to be exempt from paying ministerial taxes was achieved with greater difficulty.

Support for disestablishment was not as strong in Massachusetts as it was in Virginia; therefore it took more time for religious dissenters to persuade a majority of the people of the injustice of the state-supported system. In addition, once this view had obtained the support of a majority of the citizens and legislators, their efforts to secure religious liberty were hampered by a variety of constitutional and judicial actions.

Throughout most of the seventeenth and eighteenth centuries, the relationship between church and town in Massachusetts was governed by laws that on the surface required each town to financially support a minister but in practice "granted almost complete religious freedom." In fact, during the colonial period, the "legislature had ample authority to liberalize the ecclesiastical statutes and had done so from time to time."[21] Thus in the 1720s the legislature granted explicit exemptions for Baptists and Quakers who could produce certificates of membership in one of those societies, and then in the 1770s it provided even more liberal exemptions.[22]

When the Massachusetts Constitution of 1780 was adopted, it actually had the effect of limiting the rights of religious dissenters.[23] In the first place, the constitution directed the legislature to require "the several towns . . . to make suitable provision, at their own expense, for the institution of the public worship of God, and for the support and maintenance of public Protestant teachers . . . in all cases where such provision shall not be made voluntarily."[24] Additionally, although the constitution provided that certain persons could be exempt from this requirement, the clause was "so laden with quasi-statutory provisions that the General Court, unlike its provincial predecessor had only the most peripheral opportunity to enact useful interpretative legislation that would meet the changing needs of the times."[25]

In the next several decades, the Massachusetts General Court made several efforts to enlarge the rights of religious dissenters. In 1797 it enacted a law to "exempt the people called Quakers from paying taxes for the support of public worship."[26] It then provided another measure of liberalization in 1800, by exempting members of all other denominations who regularly attended the worship services of an incorporated religious society.[27]

The precise extent of these statutes remained unclear, however. Some argued that the legislature intended to permit dissenters to apply their tax money even in the case of an unincorporated parish, which was the status of many of the dissenting sects. Accordingly, in 1810 Thomas Barnes, a minister of one of these unincorporated societies, tried to recover the tax money to which he claimed he was entitled under the law. But the Massachusetts Supreme Court concluded that the legislature had not intended to go quite this far in securing religious liberty. When Chief Justice Theophilus Parsons examined the act of 1800, he argued: "Certainly no conclusion can be drawn from it, that the statute intended to exempt any citizen, except Quakers, from contributing to the support of some public Protestant teacher."[28] To those who argued that such an establishment offended the guarantee of freedom to worship according to one's conscience,

Parsons responded that this "seems to mistake a man's conscience for his money."[29] In his view, the results of such a disestablishment would be disastrous for the polity: "Civil government, therefore, availing itself only of its own powers, is extremely defective; and unless it could derive assistance from some superior power, whose laws extend to the temper and disposition of the human heart, and before whom no offence is secret; wretched indeed would be the state of man under a civil constitution of any form."[30] In what therefore constituted a significant defeat for religious dissenters, Parsons ruled that Barnes and similarly situated ministers could not receive the tax money that their parishioners had paid.

Public opposition to this ruling was so swift and strong that the Massachusetts General Court responded in its next session by enacting the Religious Freedom Act of 1811.[31] This law, which for all practical purposes proclaimed "the right of every man to have his ministerial taxes paid to his own religious society, corporate or not," held that any properly ordained minister could receive the taxes paid by the members of his society, and that any citizen could so designate his taxes merely by filing a form with the town clerk.[32] "After the passage of the Religious Freedom Act of 1811 the commonwealth no longer supervised the quality of religious instruction. The sects were placed on an equal basis with the Congregationalists in the matter of supporting their own ministers. They could choose their own ministers and decide on their own qualifications."[33]

When the Massachusetts Supreme Court heard a challenge to this law in 1817, the justices were presented with a number of reasons why they should uphold their previous decisions and interpret the law narrowly. Chief Justice Isaac Parker acknowledged that there would be financial and moral "mischief to be dreaded" from the "breaking up of the parochial religious establishments, by authorizing any number of individuals to withdraw themselves, in the easy and loose way which is provided in this act."[34] In a major break from previous decisions, however, he upheld the legislature's interpretation of the freedom of worship clause. Parker argued that although the law might well have the effect of reducing the level of virtue in the populace, the appropriate avenue for redress was through the legislature. "[O]ur duty is to give effect to such acts of the legislature as they have the constitutional authority to make, without regarding their evil tendency or inexpediency. Subsequent legislatures may correct the proceedings of their predecessors, which may be found to have been improvident or pernicious. And if a law, however complained of, is suffered to remain unrepealed, the only legal presumption is, that it is the will of the community that such should be the law."[35]

Several additional steps were taken to complete the process of disestablishment in Massachusetts. In 1824, in response to the entreaties of Trinitarians, Baptists, and Universalists, the General Court enacted a religious liberties act that made it even easier for religious societies to grant tax exemptions.[36] All that remained was to repeal the offensive constitutional provision altogether, which was accomplished through a constitutional amendment ratified in 1833.

This survey of the process of disestablishment in Virginia and Massachusetts yields several conclusions. In the first place, the right to be exempt from supporting an established church was not secured through judicial review of legislation. In both states, the courts were the primary defenders of the existing establishment, and disestablishment was not achieved until changes in judicial personnel led the courts to reverse their earlier decisions. Nor was this right secured primarily through constitutional provisions. The Massachusetts Constitution of 1780 actually served as an obstacle to legislative efforts to liberalize religious freedom laws, and the most significant gains in Massachusetts and Virginia were achieved without resort to the constitutional amendment process. Finally, the legislative actions that were in fact responsible for securing this right did much to vindicate the view that rights would be protected primarily through the political process. Madison, for one, believed that freedom of religion in the states "arises from that multiplicity of sects, which pervades America, and which is the best and only security for religious belief in any society. For where there is such a variety of sects, there cannot be a majority of any one sect to oppress and persecute the rest." According to Judge John Noonan, this was "[e]xactly so in Massachusetts. The multiplicity of sects was the chief obstacle to religious establishment. The split of the Congregationalists into Trinitarians and Unitarians, the Universalist defection from the Unitarians, the increase of the Baptists, and the appearance of Catholics all led to changes promoting religious freedom."[37]

The Right to Be Exempt from Military Service

Along with paying taxes, the duty to take up arms in the defense of the state has long been viewed as inherent in citizenship, and as a result, it was no small decision to exempt individuals from fulfilling this fundamental duty. In fact, though, eighteenth- and nineteenth-century legislatures consistently determined that the freedom to worship included the right of conscientious objectors to be exempt from service in the militia.

There was actually very little dispute over the general question of whether conscientious dissenters should be exempt from militia service, and each of the states enacted statutes that guaranteed this basic right.[38] The more contentious issues concerned how best to secure the right in particular circumstances. The first question to be addressed was which sects could apply for exemptions. Thus the initial Massachusetts Act of 1775 excepted only the Quakers,[39] but in 1793 this was amended to include the Shakers.[40] The Michigan Legislature provided exemptions for the Quakers and the Shakers.[41] The Virginia General Assembly also exempted the Mennonites.[42]

The next question was which members of these societies could qualify for an exemption. In 1781 the Massachusetts General Court determined that any individual who sought an exemption should provide a certificate from the town selectmen attesting to the fact that he was a conscientious objector. Then in 1809 the General Court provided that each objector would have to produce a certificate from his religious society attesting that he "is a member of our Society, and that he frequently and usually attends with said Society for religious worship, and we believe is conscientiously scrupulous of bearing arms."[43]

A final question concerned which duties dissenters would have to fulfill in the absence of performing military service. The Massachusetts General Court determined that objectors should "pay their full proportion of all expenses for raising men . . . together with an addition of ten per centum."[44] The Virginia General Assembly determined that religious societies should bear the cost of providing "proper substitutes to serve in their stead."[45] By the time of the Civil War, the price of a substitute had increased, and religious societies were no longer responsible for bearing the costs. The General Assembly found that the individual should pay "the sum of five hundred dollars, and in addition thereto, the further sum of two per cent of the assessed value of said applicant's taxable property."[46]

To the extent that courts were involved in securing this right, their role was confined to applying these statutes in particular cases. When Stacy Fletcher of Massachusetts appealed his denial of an exemption in 1815, the Massachusetts Supreme Court ruled that, "[b]y the statute," applicants were required to produce certificates stating that they *"frequently and usually"* attended society meetings; but Fletcher's society had stipulated only that he did "attend" those meetings. The court ruled, therefore, that he could not be exempt from service.[47] Another Massachusetts Quaker, John Lees, produced a certificate that included the "frequently and usually" clause but omitted the last clause, in which the elders of the society would normally state *"that they believe he is conscientiously scrupulous of bearing arms."* Lees acknowledged as much, but he urged the court to provide a more liberal interpretation of the right. The court concluded, however: "It is . . . certain that the legislature, who passed the law, were not of this opinion." These clauses were required for a particular purpose: to guard against fraud and the granting of inappropriate exemptions.[48]

The Right to Take an Alternative Oath

At first glance, the right of religious dissenters to give alternative oaths or affirmations does not appear to be as significant as various other aspects of religious liberty. In fact, though, oaths had far-reaching implications in the eighteenth and nineteenth centuries. They determined who could hold public office, serve on a jury, execute any number of legal duties, and testify in court. When one also considers the seriousness with which oaths were treated in this era, it is no surprise that legislatures were frequently called upon to deliberate over who could qualify for exemptions, under which circumstances, and with what consequences.[49]

The first question to be settled was whether religious dissenters had a right to serve on juries and in other legal capacities. The legislatures of Virginia, Michigan, and Oregon provided from the start that anyone could give an alternative oath in a legal proceeding, and that individuals who were opposed to taking an oath of any kind could give an affirmation instead.[50] The Massachusetts General Court gradually evolved to this position. In 1798 it enacted a law that permitted Quakers to take an alternative oath as jurors or witnesses,[51] and in 1811 it extended the right to apply to the "discharge of any office, place, or business, or on any other lawful occasion."[52] Then, after the Massachusetts Supreme Court made clear in 1812 that "both in the statute respecting jurors, and in the latter statute, where the more general provision is made, it is only the case of *quakers* scrupulous of taking oaths, in which the legislature have authorized an affirmation to be received instead of an oath,"[53] the General Court provided that "any person" with religious scruples could "affirm in the manner provided by law for the denomination of Quakers."[54]

It was quite another matter to provide that religious dissenters could testify in court, and in fact this right was only gradually secured in the course of the nineteenth century. Religious oaths were thought to be essential to ensuring the integrity of an individual's testimony, and great risk attached to the removal of this guarantee, in the view of many. Thus Jefferson wrote in his *Notes on the State of Virginia:* "The legitimate powers of government extend to such acts only as are injurious to others. But it does me no injury for my neighbor to say there are twenty Gods, or no God. It neither picks my pocket nor breaks my leg." When he went on to consider whether the loss of the religious sanction would impair the truthfulness of testimony in court, however, he was willing to acknowledge the force of this objection. "If it be said, his testimony in a court of justice cannot be relied on," he wrote, "reject it then, and be the stigma on him."[55] Despite these concerns and what Virginia Justice John Scott described as the "great value" placed on "the obligation of an oath,"[56] each state legislature gradually guaranteed the right of dissenters to testify without taking the required oath.[57]

Although a witness could not be declared incompetent on account of religious beliefs, it remained to be determined whether he could be questioned about his religious views and thus have his credibility impugned in the eyes of the jury. In the course of the nineteenth century, legislators decided that this too was inherent in the right to worship, and they enacted statutes to secure this extension of the right.[58]

On one final question, whether atheists could testify, the Massachusetts General Court, for one, was unwilling to interpret the right in such an expansive manner. The Massachusetts Supreme Court ruled in an 1848 case that neither the constitution nor any statute protected individuals who did not believe in any god, and the Massachusetts General Court declined to interpret this right in a different manner. Justice Samuel Wilde noted: "It would indeed seem absurd, to administer to a witness an oath, containing a solemn appeal for the truth of his testimony, to a being in whose existence he has no belief."[59]

Freedom of Worship in the Schools

Some of the most heated debates over religious liberty arose in connection with education. Questions arose, in particular, as to whether public funds could support religious schools, whether religious material could be used in public schools, and whether legislatures could regulate the operation of religious schools. As the nineteenth century progressed, these questions were increasingly answered in the negative, and in nearly every case, the advances for religious liberty were secured through legislation.

Religious liberty could be threatened, in the first place, by the appropriation of public funds to support religious schools. In Massachusetts the prohibition on the use of funds for this purpose was secured through a constitutional amendment in 1855,[60] but in the remaining states it was secured through legislation. The Virginia General Assembly enacted a series of statutes in the 1830s and 1840s to prohibit the appropriation of state funds to theological academies or institutions.[61] In similar fashion, the Michigan legislature provided that "No school district shall apply any of the money received by it from the primary school interest fund or from any and all other sources for the support of any school of a sectarian character."[62]

Religious liberty could also be threatened by the use of religious or sectarian books in the public schools. The debate concerned not so much whether the Bible would be read in the schools (this practice was largely unchallenged in the nineteenth century) but which version would be used and in which fashion. As Samuel Spear noted in an 1878 essay, two Bibles were used in America: "The English version, sometimes designated as the King James's Bible, and the Douay version. The former is the Bible of Protestantism, and the latter the Bible of English-speaking Catholics. . . . Neither uses the Bible of the other."[63]

Nowhere did this issue generate more passion than in Massachusetts, the birthplace of the modern public school system under Horace Mann. At the inception of the state public school system in 1827, the Massachusetts General Court provided that school committees "shall never direct to be purchased or used, in any of the town schools, any school books which are calculated to favor the tenets of any particular sect of Christians."[64] Controversy erupted in the 1850s, however, when Catholic attendance in the public schools increased dramatically, and Protestants responded by securing the enactment of a law that directed school committees to "require the daily reading of some portion of the Bible in the common English version."[65] Although many school committees continued to adhere to the spirit of the 1827 law and to be sensitive to the diverse religious faiths of their students, the Boston schools were the scene of one notorious deviation from this policy. In an incident that attracted a great deal of attention throughout the state, a ten-year-old Catholic boy, Thomas Wall, was beaten in 1859 for refusing to follow his teacher's orders to read from the Protestant Bible, and the teacher was subsequently acquitted at trial of any wrongdoing.[66]

Catholics secured a reversal of this policy in Boston largely through the political process. The uproar over the Wall case led to the election of the first Catholic to the Boston school committee and the subsequent repeal of the offensive rules.[67] Religious liberty in the public schools was secured on a statewide level when Catholics succeeded in persuading the legislature of the injustice of the 1855 law. In 1862, on account of the force of these arguments, as well as the strong participation of Catholics in the Union army during the Civil War, the General Court revised its Bible-reading law to omit any mention of the "English version," to provide that the Bible should be read "without written note or oral comment," and to direct that the school committee "shall require no scholar to read from any particular version, whose parents or guardian shall declare that he has conscientious scruples against allowing him to read therefrom."[68] One Catholic newspaper opined: "This is a long stride from the Know-Nothingism of 1854, the remnants of which seem to have been pretty nearly disposed of by the Civil War."[69] In 1880 the General Court further revised the law to provide that students could be excused not only from reading out of a particular version with which they disagreed but also from "tak[ing] any personal part in the reading."[70]

In Virginia, this particular aspect of the right to worship was secured in several ways throughout the course of the nineteenth century. Beginning in the 1840s, the General Assembly provided that in local school districts, "no books shall be used nor instruction given in the public schools, calculated to favour the doctrinal tenets of any religious sect or denomination."[71] With the advent of a statewide school system in 1870, the first superintendent of public schools, William Ruffner, announced that the question of Bible reading "was to be left for determination to the direction of local authorities," within proper bounds and as long as students could receive exemptions. As the historian Sadie Bell explained: "The historic position of the legal separation of church and state was not to be marred by a legal incorporation of anything that would tend to establish a definite alliance between church and state," but "where the people wished to co-operate in permitting the Church to exert a religious influence in education, it was to be allowed."[72]

To be sure, some dissatisfied parents in the nineteenth century occasionally took to the state courts to seek further exemptions, but judges routinely declined to overturn legislative determinations. For instance, the town of Woburn, Massachusetts, directed that each school day begin with a Bible reading, but that "any scholar should be excused from bowing the head, whose parent requested it."[73] In 1866, one student's father refused to request an exception, and when the student disobeyed the rule and was dismissed from school, her father challenged the dismissal in court. The Massachusetts Supreme Court ruled, however, that because the town rule provided exemptions for students with religious scruples, it was consistent with the current statutory guarantee and therefore did not encroach on religious freedom.[74]

In 1898 the Michigan Supreme Court heard a similar challenge to a Bible-reading provision in the Detroit public schools, and the court deferred in similar fashion to the legislative judgment. The judges were impressed by the fact that under the Michigan statute, as in Massachusetts, the teachers were not permitted to comment on the reading, nor were the students required to sit through the reading if their parents requested an exemption.[75]

Religious liberty could be threatened, finally, by laws that sought to regulate the operation of religious schools. In the second half of the nineteenth century, an increasing number of Catholics began to send their children to diocesan schools, and Protestants tried on several occasions to prevent them from doing so by introducing legislation that sought to impose a variety of onerous regulations on religious schools. Significantly, these bills were routinely defeated, due in large part to the operation of institutional arrangements and rules of legislative procedure that were designed to obtain the reflective, rather than the reflexive, voice of the public.

The first of these offensive bills was introduced in the 1855 session of the Massachusetts General Court and would have required that all private school teachers receive the approval of the town school committee. As Robert Lord and John Sexton noted, "One can imagine the reception that would have been given to a Catholic nun who appeared for examination."[76] The bill received the support of a majority of the Massachusetts House of Delegates, but it was rejected by the Senate and failed to become law.

Another oppressive bill was introduced in the same session, and the patrons tried to mask its true intent by burying its contents in an unrelated child-labor bill. When one senator unwittingly tried to attach a controversial rider to the bill, however, the supporters were forced to acknowledge its actual purpose. As one of the patrons argued: "The bill has a further object, a peculiarly American object. It is true we did not wish to bring that object out fully to view. We wished to bring that object out as quietly as we could, for it is a subject that has occasioned the committee more difficulty than any that has come before them this year, and this object was, if we must say it, to break up the Catholic schools."[77] The resulting publicity and subsequent deliberation were instrumental in preventing the passage of this bill as well.

A third effort to unduly restrict the Catholic schools came in the form of inspection bills that were introduced in the 1888 and 1889 sessions of the Massachusetts General Court. These bills sought to require government approval of all private schools, textbooks, teachers, and student progress and to levy fines on any individual who tried to induce parents to remove their children from the public schools.[78] Introduced in an atmosphere of great excitement, the bills were then considered by a legislative joint committee, which proceeded to hold a total of twenty hearings. With the appropriate time for reflection and deliberation, and after several distinguished Protestant leaders spoke against the bills, virtually all the offensive provisions were withdrawn.[79] In fact, "[l]ong before the hearings were ended, the bill was already condemned by public opinion."[80]

Sabbatarian Legislation

At the beginning of the nineteenth century, virtually no states granted exemptions for individuals who observed the Sabbath on the seventh day rather than the first day, which was the custom of the majority of religious observers. By the close of the nineteenth century, however, the right of individuals to be exempt from Sabbatarian laws was protected in a number of circumstances, and in nearly all cases this came about through the passage of legislation.

The movement for the reform of Sabbatarian laws began in the 1840s, when William Lloyd Garrison issued a call for an American Anti-Sunday-Law Convention that was held in Boston and was addressed to "the friends of civil and religious liberty." Garrison called attention to what he believed was a contradiction between "the right of every man to worship God according to the dictates of his own conscience" and the fact that "in all the States, excepting Louisiana, there are laws enforcing religious observance of the first day of the week as the sabbath, and punishing as criminal such as attempt to pursue their usual avocations on that day."[81] Accordingly, the convention recommended to "all friends of religious liberty throughout the country the presentation of petitions to the next Legislature, in every State in which such laws exist, and protesting against their enactment as an unhallowed union of church and state."[82]

During the course of the nineteenth century, nearly all the state legislatures responded by enacting statutes that embodied the general spirit of this resolution. Thus the Massachusetts General Court declared: "Whoever conscientiously believes that the seventh day of the week ought to be observed as the Sabbath, and actually refrains from secular business and labor on that day, shall not be liable to the penalties . . . for performing secular business and labor on the Lord's Day if he disturbs no other person."[83] A number of states provided more specific guarantees. For instance, the Michigan Legislature provided a series of exemptions from general laws for those who observed the Sabbath on the seventh day. For one thing, it directed that no conscientious observer "shall be compelled to defend any civil suit in the justice's courts of this State on that day."[84] In addition, although barbers were generally prohibited from working on Sundays, the legislature exempted all individuals "who conscientiously believe the seventh day of the week should be observed as the Sabbath, and who actually refrain from secular business on that day."[85]

Judicial activity in this area was generally confined to applying these statutes to particular circumstances, such as when the Michigan Supreme Court upheld the exception for barbers in the face of arguments that it applied only to a particular class of citizens.[86] But when litigants pleaded with courts to provide further exemptions that had not been granted by the legislature, judges routinely declined to do so. Thus in 1876, in a case involving a Jewish storekeeper, the Massachusetts Supreme Court agreed with the ruling of the Superior Court that the law "could not be extended so as to permit the act of keeping open a shop upon the Lord's day."[87] Nor would the court permit a Jewish shopkeeper to open his store on Sunday, even if it was kept open solely for the purpose of selling kosher meats to others of the Jewish faith.[88]

Freedom to Worship in the Context of Marriage, Prison, and Public Expression

At the start of the republican era, a number of laws were in place that required marriages to be performed by Protestant ministers. It was not uncommon, therefore, for Catholic priests or ministers of other faiths to be brought into court and charged with performing illegal marriages.[89] As public opinion evolved throughout the course of the century, however, legislatures enacted a series of statutes that provided exemptions for Quakers, Shakers, Mennonites, Catholics, and Jews.[90] Thus in 1784, in passing a law that was typical of those enacted across the country, the Virginia General Assembly responded to a series of memorials from religious dissenters by stipulating that "it shall and may be lawful for the people called quakers and menonists, or any other christian society that have adopted similar regulations in their church, to solemnize their own marriages."[91]

Then, in the middle of the nineteenth century, the growing reliance on religion for rehabilitative purposes prompted legislatures to address the question of religious liberty in yet another context. Because the ministers who regularly presided at the chapels of prisons and reform institutions were overwhelmingly Protestant, some people began to feel that this constituted a denial of religious liberty to juveniles and criminals. They were concerned, in particular, that "Freedom of conscience and of worship was a boast of Massachusetts, but for the Catholic inmates of her public institutions at that time it simply did not exist."[92] Thus in 1859 the Michigan Legislature acted to protect the rights of religious dissenters by ensuring that when an inmate wanted assistance, "the clergyman of his choice shall be admitted to visit such inmate."[93] Likewise, in 1875 the Massachusetts General Court responded to a series of memorials by providing that "No inmate of any prison, jail, or house of correction in this Commonwealth shall be denied the free exercise of his religious belief and liberty to worship God according to the dictates of his conscience."[94] In 1879 the General Court extended this guarantee to apply to the state's charitable and reform institutions as well.[95]

In one final area, that of religious liberty for atheists, state legislatures retained responsibility for regulating the right but failed to provide a high level of protection. The particular question before eighteenth- and nineteenth-century legislatures was whether laws that prohibited blasphemy were consistent with religious liberty. In most cases, these laws were retained, albeit in a more moderate form than in previous years.[96] Thus in 1782 the Massachusetts General Court reenacted its blasphemy law, but it omitted the penalty of "boring through the tongue" in favor of imprisonment.[97] In one notorious instance in Massachusetts in 1835, one man was even convicted under this law. When Abner Kneeland challenged his conviction in the state supreme court, Chief Justice Lemuel Shaw deferred to the legislature's view that the antiblasphemy law conformed to the guarantee of religious freedom,[98] and the General Court failed to alter this interpretation.[99] Neither the judges nor the legislators of Massachusetts, it would appear, were willing to define religious liberty in such a way as to include the right of atheists to express their views in public.

FREEDOM OF EXPRESSION

The precise understanding of free speech in the republican era has been the subject of much debate.[100] At a minimum, it meant that legislators were privileged from arrest in the performance of their official duties and that prior restraints of publications were prohibited.[101] Aside from this, there were remarkably few efforts to define the meaning of free speech in particular circumstances.[102] The few free-speech issues that did arise were resolved by legislatures, although the record is a mixed one.

The federal Sedition Act of 1798 provided the first threat to free expression, and at least one state legislature responded by better securing free-speech rights. Alongside Madison's Virginia Resolution, which made a case for the unconstitutionality of the law, the Virginia General Assembly enacted a statute that protected all legislators from arrest in the performance of their duties.[103]

Another national controversy, this time concerning the abolition of slavery in the mid-1830s, provided the impetus for another state statute, which on this occasion served to restrict rather than to expand liberty. In response to "a powerful, concerted effort of propaganda [that] had been launched against the Southern way of life by the abolition societies of the North,"[104] Virginia was one of several southern states that enacted laws that directed all "incendiary publications" to be burned and their subscribers fined.[105]

In one final area, concerning the right of defendants in libel cases to demonstrate the truth of their statements, legislatures provided a significant liberalization of free-speech rights. In a series of decisions in the early part of the nineteenth century, the Massachusetts Supreme Court adhered to the common-law rule that prohibited defendants from presenting this evidence.[106] Thus in 1808 a Boston man posted signs around the city claiming: "Caleb Hayward is a liar, a scoundrel, a cheat, and a swindler. Don't pull this down." The lawyer for the accused did not deny the charges, but he sought to "prove the truth of the matters charged in the libel," for he was confident that he could show that Hayward had in fact defrauded his client, tricked him out of money, and "had in many instances acted unfairly."[107] But the trial judge adhered to the common-law rule and denied the motion, and his decision was upheld by the state supreme court. In 1825 Chief Justice Parsons reaffirmed this interpretation: "[T]his is certainly the common law doctrine, and it never has been repealed by any decision of this court."[108] The rule had "stood before the public nearly twenty years, and successive legislatures must be presumed to have acquiesced in its wisdom and policy, or it would have been altered by statute."[109]

In its next session, however, the Massachusetts General Court accepted the judicial recommendation that the legislature declare its intention on the subject. It enacted a statute that provided: "In every prosecution, for writing or for publishing a libel, the defendant may give in evidence, in his defence upon the trial, the truth of the matter contained in the publication, charged as libellous."[110] Nor was the Massachusetts experience exceptional. The Oregon Legislative Assembly was one of a number of state legislatures to secure this free-speech right in the course of the nineteenth century.[111]

THE GUARANTEE OF A FAIR TRIAL

The nineteenth century featured a number of discussions of the precise meaning of the right to a fair trial. Some of these issues, such as the admissibility of evidence, testimony, and witnesses, were considered the proper domain of the judiciary. In general, however, legislatures were responsible for defining the most important fair-trial rights, such as the protection against double jeopardy, the privilege against self-incrimination, the right to retain counsel, the right to obtain a public and speedy trial, and the guarantee against improper searches and seizures. On the whole, legislatures established a commendable level of protection for these rights.

The Right Not to Be Twice Placed in Jeopardy for the Same Offense

Legislatures frequently secured the guarantee against double jeopardy, but as in most of these cases, the important question was not whether to protect the right but rather under which circumstances and in what manner to do so.[112] Thus the Massachusetts General Court provided in its Revised Statutes of 1835 that "A person shall not be held to answer on a second indictment or complaint for a crime of which he has been acquitted upon the facts and merits." A person could be retried only when he had "been acquitted by reason of a variance between the indictment or complaint and the proof, or by reason of a defect of form or substance in the indictment or complaint."[113] In 1848 the Virginia General Assembly enacted a law that contained nearly identical language.[114] The Michigan Legislature followed suit in its Compiled Laws of 1871.[115] Finally, the Oregon Legislative Assembly secured this right in its 1864 Code of Criminal Procedure, and it provided further that an acquittal on a charge of a "crime consisting of different degrees" shall serve as a bar to further prosecution for any degree of the crime.[116] As Jay Sigler noted, the virtue of "placing double jeopardy on a statutory or common law base" was that it made "alteration of the doctrine to suit policy needs much easier than where it may be enshrined in a constitutional provision."[117]

The Privilege Against Self-Incrimination

The privilege against self-incrimination was secured in nearly all the state constitutions, but the challenge was to define this general guarantee in particular circumstances. Once again, state legislatures were primarily responsible for securing the right, which they did by guarding against the two principal ways that the right could be violated.

The right could be violated, in the first place, if defendants were induced to confess to a crime on the basis of promises or threats. Accordingly, legislatures enacted statutes that prohibited the use of coerced confessions. The Oregon Legislative Assembly stipulated that a defendant's confession "cannot be given in evidence against him, when made under the influence of fear, produced by threats."[118] The Michigan Legislature, when it became apprised of the problem of coerced guilty pleas, directed judges to determine whether guilty pleas were made "without undue influence. And whenever said judge shall have reason to doubt the truth of such plea of guilty, it shall be his duty to . . . order a trial."[119] As the Michigan Supreme Court noted in an 1878 case: "The Legislature of 1875, having in some way had their attention called to serious abuses caused by procuring prisoners to plead guilty when a fair trial might show they were not guilty, or might show other facts important to be known, passed a very plain and significant statute designed for the protection of prisoners and of the public."[120]

The right could also be violated when defendants were forced to testify against themselves. Legislatures secured this aspect of the privilege against self-incrimination in two distinct ways in the nineteenth century. Prior to 1859, every state legislature protected the right by preventing defendants from testifying in their own behalf. Although it is difficult in the modern era to comprehend how such a prohibition could actually protect individual rights, early-nineteenth-century legislatures defended this arrangement on the ground that "if we were to hold that a prisoner offering to make a statement must be sworn in the case as a witness, it would be difficult to protect his constitutional rights in spite of every caution, and would often lay innocent parties under unjust suspicion where they were honestly silent, and embarrassed and overwhelmed by the shame of a false accusation."[121]

As the century progressed, public opinion evolved to the point that this came to be seen as a denial rather than a protection of a defendant's fair-trial rights. In 1859 Maine became the first state to permit defendants to testify in their own defense,[122] and other states soon followed suit. In 1861 the Michigan Legislature permitted any defendant "to make a statement to the court or jury."[123] The Massachusetts General Court provided in 1866 that a defendant could testify in all cases.[124] The Virginia General Assembly gradually granted defendants the right to testify. In 1872 it determined that defendants could testify in cases of assault, battery, and trespass,[125] then in 1882 it permitted testimony in a host of other circumstances,[126] and finally in 1886 it provided that defendants could testify in all cases.[127] By the close of the century, all but one state legislature had secured the right in this fashion.[128] As Joel Bodansky argued: "The extent to which the testimony of such persons is today accepted as a matter of course may obscure the fact that, at one time, the extension of competency provoked bitter controversy and was regarded by contemporaries as one of the most significant procedural reforms of the day."[129]

This new arrangement opened the possibility, however, that defendants who chose not to exercise their recently obtained right to testify could be tainted by that choice. It was at this point that legislatures began to enact statutes to ensure that a defendant would not be affected by his decision not to testify. The Virginia General Assembly provided, for instance, that a defendant's "failure to testify shall create no presumption against him, nor be the subject of any comment before the court or jury by the prosecuting attorney."[130] The Massachusetts General Court enacted a similar guarantee.[131] As the Massachusetts Supreme Court explained: "[T]he Constitution of the Commonwealth declares that no subject shall be compelled to accuse or furnish evidence against himself. The statutes allowing persons charged with the commission of crimes or offenses to testify in their own behalf were passed for their benefit and protection, and clearly recognize their constitutional privilege, by providing that their neglect or refusal to testify shall not create any presumption against them."[132]

The Right to Retain Counsel

The right of individuals to retain counsel was interpreted literally at the close of the eighteenth century; it meant that a defendant could retain the counsel of his choice. This was not an insignificant guarantee; it was, after all, a right that was "not always recognized in early English criminal cases." It did not mean, however, that an accused was "entitled, as of right, to have counsel assigned by the court to advise him relative to his plea."[133] In the course of the nineteenth century, however, legislatures interpreted this right in an increasingly expansive fashion. Legislatures first sought to secure the right more effectively, a number of legislatures provided that counsel should be appointed for indigent defendants, and finally some legislatures decided that counsel should not only be appointed to represent these defendants but also be compensated for their efforts.

Legislatures first sought to secure the right to counsel in a meaningful fashion. In 1864, for instance, the Oregon Legislative Assembly enacted a law that held that defendants must be informed of and given adequate opportunity to exercise their right to counsel. "When the defendant is brought before a magistrate upon an arrest, either with or without warrant, or on a charge of having committed a crime, the magistrate must immediately inform him of the charge against him, and of his right to the aid of counsel before any further proceedings are had." Furthermore, the magistrate "must allow the defendant a reasonable time to send for counsel, and adjourn the examination for that purpose." Only when counsel was present could the magistrate "proceed to examine the case."[134]

Several state legislatures then directed courts to appoint counsel for indigent defendants, in certain circumstances. Thus in 1820 the Massachusetts General Court directed that all capital defendants be provided with counsel,[135] and in 1877 it provided that counsel could be assigned to represent inmates of state reform schools at criminal trials.[136] The Michigan Legislature was one of several state legislatures that permitted magistrates to appoint counsel for paupers accused of a broad range of crimes, on a case-by-case basis.[137]

Appointed counsel often represented indigents on a pro bono basis, but some legislatures decided to expand the right even further by directing that counsel should be compensated for their efforts. In 1850, for instance, the Michigan Supreme Court considered whether a lawyer was entitled to recover $50 for his expenses in defending a pauper, but it ultimately found no warrant for his claim.[138] The Michigan Legislature responded in 1859 by enacting a statute that directed all counties to provide compensation. The statute provided that "Whenever any person charged with having committed any felony or misdemeanor shall be unable to procure counsel and the presiding judge shall appoint some attorney to conduct the defense, the attorney so appointed shall be entitled to receive from the county treasurer . . . such an amount as the presiding judge in his discretion shall deem reasonable compensation."[139]

To be sure, defendants occasionally urged courts to overturn their convictions on the ground that the legislature had not gone far enough in extending this right. Judges routinely declined to act, however, in the absence of specific statutory provisions. In considering one such request, the Massachusetts Supreme Court noted: "In an indictment for murder, counsel are assigned to the prisoner by the court, under the provisions of the [statute], and are expected to serve without pay, if the prisoner cannot furnish compensation; and no such prisoner has gone undefended on this ground. There is no provision of statute for assigning counsel to one indicted for a less offence."[140] The courts therefore deferred to legislatures on this subject, and as William Beaney noted, "most states have tried to solve the counsel problem by statute, rather than by constitutional interpretation."[141]

The Right to Obtain a Public and Speedy Trial

The right to a public trial was also secured through legislation. In 1846, for instance, the Michigan Legislature provided: "The sittings of every court within this state shall be public, and every citizen may freely attend the same."[142] This statute was invoked in several instances to secure a defendant's rights. In one case, a trial judge directed a court officer to "see that the room is not overcrowded, but that all respectable citizens be admitted," and as a result, a number of friends of the accused were denied admission. In an effort to sort out the rights to which this man was entitled, the Michigan Supreme Court examined the constitutional guarantee as well as the relevant statute. It concluded: "This statute has been in force since 1846. It voices the sentiment of the people at the time the Constitution of 1850 was adopted. It gives expression to what is there meant by a public trial." Accordingly, the court held that this particular defendant's trial "was accomplished in violation of his constitutional and statutory right to a public trial."[143]

The right to a speedy trial was also secured in several states through legislation, and in a particular manner. For instance, in 1814 the Virginia General Assembly provided that in the case of treasons and felonies, defendants would be released if they were not indicted and tried within a certain time, provided that the delay was not caused or desired by the prisoner.[144] In 1847 the legislature extended the right to apply to "any person held in prison on any charge of having committed a crime."[145] As President James Keith of the Virginia Court of Appeals explained in an 1895 opinion:

> To my mind, the legislature has taken ample and most satisfactory steps to secure to the accused his constitutional right of a "speedy trial," not by limiting or confining the legislature as to the mode of procedure by which it has been thought wise to guard at once the rights of the prisoner and the interest of the Commonwealth, but by providing that there shall be no undue delay in taking the successive steps in the procedure. Thus, in section 4001 the accused is discharged from imprisonment "if a presentment, indictment, or information be not found or filed against him before the end of the second term of the court at which he is held to answer," . . . [and] he shall be forever discharged if four terms of the county, corporation, or hustings court shall pass without a trial. . . . These are means which the legislature has thought sufficient to secure a "speedy trial" within the meaning of the constitution— that is, a trial without delay.[146]

The logic underlying these provisions was that rights were not self-executing. The best way to secure a right was not to specify a rule and then exhort officials to abide by it but rather to arrange institutions and incentives in such a way as to make it in the interest of public officials to protect rights. In this instance, the public interest in effectively prosecuting the case was linked with the defendant's interest in securing a speedy trial, and it was therefore not only the duty but also in the interest of public officials to guarantee the right.

The Guarantee Against Improper Searches and Seizures

The constitutional guarantee against improper search and seizure was secured in the nineteenth century in a manner that is quite foreign to the modern mind. In order to evaluate the extent to which this right was secured in this era, it is important to uncover this traditional approach and to understand its logic.

The first way in which legislatures sought to protect this right, as Akhil Amar, among others, has argued, was to limit the use of search warrants.[147] Whereas it is customary today to conceive of search warrants as a protection against arbitrary searches, individuals in the nineteenth century were prone to view warrants as dangerous to liberty. According to Telford Taylor: "It is perhaps too much to say that they feared the warrant more than the search, but it is plain enough that the warrant was the prime object of their concern. Far from regarding the warrant as a protection against unreasonable and oppressive searches, they saw it as an authority for unreasonable and oppressive searches, and sought to confine its issuance and execution in line with the stringent requirements applicable to common-law warrants for stolen goods."[148]

Accordingly, legislatures imposed strict limitations on the procedures by which warrants were obtained.[149] In 1847, for example, the Virginia General Assembly directed that all warrants would normally be in effect only in the "day time" and must designate "the place and property or things to be searched for."[150] In addition, most states restricted the purposes for which a warrant could be obtained. Thus the Oregon Legislative Assembly stipulated: "A search warrant cannot be issued but upon probable cause, shown by affidavit," and the magistrate was required to "examine, on oath, the complainant and any witnesses he may produce, and take their depositions in writing."[151]

Legislatures were not content to rely on parchment rules to secure this right, however. Although the modern view holds that the way to enforce the guarantee is to exclude illegally obtained evidence at trial, nineteenth-century legislatures determined that the right could best be secured by permitting individuals to bring civil suits against officials who conducted improper searches.[152] Civil suits offered a remedy for all citizens who were the victims of improper searches, not just those who were brought up on criminal charges. In addition, the threat of a civil suit was thought to provide a much stronger incentive for public officials to refrain from conducting improper searches. Accordingly, rights were protected by arranging the law in such a way that the interest of the official in avoiding a suit coincided with the interest of the citizen in avoiding an improper search. In fact, throughout the nineteenth century, "The idea of exclusion was so implausible that it seems almost never to have been urged by criminal defendants, despite the large incentive that they had to do so, in the vast number of criminal cases litigated in the century after Independence. And in the rare case in which the argument for exclusion was made, it received the back of the judicial hand."[153] Thus in 1841, in a decision that served as a model for other states throughout the nineteenth century, the Massachusetts Supreme Court ruled that the guarantee against improper searches and seizures did not require the exclusion of evidence. Justice Samuel Wilde noted: "If the search warrant were illegal, or if the officer serving the warrant exceeded his authority, the party on whose complaint the warrant issued, or the officer, would be responsible for the wrong done; but this is no good reason for excluding the papers seized as evidence, if they were pertinent to the issue, as they unquestionably were."[154]

State legislatures also had a number of particular occasions to deliberate over the meaning of this guarantee in practical circumstances, especially in connection with efforts to restrain behavior such as gaming and drinking. In several of these cases, legislatures failed to provide adequate guarantees, and the right was secured instead through judicial decisions. In 1854, for instance, the Massachusetts Supreme Court struck down a Prohibition law that did not sufficiently limit the use of search warrants,[155] and in 1856, the Michigan Supreme Court invalidated a Prohibition act for similar reasons.[156] In both cases, the courts ruled that the legislatures, in their zeal to stamp out liquor, had run afoul of the guarantee, and in both cases, the legislatures responded promptly by amending their laws to better safeguard the right.[157]

Except for these instances, legislatures assumed and lived up to the responsibility for securing the right. Thus, when the Massachusetts General Court enacted another Prohibition law in 1869, this time it included appropriate protection against unreasonable searches,[158] and the Massachusetts Supreme Court relied on this statutory guarantee to test the validity of future searches. As the court noted in an 1872 case, "The [statute], in accordance with the principles of the common law and of the fourteenth article of our Declaration of Rights, requires that in cases like this," certain rules shall be satisfied. Because the search failed to meet the statutory requirements, it was declared void.[159]

THE RIGHT TO EQUAL PROTECTION UNDER THE LAW

Although most state bills of rights echoed the promise in the Declaration of Independence that all men are created equal in their enjoyment of rights, the framers of the initial constitutions distinguished carefully between natural rights and civil and political rights. Every person was entitled to his natural rights, regardless of race, nationality, or sex, but the rights to vote, to sue and be sued, to marry, and to own land were conventional rights that were to be secured through legislation, when appropriate. As Delegate John Norvell argued in the Michigan Convention of 1835: "The right to vote was not entirely a natural right. It was a question of expediency." He contended that: "The right to vote comes by the law of the land. It is a conventional right. The enjoyment of liberty, property, and the pursuit of happiness, is a natural right."[160] Even at their most deliberative moments in the eighteenth and early nineteenth centuries, few individuals conceived that African Americans, Native Americans, and Asians had a right to citizenship, let alone to attend integrated schools, patronize public establishments, or intermarry with whites. In addition, women were deemed unsuited to enjoy the full rights of citizenship.[161]

In the course of the nineteenth century, however, public opinion evolved to the point that it supported the recognition of a number of these rights,[162] and legislation was invariably the vehicle for securing these changes. To be sure, some of these rights were secured through the acts of national institutions, such as the enactment of amendments to the U.S. Constitution and decisions of the U.S. Supreme Court. In general, though, when these rights were secured, as they were to a significant degree in the latter part of the nineteenth century, this took place through the actions of state legislatures.

The Rights of African Americans

The most important right that was recognized in the course of the nineteenth century was the right of African Americans to be accorded equal treatment under the law. One of the first rights to be secured was the right of blacks, mulattos, and whites to intermarry. William Lloyd Garrison's *Liberator* argued that the existing Massachusetts antimiscegenation law was "a direct invasion of our inalienable rights,"[163] and abolitionists began in 1839 to petition the legislature to repeal the law. In 1841 they secured a majority of votes in the senate and fell only seven votes short in the house. In 1842, when they obtained a majority in both houses, the law was repealed and the right was secured.[164] In 1883 the Michigan legislature recognized the right by repealing the ban on miscegenation and declaring that all previous marriages between blacks and whites would be considered legitimate.[165]

Reformers next turned their attention to securing the right of blacks to attend integrated public schools. This is perhaps the most famous instance of a right that has been secured in the twentieth century through the courts but that was protected in the nineteenth century through legislation.[166] In Massachusetts, the struggle to achieve integrated schools was fought mainly at the town level in the first half of the nineteenth century. Thus African Americans, abolitionists, and sympathetic voters fought for and obtained integration of the Nantucket and Salem schools in the 1840s.[167] Then, in 1845, the General Court took a first step toward establishing the right to attend integrated schools on the statewide level by providing that "any child unlawfully excluded from public school instruction" could sue and recover damages from a school board.[168]

The schools of Boston remained segregated, however, and in 1849 Benjamin Roberts brought suit against the Boston Primary School Committee for illegally excluding his daughter, Sarah, from attending the school closest to her home. Roberts chose as his counsel Charles Sumner, who proceeded to argue the case before the Massachusetts Supreme Judicial Court. Sumner argued, in particular, that the Boston segregation policy offended the Massachusetts declaration of rights.[169] Chief Justice Shaw declined, however, to recognize a right of individuals to attend integrated schools. He argued that the right to nondiscrimination, "as a broad general principle, such as ought to appear in a declaration of rights, is perfectly sound." But this did not mean that Sarah Roberts actually possessed such a right. "Legal rights must, after all, depend upon the provision of law; certainly all those rights of individuals which can be asserted and maintained in any judicial tribunal. The proper province of a declaration of rights and constitution of government, after directing its form, regulating its organization and the distribution of its powers, is to declare great principles and fundamental truths, to influence and direct the judgment and conscience of legislators in making laws, rather than to limit and control them, by directing what precise laws they shall make."[170] When Shaw therefore turned to "the law," in order "to ascertain what are the rights of individuals, in regard to the schools," he concluded that "[i]n the absence of special legislation on this subject, the law has vested the power in the [school] committee to regulate the system of distribution and classification."[171]

In the wake of the *Roberts* decision, abolitionists and leaders in the African American community accepted the court's advice and sought to secure legislative recognition of the right. A bill to prohibit segregated schools was introduced into the 1851 legislative session and even obtained some support before being rejected.[172] Conditions proved more favorable in 1855, when a statute was introduced providing that "no distinction shall be made on account of the race, color, or religious opinions, of the applicant or scholar" in public school admissions, and permitting excluded students to recover civil damages.[173] "In the House, the bill was ordered to a third reading with an affirmative shout, not more than half a dozen voting audibly in opposition. The Senate as readily cooperated."[174] At a banquet held to celebrate the occasion, Charles Slack noted that this was only the latest in a series of legislative successes over the last two decades.

> Well, this prejudice against colored children in the public schools has been driven out of sight—thank God for that! It was another of the triumphs which had marked the struggle for the elevation of the colored race in this Commonwealth. First came the abrogation of the laws against intermarriage—not that many desired that privilege, but they could not consent that a mark of inequality should be placed upon either race, white or black; then the "Jim Crow" car was abolished, and the privilege of travel in every public conveyance fully maintained; then the places of amusement were thrown open to the colored race equally with the white; then followed, in Boston, the abolition of the "negro pew" in the City Directory, and the record of all the citizens alike, without distinctions of color or race.[175]

Legislative statutes were also the vehicle in Michigan for establishing the right to attend integrated schools. In this case, the Detroit schools were the primary battleground. In 1842 the Michigan Legislature took the first step toward ending segregation by combining the separate black and white Detroit school districts into a unitary district, whose schools were to be "public and free to all children."[176] But when the Detroit schools and several other districts remained segregated, the father of one excluded student initiated a lawsuit in 1867 against one of the offending school boards.[177] The legislature acted quickly to amend its statute to make it clear that "all residents of any district shall have an equal right to attend any school therein."[178] Michigan Chief Justice Thomas Cooley examined the statute and concluded: "It cannot be seriously urged that with this provision in force, the school board of any district which is subject to it may make regulations which would exclude any resident of the district from any of its schools, because of race or color, or religious belief, or personal peculiarities. It is too plain for argument that an equal right to all the schools, irrespective of all such distinctions, was meant to be established."[179]

Legislation was the means, finally, of securing the right to nondiscrimination in public accommodations. In the antebellum era, several efforts were undertaken in northern states to establish a right to equal treatment on railcars and steamboats, but these met with little success. The Massachusetts Anti-Slavery Societies tried, unsuccessfully, to persuade the Massachusetts General Court in 1842 and 1843 that segregated railway cars ran afoul of the declaration of rights and should be prohibited.[180] Likewise, a Michigan man was defeated in his 1858 efforts to persuade the Michigan Supreme Court to recognize a right to equal accommodations on steamboats.[181]

With the close of the Civil War, state legislatures became more active in securing these rights. In 1865 the Massachusetts General Court prohibited discrimination on the basis of race "in any public place of amusement, public conveyance or public meeting," or other licensed establishment.[182] This was extended in a series of statutes to cover theaters in 1866,[183] skating rinks and other unlicensed establishments in 1885,[184] barber shops in 1893,[185] and assorted other public places in 1895.[186] The penalties were increased at each step of the process. The original 1865 statute imposed a $50 fine on those who were guilty of discrimination, but this was raised to $100 in 1885, to which was added a maximum civil penalty of $300 in 1895. Moreover, the Massachusetts General Court was dedicated to ensuring that these rights were secured in practice. In 1896 the legislature noted with dismay that an Ohio minister "was refused entertainment at reputable hotels in the city of Boston, because he is a colored man, in spite of statute law against discrimination on account of color." It indicated "that a vigorous campaign for statute rights by the persons most aggrieved will meet the hearty approval and co-operation of the two branches of the general court."[187]

The Michigan Legislature enacted a comprehensive statute in 1885 that established a right to equal treatment in "inns, restaurants, eating-houses, barber shops, public conveyances on land and water, theatres, and all other places of public accommodation and amusement," as well as in service as a "grand or petit juror in any court." Violators of either section could be found guilty of a misdemeanor and penalized by fine or imprisonment.[188]

In an analysis of the right to nondiscrimination in Massachusetts, Francis Fox noted that, although in the present era "one is apt to think of civil rights as being predominantly, if not exclusively, the private preserve of the courts," the recognition of the right to equal treatment "has been a legislative march." Fox argued: "When advances were made they were for the most part, legislative advances. When legislative regressions occurred, they were cured, if at all, by legislative repeal. [The Massachusetts judiciary has] largely cooperated with whatever programs and policies the people, through the General Court, have enacted into law."[189] Fox's analysis of Massachusetts can be said to apply equally well to the other states.

The Rights of Women

At the start of the republican era, married women did not possess full rights of citizenship, and women could not practice law, hold public office, or vote in school board and municipal elections. By the century's close, however, virtually all these states had secured each of these rights, and once again, legislation was the primary means by which these gains were achieved.

In the first place, legislatures removed the disabilities that prevented married women from exercising the same rights as unmarried women. In 1844 Massachusetts became one of the first states to secure the property rights of married women when the General Court enacted a law affirming that a married woman should "have the same rights and powers, and be entitled to the same remedies, in her own name, at law and in equity, and be liable to be sued at law and in equity upon any contract by her made . . . in the same manner and with the same effect as if she were unmarried."[190] In similar fashion, in 1880 the Oregon Legislative Assembly repealed "[a]ll laws which impose or recognize civil disabilities upon a wife which are not imposed or recognized as existing as to the husband."[191]

Women also demanded recognition of the right to practice law. In Michigan and Oregon, this issue was first raised in the legislatures, which enacted statutes that secured the right.[192] In Massachusetts, this question was first taken up by the Supreme Court, which concluded in 1881 that the legislature had not stated its express intention to declare such a right. The court ruled: "It is hardly necessary to add that our duty is limited to declaring the law as it is, and that whether any change in that law would be wise or expedient is a question for the legislative and not for the judicial department of the government."[193] The Massachusetts General Court responded to this invitation at its next session by passing "An Act to permit women to practise as attorneys at law."[194]

The next question was whether the right to equal protection encompassed the right of women to hold public office. In 1883 the Massachusetts General Court determined that women could perform most of the duties of a notary public.[195] When the question then arose whether women could serve on school committees, the Massachusetts General Court also voted yes in 1874,[196] as did the Oregon Legislative Assembly in 1893.[197] Although the Massachusetts statute was permitted to stand,[198] the Oregon law was deemed by the Oregon Supreme Court to be "plainly in violation of the provisions of the constitution, and to that extent void."[199]

When the question arose, finally, whether women could vote in certain representative elections, legislatures again secured the right, although they were occasionally stymied by judicial decisions. The legislatures of Michigan, Oregon, and Massachusetts enacted statutes that permitted women to vote in school elections.[200] But when the Michigan Legislature moved even further and permitted women to vote in all school, village, and city elections,[201] the Michigan Supreme Court invalidated the statute.[202]

The Rights of Native Americans and Aliens

Neither Native Americans, by tradition, nor aliens, by definition, were vested with the same rights enjoyed by the citizens of the various states. In the course of the republican era, though, legislatures enacted statutes that secured full civil rights for Native Americans, as well as the rights of aliens in particular circumstances.

Because Native Americans did not initially qualify as citizens at the start of the nineteenth century, they were not guaranteed the rights to sue, testify in court, or hold land, let alone vote. But as public opinion evolved, legislatures responded by recognizing each of these rights. The Michigan Legislature directed in 1841: "That any Indian shall be capable of suing and being sued in any of the courts of justice of this State, and shall be entitled to all of the judicial rights and privileges of other inhabitants thereof."[203] Likewise, the Virginia General Assembly provided in 1867 that criminal proceedings against Indians "shall be as against a white person."[204] In similar fashion, the Massachusetts General Court enacted a series of statutes between 1859 and 1869 that secured the right. Among other actions, the General Court directed a commissioner to determine the most appropriate means of "conferring civil and political rights in the Indians," then it conferred citizenship on some Native Americans, and eventually it declared all Native Americans to be citizens of the commonwealth.[205]

Aliens were placed in a slightly different situation, in that they could become citizens merely by following the appropriate naturalization requirements. Even so, legislatures acted in certain circumstances to secure their rights when it was appropriate. Thus the Oregon Legislative Assembly provided in an 1872 law that "Any alien may acquire and hold lands, or any right thereto, or interest therein by purchase, devise, or descent, . . . as if such alien were a native citizen of this State or of the United States."[206] Likewise, the legislatures of both Oregon and Massachusetts declared that aliens could be admitted as attorneys to the state bar on the same terms and conditions as citizens, as long as they made it clear that they eventually intended to become citizens.[207]

CONCLUSION

Admittedly, this survey of rights protection in the eighteenth and nineteenth centuries falls short of being comprehensive. A complete evaluation would take account of an even greater number of rights and would include other states. In addition, it would go even further in measuring the extent to which these rights were secured in practice as well as in law. Nevertheless, the existing record is sufficiently rich to support several conclusions about the strengths and weaknesses of republican institutions.

On the one hand, legislatures demonstrated a capacity to secure a reasonable level of protection for a broad array of rights. Legislatures protected virtually all areas of religious liberty, some areas of free speech, and most fair-trial rights. Moreover, as the century progressed, the legislatures of Massachusetts and Michigan secured the legal rights of African Americans to a significant degree, and the legislatures of Massachusetts, Michigan, and Oregon gradually provided rights for women in a number of areas.

On the other hand, legislatures fell short in several areas. There were, of course, some rights that were left unsecured throughout the whole era, such as the rights of atheists in Massachusetts, the rights of women in Virginia, and the rights of blacks in Virginia and Oregon. It is unclear, however, that these deficiencies can be attributed to the prevailing institutional arrangement. The failure to secure these rights was more likely due to an immature conception of rights that prevailed on these particular issues in these states. It is at least an open question whether any other institution would have been more effective in securing the people's liberties in these cases.

Certain failures can be fairly ascribed to republican institutions. In the first place, legislatures did not always regulate the right to vote in an effective manner, and as a result delegates at constitutional conventions occasionally acted to secure this right. In addition, there were various periods when legislators were dominated by a momentary passion and failed to secure rights that were then protected by the judiciary. This took place in particular during periods of Prohibitionist fervor in a number of these states with respect to search-and-seizure rights.

It is important, though, to stress the limited nature of these deficiencies. Legislatures were incapable of securing rights when their self-interest predominated, as in the case of regulating the suffrage. Additionally, they did not always succeed in resisting momentary passions, as was the case in certain periods of social or political agitation. In virtually all other areas, legislatures demonstrated the capacity to secure a reasonable degree of rights protection.

4

The Theory and Design
of Populist Institutions

Legislatures were viewed throughout the nineteenth century with a certain degree of distrust, and in fact as the century progressed, legislators who had once been constrained only by their capacity for self-restraint were increasingly hemmed in by a series of procedural and substantive restrictions. In the last decade of the nineteenth century and the first two decades of the twentieth century, this existing distrust of representative institutions was elevated to a qualitatively different level. Social, economic, and political reformers became increasingly frustrated by the defeat of their proposals in the legislatures and, occasionally, in the courts, and they concluded that these institutions had become more responsive to particular interests than to the public interest.

Confronted with a choice between restoring the original character of these institutions and redesigning them according to a new model, leaders of intellectual opinion chose to reconstitute these institutions on a foundation other than republicanism. Accordingly, a series of constitutional conventions that were held between 1900 and 1920 established populism rather than republicanism as the measure of institutional legitimacy, and they restructured governing institutions to conform to the view that the people were the best keepers of their liberties.[1] The overall effect was to limit representative institutions and to empower the collective citizenry, whose voice would now be expressed through direct democratic institutions.

CRITIQUE OF THE OLD REGIME

The impulse to reform institutions has been present in virtually every era in American history, and calls for reform have generally been greeted more favorably than arguments for conservation. At the turn of the twentieth century, however, a new set of social and economic conditions provided a particularly fertile reception for proposals to reform existing political institutions. Foremost among these changes was an increase in the number and size of corporations and the growing corruption of the political parties.[2]

These new conditions suggested that the existing conception of rights was outdated and would have to be revised. In the view of J. Allen Smith, one of the intellectual leaders of this reform movement, the founders' conception of liberty "was a purely negative conception. It involved nothing more than the idea of protection against the evils of irresponsible government."[3] Accordingly, political institutions had been designed with an eye toward preventing government action, thereby reducing the chance that this action would be irresponsible. In the twentieth century, however, irresponsible actions and threats to individual liberty were likely to emanate not so much from political institutions as from economic entities. As Walter Weyl argued: "The political weapons of our forefathers might avail against political despotism, but were farcically useless against economic aggression. The right of habeas corpus, the right to bear arms, the rights of free speech and free press could not secure a job to the gray-haired citizen, could not protect him against low wages or high prices, could not save him from a jail sentence for the crime of having no visible means of support."[4]

The rights that people were now concerned with protecting—"rights, for instance, of labor, women, children, and of electorates in respect to their definite control over all governmental agencies"[5]—were of an entirely different character than those that preoccupied previous generations. As Arthur Holcombe argued, what was needed was "a more positive conception of liberty. It is coming to mean more than the mere absence of physical restraint upon the physical person. Real liberty is not the antithesis of social control. Rather, rightly directed and effective social control is the condition of such liberty."[6] In particular, securing liberty in the early twentieth century required that the government take action. Government action was needed to secure the right to safe working conditions, which meant in practice the elimination of the fellow-servant, contributory-negligence, and assumed-risk doctrines on which corporate counsel had relied to prevent workers from receiving compensation for on-the-job injuries. Steps would also have to be taken to limit the number of hours that an employee could be required to work in a day or week. Finally, it was thought to be incumbent on government to provide pensions to those who were widowed, disabled, or unemployed.

Existing governmental arrangements were deficient, in the view of the populist reformers, not only because they were ill-designed to secure these rights in a timely fashion but also because special interests had grown so numerous and party bosses had become so powerful that they made passage of these laws nearly impossible. The populists were aware that theirs was not the first generation to complain about the capacity of party bosses and economic interests to corrupt the political process. In their view, however, the corruption that pervaded the system in the early twentieth century was different in kind from that of previous eras.

Legislatures were considered to be particularly susceptible to corruption by special interests. According to Sherman Whipple, a delegate to the Massachusetts Convention of 1917–1918:

> There exists a belief that special privileges and special favors have been granted to those who have had the influence to get them; a belief that much of our legislation has been framed by lobbyists in their own offices or by skilled and trained lawyers in the offices of the corporations or the offices of the attorneys themselves, and that that legislation has been directed not to promoting the general public welfare of all the people alike, but has been for the purpose of promoting the interests of those who stood behind—secretly stood behind—the measures and the legislators who put them through.[7]

To be sure, legislators in the nineteenth century had been subjected to the same kinds of pressures from special interests, and the response at that time had been to impose certain requirements on the legislative process to ensure that the majority will would prevail. In the view of the populist reformers, however, special-interest pressures were growing in scale. Lawton Hemans, a delegate to the Michigan Convention of 1907–1908, argued:

> The time was when the right of petition was considered sufficient to keep the member in the legislative branch of the government in close touch and responsibility with his constituency. . . . This relationship has in a large measure been lost or destroyed, and to my mind there are two great factors that have entered into the question as to why this relation has been lost or no longer obtains. One of them is in the growth of great political parties, which hold over the imagination and the wills of men a power and an influence unknown in the earlier days of the state of Michigan and this republic. The other is the great growth of commercial and industrial things throughout this great country of ours.[8]

As a result, existing procedural restrictions on the legislature were increasingly seen as inadequate to promote responsive lawmaking. Rules forbidding inaccurate titles, dual subjects, and late-session amendments enabled representatives who desired to legislate in the public interest to do so, by providing a way to fend off the advances of the special interests. But once the character of the legislators declined, as many reformers believed it had, these provisions were less effective. Accordingly, in 1914 Alabama Governor Emmet O'Neal took note of the "open contempt for our lawmaking bodies. In many, if not a majority, of the States, a session of the Legislature is looked upon as something in the nature of an unavoidable public calamity." He argued: "It is claimed that there has been a steady decline in the average standard of ability, independence, and intelligence of the membership of our State legislatures. That this is true, students of our government all agree."[9] Charles Beard concurred: "It is incontrovertible that the popular estimate of the ability and common honesty of legislators is by no means high. That the popular judgment is often unjust and based upon an exaggeration of the facts in any particular case will be conceded. It is needless, however, to argue the point as to whether the judgment is altogether just and righteous; it stands nevertheless."[10] Thus the view took hold, in the words of James Dealey, that the sheer complexity of modern problems "demands more wisdom and knowledge than is usually found in legislatures, which are often incompetent and sometimes venal."[11]

Populist reformers were no more sanguine about the capacity of courts to secure rights. Even when the public interest did prevail over particular interests in the legislature, and the passage of appropriate legislation was achieved, the courts posed an additional obstacle to the operation of these laws. Judges were roundly and repeatedly criticized during this era as being captive to special interests or to out-of-date constitutional doctrines, and in fact, it was difficult to determine in some states whether the judiciary or the legislature was viewed as the more corrupt institution.[12]

By the early twentieth century, reformers could point to a number of state court rulings that stood in the way of legislative efforts to secure the rights of working men, women, and children.[13] Herbert Kenny, a delegate to the Massachusetts Convention, complained that the "[s]tate courts, by their ultra-conservative interpretation of the police power, are preventing the enforcement of many progressive industrial and social laws." He noted: "When our State Constitution was adopted the factory system and other products of capital were in an embryonic condition. Now times have changed. . . . Yet our courts are basing many of their opinions which determine the constitutionality of social legislation upon instruments which in their inceptions of social justice are now obsolete."[14] Kenny was particularly troubled, as were many of his contemporaries, by two decisions—*Ritchie v. The People,* an 1895 Illinois Supreme Court ruling that struck down a maximum-hours-for-women law, and *Ives v. South Buffalo Railway Co.,* a 1911 New York Court of Appeals ruling that invalidated a workmen's compensation act—that were universally regarded as instances of knight-errantry. He made it clear, however, that these were only two of a number of egregious examples. Louis Boudin therefore concluded in 1911: "We have thrown to the winds all those great limitations, embodied in principles and rules of interpretation, which the earlier judges imposed upon their own power—a power which they deemed necessary for our orderly development, but the danger of which, when not properly limited, they clearly foresaw. One cannot read the latest decisions of our courts, either state or federal, without being forced to admit that they have usurped supreme legislative power, and that we have reached the condition of 'judicial despotism.' "[15]

In general, then, republican institutions were no longer thought to be capable of securing the people's most important liberties. Legislatures were frequently indifferent to efforts to secure popular rights, and overzealous judges occasionally posed an obstacle to the enforcement of rights. In his presidential address to the American Political Science Association in 1908, Professor Frederick Judson therefore alerted the members of the profession to the significant loss of confidence in representative institutions: "Our citizens are realizing that the representation provided by our existing conditions is not true representation, and as they feel their inability to control these tendencies they are prepared to welcome any remedy."[16]

The remedy for this state of affairs was not readily apparent, however. More precisely, there were several courses of reform that could be pursued. In one view, which was implicit in some of these critiques, representative institutions had at one time served to secure rights, but circumstances now rendered them incapable of performing their intended function. According to this line of reasoning, the failure of representative institutions could be attributed to a temporary disjunction between the theory and the practice of republicanism. Insofar as the flaw was identified in this way—that representative institutions had deviated from their true purpose—the appropriate remedy would be a return to fundamental principles.

Some public officials adhered to the logic of this position. They contended that the failure of representation could be attributed to particular circumstances, such as the corruption of the political parties and the predominance of special interests.[17] Accordingly, they delivered a moderate critique of republican institutions and sought primarily to restore these institutions to their original purpose. Woodrow Wilson, for instance, made it clear that he proposed reforms not so much "as a *substitute* for representative institutions, but only as a means of stimulation and control." He desired to find "a means of bringing our representatives back to the consciousness that what they are bound in duty and in mere policy to do is to represent the sovereign people whom they profess to serve, and not the private interests which creep into their counsels by way of machine orders and committee conferences." He sought therefore to provide "a sobering means of obtaining genuine representative action on the part of legislative bodies."[18]

Another group of populist reformers went even further in its critique of republicanism and maintained that existing difficulties were not the product of particular circumstances but were indicative of the poverty of republican principles. According to this line of reasoning, the current state of affairs could be attributed not so much to the corruption of republican institutions but rather to their design. In this view, which eventually provided the intellectual grounding for the populist reforms, the principles of the republican regime were faulty at their core, and rights could be secured only by restructuring institutions on a foundation other than republicanism.

In particular, those who leveled this strong critique challenged the wisdom of institutional arrangements such as constitutionalism, separation of powers, checks and balances, and bicameralism, on which the republican regime had chiefly relied for the protection of rights. Whereas constitutions had once been thought to impose limits on popular majorities, the populist reformers argued that this unduly restricted the popular will. Thus Theodore Roosevelt argued in an address to the Ohio Constitutional Convention of 1912 that he was "emphatically a believer in constitutionalism," but he also believed that "[i]t is impossible to invent constitutional devices, which will prevent the popular will from being effective for wrong without also preventing it from being effective for right."[19] The principle of separation of powers was criticized on similar grounds, because it was thought to thwart rather than secure the public interest. *Equity* magazine therefore lamented that the founding fathers had been "misled into adopting Montesquieu's mischievous theory of the separation of the legislative, executive and judicial functions of government," and furthermore, "that this restrictive and faulty theory of government, like grandfather's overcoat, which was ill-fitting at best, has been imposed on all our states!"[20] As for institutional arrangements that sought to secure the proper exercise of powers through a system of checks and balances, the populist reformers followed California Governor Hiram Johnson in contending that "The historic system of checks and balances guarded against the old danger of governmental aggression, but not sufficiently against the new danger of aggression, and because that old system did not guard it sufficiently in the West against private aggression, we found it necessary that the system of checks and balances that some view with such idolatry and with such pride, should be eliminated in our constitution."[21] In addition, bicameralism was now viewed as advancing the cause of particular interests rather than securing the deliberative sense of the community. In fact, many came to believe that "the bicameral system is somewhat or even largely responsible for the inefficiency and corruption of many states."[22]

In short, whereas the founders of the republican regime contended that the majority should rule but that it must be reasonable, the populist reformers detected in every institution that sought to obtain this reasonable expression of public opinion an attempt to limit the majority in favor of the minority. "There is, in fact, no middle ground," J. Allen Smith argued. "We must either recognize the many as supreme, with no checks upon their authority except such as are implied in their own intelligence, sense of justice, and spirit of fair play, or we must accept the view that the ultimate authority is in the hands of the few. Every scheme under which the power of the majority is limited means in its practical operation the subordination of the majority to the minority."[23]

ADVENT OF THE POPULIST REGIME

This dissatisfaction with the existing model of representation coalesced into a nationwide movement that sought a national audience and highlighted the shortcomings of national institutions. The reformers therefore reserved their strongest rhetoric for the federal Constitution, which was thought to contain "the political wisdom of dead America," as well as for national institutions such as the Senate, the Supreme Court, and the presidential selection process.[24] At the same time that the populists highlighted national institutions in their critiques, they concentrated on reforming *state* constitutions, which were more flexible and therefore more susceptible to change. As Smith argued: "It is through our state governments that we must approach the problem of reforming the national government. Complete control of the former will open the door that leads to eventual control of the latter."[25]

Smith was perhaps the most articulate proponent of the populist reform program. He argued that the first step toward reconstituting governing institutions, which had already been taken, was to deprive the legislature of "its power to enact constitutional legislation." The next step was "to diminish the power of the legislature by including in the constitution itself much that might have taken the form of ordinary statutory legislation." Another step was to "requir[e] that some of the more important acts passed by the legislature should receive the direct assent of the voters." Finally, "the initiative combined with the referendum would make the majority in fact, as it now is in name only, the final authority in all matters of legislation." He concluded: "The logical outcome of this line of development is easily seen . . . [C]onstitutional development first limits and eventually destroys irresponsible power, and in the end makes the responsible power in the state supreme."[26]

The populist reformers sought first to limit the irresponsible power of the legislature. As Amasa Eaton noted in 1892 in a review of the work of several late-nineteenth-century conventions: "One of the most marked features of all recent State constitutions is the distrust shown of the legislature."[27] He argued that the delegates to these conventions had thus rejected the advice of Thomas Cooley and James Bradley Thayer to refrain from legislating too much in their constitution making. "It would seem instead as if the theory underlying [these constitutions] were that the agents of the people, whether legislative, executive, or judicial, are not to be trusted; so that it is necessary to enter into the most minute particulars as to what they *shall not* do."[28] The delegates to these conventions considered, and in a number of cases enacted, a variety of proposals to reduce legislative power, ranging from limiting the length of legislative sessions to reducing the frequency of legislative meetings to limiting dramatically the discretion of legislative assemblies.[29]

Populist reformers also sought to limit the irresponsible power exercised by the judiciary. A number of delegates to these conventions searched for ways to prevent the judiciary from exercising any check over the people or their representatives. The proposals included abolishing judicial review altogether; requiring a unanimous bench to declare a statute unconstitutional; requiring the votes of all but one of the justices, or a supermajority of the justices, to invalidate a statute; and stipulating that all sitting justices be present before such a decision could be issued (which was adopted in the Virginia Constitution of 1870 and remained in effect in the Constitution of 1902 and was the only one of these proposals to be implemented by any of these particular states).[30] Another group of proposals, which were not ultimately enacted in any of these states, sought to ensure that the judiciary was more responsive to the popular will by providing for popular selection of the judges (where this was not already in effect), permitting the people to recall judicial decisions, or providing for recall of the judges themselves.[31]

Although the populist reformers were unable to secure the enactment of many of these proposals, they had more success in their efforts to implement the second prong of their reform program, which centered on increasing popular participation in lawmaking. In addition to enacting the statewide legislative referendum, which would permit the legislature to obtain the judgment of the people on controversial legislation, convention delegates introduced the popular referendum and initiative, as well as the constitutional initiative.

The logic underlying these institutions was that the popular referendum would permit the people to overturn oppressive laws, the popular initiative would permit the people to enact laws independently of the legislature, and the constitutional initiative would give the people the independent means to repeal oppressive statutes, constitutional provisions, or judicial decisions. To the extent that individuals had in previous years relied on legislatures or judges to overturn oppressive acts, they could now rely on the initiative and referendum to secure their rights. As delegate Charles Morrill of Massachusetts argued, the principle of popular sovereignty required that "the people [should] be the ones to say whether or not a law shall remain in force[.] They should give their consent, either by acquiescence or through a referendum if they are not satisfied to silently consent to a law becoming operative or remaining so."[32] He argued that if an oppressive law were enacted, "the people through the initiative and referendum could repeal that law far more expeditiously than the Supreme Judicial Court could, before it reached them and was decided by them, judging from a great many past instances."[33]

A number of individuals played prominent roles in securing the enactment of these direct democratic institutions in the various states, but none was more influential than William Simon U'Ren of Oregon.[34] In 1891, as a member of the Milwaukie Alliance, U'Ren read a study by J. W. Sullivan on the operation of the initiative in Switzerland, and he became an instant convert to the direct democratic movement.[35] In the belief that his favorite economic reforms could be achieved only through the initiative, U'Ren formed the Direct Legislation League and was instrumental in persuading the Oregon Legislative Assembly to adopt direct democracy. U'Ren explained:

I went just as crazy over the single tax idea as any one else ever did. I knew I wanted single tax, and that was about all I did know. . . . I learned what the initiative and referendum is, and then I saw the way to single tax. So I quit talking single tax, not because I was any the less in favor of it, but because I saw that the first job was to get the initiative and referendum. . . . All the work we have done for direct legislation has been done with the single tax in view, but we have not talked single tax because that was not the question before the house.[36]

As a result, although South Dakota was the first state to adopt direct democracy, the movement enjoyed its most significant early success in Oregon.[37] In 1902, as a result of the political maneuvering of U'Ren, whom the *Portland Oregonian* referred to as the fourth branch of Oregon's government, Oregon voters ratified an amendment that introduced the popular initiative and referendum, as well as the constitutional initiative.[38]

Michigan was the next of these states to adopt direct democracy. The delegates to the Michigan Convention of 1907–1908 were determined to transform the character of their governing institutions. Delegate Frederick Ingram argued that there was no need to "go into detail regarding present political evils, they are known of all men. The remedy is always the same—more democracy."[39] Similarly, William Manchester argued that the question of whether to adopt the initiative was "the only question of real interest that we have before this body."[40] The convention delegates adopted the constitutional initiative, and four years later, the citizens made use of this power to enact the statutory initiative.[41]

In addition, direct democracy was one of two issues (the other concerned public aid to religious institutions) that dominated the proceedings of the Massachusetts Convention of 1917–1918. In fact, Governor Samuel McCall noted in his opening address to the convention that: "The democratic idea will be, I think, the animating principle in your deliberations."[42] The popular initiative and referendum enjoyed the overwhelming support of the delegates, and their passage was virtually assured from the start. The only questions left to be determined were whether the constitutional initiative would be adopted and what form these institutions would take. In the end, the convention decided that the initiative should apply to statutory as well as constitutional matters, but that it would be adopted in a modified form. In particular, Massachusetts decided to enact an indirect initiative, in that propositions would first be considered by the legislature, and it stipulated that the people would be prohibited from voting on propositions that were, among other guarantees, "inconsistent" with "the rights of the individual as at present declared in the Declaration of Rights."

Only Virginia failed to adopt any form of direct democracy. The initiative was not at the top of the agenda of the Virginia Convention of 1901–1902, which, delegate Joseph Stebbins argued, was "called into being primarily for the specific purpose of disfranchising a large number of voters."[43] In addition, although several initiative and referendum proposals were introduced into the General Assembly over the next several years,[44] Virginia, much like the rest of its southern neighbors, remained impervious to the movement toward direct democracy.[45]

PRINCIPLES OF THE POPULIST REGIME

The institutional reforms of this period can be attributed in part to social and economic conditions that led to a reassessment of existing political institutions, and in part to the public officials who secured the enactment of the appropriate constitutional changes. But these reforms could not have been enacted, much less sustained, without a corresponding change in the norms of institutional legitimacy. As Eldon Eisenach has written:

> On both sides of this conflict competing interests and values had to legitimate the power and purposes of their respective institutions and practices. But the only way justification or legitimation of these institutions and practices can take place in a democratic political forum is in the form of a coherent "discourse" that mobilizes followers and empowers the leaders through their respective institutions. The creation and articulation of this institution-legitimating discourse . . . also serves to constitute or "found" these institutions.[46]

In this case, the justification and legitimation of these new institutional forms took place primarily through debates in state constitutional conventions. The advocates of populist reforms challenged the republican understanding of representation, deliberation, and compliance, and they undertook to redefine these terms. The critics sought to defend republican principles, and though they lacked the votes to defeat the proposed reforms, they succeeded in highlighting the contrast between republican and populist principles.

Representation

The populist reforms constituted a clear rejection of the republican view of representation. It fell to William Kinney of Massachusetts, a critic of the reforms, to articulate the extent of the disagreement between republican and populist views of representation.

> We believe to a certain point together, that is, that the final test upon constitutional and upon legislative matters is the convictions of a majority of the people of Massachusetts. *We differ as to the method of ascertaining that will.* We believe, and the framers of the Constitution of Massachusetts believed, that the system of government which we have adopted, with all its checks and balances, is the system which in the long run and in the majority of cases will secure the expression, in constitutional provision and in legislation, of the settled, well-founded, well-considered views of the people of Massachusetts. We believe that the adoption of the initiative and referendum in any form is the taking away of those safeguards, and substituting for the old system a system by which there may be enacted into law, or into constitutional provision, the hasty, the intemperate, the ill-considered, the temporary and

not the permanent, convictions of the people of Massachusetts. We believe that this change will result in the destruction of our institutions. We believe that it is opposed to, and cannot exist in connection with, the system which I have outlined.[47]

Although the populists naturally took issue with Kinney's critique, they did not necessarily disagree with his characterization of the differences between the two groups. In particular, they agreed that the crucial difference between populism and republicanism centered on the best method of ascertaining the popular will: whereas republicanism assumed that the public will was obtained through representative elections, populism sought to obtain a more direct expression of public opinion.

Accordingly, one group of populist reformers supported the initiative and referendum on the ground that this represented the most effective way to restore indirect representation. This group of delegates argued that, at least in the early part of the twentieth century, the representative principle could be upheld only by adopting the institution of direct democracy. As Michigan delegate Floyd Post argued, "It is not *representation,* but *misrepresentation* that is being complained of."[48] Similarly, Walter Creamer of Massachusetts argued that it was possible to adopt populist reforms without departing from the representative principle. "[I]s our General Court as at present constituted really representative of the public will or sufficiently responsive to it? It is because some of us believe that it is neither of these things that we look with so much favor on the initiative and referendum, and that we are willing to consider the somewhat radical changes therein involved in order that we may get representative government."[49]

According to this view, the presence of the initiative and referendum would restore representation by forcing legislators to take account of public opinion in their deliberations, out of a fear that unrepresentative legislation would be overturned by the people. The existence of direct democratic procedures would also help legislators to fend off groups and individuals who advocated measures adverse to the public interest. In addition, by providing a forum for resolving particularly controversial questions independently of representative elections, the initiative would permit these elections to focus on a wider array of issues, thereby increasing the quality of representation across the board. As Joseph Walker argued in the Massachusetts Convention: "I have seen some of the best legislators in Massachusetts defeated because they opposed a certain law. They might have been wrong on that, but on all other matters they were strong and stalwart and good. Have you got to defeat such men as that in order to bring the will of the people to bear in favor of one particular measure or another? How much better to take that measure out of the Legislature, submit it to the people, let them pass upon it, and then they can express their will."[50]

A number of populist reformers went even further, however, and challenged the representative principle itself. Several delegates acknowledged that they were advocating a departure from the founding view of representation, but they contended that they were merely following the founders in spirit, if not in form. According to this group of delegates, the founders had chosen to adopt republican institutions in the 1780s largely because existing conditions rendered direct democracy an implausible choice. Now that public schools, newspapers, and civic associations had produced a well-informed community of citizens, the descendants of the framers were free to make the decisions that their forefathers would have made if not constrained by circumstances. Massachusetts delegate Gerry Brown therefore "desired to impress upon this Convention, and more particularly upon those who are opposed to the initiative and referendum . . . that when the Constitution was adopted representation was from the town; it was a direct democracy."[51]

Still other delegates made no apologies for their preference for direct rather than indirect representation. They argued that indirect representation was as ill suited in the early twentieth century as it had been for the founding generation in the late eighteenth century. In a speech that was in one sense reminiscent of Alexander Hamilton's address to the federal convention of 1787, Brooks Adams of Massachusetts articulated the most extreme form of the populist position, and thereby expanded the spectrum of reforms that could be considered reasonable. In his typically colorful manner, Adams urged his fellow delegates: "[W]e have got to get rid of all this old, elaborate, complicated theory of representative government with its dry-nurse of courts and lawyers which everybody knows is exploded. Everybody knows that the thing is dead; we cannot get along with it. It will not move, it cannot march. . . . The legislature is like a dying animal. Representative government with grandmother courts is like an agonizing animal, and it has got to be replaced by something with vitality in it."[52]

Although few of the populist reformers adopted such forceful rhetoric, a number of delegates shared Adams's view that direct representation secured rights more effectively than indirect representation. For one thing, direct democracy could more effectively prevent public officials from encroaching on the rights of the citizens. David Walsh of Massachusetts argued: "We are not opposed to representative government, but when organized human selfishness controls representative government then we demand the right of appeal to the people for the judgment of a majority of the citizens of the State. . . . As an additional protection, as another safeguard to our inalienable rights, when we are deserted or betrayed by our public officials we will rest content and satisfied only with the verdict of a majority of our fellow citizens."[53] Second, the populists confronted Publius's argument in Federalist No. 10 that a republic was better suited than a democracy to control the effects of factions. The populist reformers contended, to the contrary, that a direct democracy actually offered more protection against factions. John Bodfish of Massachusetts argued:

> It cannot be denied that we are all of us selfish, that we all of us approach every question from our own selfish viewpoint or from the viewpoint of the

particular group in which we live and move and have our being. And the safety of democracy lies in keeping the laws out of the hands of any of these groups, and how shall you keep them out of the hands of these groups except you place them in the hands of the majority? So, Mr. Chairman and gentlemen, I call to your attention the fact that the representative system has failed at the very point where it became representative, at the very point where the people lost control; at that very point the selfish,—I will not call them sinister,—influences gained control.[54]

Direct democracy would be at least as effective as a republican government, therefore, in preventing factions from forming. Moreover, it would provide a more effective mechanism for ensuring that legislation conformed to the public interest rather than to individual or special interests. Justin Sutherland of Michigan believed that the public interest was more likely to emerge from direct democracy than from indirect representation, because initiative and referendum proposals would have to obtain numerous signatures before they could even appear on the ballot.

> [T]here is not a chance nor an opportunity for error or private interests to creep in where a matter is proposed by the electors of the state in a collective capacity, that there is in any small or appointed body from the people. We must remember this that truth is a unit, and that when a great aggregation of people pass upon a matter proposed and agree upon the exact words of that subject matter as it may be proposed in the amendment in that proposal, that there are from eighty to a hundred thousand qualified electors of the state in the very beginning who have agreed upon the principle of that proposal. That where there is that multitude of individuals who must agree, that there must be eliminated from that process of agreement, the errors of each individual and the private interests of each individual.[55]

The subsequent campaigns would also help to eliminate the possibility that particular interests would prevail. According to Jonathan Bourne of Oregon: "Where individuals act collectively or as a community,—as they must under the Initiative, Referendum, and Recall,—an infinite number of different forces are set in motion, most of them selfish, each struggling for supremacy. . . . No one selfish interest is powerful enough to overcome all the others; they must wear each other away until general welfare, according to the views of the majority acting, is substituted for the individual selfish interest."[56]

In response to these arguments, the supporters of republicanism mounted a series of defenses of the virtues of indirect representation. They argued that although direct democracy might secure certain rights, it would place others at greater risk. Robert Luce reminded the Massachusetts Convention that, through the initiative, "in Switzerland the people passed a law in regard to the Jewish method of slaughtering cattle, that never could have received enough support in the Assembly." He feared that similar initiative measures would be targeted in Massachusetts toward "Christian Science" or "the negroes." Measures would pass that "would appeal to the passion and to the prejudice of the people" but that would never prevail in "the cool, calm reasoning of our Legislature."[57] Benjamin Heckert of Michigan objected to the initiative on the ground that "history is full of instances where demagogues and walking delegates have fooled the people and led them on to untenable ground; led them into currents of thought which resulted in losses and injuries which they could not recoup or escape from."[58] Massachusetts delegate Albert Pillsbury also turned to the lessons of previous direct democracies.

> "Will you not trust the people?" This has been the capital of every demagogue from Cleon of Athens down to this day and hour. I would trust the "sober second thought" of the people when they are not deceived or misled, but this we shall not have. I would trust the people if the demagogues would let them alone. I would not trust them when they are lied to, as they are and will be, and believe what they are told because it is their interest to believe it, though it may be the plainest falsehood or folly. . . . There is not a man among the loudest advocates of this scheme who, under popular attack, would trust his life, his liberty, his character or his property to the unbridled edict of the people at the polls if he could avoid it.[59]

Arguments in defense of republicanism were advanced to no avail, however. The populists countered that the experience with the initiative and referendum in the American states disclosed no such occasions "where religious freedom has been attacked, where civil rights have been assailed, or where the rights of the minority have been ruthlessly sacrificed because of the rule of the majority."[60] David Walsh, for one, argued: "I am willing to leave the protection of my religious convictions and my judicial rights to a majority of my fellow citizens. [Applause.] I am willing to trust the protection of our institutions to the fairness, the honesty, the integrity of the judgment of a majority of our fellow-citizens."[61]

According, then, to the populist view of representation that prevailed in each of these conventions, direct democracy would leave existing rights undisturbed. Moreover, it would better secure the popular will with regard to newly discovered rights. Joseph Walker of Massachusetts concluded: "[I]f you do not give this power into the hands of the people there is real danger in regard to the liberty and the property of the people of this Commonwealth. What restrictions on the liberty of men and women and children are feared by this appeal to the people? It is laws directly limiting the hours of labor for men and women and children. It is laws that provide that young girls shall not be employed in our factories and mills at a wage which will not support them and keep the life in their bodies."[62]

Deliberation

At one point in the Massachusetts Convention of 1917, Frances Balch argued: "Much has been said of *representative* government and the effect on it of these proposed governmental innovations. Very little has been said of *deliberative* government. Now the real *point* to my mind is,—the real virtue of the present system is,—its *deliberative* character; and that is precisely what we are going to lose."[63] The populists contended that they were, in fact, intimately concerned with providing opportunities for deliberating over rights, and that they disagreed only on the best manner of providing this deliberation. Whereas republicanism placed a premium on providing a proper institutional forum for deliberation, the populists argued that deliberation could best take place among the collective citizenry.

The populists argued that the republican view of deliberation rested on an idealized notion of the legislative process. Even if the legislature had at one time been the scene of reasoned deliberation, Massachusetts delegate Francis Horgan argued, by the end of the nineteenth century, "The 'calm deliberation' of representative assemblies is a figment of the imagination."[64] Thus George Webster of Massachusetts recalled the exchange during which Thomas Jefferson asked George Washington why he had permitted the establishment of a bicameral system. " 'Why did you give your consent, and why did you adopt the bi-cameral system? Why did you have a Senate?' Washington said—or so runs the story— 'Why do you turn your tea out into your saucer?' . . . Jefferson of course naturally made the reply, the only reason a man could give for the practice: 'To cool it.' 'That is just what we are going to do with our Legislature,' said Washington. 'We are going to furnish, in the senatorial saucer, the cooling.' " After recounting this tale, Mr. Webster pleaded with his fellow delegates: "The senatorial saucer, sir, has reached such a degree of refrigeration that it freezes every beneficial piece of legislation that is brought up in the Commonwealth."[65]

The populist reformers did not seek, however, to restore the traditional view of deliberation. Rather, they maintained that the republican understanding of deliberation had been flawed from its inception, and that the institutional devices that had been adopted for the purpose of securing the deliberative sense of the community had in fact had a quite different effect. Whereas the republican view held that these institutional arrangements created constitutional space between the people and their representatives out of which the public interest could emerge, the populists argued that these institutions served in practice to increase the influence of special interests and to reduce the likelihood that legislation would conform to the public interest. Consequently, they believed that republican institutions served more often to violate than to secure individual rights. Eugene Sawyer argued in the Michigan Convention:

> [I]f a majority of the people shall not rule, then pray who will? Who shall be the high priest, who can enter the holy of holies and perform for us the sacrifice which shall take away our blindness and open our eyes that we may see what is good for us? Who is this high priest? Yonder he comes in his robe of office, dressed in purple and fine linen, faring sumptuously every day. He is the party boss, the political manager. He will show us the way. Danger in

majorities, gentlemen of the Convention, and yet no danger in party bosses? Oppressed by the majorities, but no fear of being oppressed by political leaders? The people must be protected from themselves, but no need of being protected from the party machine? This is absurd.[66]

For the populist reformers, the implication was clear: deliberation could no longer take place in representative assemblies. Willis Townsend of Michigan argued: "Now if you want deliberation, gentlemen, if that is an essential in order to permit these amendments, let us have deliberation, but do not in the name of reason and common sense leave it to one branch of the government to make these deliberations, and especially that branch of the government which we have spent half or two-thirds of our time in this Convention in considering measures of limitation upon."[67] Technological advancements now made it possible for deliberation to take place outside of formal institutions, among the general public. According to Herbert Croly:

[Citizens] have abundant opportunities of communication and consultation without any actual meeting at one time and place. They are kept in constant touch with one another by means of the complicated agencies of publicity and intercourse which are afforded by the magazines, the press and the like. The active citizenship of the country meets every morning and evening and discusses the affairs of the nation with the newspaper as an impersonal interlocutor. Public opinion has a thousand methods of seeking information and obtaining definite and effective expression which it did not have four generations ago. . . . Under such conditions the discussions which take place in a Congress or a Parliament no longer possess their former function. . . . Thus the democracy has at its disposal a mechanism of developing and exchanging opinions, and of reaching decisions, which is independent of representative assemblies, and which is, or may become, superior to that which it formerly obtained by virtue of occasional popular assemblages.[68]

The initiative and referendum would therefore actually provide more opportunities for deliberation, as well as a higher quality of deliberation, than would ordinarily take place in legislative assemblies. In the first place, deliberation would take place in the course of securing signatures for initiative and referendum petitions. "They say we need a deliberative body, that we need the great safeguard of a deliberative body, and in that connection they refer to this matter of initiative on constitutional amendments as though it were something that was going to be done quickly," argued Frank Pratt of Michigan. "Now, we propose to circulate a petition—it is not going to be done in a week nor in two weeks, nor in a month. . . . Where is the haste? Isn't this deliberate? I submit to you gentlemen of the Convention, that it is very deliberate."[69] Deliberation would also take place in the meetings, associations, and conversations that would inevitably be held in the months leading up to the election. In the view of Michigan delegate Charles

Thomas, the typical citizen "thinks about [an initiative], he talks about it with his neighbors, or with the men who are working beside him, with the result that when the day of voting comes, the voters are not surprised by having something placed before them of which they never have heard, but are prepared to stamp upon it their approval or rejection after mature deliberation."[70] In fact, reports circulated from John Randolph Haynes in California that in the days leading up to a vote on an initiative or referendum, "school children talked about them on the playground, some of them saying that their parents spoke of nothing else at their meals."[71]

The defenders of republican institutions thought that these stories of citizen deliberation were "a Utopian dream." Even if this discussion and education did take place as promised, these delegates still contended that this could never substitute for the type of deliberation in which legislators engaged in representative assemblies.[72] As Henry Campbell of Michigan argued, the initiative process lacked any opportunity for compromise, because "[w]hatever is proposed must be voted upon precisely as presented, without modification or change."[73] Nor did press coverage of these initiatives provide an adequate forum for reflection. "With all that is proposed as a means of information, one great means is lacking, namely, real debate."[74] Charles Choate argued in the Massachusetts Convention: "We every one of us know the advantage which each of us individually obtains from the discussion of subjects on this floor. We know the reaction produced upon our own minds by the views of other men. We know the light that comes to any body like this by the presentation of the views of many minds which look at a subject from many different viewpoints. Now, it is perfectly obvious that the people, who are to be made the legislators by this measure, will have none of that benefit."[75] Walter Wixson of Michigan concluded, similarly, that although "it is somewhat in fashion nowadays with many upon every occasion to throw bricks at the legislature, . . . in some very notable and conspicuous instances at least, the criticised are entitled to far more commendation than are the critics." He thought that there was much to be recommended in "a deliberative body whose business it is to consider carefully and calmly all the changes they will originate in the fundamental law and submit to the people for rejection or adoption. I say, gentlemen, *carefully, deliberately, and calmly consider,* not in the haphazard, careless, happy-go-lucky, devil-may-care sort of fashion, and with the alacrity with which most men sign petitions."[76]

In the view of these defenders of republican principles, deliberation amounted to more than discussion, publicity, and education. Deliberation could take place only in an institutional setting that permitted the orderly exchange of views, the consideration of unintended consequences, the comparison of costs and benefits, and the forging of reasonable compromises. As Elihu Root argued: "[T]he only method by which intelligent legislation can be reached is the method of full discussion, comparison of views, modification and amendment of proposed legislation in the light of discussion and the contribution and conflict of many minds. This process can be had only through the procedure of representative legislative bodies."[77]

In the end, the populist view of deliberation prevailed. When the populists compared the respective abilities of the citizens and legislators, they determined that, "On the whole, laws enacted by the people are more carefully prepared, more widely discussed, and more thoroughly considered than are the acts of a legislature."[78] Moreover, insofar as deliberation consisted of providing sufficient time for reflection, due opportunity for discussion, and adequate education of the public, this could be achieved through the initiative procedure more effectively than through the legislature. Charles Thomas of Michigan therefore concluded, "The argument for conservatism and safety and intelligence is on the side of the initiative."[79]

Compliance

The populists undertook, finally, to challenge the republican understanding of the relationship between public opinion and the protection of rights. Individuals in the republican regime understood that legal guarantees were not self-executing, and they had been concerned to some extent with ensuring that legal guarantees were secured in practice. In their view, it was important that the people have an opportunity to participate in drafting the laws under which they were governed, but this requirement was fully satisfied by permitting the people to vote in representative elections and ratify constitutional amendments.

The populist reformers charged, however, that the republican view was insufficiently concerned with ensuring that legal guarantees were secured in practice. Moreover, the populists argued that to the extent that individuals in the eighteenth and nineteenth centuries had been concerned with the problem of compliance, they relied too heavily on formal institutional arrangements. According to the populists, republicanism failed to acknowledge that competing claims of right were resolved far more frequently through ordinary interactions among citizens than through institutions. As Brooks Adams argued: "It is not a scrap of paper that is going to make you safe. What does a scrap of paper mean, and who gives you the protection? Is it a bench of judges, who sit up in a lot of armchairs and go to sleep? Not a bit, you know. That is not what gives you safety. It is because your contemporaries do not want to have you injured. It is because public opinion will not permit that you shall be injured, and it does not make any difference whether you have got a lot of constitutional guarantees or not."[80]

When the question of securing rights was raised in a direct fashion, the populists argued that republican institutions were incapable of developing a level of public opinion that could support legal guarantees. It was not enough for the people merely to elect their representatives. In order for the people to have a stake in obeying the law, they would have to be afforded a more direct form of participation. According to Joseph Walker of Massachusetts: "[T]he real protection of the citizens of this Commonwealth does not lie in a written document, does not lie merely in a 'scrap of paper.' It lies in the fact that back of that 'scrap of paper' is a contented people, a majority of the people approving of those restrictions, approving of that Constitution; and the minute the support of a majority of the people is withdrawn from the Constitution of this Commonwealth then indeed will it become a 'scrap of paper.' "[81]

The best way to produce this popular support for rights, according to the populists, was to adopt the initiative and referendum. According to Walker, once these measures were in place, "then you get a body of public opinion, enlightened, educated by discussion, back of our Constitution, that will indeed make it secure, and make the liberties of every one of us more secure than they are today."[82] At a basic level, individuals would be more likely to uphold legal guarantees that were secured through the initiative, because, as Robert Crosser of Ohio argued, "Any man has more pride in a thing which he has created than in that which someone else has created for him."[83] In addition, individuals would be more likely to comply with laws, because they would know that "the will of a real majority of the people is behind that law which gives it its force, and if for no other reason than the mere selfish one that they feel they are outnumbered they are inclined to respect it, which is not usually the case when the law is the result of some legislative action, always more or less the result of machination and tricks."[84] Individuals would also respect rights secured through direct legislation because they would have benefited from "the discussion which has gone on before the people," which is "bound to make the citizen understand the law better than he would if it were passed here by the general assembly. He knows the reason for it, and knowing the reason he sees the justice or what is claimed to be justice by the great majority who have approved it."[85] Finally, in response to those who argued that under a system of direct democracy, passion would prevail over reason, the populists argued that "where we have the people's will expressed in the form of law as the direct initiative would permit it to be, we have the surest bulwark against anarchy and appeal to passion. How many men do you suppose are going to take chances in the violation of law if they know that the great majority of their fellow men have personally expressed their approval of that law instead of giving someone carte blanche to pass such a law without their knowing anything about it?"[86]

CONCLUSION

The populist reform project sought, therefore, to supplant the governing institutions and principles that were central to the republican regime. Whereas republicanism held that the legislature best represented popular opinion with respect to rights, the populists advocated a more direct expression of the popular will. Whereas republicanism understood that the legislature provided the best opportunity for deliberating over rights, the populists thought that deliberation would take place through initiative and referendum campaigns. Finally, the republican regime had operated on the view that compliance would be secured insofar as citizens had an opportunity to participate indirectly in drafting the laws under which they were governed. The populists held that people would be even more likely to comply with legal guarantees when they had participated directly in approving or rejecting them.

5

Populist Institutions and the Protection of Rights

The most significant institutional development between 1900 and 1940 was the introduction of the initiative and referendum as an additional means by which citizens could secure their rights. As Herbert Croly wrote:

> Instead of continuing the attempt to make government by Law democratic, they are trying really to organize popular government and make it effective. They have fallen back on the power behind the Law. They are proposing to withdraw from Law the responsibility under which it has been suffering, and to exercise this responsibility themselves. They are proposing to take the Law into their own hands. Instead of embodying their program in a constitution which either accomplishes too much or not enough, they propose to retain the power to legislate and to prevent legislation from being adopted. The local democracies have suddenly decided or discovered that they themselves are free men worthy of confidence—even if their agents are not.[1]

The populist spirit also had an effect on the way in which other individuals conceived of their role in protecting rights. Although legislators continued to secure some rights by enacting statutes, as they had done throughout the nineteenth century, they also began to defer more frequently to popular judgments and became less active in redressing grievances. Judges were also influenced by the populist ethos, but in a complex manner. For the most part, judges continued to secure rights in the same way that they always had, by issuing statutory and common-law decisions and superintending the forms of legislation. In certain cases, however, they departed from this traditional practice and began to issue constitutional decisions that removed rights from the political process. Significantly, this behavior was recognized as deviant, and in fact was partly responsible for the enactment of the populist reforms that eventually enabled the people to bring a halt to these decisions.

THE ROLE AND BEHAVIOR OF CITIZENS

In light of the grandiose predictions on the part of the supporters and critics of direct democracy, the actual record did not live up to its billing. The initiative did not replace the legislature, nor did it render the judiciary irrelevant. Nevertheless, it had a significant effect on the way in which citizens conceived of their role in protecting rights. For the first time, as Oregon Governor George Chamberlain argued, the people assumed responsibility "not only for laws which are written in our statute-books and which ought not to remain there, but for failure to enact those laws which ought to be enacted. . . . Blame for bad laws was accustomed in those days to be visited upon the legislature, but now responsibility rests with the people themselves."[2]

In the first place, the initiative and referendum enabled the people to overturn statutes that were the product of inadequate reflection. To be sure, the mere presence of direct democratic institutions increased the probability that legislatures would undertake a reasonable amount of deliberation. Even so, occasions would inevitably arise when legislators would fail, for any number of reasons, to consider the deleterious consequences of proposed bills. In these cases, the people would be well positioned to render a more reasoned judgment. A prime example occurred in 1921, when the Massachusetts General Court enacted a law that required all movies to be licensed by the commissioner of public safety, who was charged with regulating their moral content and upholding standards of decency.[3] Shortly after the law was passed, citizens began to express concerns about the wisdom of vesting this public official with such power, a requisite number of signatures was secured to force a referendum on the bill, and at the 1922 election, the voters secured its repeal by a large margin.[4]

Direct democratic institutions also permitted the people to overturn statutes that were insufficiently representative of the popular will. Again, the mere presence of the referendum went some way toward guaranteeing that legislators would remain attuned to public opinion. Nevertheless, there were bound to be cases in which legislatures would fail to measure public opinion adequately, and the people could rely on the initiative process to register their views. The initiative was used for just such a purpose in Oregon, when in 1899 the legislature enacted a law that permitted prosecutors to proceed to trial by filing information against a defendant rather than securing a grand-jury indictment. Although the legislators apparently believed that this measure would better secure individual rights, in that the grand jury had come to be viewed by many people as an increasingly arbitrary institution, it turned out that the citizens had a different view of the matter. Accordingly, in 1908 the citizens initiated and approved a ballot proposition that reinstated the right not to be prosecuted for a crime without first having been indicted by a grand jury.

The people also relied on the initiative to secure rights when legislators proved to be more responsive to their own particular interests than to the public interest. Prototypical cases included the failure of legislators to expand the suffrage in a timely manner, to redraw electoral district lines in an equitable fashion, and to regulate the conduct of elections. In each of these instances, legislators' self-interest in maintaining their offices occasionally prevented them from enacting laws that were consistent with the general welfare. The initiative not only reduced the probability that legislators would succumb to this temptation, but if the legislature failed to resist the temptation, it also provided a vehicle by which the people could secure enactment of the necessary laws.

Direct democratic institutions permitted the people, finally, to secure rights in cases in which legislators proved inordinately responsive to special interests. This was perhaps the most common type of legislative failure during this era, and it produced a number of ballot propositions. Thus when railroad and other business groups succeeded in preventing the passage of a comprehensive workmen's compensation plan in Oregon, the people resorted to the initiative process to secure their rights.[5] Similarly, when the liquor interests wielded their influence to prevent the enactment of a women's suffrage law in Oregon, the initiative provided a vehicle by which the people could secure this right.[6]

The constitutional convention offered an additional avenue through which citizens could secure rights independently of legislatures. In the nineteenth century, the people had largely refrained from resolving issues through constitutional action, just as they refrained from making use of direct democratic institutions. In the populist era, however, the people and their representatives in constitutional conventions exercised no such restraint. In fact, as James Dealey noted in 1915, the constitutional convention was viewed, along with the initiative, as one of the primary governing institutions during this period. He argued, "If general tendencies in the making of constitutions may be condensed into a sentence, we may say that the governmental powers of the states are centering into their electorates, which voice themselves through the ballot and the constitutional convention."[7]

To be sure, a number of convention delegates continued to adhere to the view that rights were best protected through representative institutions. Thus Roswell Bishop proclaimed in the Michigan Convention of 1907 that "representative government is not a failure." He argued: "If the people of the state cannot trust their representatives to legislate for them and must tie their hands in advance, then the principles that lie at the very foundation of our government stand upon a false basis."[8] Similarly, some delegates still maintained that legislatures were the ideal forum for conducting discussions and forging compromises. Michigan delegate Henry Walbridge argued that the legislature "is where subjects of this kind and character can receive adequate consideration, not in the hurried manner this Convention must do its work."[9] Finally, several delegates still put their faith in statutes as the best vehicle for securing rights and cautioned that constitutional provisions lacked the flexibility of legislation. As Gordon Robertson argued in the Virginia Convention of 1902: "I have never known the Legislature to pass any law involving any great right—take for instance the married woman's law or any law, I care not what—when it has not become apparent within a few years that that law does not meet the requirements of the case, does not fully carry out the objects which its promoters had in view. . . . These sorts of things have to be amended until experience teaches us they need no further amendment."[10]

In general, though, these men were fighting a rearguard battle against a majority of delegates who were not as sanguine as their predecessors about the capacity of republican institutions to secure their rights. In a pair of articles published in 1891, Frances Newton Thorpe and Ellis Oberholtzer surveyed the work of several contemporary conventions and took note of the attitude that had begun to take hold among constitution makers. Thorpe noted, "The perusal of these new constitutions suggests that the people have lost confidence in their state legislatures."[11] Meanwhile, Oberholtzer discerned "a tendency toward taking our laws in bulk from a convention instead of in small lots each year from a legislature."[12] This was the view that predominated throughout the first several decades of the twentieth century.

Whereas republican-era delegates had disclaimed any greater wisdom or purity than legislators, the view predominated in the populist era that convention delegates were on the whole more trustworthy and capable. Oberholtzer noted, "The legislatures of the States are filled with men who, with the rarest exceptions, are of mediocre ability." But: "The conventions, chosen more rarely and for a rather unusual purpose, have up to this time been kept comparatively free from those who are 'party men' in the bad sense, politicians who are seeking personal profit."[13] Charles Beard agreed. He thought that convention delegates, "being elected for the particular purpose and usually composed of more disinterested citizens than the ordinary legislature, gave special attention to building defences against the unscrupulous manipulators who were sure to find their way into the state assemblies."[14] Arthur Holcombe reached a similar conclusion—"that the constitutional convention, considered as an organ of state government, has been more successful than the legislature"—which led him to raise the question "whether the legislatures might not do more satisfactory work if their organization and procedure more closely resembled that of the conventions."[15]

As a result, efforts to engage in constitutional legislating encountered none of the stigma that had previously attached to this activity in the nineteenth century. Proposals to amend the constitution so as to restrict the legislature had once been considered deviant and required special justification, but by the twentieth century no apologies were necessary. When Michigan delegate Louis Tossy was charged with "doing work that should be in the hands of the legislature," he responded with an unabashed defense of constitutional legislating: "Mr. Chairman, it seems to me that that is a pretext that has been offered and will be offered as long as this Convention holds. . . . I believe that we ought to have the courage of our convictions in regard to this matter, and with the belief that we ought to legislate, if you desire to call it legislation, I hope that the [measure] will prevail."[16]

Consequently, convention delegates were emboldened to propose constitutional amendments in a variety of areas, including the right to health insurance, unemployment compensation, an old-age pension, a minimum wage, and one day's rest in seven, among others.[17] No longer would delegates presume that this behavior was in any way improper. They were convinced that they were at least as qualified as legislators, if not more so, to regulate rights, and that constitutional provisions were generally preferable to statutes as vehicles of rights protection.

This attitude is perhaps best illustrated by a series of debates in the Massachusetts, Michigan, and Virginia Conventions over the wisdom of amending the constitution to prohibit public appropriations to religious charities, hospitals, and associations.[18] These amendments, which were eventually enacted in both Massachusetts and Virginia, departed significantly from the tradition that had governed nineteenth-century conventions, and as a result, they inspired a good amount of reflection about the proper role of constitutional conventions in securing rights.[19]

Some delegates opposed these amendments on the ground that legislators were quite capable of making reasonable judgments about how best to secure freedom of worship in particular situations. William Feiker of Massachusetts argued: "I believe in a representative democracy and the Legislature as a fair and honest representation of the people. Some people harp upon and criticize its action, and some people say it is subject to prejudice and narrow-mindedness and that it lacks discretion; but I do not believe this. Great questions have been settled fairly and on the merits of the case. Can it be shown that in this case the Legislature has betrayed its trust?"[20]

Moreover, some delegates still believed that legislatures were a superior forum for resolving questions of this kind. George Anderson of Massachusetts argued: "I cannot easily accept the proposition that in the important work of education we are so torn by distrust of each other, by a subterranean but yet existent jealousy of each other's religious convictions, that we cannot trust the Legislature to deal in the important work of combining public funds and private funds in the tremendously important work of education."[21]

These institutional concerns were eventually overcome, however, by a majority of delegates who were convinced that legislators could no longer be trusted to deliberate responsibly. Massachusetts delegate Frederick Anderson argued that the virtue of enacting this constitutional amendment was that "it takes the last irritating, debatable question out of politics."[22] W. F. Dunaway of Virginia concluded similarly:

> It is said that we have never had this provision before. "Why not leave the Legislature free as it has always been?" I think, sir, that the transgression of our Constitution and the act for establishing religious freedom is something of recent growth in the Commonwealth of Virginia, and that is the reason why this great principle has never been raised for discussion in a previous Constitutional Convention of Virginia.

We are confronted by altered conditions to-day. There are new institutions growing up in our midst and new claims made upon the public treasury. I would restrain the Legislature, because if they pass these acts . . . it is committing a wrong. The principle for which I contend is fundamental. It is inalienable, and therefore is entitled to a place in a Constitution.[23]

THE ROLE AND BEHAVIOR OF LEGISLATORS

Legislatures were held in such low regard at certain points in the early twentieth century that some commentators were led to speculate about whether they might be superseded altogether. Dealey argued: "The relative importance of legislatures is therefore decreasing, not in a few but in all the states, and that, too, in spite of the fact that legislatures are much more democratic than formerly. . . . A powerful executive with ordinance privileges, a convention meeting periodically, and the use of the initiative and referendum as in Oregon, certainly seem to leave no pressing necessity for a legislature."[24] Likewise, Frank Parsons predicted that with the advent of direct democracy there was no need for the legislature to play any more than a minor role. Under such a system, "The Legislature becomes the *emergency ruler* and the *universal advisor*—the most important advisory body in the commonwealth."[25] Allen Eaton believed that "Unless the people and their representatives resolve to work together the time is not far off when there will be a new issue in Oregon and that issue will be the abolition of the Legislature. Such a statement may seem absurd, but it is not an unlikely result. Indeed, such a proposal has been seriously made by some of the Oregon press and under the present conditions there would seem to be no difficulty in getting a petition for this purpose. It would undoubtedly receive an astonishing support."[26] Gilbert Hedges was of the same mind-set. At a time when the citizens of Oregon were considering a proposal to adopt a unicameral legislature, he predicted: "Should the State Senate be abolished the next step will be the elimination of the House of Representatives. . . . Should a State government without a legislature be held to be a republican form of government, the city councils and boards of aldermen will go, and the initiative method of enacting laws at the polls will become absolute and supreme."[27] As the Oregon Supreme Court concluded, "In time the people may strip the legislature of every power it once enjoyed, leaving it but a place in memory, and themselves exercise directly within the state all of the powers formerly committed to the legislature."[28]

In retrospect, of course, it is clear that the demise of the legislature was greatly exaggerated. Legislatures were not eliminated, nor did they abdicate complete responsibility for securing rights. They continued, for instance, to give practical meaning to general guarantees of rights. Thus the Massachusetts General Court determined during this period that the freedom to worship required that legal protection be accorded to a variety of activities. As a result, the legislature provided that individuals could sell kosher meats on Sundays, as long as they closed their shops on their preferred day of religious observance, and that produce shops could remain open when a Jewish holiday fell on a Sunday.[29] Statutes were also enacted to protect the religious freedom of prisoners and members of religious organizations seeking to hold extracurricular meetings in public school buildings.[30]

Legislatures also sought to devise more effective means for securing rights. For instance, when members of the Virginia General Assembly heard complaints from a number of citizens who "were being harassed and humiliated by having their houses, vehicles and baggages searched, upon mere suspicion, by officers and other persons seeking to discover infractions of certain laws,"[31] they responded by requiring search warrants to meet specific and demanding requirements and levying stiff penalties on individuals who violated these rules.[32]

In addition, as the public understanding of rights evolved during this period, some citizens continued to turn to the legislature to seek their protection. For instance, legislatures enacted statutes that limited the number of hours that employees could be required to work in a day or a week, and thereby recognized the right to reasonable working conditions. Thus Massachusetts, which in the nineteenth century had enacted a law mandating a ten-hour day and a sixty-hour week for women and children, gradually reduced the workweek even further and made appropriate accommodations for specially situated workers.[33]

Moreover, legislatures continued to respond to judicial invitations to clarify their intent on various subjects. Until Samuel Warren and Louis Brandeis wrote their famous article in the 1890 edition of the *Harvard Law Review* entitled "The Right to Privacy," few persons thought that privacy merited legal protection.[34] But in one of several suits brought in the wake of this article, a Michigan woman argued that her right to privacy prohibited a cigar manufacturer from advertising the "John Atkinson cigar," which was named after her recently deceased husband. The Michigan Supreme Court took note of the fact that "prominence was given to this subject" by the Warren-Brandeis article, in which "[t]he right to privacy in a broader sense than before known to the common law is asserted."[35] The justices concluded, however, that if such a right did deserve recognition, it should come as a result of legislative action. Should this ruling meet with dissatisfaction, Justice Frank Hooker noted: "[I]t is only necessary to call attention to the fact that a ready remedy is to be found in legislation. . . . The law does not remedy all evils; it cannot, in the nature of things; and deliberation may well be used in considering the propriety of an innovation such as this case suggests."[36] The Virginia General Assembly was one of many state legislatures that responded by enacting such a statute, which in this case declared that any person who used a picture or name for advertising purposes without permission could be found guilty of a misdemeanor and forced to pay damages to the person wronged.[37]

Although legislators therefore continued to play a role in securing rights in the populist regime, this role was reduced in significant respects. In particular, because legislators were no longer viewed as the legitimate interpreters of the popular will, they began to protect rights in a provisional manner, either by relying on the legislative referendum or by deferring to the popular initiative and referendum.

The introduction of the legislative referendum meant that legislators who lacked confidence in their ability to interpret a right could now defer responsibility by enacting statutes that took effect only if approved by the people. Throughout the better part of the nineteenth century, this option had not been available to legislators, because the referendum had been considered inconsistent with the principles of republican government. But the populist regime required obeisance to the direct expression of the popular will. Thus, when the Michigan Supreme Court considered the validity of a particular referendum at the close of the nineteenth century, Justice Allen Morse was the only member of the court to oppose the law, on the traditional ground that "[t]his would be a convenient thing for a Legislature wishing to shirk responsibility," but "[o]ur system of State government under the Constitution is not a pure democracy, but a representative one."[38] A clear majority of the justices disagreed with Morse and concluded that the legislative referendum was entirely consistent with a democratic form of government and, moreover, was actually superior in several ways to ordinary legislation.[39]

The legislative referendum was thought to be particularly appropriate for laws that were controversial and therefore difficult to enforce. Prohibitory liquor laws were a prime example, and in the first several decades of the twentieth century, legislatures began to rely heavily on the legislative referendum in this area. Thus when the question surfaced during this period, the Virginia General Assembly, which had grappled with the liquor question throughout the nineteenth century, declined for the first time to exercise responsibility for resolving the matter. Instead, it established an elaborate procedure for gauging public opinion. If one-quarter of the citizens petitioned the governor to hold a referendum on the subject, he was to call a statewide election, at which time the voters would approve or disapprove of statewide Prohibition; if a majority of voters approved the proposal, which it turned out that they did, the law would take effect.[40] The advantage of submitting this type of measure to a popular vote, as Michigan Chief Justice John Champlin argued, was that "experience has demonstrated that a prohibitory law cannot be enforced unless the law itself has the moral support of the majority of its electors. If public sentiment is not in favor of such a law, it ought not to be forced upon the public."[41]

As one might expect, the legislative referendum was not confined to these cases. Charles Morrill noted in the Massachusetts Convention of 1917 that the referendum also served a variety of other purposes: "In some cases, a politic wish to shift responsibility in a difficult situation; in others a democratic deference to the unknown will of the majority; in others, uncertainty as to how the interests of the public would be affected by the measure, or a desire to secure for it the backing of a declared public opinion."[42] In particular, legislatures during this period employed the referendum to determine whether the right to reasonable work hours should extend to public employees,[43] as well as whether the right to equal protection required that male and female teachers receive the same salary.[44]

As a result, whereas legislators in the nineteenth century had resolved questions merely by canvassing their constituents, they now felt compelled to refer bills to the people for their resolution. Horace Bartlett of Massachusetts concluded that the legislative referendum was "the most effective instrument for taking the backbone out of legislators that has ever been invented."[45] Another former member of the Massachusetts General Court, Samuel Collins, agreed. He thought that the chief effect on the legislature had been "to relieve it of practically all responsibility. . . . On any proposition in the legislature which was State wide in its provisions and which any member of the legislature thought might get him in wrong . . . they said: 'The great cry in this State today is for the people to rule. Now here is an opportunity. We will kill two birds with one stone. We will dodge responsibility and we will let the people rule.' And I want to say to you, sir, that for an up-to-date, absolutely-on-the-minute surgical operation to relieve the legislature of any backbone, this had the call."[46]

The presence of the statutory initiative had a similar effect. In previous years, legislators had been able to overcome doubts about their ability to register public opinion by reflecting on the fact that they were the only officials who could act. But with the advent of the initiative, legislators could respond to individual grievances not by enacting the desired statutes but by urging the petitioners to take their case to the people as a whole.

Although it is difficult in the end to gauge the precise effect of the initiative and referendum on legislative behavior, there were some indications, particularly in the first decade of the twentieth century, that legislatures became less likely to assume responsibility for securing rights. Thus in his study of direct democracy in Oregon, Eaton noted that the legislature displayed a tendency to "shift upon the people responsibilities very properly belonging to themselves."[47] James Barnett noted, similarly, that although the evidence was mixed, "a tendency to avoid responsibility does at times appear in the legislative assembly." Moreover, this was occurring despite the fact that legislatures were enacting an increasing number of laws. "[A]lthough the increase in the volume of legislation might be interpreted to prove that the assembly does not refrain from action in view of the power of the people to obtain desired legislation independently of the assembly through the initiative, it might as well be interpreted to indicate that the assembly is becoming less conservative and tending to cast the final responsibility for action upon the people in view of their power to nullify undesired legislation by the referendum."[48]

THE ROLE AND BEHAVIOR OF JUDGES

The relationship between populism and the courts was a complex one, and it is important to distinguish between two kinds of judicial behavior in the populist era—one that conformed to and another that deviated from regime principles. For the most part, judges were unaffected by the introduction of direct democracy, in that they continued to protect rights as they always had, by superintending the form of legislation and interpreting statutes and common-law principles. In one area, however, judges departed from their traditional behavior and began to interpret state bills of rights in such a way as to overturn legislative judgments and remove issues from the political process. When judges engaged in this type of behavior, they were condemned by citizens and public officials alike, who sought to overturn these errant decisions by bringing to bear the force of public opinion or by relying on the constitutional amendment process.

In many ways, judges in the populist era conceived of their role much the same as they had in previous years. They assumed that legislators were generally competent to interpret general guarantees of rights and that representative institutions were generally capable of securing protection for these rights in particular situations. The role of the judge, then, was to ensure that legislative statutes conformed to constitutional requirements and to apply these statutes in particular situations.

As a result, judges continued to secure rights indirectly, by enforcing majoritarian restrictions of the legislative process. Thus judges continued to guard against statutes with inaccurate titles and multiple subjects, as well as against statutes that had been enacted without adequate publicity or deliberation. In one case, for instance, the Michigan Supreme Court overturned a law whose title announced that it was "An act relative to the loaning of money and prescribing rates of interest" but that actually permitted the issuance of search warrants "for recovering stolen property from pawnbrokers."[49]

Judges also remained vigilant for statutes that granted special privileges or aided classes of citizens. The idea was that these laws were suspect because they were more than likely a product of undue influence on the part of a particular group of citizens and therefore a perversion of the majoritarian process. In one case in 1915, for instance, the Oregon Supreme Court overturned an ordinance that imposed a tax on certain peddlers but not on others. Chief Justice Frank Moore concluded that "the business in which the plaintiffs are engaged is identical with that of some of the merchants of Salem . . . except that the plaintiffs do not have a regular place of business in that city," and as a result, the ordinance was constitutionally invalid.[50]

The courts were also on guard for legislation of this kind that granted certain groups or individuals unfair advantages in the judicial or political process. Thus the Michigan Supreme Court voided one piece of legislation not only because it was an "unwarranted interference in purely local affairs and an invasion of the principles of local self-government" but also because it prevented a popular majority from governing. The view was that members of a general assembly were less likely to possess the requisite "intelligence and judgment" to deliberate responsibly on purely *local* matters.[51]

Judges were concerned above all with ensuring that laws were not enacted or enforced in an arbitrary fashion. The prevailing view in this period, which was perhaps best expressed by the Massachusetts Supreme Court in a 1914 opinion, was that "Liberty is immunity from arbitrary commands and capricious prohibitions."[52] Accordingly, the Virginia Supreme Court found "most objectionable" a statute that permitted Prohibition officers, but no other individuals, to receive an automatic change of venue for their trials. The court noted: "It discriminates against all other officials who are equally charged with making arrests for alleged violations of all other criminal laws, and against all other persons who are not officials who may be charged with crime—that is, against all others who are so unfortunate as to be similarly situated."[53]

It is significant, therefore, that in most of these cases, judges did not intend to overturn the considered judgment of the legislature. Rather they sought to ensure that statutes conformed to accepted standards and principles of legislation. As Howard Gillman argued: "[T]he decisions and opinions that emerged from state and federal courts during the *Lochner* era represented a serious, principled effort to maintain one of the central distinctions in nineteenth-century constitutional law—the distinction between valid economic regulation, on the one hand, and invalid 'class' legislation, on the other—during a period of unprecedented class conflict."[54] To the extent that courts were more active in this era than in previous years, this could be attributed in large part to "the increase in the number of limitations imposed by the constitutions themselves upon state legislatures," as well as to changing conditions that required greater supervision of these limitations.[55]

When judges had an opportunity to reflect on the particular rights to which individuals were entitled, they generally proceeded as they had in the nineteenth century—by interpreting statutes and common-law principles. Thus when one man tried to persuade the Virginia Supreme Court that he had been denied his right to a speedy trial, the judges repaired to the statute books. The court took note of the importance of the right to a speedy trial, arguing that it "has been carefully safeguarded by the Constitution of this State and has constituted a part of its Bill of Rights from the earliest history of the Commonwealth, and its enforcement is not less important today than it was then." The court concluded: "What constitutes a 'speedy trial' within the meaning of the Constitution has been interpreted by the legislature in section 4926 of the Code, the substance of which has long been a part of the statute law of this State."[56] In particular, the legislature had determined that the best way to secure the right was to provide for the release of any person not tried after three terms of the court. Insofar as these statutory requirements had been satisfied, the defendant's rights were deemed to have been protected.

Similarly, when an Oregon man claimed that he had been denied his constitutional right to counsel, this prompted the Oregon Supreme Court to look to the statute books for guidance. The court concluded that "[a]n aid to the enforcement of the above constitutional provision is found in Section 1772, Oregon Laws, which provides that, when the accused has been arrested, charged with crime, and is brought before the magistrate . . . the magistrate must immediately inform him of the charge against him and of his right to counsel."[57] To the extent that this statutory requirement had been met, the defendant's rights were deemed to have been adequately secured.

To be sure, there were numerous instances during this period when individuals petitioned judges to overrule statutes on the ground that they ran afoul of provisions in bills of rights. But judges were generally hesitant to do so, in the belief that the legislature remained the proper forum for interpreting bills of rights and determining the best means of securing their provisions.

This continued deference to legislative judgment is perhaps best illustrated by a Virginia case dealing with search-and-seizure rights. In this particular instance, one of many persons charged with violating a prohibitory liquor law argued that certain pieces of evidence had been improperly obtained and therefore should be excluded from the trial, in order to guarantee the constitutional prohibition against improper searches and seizures. The Virginia Supreme Court acknowledged the importance of the constitutional guarantee but pointed out that "The Virginia search and seizure act of 1920 was manifestly passed to protect and enforce the rights of the citizens guaranteed to them by article 10 of the Virginia Bill of Rights."[58] In particular, the General Assembly had concluded that the most effective way to enforce the right was not to exclude improperly obtained evidence at the trial, but rather to impose financial and civil penalties on the person who had conducted the illegal search. The court therefore concluded: "Had the legislature deemed further penalties necessary for the protection of the citizens against illegal searches and seizures, it would doubtless have prescribed them. Having failed to do so, the duty does not rest upon the courts to inflict additional penalties."[59]

The court was especially confident in reaching this conclusion because, in doing so, it was following the judgment of a number of other state courts. To buttress their holding, the judges borrowed heavily from several of these opinions, including one from the Georgia Supreme Court that stated:

The office of the Federal and State Constitutions is simply to create and declare these rights. To the legislative branch of government is confided the power, and upon that branch alone devolves the duty, of framing such remedial laws as are best calculated to protect the citizen in the enjoyment of such rights, and as will render the same a real, and not an empty, blessing.

Whether or not prohibiting the courts from receiving evidence of this character would have any practical and salutary effect in discouraging unreasonable searches and seizures, and thus tend towards the preservation of the citizen's constitutional right to immunity therefrom, is a matter for legislative determination.[60]

When the Virginia Supreme Court had another occasion several years later to interpret the search-and-seizure law, the judges again deferred to the legislative judgment of how best to secure the right and it again reminded the litigants that the legislature remained the proper forum for remedying any defects in the law. The court noted: "That the language employed is perhaps too broad in its scope may be conceded. But this fault, if fault it be, is not to be corrected by the court, as correction lies within the exclusive province of the law-making branch of the government."[61]

In similar fashion, the Massachusetts Supreme Court declined to recognize the right of individuals to purchase contraceptives. The current legislative prohibition, which had stood on the books since the nineteenth century, made no distinction based on whether or not the contraceptives had been prescribed by a physician, and one doctor challenged the validity of the law on this ground. The court concluded that "such an exception cannot be read into our statute by judicial interpretation." If any individual believed that the current law failed to protect his rights adequately, "The relief here urged must be sought from the law-making department and not from the judicial department of government."[62]

There were, finally, several judicial decisions during this period that departed from this general approach in that they neither enforced limitations on the legislative process nor interpreted statutory and common-law principles. In particular, judges occasionally relied on an expansive interpretation of the due-process clauses of state and federal bills of rights in order to substitute their views of rights for those of legislators. In considering the significance of this final category of cases, it is helpful to distinguish between behavior that is consistent with regime principles and behavior that takes place during a particular era but is inconsistent with the principles of the regime. A closer examination of these cases suggests that this behavior was widely regarded as inconsistent with the spirit of the regime.

In the first place, these decisions were delivered relatively infrequently. Thus in 1891 the Massachusetts Supreme Judicial Court handed down a decision in *Commonwealth v. Perry* that invalidated an obscure law governing the wages of weavers.[63] But one finds very few of these cases in the populist era. In fact, the *Perry* case was literally the only instance when the Massachusetts Supreme Court relied on the state bill of rights to overturn a law of this kind. As Henry Lummus argued in the Massachusetts Convention of 1917, "I can find no case in the last twenty-five years in which any labor or social legislation has been held contrary to the provisions of the State Constitution."[64]

As a number of legal historians have demonstrated in recent years, state courts did not present a significant obstacle to legislative recognition of rights during this period. According to Melvin Urofsky: "In surveying state court decisions prior to World War I involving the basic elements of the Progressive program to protect workers—laws involving child labor, maximum hours, minimum wages, employer liability, and workmen's compensation—one finds that, with only a few exceptions, state courts moved consistently toward approval of a wide range of reform legislation. In attempting to enact their program, Progressives, although occasionally delayed in the courts, were not blocked there."[65]

Nor, as legal historians have also shown, did federal court interpretations of the due-process clause of the federal Bill of Rights result in the overturning of a significant number of state statutes.[66] To be sure, the Massachusetts Supreme Court in 1915 relied on the U.S. Supreme Court's decision in *Lochner v. New York* to invalidate a nine-hour-day law for railroad workers, on the ground that "the case at bar is indistinguishable from and is governed by *Lochner v. New York*."[67] But this was an unusual decision, not only in Massachusetts but across the country. In fact, most state courts "either ignored *Lochner* or distinguished it from the cases before them."[68]

These rulings were not only delivered infrequently but were also acknowledged to be inconsistent with established regime principles and roundly criticized as illegitimate. The *Perry* decision engendered significant and severe criticism from leaders of legal and intellectual opinion. Seymour Thompson argued in the next year's edition of the *American Law Review* that "[j]udges who render such decisions are not fit for the offices to which the people have elected them."[69] In an article published the same year in the *Harvard Law Review,* Herbert Darling argued that the issue decided by the court in the *Perry* case "is a political question to be discussed in the Legislature."[70] At a minimum, these decisions attracted few supporters in the legal community.[71]

In fact, most commentators actively discouraged this type of judicial behavior and fully expected populist principles to have an indirect influence—and populist institutions to have a more direct effect—in halting and overturning these decisions.[72] Walter Dodd, for instance, was convinced that "[t]he popular will must finally control in any popular government, either through the education of the courts or through an express change in constitutional texts."[73] That, according to William Allen White, is precisely what took place in the first few decades of the twentieth century. He argued that these judicial decisions constituted "a fine game of political hide and seek; but democracy has caught and is catching so many of the hiders, that within a decade at the most the game will be played out."[74] George Alger therefore argued:

> The forces of reaction . . . find themselves arrayed in defense of a theory of judicial power which is out of harmony with the new programme of democracy.
>
> This programme has for its initial purpose the more direct participation of the people in their own government, and in the selection of their representatives, and in a more direct sense of responsibility by those representatives to the people. . . . The part of this programme which affects the courts is that which seeks to bring them in line with this movement by compelling them to recognize a shift in the balance of power, a necessary change in their

relation to a system which must depend for its strength, its efficiency, and its growth upon the power to create, and not upon the power to complicate or prevent.

The Ark of the Constitution is not to be destroyed, the priests are not to be driven from the temple of justice. But the Ark exists not for the priests and the Levites, but for an expanding nation. Its safe place is not a temple, but the hearts of a people whom it guides, protects, and serves.[75]

CONCLUSION

The populist regime can be generally distinguished from its predecessor in that its animating spirit was democratic rather than republican. It is also possible to compare the two regimes by identifying the constitutional provisions that served as the principal guarantors of rights in each era, the institution that was counted on to secure the people's most important liberties, and the manner in which rights were ideally secured.

In the populist regime, the constitutional provisions that were thought to provide the chief security for rights were restrictions on representative institutions. Although the republican regime had relied primarily on institutional arrangements such as separation of powers and bicameralism to secure individual rights, these arrangements were no longer thought to be capable of preventing the passage of oppressive legislation. Nor did citizens in the populist regime place their faith in bills of rights, which were generally viewed as posing obstacles to the protection of liberty. To the extent that citizens in the populist regime placed their faith in constitutional provisions—and, to be sure, one strand of populist thought rejected the importance of constitutions and institutions altogether—they relied on clauses that circumscribed legislative and judicial power.

The initiative and referendum were the institutions in which people placed their faith in this era. Whereas the republican regime understood that claims of right were properly advanced, debated, and resolved in representative institutions, the populist regime held that legislators were too far removed from popular opinion to deliberate intelligently about rights. Accordingly, rights were believed to be safeguarded most effectively through initiative campaigns, which offered a direct and unmediated expression of the popular will. It could be said, therefore, that the populist regime understood that the public voice would be more consonant to the public good when pronounced by the people themselves than by their elected representatives.

Finally, ballot propositions were the ideal vehicles for securing rights. During the republican regime, legislative statutes were thought to embody the appropriate measures of responsiveness and reflection; in the populist regime, initiatives and referendums were viewed as inherently superior means of securing rights. Because they could be enacted independently of the legislature, they were more responsive to the popular will, but because they could not be enacted hastily, they were thought to be the product of adequate deliberation, albeit of a different character from that in the previous regime.

6

Populist Institutions as Keepers of the People's Liberties

There has been no shortage of efforts to evaluate the capacity of populist institutions to protect rights. In fact, the initiative and referendum have been evaluated in the infant, middle, and mature stages of their development;[1] on the basis of individual and multistate analyses;[2] and through empirical and public-choice analyses.[3] The difficulty is that these studies have produced a variety of conclusions.

Early scholarship, although not unanimous in its approval, could be said up until the middle of the twentieth century to have generally endorsed direct democracy. As Arthur Holcombe wrote in 1926: "There is as yet no convincing evidence that the initiative has tended to demoralize the electorates by exposing casual majorities of voters to the temptation of abusing the rights of helpless minorities under the lead of irresponsible and reckless agitators. Either there have been legislative precedents for the radical measures submitted by means of the initiative, or they have been rejected at the polls."[4] James Pollock reached a similar conclusion in 1940: "[T]here is quite as likely to be a judicious and rational decision on popular votes as on legislative votes," and on the larger questions, "the people have been much more likely [than the legislature] to arrive at an acceptable conclusion."[5] With the exception of several early setbacks in Oregon,[6] the view predominated that voters had "stood the test remarkably well."[7]

The scholarly consensus shifted in the second half of the twentieth century, primarily in response to a series of ballot propositions that sought to regulate civil rights. Beginning in the 1960s, scholars took note of several initiatives, primarily in California, that had the effect of reversing fair-housing and busing measures. Populist institutions were now deemed to "present a threat to minority rights,"[8] to "commonly usurp minority rights,"[9] and to "provide a procedure whereby legislative decisions can be made exclusively along the lines of racial prejudice."[10] In the early 1990s a series of anti–gay-rights measures, some of which were approved, led to another reassessment of populist institutions. More scholars joined the discussion, and many now concluded that plebiscites "pose a greater threat to minorities than laws enacted by legislatures."[11]

Although the capacity of populist institutions to protect rights is therefore now generally held in low esteem,[12] a fair number of scholars interpret the record in a different manner. Ronald Allen concludes, "The history of the initiative is remarkably free of the enactment of abusive legislation."[13] David Butler and Austin Ranney contend that "[i]f elected representatives are more protective of minority rights than popular majorities voting in referendum elections, the difference is at most marginal."[14] Additionally, as Janice May pointed out, "the fact that the device has been used to promote rights has been overlooked."[15] Furthermore, it has been noted that the initiative has "provided a valuable political tool to force the enactment of laws that the elected legislature has been unwilling to adopt" and "has protected the voters from laws that they were unwilling to accept."[16] On this reading of the evidence, then, representative institutions are not clearly superior to direct democracy. In fact, some scholars go even further and conclude that, "at least in certain situations, direct legislation may be more ameliorative than harmful,"[17] and "that the work-product of the initiative process overall is at least the equal of, and often superior to, that of the legislative process."[18]

It would be fair to say that "[t]he social science literature furnishes no definitive resolution of the controversy,"[19] and on the question of whether the initiative and referendum are more likely to secure or to endanger rights, "[r]eliable empirical studies do not exist."[20] What is needed, then, is an empirical study that can address the deficiencies in the unit of analysis, as well as in the scope and framework, of previous studies.

With respect to the unit of analysis, there are a number of capable studies of the constitutional initiative, the statutory initiative, *or* the popular referendum. But few studies have considered in a comprehensive manner the way in which all these direct democratic institutions have been used to regulate rights. Nor has adequate attention been given to the way in which the *presence* of these institutions has contributed indirectly to the security or insecurity of individual rights. After all, the founders of these institutions thought that their utility would be demonstrated "in the long run, not in the legislation placed by its use directly upon the statute books, but in the improvement of the legislation placed there by the legislatures."[21]

With respect to the scope of analysis, this study is both more broad and more narrow than existing accounts. It is more expansive in that it considers the record of populist institutions across several states and time periods. Because institutional tendencies are sometimes revealed only by analyzing a wide range of cases and situations, studies that focus on the record of direct democracy in a particular state or period are of limited utility. It is important, therefore, to examine the record of populist institutions in several states (Massachusetts, Michigan, Oregon, and Virginia) over an extended period (from 1900 until 1970).[22] Evidence from other states and other periods is considered insofar as it can shed light on the general tendencies of these institutions.

Although it is expansive in this sense, the project is necessarily confined to cases in which populist institutions were used to protect *rights*. Accordingly, this study does not discuss the various other innovations that have been enacted through direct democratic procedures, including the Missouri judicial selection system, which was adopted by initiative in 1940 and then copied by numerous other states; bottle-deposit laws, which were passed by initiative in Michigan in 1965 and proposed in numerous other states; California's influential Proposition 13 tax-limitation measure, which passed in 1978 and inspired countless other tax-cutting measures; Arizona's motor-voter bill, which was enacted in 1982 and then adopted by a number of other states as well as by the U.S. Congress; and legislative term limits, which have been enacted almost entirely through the initiative procedure.

Finally, the framework of this analysis is designed to achieve greater clarity than previous studies. Whenever one encounters such dramatically divergent assessments in the literature as in this case—with some scholars concluding that populist institutions pose a grave threat to rights, and others maintaining that they actually safeguard rights—there are two possible explanations. These scholars could either be talking past one another, by ostensibly referring to the same kinds of rights but actually speaking of different sets of rights, or be relying on different standards to evaluate the same data. To guard against the first possibility, this study examines a broad array of rights. This permits us to test the possibility that populist institutions may be quite effective in protecting certain rights but less effective in other cases, and in a patterned and predictable manner. Second, to provide a reasonably clear and consistent standard of measurement, it is advisable to compare the results of initiatives and referendums with the outcomes achieved through legislatures. Previous studies have not always undertaken such a comparison; consequently, they have been unable to address the question of the relative capacities of populist versus republican institutions.[23]

FREEDOM TO WORSHIP

The critics of direct democratic institutions at the time of their inception were perhaps most fearful for the fate of religious liberty. Henry Campbell argued in 1912, in comments that were echoed in a number of early-twentieth-century constitutional conventions: "In times of excitement, when the passions of the populace are aroused and those disposed to conservative views are intimidated by popular clamor, almost any measure might be adopted, which perhaps many of its supporters in their more sober moments would afterwards regret."[24] In one important religious freedom case, these predictions proved to be quite accurate. In addition, in several instances the initiative provided slightly less protection than representative institutions. At the same time, however, voters rejected most of the ballot measures that would have encroached on religious freedom, and in several cases the people secured religious liberty more effectively than the legislature.

Schools were the primary battleground for religious liberty in the populist era, and the early 1920s featured several controversies over the proper means of securing this right. The First World War, which inspired numerous efforts to distinguish American culture from that of its foreign combatants, combined with an influx of immigrants to produce a nationwide movement to "Americanize" the foreign-born. Many of these efforts were genuinely designed to help newcomers assimilate. Massachusetts, among other states, appropriated funds for night classes to teach adult immigrants the English language and basic civic skills.[25] Several states also directed their school systems to strengthen the American history curriculum and require students for the first time to recite the National Anthem and Pledge of Allegiance.[26] Compulsory-schooling laws were also enacted to require that all children receive some form of public or private education.

At a certain point, "a change in the approach to Americanization was taken by many in the movement. A definite emphasis was assumed which sought to stamp out the remnants of foreign culture still in existence in America."[27] This latter movement sought to instill American and Protestant values into the public-school curriculum in ways that occasionally infringed on the rights of religious minorities. In particular, because many Catholic immigrants attended parochial schools and therefore were deprived of the benefits of these measures, the Americanization movement next turned to regulating the private schools. "Not all children went to public schools where they could be shaped to fundamentalist specifications. Nativists wondered what went on in Catholic parochial schools, in German Lutheran classrooms, in elite academies."[28] Thus in 1921 the Michigan Legislature made the state superintendent of education responsible for regulating both the public and the private schools,[29] and several other state legislatures acted to permit public inspection of private schools.[30]

Although legislatures of this period were not particularly solicitous of religious minorities, their superiority to the initiative and referendum is evident when we examine the most extreme Americanization measure: the movement to ban private schools altogether. No legislature came close to adopting such a drastic law, but private-school bans were proposed through the initiative process in Michigan in 1920 and 1924, Oregon in 1922, and Washington in 1924. Although these measures were portrayed by their supporters as being neutral toward religion, they were clearly targeted against Catholics. In Oregon, the Ku Klux Klan initiated and campaigned strongly for the measure.[31] In Michigan: "All the old arguments based on bigotry were collected and used against the Catholic church and the parochial school. Slander and vilification came from platform and pamphlet. 'Ex-nuns' and 'ex-priests' were utilized to spread the propaganda. Absurd appeals to prejudice and sectarian hate were shouted abroad."[32] Both Michigan measures were defeated soundly, as was the Washington proposition, but the voters in Oregon approved a ban on private schools by a relatively comfortable margin.[33]

Although direct democracy served as a vehicle for limiting the free exercise of religion in this case, as well as in several others,[34] the initiative was occasionally used to a different effect. Perhaps the most notable case involved a constitutional amendment initiated and ratified by the citizens of Michigan. In its 1970 session, the Michigan Legislature resolved that the state's private schools contributed significantly to the state's educational goals and should therefore be entitled to public assistance.[35] In November 1970, however, the citizens ratified an initiated amendment that prevented the use of any public money to support private education, except in the case of transportation.[36] Initiatives were also used during this period to secure the repeal of Sabbatarian legislation, including in Oregon, which in 1917 abolished its ban on Sunday amusements,[37] and in Massachusetts, which in 1928 voted to permit Sunday sporting events.[38] In addition, North Dakota voters permitted Sunday baseball in 1920[39] and movies in 1934,[40] and Washington repealed its blue laws altogether in 1966.[41]

FREEDOM OF EXPRESSION

Free-speech controversies flared up on a number of occasions during this period, but direct democratic institutions played a relatively minor part in these deliberations. In the few cases in which initiatives were employed, they generally provided less protection than the legislative process.

Several initiatives were enacted that curtailed the right of association of members of labor unions. In 1938 the citizens of Oregon voted to impose numerous restrictions on picketing and to prohibit any form of picketing "unless there is an actual bona fide existing labor dispute between said employer or employers and his or their employees."[42] Then in 1946 Massachusetts voters approved a ballot proposition that banned unions from operating unless they provided, for the public record, the names of all officers and their salaries, as well as all sorts of information about the internal operation of the union.[43]

It should be noted, however, that although these initiatives were not particularly favorable to the right of free expression, they were not significantly more restrictive than measures adopted by legislatures and upheld by a number of state courts.[44] In addition, a number of oppressive initiative proposals were defeated at the polls. Thus a proposition to abolish boycotting was defeated in Oregon in 1912,[45] as was a California initiative that sought to impose significant limits on picketing in 1938.[46] Also defeated were a pair of measures on the ballot in Massachusetts in 1948 that sought to regulate internal union rules governing election procedures and strike votes.[47]

Initiatives were also used sparingly in a second area in which populist-era legislatures were quite active: to restrict the activities of anarchists, communists, and members of other political movements.[48] North Dakota voters enacted a ban on the display of red and black flags in 1920,[49] but although this measure was not particularly protective of free-speech rights, it was not markedly different from restrictions imposed by numerous other legislatures during the period.[50]

Additionally, the people rejected the more oppressive ballot measures, as in 1912, when Oregon voters rejected a proposal to give mayors the power to license street speeches,[51] and in 1962 when California voters disapproved an initiative that would have banned the Communist Party.[52]

Finally, on one occasion, direct democracy secured free-speech rights more effectively than did representative institutions. At the beginning of the twentieth century, a number of legislatures enacted statutes to require licensing of motion pictures, and the courts routinely ruled that these measures constituted reasonable protections against indecency.[53] In Massachusetts, however, the people relied on the referendum process to disapprove such a measure. In 1921 the Massachusetts General Court enacted a law providing that no film could be shown in the commonwealth unless it was first submitted to a commissioner of public safety, who could "disapprove any film or part thereof which is obscene, indecent, immoral, inhuman or tends to debase or corrupt morals or incite to crime."[54] A sufficient number of signatures was obtained to force a referendum on the law. During the ensuing campaign, "[s]carcely a paper failed to condemn the proposed law editorially,"[55] and in the 1922 election, Massachusetts voters rejected the censorial law by an overwhelming margin.[56]

THE GUARANTEE OF A FAIR TRIAL

The initiative was also used for multiple purposes and with mixed effect in regard to the right to a fair trial. The most significant initiative in this area sought to regulate the grand jury, an institution whose utility was the subject of much debate in the late nineteenth and early twentieth centuries. The grand jury had originally been viewed as a significant source of protection for individual rights, because it prevented state officials from undertaking arbitrary prosecutions. By the latter half of the nineteenth century, however, the grand jury had come to be viewed in some quarters as a source of unaccountable power rather than as a guarantor of individual liberty.[57] Therefore, when in 1899 the Oregon Legislative Assembly permitted district attorneys to proceed to trial by filing information instead of having to obtain an indictment through a grand jury,[58] it was not clear whether this would be viewed by the citizens as having secured or violated rights. A majority of legislators undoubtedly believed that in bypassing the grand jury they were securing rights, but as it turned out, a significant percentage of the Oregon populace still looked upon the grand jury as an institution that protected its rights.

These conflicting views of the grand jury were initially brought before the Oregon Supreme Court in 1900, when a defendant challenged the new procedure on the ground that it violated his fair-trial rights. The court rejected his claim and argued that:

> [The Bill of Rights] has secured to the accused the right of public trial by an impartial jury; to be heard by himself and counsel; to demand the nature of the accusation against him, and to have a copy thereof; to meet the witnesses face to face; and to have compulsory process for requiring the attendance of witnesses in his favor. This constitutes the chief palladium of civil liberty under the constitution. The manner of preferring the accusation is of preliminary import, and whether it shall be done by a grand jury or by a public prosecutor, or concurrently by both, has, whether wisely or not, been left to the wisdom of the legislature to determine.[59]

Justice Charles Wolverton concluded that, "while the wisdom of the law may be a subject of dispute, the authority to enact it cannot be gainsaid."[60] In previous years, citizens would have had no other means of redressing their grievance, short of calling a constitutional convention. But the advent of the initiative offered the people another opportunity to implement their view of the grand jury independently of the legislature or the judiciary, and in 1908 Oregon voters relied on the initiative procedure to enact a constitutional amendment that reinstated the requirement of a grand-jury indictment.[61]

The only other fair-trial right that was regulated through the initiative procedure was the privilege against self-incrimination, which had also been secured in several ways throughout the nineteenth century. Initially, defendants were protected by not being permitted to testify in their own defense. Then, midway through the century, legislatures changed course and permitted the accused to testify but stipulated that his refusal to do so could not be held against him. In the early twentieth century, this arrangement came under attack, and a number of proposals were advanced to permit prosecutors to comment on a defendant's failure to testify.

This criticism became particularly intense in the 1930s. Roscoe Pound argued in a 1934 law review article that the privilege had become "of little or no use to the innocent and is one of too many advantages of which the habitual defender of professional and organized criminals and the malefactors of means know how to avail themselves."[62] He argued that this bred disrespect for the privilege among law-enforcement officers, which in turn led to "a systematic development of extra-legal or downright illegal examinations by officials, with every external appearance of legality."[63] Pound, among others, recommended as an alternative that "[t]here should be express provision for a legal examination of suspected or accused persons before a magistrate; that those to be examined should be allowed to have counsel present to safeguard their rights; that provision should be made for taking down the evidence so as to guarantee accuracy."[64] The initiative was the vehicle by which the citizens of California enacted such a plan in 1934. The voters permitted prosecutors to comment on the failure of a defendant to testify,[65] but they secured the defendant's rights by directing that he be examined immediately after his arrest, before a magistrate, in the presence of counsel, and with all the guarantees that Pound envisioned.[66]

THE RIGHT TO EQUAL PROTECTION UNDER THE LAW

Significantly, these four states do not yield a single example of an initiative or referendum that violated the right to equal treatment under the law. When we broaden the study to include all the states, we are generally confirmed in our judgment that the initiative has been employed infrequently in order to encroach on minority rights. This broader sample does suggest, however, that in certain circumstances, the right to equal protection has been placed at greater risk in the initiative procedure than in the legislative process.

On several occasions the initiative provided diminished protection for the rights of aliens. Arizona voters limited the right of aliens to work by enacting an initiative in 1914 that required that at least 80 percent of an employers' workforce be composed of naturalized citizens.[67] The most notorious initiative affecting aliens concerned their right to own land. At the height of anti-Japanese sentiment in 1920,[68] California voters approved an initiative that "declare[d] that an alien ineligible to naturalization shall have no rights whatsoever with respect to 'real property' in California other than those secured to him by a 'now existing treaty' between the United States and his country."[69] The right of aliens to vote was also limited by an initiative that was enacted in California in 1920 and imposed a $10 poll tax on all aliens.[70]

Initiatives were introduced to regulate the rights of African Americans in two kinds of cases. In Oklahoma in 1910, an initiated amendment was the vehicle for the disenfranchisement of African American voters. The amendment, which was approved by a significant margin, instituted a universal literacy test for voting but then "grandfathered" virtually all white residents. Although this amendment, which was declared unconstitutional by the U.S. Supreme Court in 1915,[71] clearly oppressed African Americans, there is reason to be cautious about drawing any general conclusions about the tendencies of direct democratic institutions. According to David Schmidt: "[R]acist state officials, instead of printing 'yes' and 'no' on ballots, printed in small type: 'For the amendment.' Anyone wishing to vote against it was supposed to scratch out those words with a pencil. If they left their ballot as it was, it was counted as a vote in favor. In some precincts voters were not even provided with pencils. Casting further doubt on the accuracy of the 1910 vote count was a 'literacy' test measure placed on the ballot by the legislature in the 1916 primary, six years later: voters rejected it by a 59 percent margin."[72] It is also noteworthy that in states such as Virginia, where constitutional conventions were the agents of disenfranchisement, the delegates to these conventions frequently declined to submit these measures to the people for ratification, and instead declared them to be immediately operative.[73] This would suggest that the people could not be counted on to vote for these measures, and therefore that the general citizenry was not ordinarily disposed to approve limitations on the franchise.

Initiatives were also introduced later in the century to regulate the right of African Americans to equal treatment in employment, schooling, and housing. In the 1940s the voters of California rejected a ballot proposition that sought to prohibit all racial discrimination in employment.[74] Then, in the 1950s, Arkansas voters approved an initiative that urged the legislature to resist *Brown v. Board of Education* by all legal means. The 1960s was the occasion for the only successful statewide initiative of any practical importance. In 1964 California voters enacted an initiative to disapprove the 1962 Rumford fair-housing law.[75] According to Raymond Wolfinger and Fred Greenstein, the "disparity in the outcomes" of the legislature and the initiative in this case was "remarkable."[76] In 1964 "there were no signs that either the governor or the legislature was giving serious consideration to repealing the Rumford Act."[77] Yet later that year the repeal initiative prevailed by a two-to-one vote at the polls.[78]

THE RIGHT OF THE ELECTORATE
TO CONTROL GOVERNING INSTITUTIONS

The chief concern of the populist reformers was not so much to protect existing rights as to secure recognition of a new set of rights. The populists were perhaps most concerned with securing the right of the electorate to exercise effective control over governing institutions, which could be frustrated in several ways: by the self-interested actions of legislators, the disproportionate influence of certain groups, and the absence of institutional mechanisms for enforcing the majority will. The initiative process provided a means to overcome each of these deficiencies, first, by enabling the people to limit the influence of individual and special interests, and second, by ensuring that the popular will would be implemented more immediately and concretely.

In the first place, populist institutions were believed to "open the way for dealing with constitutional and political questions directly and effectively, without the necessity of reversing the laws of human nature in order to compel the legislature to act unselfishly in matters peculiarly affecting its members."[79] As Delos Wilcox argued: "How can we appeal to a state legislature to divest itself of the powers of interference in municipal affairs? How can legislators and aldermen be expected to forbid themselves to use railroad passes?"[80] The logic of the populist regime was that on most questions, representatives could act reasonably, but on certain issues, their particular interests rendered them incapable of deliberating reasonably.

The primary issue that legislators were deemed incompetent to regulate concerned the electoral process itself. When the Oregon Legislative Assembly declined in its 1907 session to enact a law for the regulation of campaigns and elections, the people in the next year initiated and approved a corrupt practices act that limited campaign expenses, required full disclosure of all candidate expenditures, and prescribed a comprehensive set of rules to govern campaign and election behavior.[81] Allen Eaton concluded that "of all the measures passed by the people it is without doubt one of the best."[82]

Another issue that legislators were deemed incapable of regulating is one to which Wilcox alluded but whose significance may no longer be apparent. In an era when the railroads constituted one of the most powerful special interests, the free rail pass was one of the chief means of wielding influence in the political process. Not suprisingly, one of the chief populist reform goals was to abolish the free pass. As William Allen White noted:

> [T]he anti-pass movement was based, not on economics, but upon politics. The movement was really connected with the growth of fundamental democracy. For the pass of the politician gave him power. He could run on errands against free government, and he became by reason of his pass the political agent, not merely of the railroad, but of all the foes of progress in the community. Railroad passes packed conventions, corrupted legislatures, colored the view of administrative officers, and biased courts. The pass was one of the most formidable weapons of the aristocracy of politics against the democracy.[83]

A number of state legislatures moved to ban the free pass during the first decade of the twentieth century, but where legislators declined to ban rail passes, as in Oregon,[84] the people resorted to the initiative to eliminate them.[85]

The initiative was also used to overcome the improper influence of special interests. In particular, populist institutions were employed to ensure that "[t]he clamor of loud-voiced minorities would have less effect upon the people at large than it now has upon their representatives. From the eye of the legislator at the state capital prevailing sentiment is often hidden by the mist arising from the fierce breath of the militant few who fill the corridors. . . . The Referendum removes the ultimate control of legislation from the artificial storm center at the capital to the wider fields of common life where average weather conditions prevail."[86] In a broad sense, of course, the initiative and referendum performed this checking function in ways that cannot accurately be detected or measured. U'Ren, for one, thought that these institutions had such an influence on the 1903 session of the Oregon Legislative Assembly, which was the first to be held after the adoption of the initiative. He thought that this session was the first one in a long time that reflected the majority will rather than that of special interests, because of the representatives' "fear that the referendum would be demanded on any legislation obtained by [improper] methods."[87]

The initiative also performed this checking function in several specific ways, two of which are only marginally related to rights. First, Oregon and Michigan were two of many states where voters living in the fields battled those residing closer to the legislative corridors over the merits of daylight versus standard time. After the Oregon Legislative Assembly adopted daylight saving time in 1949, citizens resorted to the initiative process and in 1952 forced the state to revert to standard time.[88] In Michigan, it was the partisans of daylight saving time who relied on the initiative to effect a change from standard back to daylight time.[89] Second, geographic splits were responsible for the efforts in some states to physically move the capital in order to bring it closer to the fields.[90]

In addition to using the initiative to reduce the power of particular interests, populist reformers secured popular rights by transferring governing powers from the legislatures to the electorate. In 1908, for instance, the citizens of Oregon used the initiative to obtain the power to recall public officials,[91] and in 1939 Michigan voters relied on the initiative to obtain the power to select their judges, through nonpartisan elections.[92] The initiative was also the means by which the electorates of several states secured the direct election of U.S. senators. In 1904 Oregon voters required state legislators to pledge to vote for the Senate candidate of the people's choice,[93] and in 1908 they approved an initiative that formally instructed legislators to honor the results of the popular vote.[94] The direct primary, another favorite Progressive reform, was also adopted in a number of states through the initiative. Oregon voters adopted the direct primary for state officeholders in 1904,[95] and then extended this to national offices in 1910;[96] Massachusetts voters in 1932 enacted an initiative that reformed party nomination procedures.[97]

The initiative also transferred control of the constitutional revision process from the legislators to the citizens. In Oregon, the people feared that the legislature might call a constitutional convention without first obtaining their approval. Thus in 1906 Oregon voters approved an initiative that required that the legislature hold a popular referendum before it could hold a constitutional convention.[98] In Michigan, the voters feared just the opposite—that the legislature would not permit a convention to be held, even when this was supported by a majority of the people. Thus, after the Michigan Legislature rejected repeated calls for a constitutional convention throughout the 1950s, Michigan voters in 1961 approved a constitutional initiative that required a popular referendum to be held the following year, and every sixteenth year thereafter, on whether or not to hold a constitutional convention.[99] In 1968 Massachusetts voters approved a similar initiative to force a popular vote on holding a constitutional convention.[100]

Finally, the initiative was used to reduce the size of legislative assemblies, as well as the frequency and duration of their sessions. Reducing the size of the legislature by abolishing the state senate, as many citizens proposed during this era, was seen as not only cutting expenses but also increasing legislative responsiveness and therefore indirectly securing popular rights. But because this would naturally deprive many legislators of their seats, it was routinely rejected by state legislatures. Accordingly, Oregon voters went to the polls to vote on ballot measures to abolish the state senate in both 1912 and 1914, but the initiatives failed each time.[101] These proposals were greeted more favorably in other states. Nebraska voters followed George Norris's lead and approved a unicameral-legislature initiative in 1934.[102] In addition, when the citizens of Massachusetts in 1968 sought to reduce the size of their house of representatives from 240 to 160 members, they initiated a constitutional amendment that eventually provided the necessary spur for legislative action.[103]

Legislators were equally chary of cutting the length or frequency of their sessions, in part because of the resulting reduction in their salaries. Therefore, when these changes were made, they were usually adopted in constitutional conventions or through initiatives, such as the 1938 ballot measure through which Massachusetts voters adopted biennial legislative sessions.[104]

THE RIGHT TO VOTE

State governments in the nineteenth century had extended the suffrage in a variety of ways. Constitutional conventions had enfranchised African Americans, removed property and freehold requirements, and secured the right to an equal vote for residents of rural areas. The early twentieth century witnessed some of the same debates, including over the extension of the suffrage (to include women), the removal of exclusionary policies (the poll tax), and the passage of measures to ensure an equality of apportionment (to secure an equal right to vote for urban and suburban voters). Populist institutions were employed to secure voting rights in each of these cases.

The initiative served in the first place as the vehicle for extending the suffrage to women. It was one thing to permit women to vote in school board and municipal elections, as some states did in the late nineteenth century. This could be justified on the ground that women possessed expertise in these particular areas. Voting for state and federal officials was something else entirely, and it was only in the course of the populist regime that these rights were recognized. To be sure, the right was usually secured through constitutional amendments that were proposed by legislatures and approved by the people,[105] but in several states women's suffrage was stymied in the legislature and could be obtained only through the constitutional initiative.

The problem was that the fate of the women's suffrage movement was so closely connected with other social reform efforts, such as Prohibition, that it provoked intense opposition from opponents of these policies, such as liquor companies and saloon keepers. These groups occasionally exerted such inordinate influence on the legislative process that legislatures failed to approve amendments, even when they were supported by a popular majority.[106] In these cases, the initiative provided a way to bypass the special interests and to secure the right independently of the legislature. Whether because the suffragists had misjudged the strength of popular sentiment, or because the liquor interests had corrupted even the electoral process,[107] these initiated measures were sometimes rejected at the polls, as was the case in Oregon in 1906, 1908, and 1910.[108] In

1912, however, the voters of Oregon finally ratified an initiated amendment that secured for women the right to vote.[109]

In addition to removing the prohibition on women voting, the initiative served as the means of abolishing of the poll tax. The populist reformers neither expected nor desired that the initiative would remove all voting qualifications. Wilcox, for instance, was "reasonably certain that the majority of the present electorate in most American communities would vote for such moderate restrictions as would exclude from the suffrage the obviously undeserving and unfit," including "those persons who cannot read and write." But he thought that it was "not likely that a property qualification could be established by vote of the electors."[110] Wilcox turned out to be prescient on both counts, in that voters generally retained literacy and citizenship tests but moved in certain cases to eliminate the poll tax. In 1910, for instance, the citizens of Oregon initiated and ratified a constitutional amendment that prohibited the poll tax.[111] Similar measures were proposed in other states and ratified every time they appeared on the ballot.[112]

Finally, voters relied on the initiative to secure the right to an equal vote, especially when legislative intransigence prevented a timely or equitable redistricting. The failure of legislatures to secure an equitable apportionment had been a long-standing problem, dating back to the early nineteenth century. Hence the occasional use of the constitutional convention to remedy extreme malapportionment. Citizens in the twentieth century faced the same problem, only in a more dramatic fashion, as some states failed to reapportion for nearly five decades.

> The reasons for such a widespread failure of legislatures to live up to state constitutional redistricting requirements are not difficult to find. In almost any reapportionment a number of legislators would be personally affected through the abolition or consolidation of districts. A legislator naturally finds the status quo under which he was elected to be satisfactory and usually dreads the prospect of a new and unknown constituency. Also, many refuse to move because their particular party would lose strength. In almost all cases a dominant consideration has been the increasing disparities in rural and urban popular strength, with legislators from smaller communities showing a hostility to growing cities. Finally, interest groups benefiting from the status quo have fought reapportionment.[113]

With the advent of the initiative and referendum, the people obtained a new tool for securing an equitable apportionment, one that permitted them to bypass the legislature as well as the cumbersome and unpredictable process of calling a constitutional convention.[114]

The initiative could be used to simply redraw district lines. Although a number of states across the country used the initiative for this purpose, none of the states in this sample used the initiative in this way. In 1930 and 1932, Michigan voters had an opportunity to do so, as did Oregon voters in 1950, but each of these proposals was rejected.[115]

Some states also used the initiative to set up alternative mechanisms for redrawing district lines. The usual strategy was to construct a reapportionment procedure that either bypassed the legislature altogether or provided a backup plan in case the legislature failed to act promptly. Thus in 1952, after the Oregon Legislative Assembly had failed to reapportion for some five decades,[116] Oregon voters turned to the initiative, in what Gordon Baker referred to as "a fruitful case study of how effective this direct democratic device can be in circumventing legislative inaction on a fundamental problem of free government."[117] In particular, the citizens established a formula for measuring the equity of future apportionments, directed the secretary of state to use this formula to draw the district lines in the event the legislature failed to do so, and gave the state supreme court original jurisdiction to review any contested apportionment plans.[118] Ironically, Clay Myers, who as a student at the University of Oregon had been one of the chief advocates for this amendment, had the opportunity in 1966 as the Oregon secretary of state to comply with the amendment by redrawing the state district boundaries after the legislature failed to do so.[119] Citizens in other states took to the polls to vote on similar schemes for bypassing legislatures. In 1952 Michigan voters approved an amendment that mandated decennial apportionment, required that boundary lines be drawn on an equitable basis, and directed the board of state canvassers to assume responsibility in the event the legislature failed to take prompt action.[120]

The use of the initiative to remedy malapportionment became so prevalent that this figured prominently in the landmark 1962 U.S. Supreme Court case *Baker v. Carr.* The Court determined that this particular case, which concerned the failure of the Tennessee General Assembly to reapportion for some six decades, was justiciable only after noting that Tennessee lacked an initiative procedure, and therefore the voters lacked any effective recourse. Justice William Brennan noted in his majority opinion that the Tennessee General Assembly was unlikely to "submit reapportionment proposals either to the people or to a Constitutional Convention," and that "[t]here is no provision for popular initiative in Tennessee."[121] Likewise, Justice Tom Clark argued in his concurring opinion that he "would not consider intervention by this Court into so delicate a field if there were any other relief available to the people of Tennessee. But the majority of the people of Tennessee have no 'practical opportunities for exerting their political weight at the polls' to correct the existing 'invidious discrimination.' Tennessee has no initiative and referendum."[122]

Several commissions on governmental organization also took note of the value of the initiative for reapportionment purposes. The Connecticut Commission on State Government Organization reported in 1950: "To ask the General Assembly to reconsider its own basis of apportionment is to ask a man to judge his own case. He can scarcely rise above his own interest if he does, and he cannot escape the charge of bias however he decides." As a result, the commission recommended that states adopt "an additional method of constitutional change, by initiative petition and popular referendum."[123] Likewise, when the National Municipal League proposed its Model State Constitution in 1961, it also recommended that states adopt the initiative, on the ground that "[s]ome way should be provided by which the people may directly effect constitutional change without depending on existing governmental institutions."[124]

THE RIGHT TO ECONOMIC AND SOCIAL SECURITY

In addition to securing an assortment of new political rights, populist reformers sought to recognize a variety of economic and social rights. The view took hold that women, children, and laborers in dangerous industries had a right to reasonable working hours. In addition, all workers had a right to safe working conditions. Senior citizens, disabled individuals, and mothers with dependent children were also entitled to be protected from economic insecurity. Finally, as the century progressed, the view took hold in some states that individuals had a right to work without having to join a union. The majority of these rights were recognized through legislation, but when legislatures failed to act promptly or were incapacitated by the disproportionate influence of interest groups, the people turned to the initiative to secure their rights.

The Right to Reasonable Work Hours

Of all the rights to which workers were entitled, the one that was established the earliest and with the least resistance was the right to limited work hours. According to Theda Skocpol: "The typical pattern was for subnational labor bodies to campaign first for legal hours limits for children, women, and particular male occupations, following up victories in these areas with campaigns for general eight-hour statutes."[125] Thus children's hours were first limited by a law enacted by the Massachusetts General Court in 1842,[126] and by the start of the twentieth century, there was a near consensus among the states in favor of child-labor laws.[127] Limiting women's hours was the next reform goal. The Massachusetts General Court enacted the first such law in 1874, and most other states again followed suit.[128] Reformers sought, finally, to limit the hours of all workers in particular industries such as railroads, mines, and public works.[129]

The representative process was generally effective in securing these rights, but when legislatures proved unresponsive the people turned to the initiative. Thus in 1912 Oregon voters proposed and enacted an eight-hour-day law for public workers, and Colorado voters approved a pair of initiatives that mandated eight-hour days for women and for miners.[130] Then, in 1914, the American Federation of Labor branches in Oregon, California, and Washington proposed universal eight-hour-day initiative measures. In the end, these propositions were defeated soundly, but interestingly enough, not necessarily on account of opposition from business groups. Following a 1913 AFL West Coast convention at which labor leaders were seemingly united in their support for these initiatives, it soon became apparent that national union leaders were ambivalent toward, if not opposed to, these measures. Between the 1913 convention and the 1914 vote, "AFL President Gompers spoke out against general eight-hour laws, infuriating unionists in California, Oregon, and Washington, who had to watch business interests put quotes from Gompers on billboards and on pamphlets distributed during successful efforts to defeat eight-hour laws by popular referenda in those states."[131] As a result, state union leaders had to remain content with their limited gains achieved through prior initiatives. With the exception of a forty-eight-hour-workweek that was secured through the initiative in Maine in 1923, all future maximum-hours laws were pursued and obtained through the legislative process.

The Right to Safe Working Conditions

The right to safe working conditions was the next to be secured, and it was established in two stages. The first step was to repeal the common-law rules that absolved employers of virtually all liability for work accidents. According to these rules, the employer was held blameless if the worker knew about and therefore could be said to have assumed the risk involved in the job (the assumption-of-risk doctrine), if the worker himself contributed in any way to the accident (the rule of contributory negligence), or if a fellow worker's negligence contributed to the accident (the fellow-servant rule).[132] The second step toward securing this right was to establish workmen's compensation bureaus that provided compensation to disabled employees.[133]

For the most part, these changes were implemented through statutes that were enacted in the first two decades of the twentieth century.[134] The relatively smooth passage of these reforms was due, in part, to the fact that "workmen's compensation, in contrast to other forms of social security, represented a redefinition or expansion of certain limited rights the worker already had."[135] In addition, these reforms attracted the rare support of both labor and business groups.[136]

At times, however, railroads and other interest groups wielded such inordinate influence on the legislative process that they succeeded in blocking reform of workmen's compensation laws. In these cases, the initiative and referendum proved helpful. Thus in its 1901 session, the Oregon Legislative Assembly defeated a bill that would have abolished the fellow-servant rule for railroad workers, but in 1903, in the first session after the adoption of the referendum, the law passed easily.[138] Several years later, when the 1909 session of the Oregon Legislative Assembly refused to enact a more comprehensive workmen's compensation plan, the issue was placed on the ballot through the initiative process,[139] and in 1910 Oregon voters enacted workplace safety rules and abolished the contributory-negligence and fellow-servant rules.[140] When these gains came under attack in the next assembly session, the threat of a referendum was instrumental in preventing their repeal.[141]

The Right to Financial Subsistence

Throughout the first several decades of the twentieth century, labor leaders and progressive reformers pressed for broad-based European-style social insurance plans that would guarantee workers and their families a reasonable wage and pension. What the states eventually enacted, however, was a number of specific pension plans that targeted the disabled, mothers of dependent children, widows, and the elderly. The most successful campaigns, as well as those in which the initiative played the most prominent role, concerned mothers' and old-age pensions.

Although support for mothers' pensions did not take hold until as late as 1909, after President Theodore Roosevelt's Conference on the Care of Dependent Children,[142] it spread like "wildfire," and by 1915, mothers' pension laws had been enacted in twenty-three states.[143] In some state legislatures, however, opposition from business and philanthropic groups was so strong that mothers' pension supporters resorted to the initiative.[144] Thus in 1912 Colorado voters enacted a comprehensive reform of the state's dependent children act, complete with a mothers' pension plan,[145] and in 1914 Arizona voters approved an initiative measure that provided for mothers'—as well as old-age—pensions.[146]

Proposals to secure the right to an old-age pension generally endured a significantly longer gestation period and engendered even stronger opposition. Old-age pension proposals were introduced into state legislatures as early as 1903,[147] but by 1920, Arizona remained the only state to have actually enacted such a proposal, which was accomplished through the 1914 initiative.[148] Supporters of old-age pensions enjoyed somewhat more success through state legislatures over the next decade and a half, during which time they secured the enactment of pension plans in half of the states,[149] but in the late 1930s they began to press their case through the initiative procedure.

Although voters in several states had voted on old-age pension initiatives prior to this period,[150] the primary impetus came from Dr. Francis Townsend, who proposed to stimulate the economy by giving a $200-per-month pension to all Americans over age sixty on the condition that they spend it immediately.[151] In part because it was significantly more expensive and more economically suspect than the standard pension proposals, Townsend's plan was ill received by Congress and by most state legislatures. Then, in 1938, he began to consider the possibility that his plan could be enacted through the initiative. "The 'initiative' enabled the pressure group to appeal directly to the electorate for a vote on the Townsend Plan and thus to circumvent both the state legislature and the political parties. In addition, the pension advocates discovered common ground upon which to cooperate with other interest groups."[152] In particular, the initiative permitted old-age pension supporters to make common cause with labor unions and to overcome the strong opposition of "business and conservative groups, who, ironically, were joined by the Communist press."[153]

Accordingly, in 1938, Oregon voters approved an initiative that endorsed the Townsend movement,[154] and between 1944 and 1950, Townsend clubs initiated constitutional amendments in a number of states across the country. Although the Townsend Plan itself met with little success, the initiative campaign was instrumental in securing the passage of a number of more modest old-age pension plans.[155] In 1946 Massachusetts voters approved the creation of the Old Age Pension Commission, which provided a minimum payment of $48 per month.[156] Another successful initiative in Massachusetts in 1950 increased the pension to $75 per month, and $85 for blind seniors.[157] Oregon voters, after rejecting several extravagant pension initiatives in 1944 and 1946, enacted a proposition in 1948 that paid $50 per month.[158]

The Right to Work

The positions of the supporters and critics were reversed in the case of right-to-work proposals. Whereas these other economic rights were generally supported by unions and opposed by businesses, the right to work was supported by business interests and bitterly opposed by labor groups.

Of the states in our sample, Virginia is the only one that actually secured the right, and it did so through a legislative referendum approved by the voters in 1947. Massachusetts was the only state in the sample that featured an initiative campaign to establish the right, and the voters defeated the measure by a resounding margin.[159] This is one area, however, where it is particularly instructive to look beyond our primary data set, because right-to-work initiatives generated significant activity in a number of states around the country. In fact, between 1944 and 1964, a total of eleven states debated the right to work in at least one initiative campaign, and four of these states voted on the issue in multiple elections.[160]

In the belief that labor unions had been the beneficiary of particularly favorable legislation on the national level in the late 1930s, right-to-work supporters tried to persuade a number of state legislatures to enact right-to-work laws.[161] They generally failed in their initial efforts, but because they attributed these defeats to the disproportionate influence of labor unions on the legislative process, they turned to the initiative.[162] For a time, this strategy proved to be quite effective. Of the first five states to enact right-to-work laws, three did so through the initiative: Arkansas in 1944, Nebraska in 1946, and Arizona in 1946.[163] In addition, Nevada voters approved a right-to-work initiative in 1952 and upheld the right by rejecting counterinitiatives in 1954 and 1956.[164] Not all right-to-work initiative campaigns were successful, though, and in fact propositions were defeated on eight occasions.[165] But every state that secured the right did so through a popular vote of some kind, through an initiative, a legislative referendum,[166] or a constitutional amendment.[167]

CONCLUSION

Admittedly, this survey falls short of being comprehensive in several respects. A complete evaluation would examine a greater number of states and would go even further in identifying the indirect effects of populist institutions. Even so, the existing data are sufficiently rich to advance several conclusions about the capacity of populist institutions to secure rights.

In the first place, populist institutions provided a superior level of protection for the right to vote and the right of the electorate to control governing institutions. The pull of self-interest was simply too strong in a number of cases to permit legislators to deliberate reasonably about these matters, and the initiative provided an effective way to secure these rights independently of the legislature. Thus the initiative was the vehicle for securing an equal apportionment, abolishing the poll tax, banning the free rail pass, regulating campaigns and elections, removing legislative control over constitutional conventions, and reducing the size, frequency, and duration of legislative sessions.

In another set of cases, popular institutions secured rights more quickly than or in a slightly different manner from legislatures, but they did not provide a markedly better level of protection. Thus the initiative secured women's suffrage when it was blocked by the liquor interests, it secured the right to workmen's compensation when it was stymied by the railroad interests, and it secured the right to an old-age pension over the opposition of a diverse coalition of groups. It is not clear, however, that one can draw any general conclusions from these particular cases. To be sure, these rights were secured in a more timely fashion through the initiative than through the legislature, but legislatures across the country generally secured them in a suitable manner. In another group of cases, concerning movie censorship and the grand jury, the initiative and referendum protected rights in a slightly different manner from the legislature, but again, these cases do not necessarily indicate any general superiority on the part of populist institutions.

In one final group of cases, concerning liberties in crisis times, populist institutions provided decidedly less protection than legislatures. To be sure, there were only a limited number of cases when the initiative process served as the vehicle for violating individual rights. Nonetheless, there were several periods when popular majorities were gripped by a momentary ill humor and the initiative process failed to provide the type of deliberation that ordinarily characterized legislative assemblies. In particular, the initiative provided inferior protection for the rights of Catholic schoolchildren in Oregon in the 1920s at the height of the Americanization movement, for alien landholders in several western states in the 1910s, and for African Americans in several periods.

In the majority of cases, therefore, there was only a marginal difference between the capacity of republican and populist institutions to secure rights. In several cases, however, certain differences emerge. With respect to the right to vote and the right of the electorate to exercise control over governing institutions, the initiative provided a higher level of protection than the legislature. With respect to the rights of individuals during periods of political or social ferment, the initiative provided inferior protection.

7
The Theory and Design
of Judicialist Institutions

The idea that judges might play a prominent role in the protection of rights was not unprecedented in the nineteenth and early twentieth centuries. During this period, judges had occasionally protected rights by issuing constitutional decisions that rested on interpretations of bills of rights. Some judges had even gone so far as to suggest that the political process was incapable of securing certain rights. In general, though, constitutional decision making was confined to particular areas of law and was not thought to represent the ordinary form of judicial behavior. Moreover, to the extent that certain judges sought to remove issues from the political process on a routine basis, this behavior was discouraged.

In the course of the twentieth century, a different view took hold. Whereas constitutional decision making was once thought to be occasionally appropriate, it now became the ordinary means of securing rights. Whereas legislative protection of rights had once been considered the norm and legislative failure the exception, legislatures were now deemed to be generally incompetent to secure rights. Furthermore, it was no longer necessary for judges to justify instances of constitutional decision making, because this type of behavior was now accepted and even encouraged by leaders of intellectual opinion.

The emergence of this judicialist regime of rights protection between 1940 and 1990 differed in several ways from previous regime changes. In the first place, this transformation did not originate in the states, but rather at the national level—in the leading national law schools and in the decisions of the U.S. Supreme Court. Nor did it emerge out of deliberations among and within political institutions. In particular, there were none of the constitutional conventions that heralded the start of previous regimes; rather, the significant changes occurred primarily in the academy and in the realm of thought. Nor, finally, was this regime implemented at a precise moment, as was the case with previous regimes; instead, it took hold gradually over a long stretch of time.

Because this regime emerged at the national level, an account of its origins should focus on developments in the nation as well as in particular states. The fact that professors, rather than public officials, supplied its principal theoretical grounding suggests, furthermore, that such an account will benefit more from a reliance on journals of law than from a reliance on journals of constitutional convention proceedings. Finally, because the implementation of the regime was such a gradual and lengthy process, it is important to reconstruct the debate over regime principles not by including every significant contribution but by presenting only the most cogent and influential arguments.

CRITIQUE OF THE OLD REGIME

At the turn of the twentieth century, the republican regime had come under attack from populist reformers who were concerned with the incapacity of republican institutions to secure a particular set of rights (namely, the right to social and economic security), and who eventually undertook a reevaluation of republican principles. In the period between 1920 and 1940, the republican regime, as modified by the subsequent populist reforms, came under attack from a different front. In particular, republican institutions were charged with providing inadequate security for another set of rights (civil liberties). This, in turn, led to a similar reassessment of republican principles.

More than any other events, the First World War and, to some extent, the Second World War were responsible for the reevaluation of existing institutions of rights protection. As Osmond Fraenkel wrote, from the vantage point of the Second World War, "Since modern war occasions vast alteration in civil life, it is not strange that the prosecution of war tends to restrict civil liberties."[1] The First World War brought a significant number of such restrictions, as both Congress and the state legislatures enacted a series of laws banning sedition and anarchy.[2] The war's end, far from bringing a halt to this type of legislation, produced a "disheartening" outpouring of laws designed to stamp out dissent, sedition, and syndicalism.[3]

This ferment of legislative activity and subsequent restrictions on civil liberties had several consequences.[4] In the first place, they led to a newfound concern for the protection of civil liberties. According to Leon Whipple, "the phenomena of conscription and the punishment of conscientious objectors, of the postal censorship, of new laws that sent economic or social radicals to jail for twenty years or more, of the 'deportation delirium' challenged liberal-minded men to a new study of the meaning of civil liberty."[5] Perhaps the most prominent of these men was Zechariah Chafee, who produced a series of law review articles and monographs that tried to distinguish between proper and improper regulations of civil liberty.[6]

This concern also led in 1917 to the creation of the Civil Liberties Bureau of the American Union Against Militarism, the precursor of the American Civil

Liberties Union (ACLU).[7] "I don't think anyone had ever called anything civil liberties in the United States before we did," recalled Roger Baldwin, the founder of the organization.[8] As a result, "For the first time civil liberties became a central political issue debated in the nation's highest chambers and in the nation's press."[9]

These early civil libertarians were concerned initially with protecting the free-speech rights of political and religious dissenters, because these were most immediately threatened in the post–First World War era.[10] But when Whipple was commissioned by the ACLU in 1927 to produce a national study of civil liberties, he detected a growing concern not only for these particular rights but also for a broad range of civil liberties.

> The true note of the period is an increased interest in and a vigorous defense of civil liberty. There has been a growing sense that we had too complacently accepted liberty as an inheritance, won by our forefathers, and somehow mysteriously embodied in the parchment of constitutions. This new interest in civil liberty arose partly out of a new realization of its essential value in our complex industrial age; partly out of the common experiences of the social reformers; partly because of the increased number of cases in which liberty was sacrificed to the interests of powerful conservative groups. Something had to be done to resist stifling encroachments and to extend the bounds of liberty for new classes and purposes.[11]

Perhaps the most important consequence of this newfound concern for civil liberties was that leaders of intellectual opinion were led to reassess the suitability of existing institutional arrangements. Although civil liberties organizations sought initially to press their case within the legislatures and in the court of public opinion,[12] the failure of legislatures to secure adequate protection for these liberties eventually led to dissatisfaction with the republican model of rights protection. As a result, by the 1920s, civil libertarians had begun to focus their attention on courts rather than legislatures as the means by which these liberties might be secured.[13]

At the same time that this growing awareness of civil liberties was leading to a reevaluation of the traditional reliance on legislatures for their protection, developments in the field of jurisprudence were indirectly producing the same result. Legal thinkers, beginning with Massachusetts and later U.S. Supreme Court Justice Oliver Wendell Holmes, began to argue that law could no longer be understood as the product of legislation and formal rules, as it had been throughout the nineteenth century. "The prophecies of what the courts will do in fact, and nothing more pretentious, are what I mean by the law," Holmes argued in an 1897 article in the *Harvard Law Review*.[14] To continue to describe law as the process of applying legislative statutes to concrete cases, Jerome Frank suggested several decades later, would be to discount the knowledge that "formal law frequently conceals what judges do in fact and what makes them do it."[15] Although there was some disagreement about the precise content of this school of legal realism that emerged in the 1930s, Karl Llewellyn believed that all could agree, at least, on "[t]he conception of law in flux, of moving law, and of judicial creation of law."[16]

All told, the legal realist movement had a variety of purposes, none of which was directly connected to promoting a heightened role for the courts in securing civil liberties.[17] In fact, the aim of most legal realists was not to encourage but rather to limit judicial creativity. Developments in the realm of jurisprudence inevitably have an effect, however, on students and practitioners; or, as Holmes argued, "Theory is the most important part of the dogma of the law, as the architect is the most important man who takes part in the building of a house."[18] Moreover, the most important effects are not always those that are immediately intended by the theorists. In this case, one of the long-term effects of the legal realist movement was to call attention to the creative power of judges and to alter the legal curriculum to reflect the importance of this judicial creativity. We are all realists now, and in a variety of respects, but perhaps most importantly in the sense that law professors no longer turn initially to legislative statutes in order to understand the rights to which individuals are entitled. As Oregon Supreme Court Justice Hans Linde noted, in the wake of the realist movement, first-year law students are now taught the "identity between the law in operation and the role of the courts," with the result that "questions of constitutional law and questions of the role of the Supreme Court are generally treated as the same thing."[19] As for judges, even if they would not go quite as far as U.S. Chief Justice Charles Evans Hughes and proclaim that "the Constitution is what the judges say it is,"[20] they have at least come to think of themselves, rather than legislators, as the principal creators of law and rights.

Another long-term development, the nationalization of civil liberties, provided a final, indirect spur to a reassessment of the traditional reliance on legislatures for the protection of rights. For a number of years, and for a variety of reasons, Americans had been increasingly inclined to consider themselves members of one national community rather than of numerous state and local communities. But the first several decades of the twentieth century brought calls for a centralization of governmental functions that were more frequent and more bold than in previous years. By the late 1930s, Harold Laski could refer to "the obsolescence of federalism,"[21] and George Benson could write: "Perhaps the most critically defective part of our present system is the state government. Constitutionally, politically, and administratively the states are the core of American government—but at times there seems discouraging evidence that the core is rotting."[22]

In subsequent decades, the view took hold that state polities were generally incapable of protecting a whole host of rights. According to John Kincaid:

"[S]tates came to be associated more with coercive deprivations of rights than with protections of individual rights, while the federal government came to be seen as a potential liberator of persons from the tyranny of small places."[23] Underlying many of these concerns was, of course, the issue of race, and the belief that a number of state communities were incapable of protecting the civil rights of African Americans. In William Riker's formulation: "If one approves the goals and values of the privileged minority, one should approve the federalism. Thus, if in the United States one approves of Southern white racists, then one should approve of American federalism. If, on the other hand, one disapproves of the values of the privileged minority, one should disapprove of federalism. Thus, if in the United States one disapproves of racism, one should disapprove of federalism."[24] As a result, a growing number of citizens began to join Monrad Paulsen in concluding that "[i]f our liberties are not protected in Des Moines the only hope is in Washington."[25]

The view that the national community could secure rights more effectively than state communities was important in its own right. But the shift in the *level* of government to which individuals looked for the preservation of their liberties also had significant implications for the *institutions* on which citizens came to rely for the security of those liberties. In particular, because the United States is a government of enumerated rather than reserved powers, Congress lacks the clear statutory authority under which the state legislatures are empowered to protect rights.[26] As a result, the choice of the nation over the states as the proper level of rights protection led necessarily to a reliance on courts rather than legislatures as the institution that could secure rights. What is significant for an institutional analysis of rights protection, therefore, is not so much that citizens began to turn to Washington rather than Des Moines to redress their grievances. The crucial difference was that they had at one time traveled primarily to the statehouse in Des Moines to secure their rights, but when they turned to Washington, the inability, and in some cases the unwillingness, of the legislature to redress their grievances drove them instead to the courthouse.

The concern for the protection of civil liberties, the influence of the legal realist movement, and the nationalization of civil liberties—all these combined in the mid-twentieth century to bring about a challenge to the reliance on representative institutions to protect rights. Individuals had previously turned to the courts in particular cases and in particular legal areas for the preservation of their rights, but they had never viewed the courts as the chief protectors of their rights. The demise of the *Lochner*-era U.S. Supreme Court in the late 1930s had the effect, however, of altering the popular image of courts as obstacles to the protection of rights, and several decisions even raised the possibility that courts might play a prominent role in safeguarding individual rights. Bills of rights also enjoyed a renaissance during this period. They were no longer viewed, as they had been in the early part of the twentieth century, as "stationary and, relatively speaking, retrogressive" documents[27] but rather as important guarantees of liberty.[28] In 1938 the American Bar Association established its Committee on the Bill of Rights; in 1939 *The Reader's Digest,* which had never before mentioned the Bill of Rights, published two articles on the subject, and three of the original thirteen states belatedly ratified the federal Bill of Rights; in 1940 a number of state legislatures for the first time established bill-of-rights weeks; and in 1941 the sesquicentennial of the U.S. Bill of Rights led to the founding of a number of organizations dedicated to the commemoration of bills of rights.[29]

Still to be determined, though, was whether these developments would lead to a mere revision or a wholesale replacement of republican principles. One prominent body of thought held that, although the republican regime was deficient in several important respects, its core principles were still generally valid. According to this view, legislative failures existed, but they were confined to particular occasions when the political process did not afford full, effective, or informed representation.

This view found its clearest expression in 1938 in footnote four of the U.S. Supreme Court's opinion in *United States v. Carolene Products.*[30] Authored by Justice Harlan Fiske Stone's law clerk, Louis Lusky, the footnote outlined a series of instances when courts should play a prominent role in superintending legislation.[31] Judicial scrutiny would be in order in the case of "legislation which restricts those political processes which can ordinarily be expected to bring about repeal of undesirable legislation."[32] Of particular concern were laws that imposed restrictions on voting rights, the dissemination of information, political organizations, or peaceable assembly. Heightened scrutiny would also be appropriate in cases in which "prejudice against discrete and insular minorities" had the effect of "curtail[ing] the operation of those political processes ordinarily to be relied upon to protect minorities."[33]

This challenge to the republican regime was a moderate one that presumed that the political process would ordinarily be expected to remedy violations of rights. Courts would defer to legislatures "unless there is some reason for assuming that the processes of the legislature are inadequate."[34] This approach "assumed the supremacy of the elected branches of government and of limited judicial review. . . . The Justices would not be substituting their values for that of the legislature."[35] In the belief that legislatures were generally capable of securing rights, this approach differed from republicanism only in its view that legislative failures were likely to be more frequent than had previously been supposed.

Another view soon took hold, however, that was more severe in its critique of republicanism and that challenged the principles that formed the core of the republican regime. According to this line of reasoning, legislatures did not merely fail on occasion to secure rights; rather, they failed frequently and in dramatic fashion. In this view, legislatures were inherently ill suited for the business of securing rights; this task should, instead, become the province of the judiciary, which could issue constitutional decisions based on interpretations of bills of rights.

This strong critique of republicanism was expressed most clearly by Justice

Robert Jackson in 1943 in the Supreme Court's decision in the compulsory flag-salute case, *West Virginia Board of Education v. Barnette.*[36] Several years earlier, in the case of *Minersville School District v. Gobitis,* the Court had let stand a similarly framed Pennsylvania flag-salute law, in part on the ground that, as Justice Felix Frankfurter had argued, this was "a field where courts possess no marked and certainly no controlling competence," and "to the legislature no less than to courts is committed the guardianship of deeply-cherished liberties." Frankfurter had written: "Where all the effective means of inducing political changes are left free from interference, education in the abandonment of foolish legislation is itself a training in liberty. To fight out the wise use of legislative authority in the forum of public opinion and before legislative assemblies rather than to transfer such a contest to the judicial arena, serves to vindicate the self-confidence of a free people."[37] After several justices publicly repudiated their votes in the *Gobitis* case, the Court revisited the issue and reconsidered the view that the political process was the proper forum for the vindication of rights. In his majority opinion in the *Barnette* case, Justice Jackson quoted the relevant section from the *Gobitis* opinion and responded: "The very purpose of a Bill of Rights was to withdraw certain subjects from the vicissitudes of political controversy, to place them beyond the reach of majorities and officials and to establish them as legal principles to be applied by the courts. One's right to life, liberty, and property, to free speech, a free press, freedom of worship and assembly, and other fundamental rights may not be submitted to vote; they depend on the outcome of no elections."[38]

This would become one of the most oft-quoted Supreme Court opinions over the next fifty years and would supply the intellectual grounding for the judicialist regime, but it was left to future judges and law professors to articulate the precise extent to which the new regime sought to supplant republicanism. Some individuals went so far as to claim that legislatures were generally inferior to courts, and that statutes and common-law decisions should be presumed to be inferior to constitutional decision making.[39] The argument was even advanced that rights were not only generally safer in the courts but were in fact the *exclusive* domain of judges, and that, "as a general matter, the scope of a constitutional norm is considered to be coterminous with the scope of its judicial enforcement."[40] Despite these various formulations, there was widespread agreement on several points. At the least, it was understood that "decisionmaking by electorally accountable institutions should no longer be presumed to be superior to that by the judiciary,"[41] and that "there are some phases of American life which should be beyond the reach of any majority, save by constitutional amendment."[42]

ADVENT OF THE JUDICIALIST REGIME

The judicialist regime was implemented in three stages. In the first period, comprising roughly the 1940s, the federal courts issued a series of constitutional decisions that sought to remove free-speech rights from the political process, and these decisions were enforced by state courts, albeit at times unwillingly. In the second period, which lasted from 1950 until 1970, the federal courts issued constitutional decisions that secured the protection of a broad range of rights, and these decisions were implemented by generally acquiescent state courts. In the third stage, which lasted roughly from 1970 to 1990, state judges adopted the federal approach and began on their own to issue constitutional decisions grounded in interpretations of state bills of rights.

State legislatures had been governed by judicial decisions prior to the 1940s, but these decisions were usually either grounded in common-law principles or designed to ensure that the process of making and applying the law was neither arbitrary nor capricious. Because decisions were cast in this way, legislatures had retained the ability to modify common-law rulings or to redraft deficient statutes. The advent of a new and quite different form of decision making was heralded by a series of free-speech rulings that were delivered by the U.S. Supreme Court in the early 1940s and that departed in significant ways from traditional judicial behavior.[43]

These decisions were noteworthy because they overturned statutes that had been the subject of extensive consideration in state legislatures. In the past, when the U.S. Supreme Court struck down a state law, it was usually overturning a deviant piece of legislation that had been enacted by a limited number of states. In this round of cases, however, the Court overturned statutes that had been enacted by a number of state legislatures and were the product of extensive deliberation. Thus in one 1940 case concerning the legality of picketing, Michigan Justice Henry Butzel noted that the Michigan Supreme Court had relied since 1898 on a common-law rule to prohibit such activity. Moreover, Butzel wrote, "the legislature has not seen fit to change by statute the common-law conclusion since this court rendered its first opinion prohibiting all picketing." He concluded: "Although the question has been presented to the legislature, no law permitting peaceful picketing has been enacted." In light of a pair of recent U.S. Supreme Court decisions, however: "The right of peaceful picketing has been upheld as an exercise of the right of free speech by the highest court in the land. Our legislative inactivity is no answer for denying a right secured by the fundamental law of the United States."[44]

Similarly, in the course of considering a challenge to a city ordinance by a member of the Jehovah's Witnesses, Massachusetts Justice Stanley Qua noted that the ordinance was a long-standing one that had been upheld by the Massachusetts Supreme Court in several recent decisions. But because these decisions had just been "disapproved by the Supreme Court of the United States" in a ruling that had "been reinforced by other recent decisions of that court," and because it was difficult to "distinguish this case in principle" from these recent holdings, the Massachusetts court had no choice but to overturn the ordinance.[45] In a similar case decided later that year, Justice Qua explained: "Notwithstanding the former decisions of this [Massachusetts] court . . . we feel that recent decisions of the Supreme Court of the United States require the conclusion that this ordinance is unconstitutional as an unwarranted interference with the freedom of speech and of the press."[46]

These Supreme Court decisions were also distinguished from previous rulings by the effect of their holdings. When Courts had previously invalidated statutes, they had usually done so on the ground that legislatures had regulated rights in an arbitrary fashion. As a result, legislatures had been able to rewrite the laws to remedy the defects. These new rulings had the effect of removing entire areas from legislative regulation altogether. Virginia Justice Henry Holt noted, for instance, that the Virginia Supreme Court was bound to apply a pair of recent U.S. Supreme Court decisions that proclaimed a right to distribute pamphlets without a license, but he took the occasion to comment on the distinctive nature of the rulings. The U.S. Supreme Court had directed that one statute be overruled, Holt pointed out, "not because arbitrary discretion was vested in the Chief of Police, but because it struck at the freedom of the press by subjecting it to license and censorship."[47] Holt argued, with respect to another decision, that "the court did not base its decision upon the fact that arbitrary power was vested in the Chief of Police but said that 'to require a censorship through license which makes impossible the free and unhampered distribution of pamphlets strikes at the very heart of constitutional guarantees.'"[48]

By the end of the 1940s, therefore, a number of areas of free-speech law had been effectively removed from legislative control. State judges who had previously been concerned primarily with interpreting statutes and common-law principles now turned their attention to following the constitutional decisions of the U.S. Supreme Court. Thus when the Virginia Supreme Court was presented with a challenge to an antipicketing law, Justice Archibald Buchanan noted, in what became an increasingly common refrain during this era: "That question is to be determined by reference to the decisions of the Supreme Court of the United States, which has the final say."[49]

Although these decisions demonstrate the growing influence of judicialist principles in the 1940s, the regime transformation was still incomplete by the end of the decade. In the first place, judicialist principles had not yet been embraced by most state judges. When these judges were forced to surrender control over an area of law that had previously been governed by statutes and common-law rules, they often did so reluctantly. Thus Michigan Justice Butzel acknowledged in one case concerning the rights of Jehovah's Witnesses: "It is unnecessary to discuss the merits of the claims of the respective parties for a Federal question has been raised and we are bound to follow the prevailing opinions of the United States Supreme Court as expressed in the later *Jehovah Witness Cases,* in an interpretation of the provisions of the United States Constitution, even though we may be in accord with the dissenting opinions filed in those cases."[50]

The judicialist regime also remained incomplete because legislatures still retained control over most rights. In the vast majority of areas of the law that were not yet occupied by the U.S. Supreme Court, the state courts jealously guarded their traditional reliance on statutory and common-law decision making. For instance, in 1949 the Michigan Supreme Court was called on to determine in one case whether an individual had a right to a grand-jury indictment. Justice John Dethmers noted that the state court had held in a prior case "that the Constitution of the State of Michigan left the subject free to legislative control, that the legislature rightly could and did provide for criminal prosecutions by information, and that such procedure constitutes due process of law."[51] Dethmers saw no reason to override the legislative judgment. He argued: "We are not persuaded that we are, as yet, constrained by the relevant holdings of a majority of the United States supreme court to hold that the Fifth Amendment applies to the States."[52]

From 1950 to 1970, the U.S. Supreme Court, under the leadership of Chief Justice Earl Warren, began to regulate an increasing number of rights on the basis of constitutional rules, and the judicialist regime spread its influence beyond the area of free-speech rights. Provisions of the federal Bill of Rights that had not previously been incorporated into the Fourteenth Amendment were now applied to the state legislatures, and the Supreme Court fashioned an ever more detailed and complex set of rules to govern these rights.[53] The state supreme courts during this period essentially read the *U.S. Reports* and transmitted them into law. The state legislatures read the state reporters and reacted accordingly.

Repeatedly during this period, the traditional reliance on statutory and common-law judging was superseded by constitutional decision making. In a typical case, Oregon Justice Arno Denecke noted: "The Oregon decisions excluding involuntary confessions have based the exclusion upon common-law rules of evidence, codified into an Oregon statute."[54] According to these rules, he concluded, the evidence in this particular instance would ordinarily be admitted. Recent U.S. Supreme Court decisions had declared, however, that "the right to remain silent at a police interrogation is a federal constitutional right."[55] Consequently, the confession was excluded from trial.

In similar fashion, after the U.S. Supreme Court ruled in 1961 that the Fourth Amendment required that states exclude evidence obtained through an improper search or seizure, Massachusetts Chief Justice Raymond Wilkins was forced to reject the state legislature's effort to adhere to the traditional statutory rule on which it had relied to secure this right. In light of *Mapp,* Wilkins argued: "We are unable to accept this argument. The *Mapp* case seems to foreclose any State fashioning the incidents of the exclusionary rule within the bounds of due process. We, accordingly, look to federal law."[56] Likewise, in a 1966 case concerning free-speech rights, Oregon Justice Ralph Holman wrote: "It is apparent from the cases heretofore discussed in this opinion that a revolution has occurred in the law relative to the state's power to limit federal First Amendment rights. Thirty years ago the statutes now under consideration would have been held to be constitutional, particularly as applied to the factual situation in the present case. This is no longer possible in view of the intervening decisions of the United

States Supreme Court."[57] As Massachusetts Justice Herbert Wilkins later explained in reference to obscenity questions, throughout the 1940s and 1950s the Massachusetts Supreme Court generally decided these cases by "reading challenged books and determining on their own—largely *apart from constitutional considerations*—whether they were 'obscene, indecent, or impure.'" But this changed in the 1960s when constitutional considerations were "forced on the court by decisions in Washington."[58]

Whereas state judges in the 1940s greeted these decisions with surprise and mild disagreement, in the 1950s and 1960s judges displayed scattered instances of hostility. Oregon Justice James Brand concluded one 1957 opinion by noting: "We are forced, not by our own reasoning, but by the necessary implications of the decision of the United States Supreme Court."[59] At the conclusion of one free-speech opinion, Massachusetts Chief Justice Qua noted: "Of course we acknowledge the binding force of these [U.S. Supreme Court] decisions while they remain the law. But we prefer not to be irrevocably committed to them as representing the true construction of our own Constitution."[60] If they were left to their "own choice," he suggested, the justices might prefer to permit the legislature to regulate the right in a different manner.[61] In one exclusionary-rule case in Michigan, Justice Dethmers referred to an opinion by Justice Holmes that predicted that, if present trends on the U.S. Supreme Court continued, he could see "hardly any limit but the sky to the invalidating of [the rights of states]." Dethmers added: "Little could he have thought, however, that in 40 short years the limit of the sky would have been so foreshortened that astronauts would be setting foot on the moon and judicial activists would perhaps go to even further reaches to put under foot precedents making constitutional interpretations."[62] Even in these cases, however, state judges ordinarily acquiesced in the implementation of judicialist principles. Dethmers concluded: "It avails little, then, to postpone decision in this Court. . . . It is not hard to read the handwriting on the wall, by whatever hand it may have been written."[63]

Judicialist principles were not fully implemented until the 1970s and 1980s, when state judges ceased to object to the U.S. Supreme Court's constitutionalization of rights, and in fact began on their own to deliver constitutional decisions based on state bills of rights. This phenomenon of independent state constitutional interpretation has been extensively documented and has received, with justification, a great deal of attention.[64] There has been a tendency, however, to focus on the consequences of this development only in the context of federal-state relations. Viewed from this perspective, of course, one could draw a sharp distinction between the period prior to 1970, in which federal courts were the primary agents of the expansion of rights, and the years after 1970, when state courts began to participate in this expansion. There is a danger, though, that an excessive focus on this shift from federal to state responsibility could mask what is, from another perspective, a continuous transfer of responsibility from legislative to judicial responsibility for rights protection.[65]

State courts in the nineteenth and early twentieth centuries had on various occasions interpreted their bills of rights to restrict legislative deliberations. But it was not until the 1970s, after state judges had witnessed the judicialist approach on display in U.S. Supreme Court rulings, that they began as a matter of course to interpret their bills of rights as a bar to legislative action.[66] Justice Hans Linde of Oregon and several other state judges were in the vanguard of this movement,[67] and U.S. Supreme Court Justice William Brennan provided encouragement in a 1977 article that urged state courts to "step into the breach" to secure rights left unprotected in the federal courts.[68]

The Oregon Supreme Court was perhaps the most active in constitutionalizing areas of law that had previously been governed by federal constitutional decisions or by state statutes and common-law rules. The Oregon Supreme Court actually began to rely on its own bill of rights in the 1960s, when it voided a movie censorship ordinance[69] as well as a local policy of providing free textbooks to parochial-school students.[70] By the 1970s and 1980s, with some prodding from Justice Linde, the Oregon Supreme Court had begun turning first and frequently to the Oregon Constitution in order to secure rights against legislative encroachment.[71]

The Massachusetts Supreme Court, which had in previous eras been one of the leaders in crafting a jurisprudence based on statutory and common-law interpretation, became in this period one of the most active in issuing constitutional rulings. Under the leadership of Chief Justice Edward Hennessey, the court suggested in several opinions in the 1970s that the Massachusetts Declaration of Rights could provide greater protection than the federal Bill of Rights for individual liberties. Beginning in 1975, the Massachusetts Supreme Court relied on these provisions to overturn the death penalty,[72] nude-dancing ordinances,[73] and the state policy against funding abortions,[74] as well as to enunciate a broad exclusionary rule and strict search-and-seizure requirements.[75]

The Michigan Supreme Court, although not quite as active as the courts in Oregon and Massachusetts, also began in the mid-1970s to turn to its own bill of rights, especially in the area of criminal procedure and search-and-seizure rights.[76] Justice James Brickley argued in 1983: "We have, on occasion, construed the Michigan Constitution in a manner which results in greater rights than those given by the federal constitution, and where there is compelling reason, we will undoubtedly do so again."[77]

The Virginia Supreme Court was the least inclined to interpret its bill of rights to constitutionalize areas of the law.[78] Although the Virginia Commission on Constitutional Revision argued in 1969 that there was "no good reason not to look first to Virginia's Constitution for the safeguards of the fundamental rights of Virginians,"[79] the court did so infrequently. During this period, the justices engaged in interpretation of the Virginia Bill of Rights on several occasions,[80] but they did not invalidate any statutes solely on these grounds.

These states varied, then, in the extent to which they embraced the judicialist approach. These differences should not obscure the fact, however, that all these state legislatures were governed in this era by judicialist principles, in the form of U.S. Supreme Court decisions that were enforced by state courts. Independent interpretation of state bills of rights on the part of several state courts meant only that some state legislatures were restrained by their state supreme courts in additional areas. For all practical purposes, legislatures had yielded control over rights protection by the 1970s. Courts became the chief institution, and constitutional decisions became the primary vehicle, for keeping the people's liberties. As John Kincaid argued: "The U.S. Supreme Court, therefore, has effected more than a legal change in rights protection and more than a change in the locus of rights protection. It has helped to effect a cultural change in the way Americans understand rights, and it is this new understanding that is finding its way into state court interpretations of state constitutional rights. In this respect, activist state courts are not filling a vacuum; they are consolidating a revolution."[81]

PRINCIPLES OF THE JUDICIALIST REGIME

The emergence of the judicialist regime can be attributed, in part, to a set of specific circumstances, in particular, the growing concern for the protection of civil liberties in the aftermath of the First World War. It can also be understood as the product of the efforts of individuals such as Justices Brennan and Linde, who introduced a new form of judicial behavior in order to better secure these liberties. The regime change was not completed, however, until members of the legal community sought to sustain the judicialist project by articulating a set of principles that could legitimate these actions. Through a series of dialogues within the legal community, the traditional understandings of representation, deliberation, and compliance were challenged and eventually supplanted by understandings that were more consistent with the behavior in which judges were engaging during this period.

Representation

It became quite common in the judicialist regime for state judges to view the judiciary as the only institution that was capable of representing the considered judgment of the public. According to Oregon Justice Walter Tooze, "The duty of seeing that [rights] are protected and preserved inviolate falls squarely upon the shoulders of the judiciary."[82] Likewise, Massachusetts Chief Justice Joseph Tauro argued in one death-penalty case that "public opinion, while relevant, is not conclusive in assessing whether the death penalty is consonant with contemporary standards of decency." In his view, only the courts were qualified to identify these standards.[83] As Chief Justice Hennessey of Massachusetts argued: "Oppressed, disfavored or unpopular minorities would be the victims of any loss of judicial independence. The minorities rely on the independence of the courts to secure their constitutional rights against incursions of the majority, operating through the political branches of government. Dependent or subservient courts render nugatory the fundamental constitutional protections which are the heart of our liberties."[84]

Although this view of representation was greeted with near universal acceptance in the judicialist regime,[85] it represented a significant departure from the republican view, which presumed that legislatures most accurately reflected popular opinion, as well as from the populist view, which considered initiatives and referendums to be the best gauge of popular opinion. A variety of factors contributed to this changing conception of representation, but perhaps the most important were a reinterpretation of the principles of the founding era, a reassessment of the representative character of legislatures, and a newfound appreciation for the ability of judges to divine the popular will. Although the new understanding prevailed, it did not go unchallenged by the defenders of republican principles, and the subsequent debates highlighted the new and the old views of representation.

The eighteenth- and nineteenth-century founding of state and national institutions was subject to a variety of reinterpretations throughout the years. Republicanism emphasized the primacy of indirect representation in the founding design. It understood the early state conventions to have designated representative institutions as best suited to obtain the *reasonable expression of public opinion* on most matters. Populism emphasized the role of popular ratification and direct representation in the constitutional structure. It focused on the importance of *public opinion* in governing institutions and believed that its direct expression was inherently reasonable. Judicialism, by contrast, attached great significance to the concern of the founding generation to create courts and bills of rights that would produce decisions that were *reasonable,* even if they were reached independently of public opinion. In particular, as Ralph Lerner argued, the founders were thought to have believed "that the courts would stand in a closer relation to the deliberate will of the people as expressed in the Constitution than would the representatives of the people. The Courts would be peculiarly fit to discover in the Constitution what the will of the people was."[86]

When the judicialists turned to the historical record, they were further fortified in their belief that legislatures were incapable of providing effective representation. To rely on legislatures to secure rights, according to Ronald Dworkin, "assumes, for one thing, that state legislatures are in fact responsible to the people in the way that democratic theory assumes. But in all the states, though in different degrees and for different reasons, that is not the case. In some states it is very far from the case."[87] Adherents to the judicialist regime pointed to a "widespread feeling among the electorate that for various reasons the legislature had ceased to be truly representative of the wishes of all the people and had become frequently a tool for certain favored classes or interests."[88] Also "contributing to this feeling of nonrepresentation was the patent under or over representation of many localities in the state or federal legislature arising from the failure properly and periodically to reapportion the seats in that body."[89] The judicialists claimed, in particular, that legislatures frequently failed to represent the interests of various minority groups. As Jesse Choper argued: "[t]he experience of history strongly suggests that vesting the majority with the ultimate power of judgment, although far from being calamitous, would not sufficiently protect minority rights."[90]

One possible response to these particular deficiencies might have been to reform the legislative process to make it more representative—to devise procedural rules to thwart special interests, to provide more equitable apportionment procedures, and to fashion institutional arrangements to address the underrepresentation of minorities. But the judicialists were uninterested in pursuing this approach; they argued that these problems were indicative of a more general and fundamental failure on the part of legislatures. In their view, institutional reforms were unlikely to address the full extent of the "malfunctioning in the political process," which included "the routine political ineffectiveness and quiescence—rooted in social and economic inequality—of masses of ordinary citizens."[91] In addition, the historical record clearly "demonstrate[d] the shortcomings of the political process in affording adequate security for fundamental personal liberties."[92] The prevailing view, as summarized by Erwin Chemerinsky, was that "[w]ithout judicial enforcement, the Constitution is little more than the parchment that sits under glass in the National Archives."[93]

Consequently, whereas the republican regime relied on institutional arrangements such as separation of powers and bicameralism to secure the "sober second thought" of the public, the judicialists turned to the courts. According to Choper:

> Since, almost by definition, the processes of democracy bode ill for the security of personal rights and, as experience shows, such liberties are not infrequently endangered by popular majorities, the task of custodianship has been and should be assigned to a governing body that is insulated from political responsibility and unbeholden to self-absorbed and excited majoritarianism. The Court's aloofness from the political system and the Justices' lack of dependence for maintenance in office on the popularity of a particular ruling promise an objectivity that elected representatives are not—and should not be—as capable of achieving.[94]

The defenders of the old regime, who mounted a series of rearguard assaults on this new view of representation, did not deny that the judicialists had identified *an* important element of the founding. They charged, however, that the judicialists focused on the fear of tyrannical majorities to the exclusion of other concerns that informed the design of state and national institutions. They argued that a more balanced appraisal would acknowledge that the founders had relied primarily on political institutions to represent the public will.[95] Nor did the defenders of republican principles deny that there were a number of instances in which the political process had failed to secure rights. They contended, however, that these examples gave no warrant for concluding that majorities were generally unrepresentative. As Henry Steele Commager wrote in 1943: "Nor is there any persuasive evidence from our own long and complex historical experience that majorities are given to contempt for constitutional limitations or for minority rights. Our majorities, state and federal alike, have been, to a remarkable extent, stable, law-abiding, and conservative."[96] Finally, the critics of the new regime did not deny that judges might occasionally represent the popular will more effectively than could the people's elected representatives, but they argued that the judicialists ignored the real and oft-demonstrated possibility that such efforts could also lead to judicial decisions that lacked popular support and therefore were not representative in any real sense.[97]

These arguments were ultimately unsuccessful, however, in stemming the judicialist advance. Due in large part to the legacy of the U.S. Supreme Court's decision in *Brown v. Board of Education*, which Robert Nagel argues was "the fulcrum on which the world of judicial review was made to move decisively," the view became widespread that courts were generally more representative than legislatures.[98] The view of representation that prevailed in the judicialist regime thus stood in stark contrast to that of previous eras. Whereas republicanism maintained that deficiencies in legislative representation were minimal and could be addressed through existing institutions, judicialism held that these failures were frequent and fundamental and necessitated a new form of representation. The judicialist view stood in even more stark opposition to the populist understanding. Judicialism held that legislatures were unrepresentative, not because they were too distant from their constituents, as the populists claimed, but because they were too responsive to the electorate and therefore incapable of representing the public effectively.

Deliberation

The judicialist conception of deliberation was perhaps most clearly expressed by Massachusetts Chief Justice Joseph Tauro, who argued in one case that "judges cannot look to public opinion polls or election results for constitutional meaning."

> Passing public passions and emotions (understandable as they may be at times such as these) have little to do with the meaning of the Constitution, as it is written. Referendums, although they serve some purpose, do not pretend to construe the Constitution. They express only ephemeral sentiments, sentiments which are highly variable over time and which may reflect public attitudes shaped by collateral problems and events of the day. Public sentiment

becomes relevant to constitutional adjudication *only* if it results in a constitutional amendment. . . . Only through an amendment can mass passions affect constitutional meaning and, absent an amendment, the Constitution stands as an unbreachable bulwark for the individual against those mass passions and the political power of the majority.[99]

According to this view, deliberation would take place primarily among justices, who were trained in the technical arcana of the law; it would take place in the judicial chambers, which permitted discussions of rights unencumbered by political concerns and compromises; and through written opinions, which guaranteed that principled decision making would occur. Deliberation would also take place among the justices and the citizens, who were invited to respond to judicial decisions, but only through the constitutional amendment process.

This view of deliberation is unexceptional in the contemporary age, but it is a striking departure from the understanding that characterized previous regimes. The republican regime presumed that deliberation over rights was an intimately political activity that properly took place within and among political institutions; in the populist regime, deliberation was believed to occur among the general public. The transformation from these older understandings of deliberation to the judicialist view can be attributed to the advent of a new conception of rights, as well as to a reassessment of the deliberative capacities of citizens, legislators, and judges.

The judicialist view of deliberation rested, at bottom, on a belief that rights should be rigidly separated from politics. Political considerations should not enter into the derivation of, the deliberation over, or the means of securing rights. As C. Herman Pritchett characterized the new view of law and politics: "Law is a prestigious symbol, whereas politics tends to be a dirty word. Law is stability; politics is chaos. Law is impersonal; politics is personal. Law is given; politics is free choice. Law is reason; politics is prejudice and self-interest. Law is justice; politics is who gets there first with the most."[100]

In one respect, this view of rights was not completely novel. After all, the republican regime did not deny that individuals possessed rights anterior to society. But whereas republicanism held that the political process was capable of determining the precise extent to which and the particular manner in which these rights would be secured, judicialism held that the protection of rights could not depend in any way on political considerations. Dworkin argued, "A claim of right presupposes a moral argument and can be established in no other way."[101] In this view, it was inconceivable that legislators or citizens could deliberate over rights; this was a task that could be performed only by judges. According to Dworkin, "Judicial review insures that the most fundamental issues of political morality will finally be set out and debated as issues of principle and not simply issues of political power, a transformation that cannot succeed, in any case not fully, within the legislature itself."[102]

At the same time that legal philosophers were introducing a new conception of rights, law professors were reconsidering the capacity of legislators and judges to engage in deliberation. They contended that the judicial selection process was designed, in a way that the legislative selection process was not, to ensure that successful candidates were knowledgeable about legal matters. According to Charles Black, "the members of Congress are not selected by a process which has any tendency whatever to ensure possession of the kinds of skill and wisdom needed for constitutional decision." Legislators "have no guarantee of long tenure, and so have no incentive, and often no opportunity, to acquire the kind of experience wanted by the skilled constitutional judge."[103]

Moreover, the nature of the judicial and legislative offices ensured that judges would have more opportunities to deliberate over rights. The judicialists believed that "officials outside the judiciary rarely reflect on the meaning of the Constitution," because "political pressures and expediencies often make it unlikely that Congress, the President, or state legislatures or executives will deal carefully with constitutional issues."[104]

Finally, the character of the decision-making process was presumed to afford more deliberative opportunities for judges than for legislators. The legislative process was thought to be oriented primarily toward political concerns, whereas the adjudicative process was structured in such a way as to insulate judges from these issues.[105] The view was that legislators "are not ideologically committed or institutionally suited to search for the meaning of constitutional values, but instead see their primary function in terms of registering the actual, occurrent preferences of the people."[106] Even if the legislative chambers had at one time provided such a forum, "the tradition has disintegrated."[107] In contrast, the court's structure made it "peculiarly well suited" to "sorting out the enduring values of a society."[108] Black summed up this view best: "The suggestion that, in regard to acquiring the qualities and skills needed for weighing constitutional policy, the members of the legislative branch are more advantageously placed than are the judiciary, must, it seems to me, function only as a facade for something else—for the abandonment of constitutionalism as we know it, of the concept of the Constitution as law binding on government."[109]

The defenders of the old regime responded that these arguments overstated the legal training and technical knowledge that were actually required to partake in deliberation about rights. It was apparent to Commager, for instance, that most of the questions that have evoked judicial nullification of majority will have turned on considerations of policy rather than of law, and that on these questions the legal learning of the legislative and executive departments has been entirely adequate."[110] The supporters of the republican regime maintained that legislators had at one time been quite concerned with ensuring that their actions accorded with constitutional guarantees,[111] and to the extent that they no longer exercised such care, this had occurred only because the view had taken hold that these concerns were the monopoly of the courts.

In addition, the defenders of the republican view charged that the judicialist conception of rights rested on a false dichotomy between legal and political considerations. On the one hand, they were confident that legislators did in fact possess "adequate resources to analyze these constitutional issues,"[112] and on the other hand, they doubted that judges were completely free of political considerations or could in fact be "trusted to act independently, objectively, and dispassionately on questions of constitutionality."[113] In any case, the critics of the judicialist project argued that the entire enterprise of maintaining a rigid separation between rights and politics was misguided. Rights were often secured as the result of political pressure and compromise, they argued, but this hardly rendered them unstable or illegitimate. The legislative process was a superior forum for deliberation precisely *because* it could better take account of political considerations than could the judicial process. As Donald Horowitz argued, the courtroom "tends to exclude interested participants" and produce "a reductionist solution"; the "generalist" character of judges "unfits them for processing specialized information"; and adjudication "inhibits the presentation of an array of alternatives and the explicit matching of benefits to costs."[114]

These arguments were advanced to no avail, however, against a judicialist view of deliberation that represented a significant departure from the understanding that governed previous regimes. Republicanism presumed that legislative assemblies were a suitable forum for deliberating over rights. In their opposition to this view, the populists and judicialists were united. Each believed that rights and politics should be separated and that legislators were therefore incapable of deliberating over rights. But whereas populism sought to eliminate the influence of special interests and political compromises by transferring deliberation to the entire electorate, judicialism preferred that deliberation take place in the isolation of the judicial chambers.

Compliance

Judge Hans Linde provided the best expression of the judicialist view of compliance when he argued that scholars and judges had become overly concerned with "public acceptance of the Court's decision."[115] In fact: "Preoccupation with the odds of effective compliance may undervalue the social importance of an announced principle for its own sake, or the social cost of failure to announce it."[116] According to Linde, "what counts is the principle itself, quite apart from its realization in some concrete situation."[117] Judges were not only well positioned to express these principles, but, because they possessed a "'mystic function' . . . that is inescapable in opinions explicating the Bill of Rights," they were also uniquely qualified to persuade people to accept these principles and therefore to bring about compliance with them.[118]

This view, although it enjoyed widespread acceptance in the judicialist regime,[119] differed significantly from the republican view, which held that people would comply with legal guarantees only when they had an opportunity to vote for the *legislators* who enacted them. The judicialist understanding was even further removed from the populist view, which held that compliance could be achieved only when citizens voted directly on the *laws* under which they would be governed. This transformation was brought about primarily by the advent of an understanding of compliance that was not grounded in citizen participation, coupled with a reassessment of the capacities of legislatures and courts to promote this type of compliance.

In place of the previous belief that compliance was generated by direct or indirect participation in drafting laws, judicialists argued that compliance depended on the *absence* of popular participation. This was, in one sense, a natural consequence of the view that rights should be rigidly separated from the political process. Once the view took hold that rights were derived solely from moral principles rather than from political deliberations, it necessarily followed that people were most likely to comply with a law that was grounded in principle, regardless of whether they had participated in its framing, and in fact precisely because they had taken no part. Thus, according to Erwin Chemerinsky, "the judiciary's method increases the legitimacy of results in particular cases and therefore increases the likelihood that the Constitution will be complied with. The written opinion demonstrates that the result is not arbitrary or just the result of political compromise." Moreover, the political insulation of the judiciary "helps people to accept that their loss was based on a consideration of principle, not on the fact that they were politically too powerless. If the legislature interpreted the Constitution and ruled against them, it would be much easier to attribute their loss to insufficient clout or political influence."[120]

The introduction of this new understanding of compliance dovetailed with another development: the view that judges were not only more likely than legislators to proclaim "principled" decisions but also better positioned to persuade people to comply with rulings to which they might initially be opposed. This view assumed that judges and citizens were engaged in a colloquy, in which the "constitutional structure gives the Supreme Court both an incentive and an opportunity to supply educative descriptions of American identity."[121] Whereas judges in the early years of the Republic educated through their grand-jury charges, modern judges taught through their written opinions.[122] In the oft-quoted words of Eugene Rostow: "The discussion of problems and the declaration of broad principles by the Courts is a vital element in the community experience through which American policy is made. The Supreme Court is, among other things, an educational body, and the Justices are inevitably teachers in a vital national seminar."[123] According to the judicialists, this education would take place even if the citizens did not actively participate in the seminar. As Christopher Eisgruber argued: "The Supreme Court may indeed conduct a 'vital national seminar' although attendance is spotty and few students do the reading. For example, even if only aspiring lawyers were to read the Court's opinions, the Court's teaching may significantly influence public opinion. Lawyers exercise considerable power in American society. If the Court were able to inculcate in tomorrow's most powerful lawyers a disposition to honor constitutional principles, that lesson could provide both the Court and the Constitution with significant protection in a crisis."[124]

Not surprisingly, supporters of the republican regime challenged this understanding of compliance and defended the traditional view that was rooted in popular consent. The movement away from the traditional view of compliance was worrisome on a moral level, republicans contended, in that participation and consent were integral to sustaining the legitimacy of the lawmaking process. They also objected on practical grounds, in particular on the ground that legal guarantees could be enforced only if they met with popular approval. Alexander Bickel, who was himself sympathetic to the notion of judicial-political colloquies, cautioned that there were limits to the courts' educative power. Judicial decisions must rest in the end, he argued, on presuppositions "to which widespread acceptance may fairly be attributed." What is meant "is that the Court should declare as law only such principles as will—in time, but in a rather immediate foreseeable future—gain general assent."[125] Moreover, Learned Hand, among others, was skeptical of the ability of judges to carry out such a seminar and, in particular, to don a professorial as well as a judicial robe. "[F]or a judge to serve as communal mentor appears to me a very dubious addition to his duties and one apt to interfere with their proper discharge."[126]

The judicialist view eventually prevailed over each of these objections. Whereas securing compliance with legal guarantees was a moderate concern for the supporters of the republican regime, and a predominant concern for the populist regime, it was of only slight concern to the judicialists, for whom the enunciation of principles frequently took precedence over the ensuring of compliance.[127] Moreover, to the extent that the judicialists were interested in obtaining compliance with these principles, they articulated a different basis for this compliance than had existed in prior regimes. Citizens would comply with legal guarantees, they argued, not because they participated in the decision-making process but because the decisions conformed with notions of justice, and in the event that the people did not immediately appreciate the justice of these decisions, judges were uniquely positioned to persuade them to adopt this position.

CONCLUSION

These principles of the judicialist regime were first enunciated by U.S. Supreme Court justices in a series of decisions in the 1940s, then debated and defended in the legal academy in the 1950s and 1960s, and eventually embraced by state courts in the 1970s and 1980s. At the center of the judicialist project was an effort to transform the public understanding of the institution that could best represent the public will, deliberate in the general interest, and secure popular compliance.

The legislature, which had been viewed in the republican regime as the proper forum for representation, deliberation, and compliance, and which had been temporarily supplanted in the populist regime by the popular initiative, was now superseded by the courts, which were seen as uniquely capable of divining the popular will with regard to rights, deliberating about their contents, and guaranteeing their security.

8
Judicialist Institutions
and the Protection of Rights

The primary intent of the architects of the judicialist regime was to alter the role and behavior of federal and state judges. Indeed, between 1940 and 1990, judges assumed primary responsibility for deliberating about rights, and constitutional decisions came to be viewed as the principal means of securing their protection. Once loosed, the judicialist spirit was not easily cabined and also began to influence the way in which other individuals conceived of their roles. Although legislators continued to enact statutes to secure some rights, they began to defer the resolution of an increasing number of issues to the courts, and when they did engage in independent interpretation of rights, they were frequently rebuffed. Similarly, although citizens still sought to regulate some rights through the initiative process, these efforts met with an increasingly hostile reception from judges and leaders of intellectual opinion.

THE ROLE AND BEHAVIOR OF JUDGES

Judges had played a prominent role in securing individual rights in the years prior to the judicialist regime, but this had taken the form primarily of issuing statutory and common-law decisions. Some judges continued during this period to decide cases in this manner, in an effort to preserve opportunities for legislative regulation of rights. Moreover, some members of the legal community continued to support and encourage this kind of decision making.[1]

Thus judges occasionally chose to decide cases on statutory rather than constitutional grounds. When in 1945 the Virginia Supreme Court considered a defendant's claim that his right to a speedy trial had been abridged, the court concluded that the commonwealth had indeed failed to comply with the relevant statute, and it ordered the defendant released. The virtue of deciding the case on statutory rather than constitutional grounds, according to Justice Edward Hudgins, was that this would permit the legislature to alter the rule if it proved unworkable. Hudgins argued, "If the statute, as written, permits guilty parties to escape justice, this fact should be brought to the attention of the General Assembly which alone has the authority to legislate."[2] In similar fashion, when the Virginia Supreme Court addressed the question in 1988 of "whether the public and, derivatively, the news media, have a constitutional, common-law, or statutory right of access to the records in a civil case," Justice Richard Poff concluded, "We find it unnecessary to conduct a constitutional analysis."[3] Relying instead on an 1820 statute that declared that "[t]he records and papers of every court shall be open to inspection by any person," Poff determined that individuals were in fact entitled to examine trial records in civil cases.

A number of judges continued, in similar fashion, to eschew constitutional decision making and to rely on common-law interpretation to secure rights. As Oregon Justice Robert Jones noted, in a 1983 case that required the court to interpret the meaning of the constitutional guarantee of a right to counsel, the practice of refraining from constitutional decision making carried certain advantages. He argued: "[T]his court is called upon from time to time to specify the procedure by which a guarantee is to be effectuated. Such specifications are not the same as interpretations of the guarantee itself, that is to say, they may not always and in all settings be the only means toward its effectuation but may be adopted or replaced from time to time by decisions of this court or by legislation in the light of experience or changing circumstances."[4] Similarly, in 1989, when the Oregon Supreme Court recognized individuals' right to solicit signatures in private shopping malls, the decision was grounded in an interpretation of the common law. Justice Jones noted that, although several other state courts had decided the issue on constitutional grounds: "We will not join in that debate, however, without first examining the parties' rights on a sub-constitutional level. Our practice is to refrain from constitutional holdings unless ordinary legal principles cannot resolve the dispute."[5] He argued: "Avoiding needless constitutional rulings is not a technical nicety of judicial etiquette. If there is no duty to decide the constitutionality of a law, there is a duty not to decide it. This rule prevents premature foreclosure of opportunities for legislators who are better equipped to consider and choose among different policies."[6]

In addition, judges occasionally chose to rely on their inherent rule-making power in lieu of constitutional interpretation. Massachusetts Justice Paul Reardon argued in a 1966 case that extended the right to counsel to encompass probation revocation hearings: "We need not rest our conclusions on this matter upon constitutional grounds. . . . We base our decision upon the application of Rule 10 of the General Rules."[7] The virtue of securing rights on the basis of judicial rules, according to these justices, was that this best preserved opportunities for either courts or legislatures to respond to various and changing circumstances. As the Oregon Supreme Court concluded in a 1960 decision, "We believe that all courts of this state have inherent power to appoint counsel for an indigent person accused of a crime when it is established that a need for counsel exists and provided that the situation is not met by one of the statutes of which we have taken notice."[8]

These decisions had once been considered the norm and constitutional interpretation the exception, but in the middle of the twentieth century, judges reversed course and began to rely primarily on constitutional decision making to secure rights. Statutory and common-law decisions were appropriate insofar as legislatures could be entrusted to secure rights, but once the view took hold that representative institutions were generally incapable of deliberating responsibly, it became necessary to remove rights from legislative control. Laurence Tribe therefore argued, in one of the most influential constitutional casebooks of the era, that although the common law contained a number of principles that could be relied on to secure rights, these principles were of "questionable origin as sources of a constitutional guarantee. More importantly, they are widely understood to be subject to legislative modification or even extinction."[9] As a leading survey of state constitutional law noted, "Although common law rulings are always subject to legislative reversal, constitutional decisions give the court the final word."[10]

Constitutional rulings were also preferred because they prevented *judges* from exercising their discretion in an errant manner. Implicit in the traditional reliance on statutory and common-law interpretation was the view that judges could usually be counted on to apply these principles in a responsible manner. But the judicialists, although they were generally inclined to trust judges rather than legislators to secure rights, did not necessarily believe that all judges would secure an adequate degree of protection for rights. In their view, constitutional decisions were significantly more effective than statutory or common-law decisions in binding judges to reach appropriate conclusions. Thus, after conducting a study of the nineteenth-century record of state courts in protecting freedom of speech, one legal commentator took note of the fact that "[c]ontroversies that clearly presented issues of freedom of speech and press were sometimes decided without a single reference to pertinent constitutional provisions." In his view, this represented a "lost opportunity." "Whether this was due to intentional avoidance of constitutional questions or to mere inadvertence, the practice hardly enhanced the value of state safeguards."[11] The fear was that these statutory or common-law decisions could not be counted on to provide the requisite security for rights. As one of the leading surveys of state constitutional law concluded: "That a police power decision reaches the same result that a constitutional decision would have reached is not enough. It is inadequate, first, because it leaves nothing behind to bind future courts to pursue a constitutional analysis. A police power decision that reaches a legitimate result today could just as easily result in a police power decision that reaches an illegitimate result tomorrow."[12]

Late-twentieth-century judges were not the first to rely on constitutional decision making. But judges in previous eras had reserved these decisions primarily for cases in which representative institutions were deemed incompetent, such as when legislators were gripped by a momentary passion or were prevented by their own self-interest from deliberating responsibly. The distinctive aspect of the judicialist era was that judges now began to issue constitutional decisions on a routine basis. Consequently, although defenses of the traditional style of statutory and common-law decision making occasionally appeared in majority opinions in this period, they were increasingly consigned to passages in dissenting opinions.

Accordingly, judges began to rely on constitutional decision making to effectuate general guarantees of rights. The Massachusetts Supreme Court was one of a number of courts during this period to rely on the search-and-seizure clause of the Bill of Rights to prevent improperly seized evidence from being admitted in trials. In one 1985 case that extended the exclusionary rule to encompass certain automobile searches, it was left to the dissenting opinion to take note of the novelty of the decision: "[T]he court creates an exclusionary rule under art. 14 for the first time in the history of the Commonwealth. The court finds in art. 14 a rule that has remained undiscovered since 1780 and that has been specifically rejected when asserted."[13] In a similar case decided by the Virginia Supreme Court in 1980, the majority noted that the guarantee against improper searches and seizures had been provided for years by a statute that "made it a misdemeanor for any law enforcement officer to search without a warrant," and that when the issue had arisen in Virginia in previous years, "the exclusionary rule was rejected." The court even mentioned "with interest the 'disenchantment' of some members of the [United States] Supreme Court with this rule," but it concluded, nevertheless, that "[o]ur own philosophical misgivings are irrelevant, and we will of course continue to apply the rule as construed from time to time by the Supreme Court."[14] Although these disagreements were expressed to no avail in these cases, they served to highlight the distinctive nature of the modern approach to securing rights, one that rests on constitutional rather than statutory or common-law interpretation.

Judges also relied on constitutional decision making to extend existing legal guarantees. In 1982, for instance, the Oregon Supreme Court joined a number of other courts in recognizing a right to equal treatment without regard to sex. Both the majority and the dissenting justices acknowledged the novelty of the ruling, which overturned an outdated law that provided public benefits to certain women but not to similarly situated men. Writing for the majority, Justice Betty Roberts noted that "[w]e are free in Oregon to begin our analysis of gender based laws on a clean slate," and she proceeded to overturn the statute and order benefits to be extended to both men and women.[15] In his dissenting opinion, however, Justice Edwin Peterson defended the traditional style of judging. He was particularly troubled by the fact that by rendering a constitutional decision the court thereby prohibited the legislature from responding to changing circumstances. He argued:

"The effect of this court's opinion is to enact a new law. . . . The point is not only that courts are forbidden to legislate, we lack the resources to make legislative decisions. Though we may possess judicial ingenuity, we have no knowledge of the fiscal implications of our opinion, and little knowledge of its other implications. . . . The legislature convenes in two months, perhaps earlier. It has the power to avoid almost every adverse effect of invalidation, even those occurring before it convenes. That is its constitutionally-appointed job, and we should let them do it."[16] Had Peterson been sitting on the bench only a half century earlier, his view of the judicial role would have formed the basis of a majority opinion from which there would likely have been no dissent. In the judicialist regime, this view placed him in a distinct minority.

A final distinctive aspect of judicial behavior during this period concerned the way in which constitutional decision making was received by leaders of intellectual opinion. When judges in previous eras had relied on bills of rights to overturn legislative judgments, they had been roundly criticized for removing matters from legislative control. By the middle of the twentieth century, this behavior was supported and even encouraged by legal scholars. As Oregon Justice Hans Linde noted, with respect to the relationship between the legal academy and the U.S. Supreme Court: "Today's theorists are at least as doubtful about the Supreme Court's premises. The difference is that, unlike their fathers in the trade, they do not aim to test and displace the Court's conclusions but to save them."[17]

THE ROLE AND BEHAVIOR OF LEGISLATORS

Legislative behavior was influenced by the judicialist regime in several ways. In the first place, so many areas of the law were now occupied by judicial decisions that when legislatures did secure rights, this frequently took the form of responding to judicial rulings rather than engaging in independent deliberation. Moreover, when legislatures sought to protect rights in areas that were unoccupied by courts, the resulting statutes were viewed as providing less security for rights than judicial decisions. Finally, in the few cases in which legislators sought to secure rights in a different manner from courts, these efforts were frequently overturned by judges who were unwilling to countenance infringements on their domain.

To be sure, legislatures did not suddenly and completely cease to secure rights in the middle of the twentieth century. They continued to enact statutes to secure some rights, and this behavior was occasionally supported by leaders of legal and intellectual opinion.[18] Nevertheless, the deliberation in which legislators partook in the judicialist era differed in kind from the deliberation that characterized the nineteenth and early twentieth centuries. When legislators deliberated over rights in previous years, they engaged in independent discussion of the meaning of constitutional guarantees, often unencumbered by judicial rulings. As a growing number of rights came to be governed by constitutional rulings, however, legislative discussions began to be conducted in the shadow of judicial decisions. As a result, legislators came to be concerned less with debating the most reasonable means of interpreting a constitutional guarantee than with satisfying or responding to a judicial interpretation of a constitutional guarantee.

Accordingly, legislatures deferred increasingly to the courts for the protection of rights and were generally content to enact appropriate laws in response to court decisions. By the late 1960s, William Keefe could identify a number of reasons "why legislatures are not suited to offer continuing leadership in state politics," not the least of which was the increased activity of the judiciary. He argued, "It can fairly be said that the Supreme Court in the early 1960s contributed at least as much as governors, political interest groups, or political parties to shaping the agendas of state legislatures."[19]

On any number of issues during this period, state legislators essentially read the *U.S.* and *State Reports* and transmitted them into law. Thus Oregon was one of a number of states that was preoccupied during this period with following judicial interpretations of the free-speech clause of the Bill of Rights. As Justice Ralph Holman of the Oregon Supreme Court noted in a 1968 opinion, "It is obvious that the legislature has experienced some difficulty in keeping up with the rapidly changing United States constitutional concept of what constitutes obscenity."[20] Similarly, the Virginia General Assembly, which had enacted statutes throughout the twentieth century to provide counsel for indigent defendants, resolved in 1972 that "there is now pending in the Supreme Court of the United States a case in which a person charged with a misdemeanor seeks to require the appointment of counsel in such cases" and that "prompt action will be required should the Supreme Court of the United States rule that counsel is required in such cases." The legislature directed a commission to determine "the most appropriate method of providing such counsel,"[21] and it revised its right-to-counsel statute in the following session.[22]

Even when the judiciary had not yet addressed an issue, legislators were still less likely to enact statutory guarantees than they had been in previous eras. This was in part an inevitable by-product of the heightened role of the judiciary, which was now considered to be the proper institution for addressing individual grievances. At a time when legislatures were considered to possess fewer attributes than courts, it is not surprising that elected representatives began to defer more frequently to judicial decisions for the protection of rights.

Legislative deference was also a natural consequence of the diminished respect for statutes as instruments of rights protection. As Tribe argued, " 'legislative rights' are creatures of the majority, theirs to give, and theirs to take away. The ultimate authority of such rights must yield more readily to other asserted interests of government than would rights ascribed to the Constitution itself."[23] It is not surprising, therefore, at a time when constitutional decision making was increasingly viewed as the preferred manner of securing rights, that legislatures were less inclined to assume responsibility for securing rights.

Finally, in the few cases in which legislators did engage in independent interpretation of constitutional guarantees, they were roundly rebuffed by the courts. Two examples from Massachusetts are particularly pertinent, one dealing with the ban on cruel and unusual punishment and the other concerning the guarantee of religious freedom.

The question of whether the imposition of the death penalty violated the constitutional ban on cruel and unusual punishment provoked a series of particularly sharp disagreements between the Massachusetts General Court and Supreme Judicial Court throughout the 1970s. Prior to 1975, the Massachusetts Declaration of Rights had never been interpreted to forbid capital punishment, but in a series of decisions handed down between 1975 and 1977, the Massachusetts Supreme Court proceeded to invalidate the state's death-penalty statute. Chief Justice Joseph Tauro noted in 1975: "We believe that the right to life is fundamental and, further, that this proposition is not open to serious debate. Aside from its prominent place in the due process clause itself, the right to life is the basis of all other rights and in the absence of life other rights do not exist."[24] The court held that the death penalty did not comport with the contemporary meaning of "cruel and unusual punishment," and, consequently, it was deemed unconstitutional.[25]

The Massachusetts General Court responded in 1979 by enacting a revised death-penalty law and defending its authority to maintain an interpretation of the Bill of Rights that differed from that of the state supreme court. The legislature argued that capital punishment was an area in which the representatives possessed more competence than the justices: "It is hereby declared that the value of capital punishment as a deterrent for crime is a complex factual issue the resolution of which properly rests with the general court, which has evaluated the results of statistical studies in terms of the local conditions with a flexibility of approach not available to the courts, and that the general court has so found and defined those crimes and those criminals for which capital punishment is most probably an effective deterrent." Not only did the legislature believe that it was more competent to decide this question, but it also thought that it was the more legitimate decision maker. "It is hereby further declared that the ability of the people of the commonwealth to express their preference through their duly elected representatives must not be shut off by the intervention of the judicial department on the basis of a constitutional test intertwined with an assessment of contemporary standards and that the judgment of the general court weighs heavily in ascertaining such standards in this commonwealth. It is hereby further declared that in a democratic society, legislatures, and here, in this commonwealth, the general court is the body constituted to respond to the will of the people." Finally, the legislators contended that the proposed statute was the product of their considered and deliberate judgment. "It is hereby further declared that the following proposed legislation is the result of long study and review of the work and experience of other jurisdictions which have satisfied all those norms demanded by the Supreme Court of the United States to safeguard against all of the elements of arbitrariness and capriciousness condemned by said court in former state death penalty statutes."[26]

In the end, the Massachusetts Supreme Court was unpersuaded by this statute/brief presented to it by the legislature. Referring once again to the importance of the natural right to life as well as to the constitutional guarantee against cruel and unusual punishment, Chief Justice Edward Hennessey's majority opinion overruled the 1979 death-penalty statute on the ground that it would inevitably be applied arbitrarily.[27]

The Massachusetts General Court was no more successful in its effort to interpret the religious-freedom clauses of the state and federal constitutions. This dispute was sparked in 1980 when the state supreme court overturned a 1979 statute that provided that each school day would begin with a moment of voluntary prayer from which any student who so desired could be excused.[28] At its 1982 session, the legislature modified the law and submitted the new version for the court's approval. In the revised statute, the legislature provided that students could offer a "meditation" instead of a prayer, and it defended its interpretation of the constitutional guarantee of religious freedom. The legislature stipulated that "[s]uch prayer shall not establish a religion in Public Schools, just as the prayer by the Chaplains of the Senate and House of Representatives, and the Crier of the Supreme Court, does not establish [a] religion in our government."[29]

The Massachusetts Supreme Court was unmoved by this argument. The justices detected little difference between this statute and the one they had previously rejected. Moreover, they dismissed the idea that legislators were competent to interpret the constitution. The court argued that the legislature, "by asserting that the school prayer bill 'shall not establish a religion in Public Schools, just as the prayer by the Chaplains of the Senate and House of Representatives . . . does not establish [a] religion in our government,' *attempts to invade the rightful province of the judiciary* to adjudicate whether a law conflicts with the requirements of the Constitution."[30]

THE ROLE AND BEHAVIOR OF CITIZENS

Although citizens during this period occasionally made use of the initiative and referendum in the same way as they had previously—to overcome failures of legislative representation or deliberation—the advent of judicial responsibility for rights protection brought changes in the purposes for which these institutions were employed, as well as in the way these institutions were viewed by leaders of intellectual and legal opinion.

As long as legislatures exercised primary responsibility for defining and securing rights, citizens concentrated on evaluating and responding to legislative acts. As a result, initiatives and referendums were invariably proposed for the purpose of restricting legislative deliberations or overturning legislative statutes.

When responsibility for securing rights was transferred from legislators to judges, citizens naturally turned their attention to the courts and began to introduce initiatives for the purpose of restraining and responding to judicial decisions.

It is not surprising, therefore, that initiatives and referendums proposed during this period were geared more toward judicial than legislative acts. Consequently, the rights that judges were most concerned with interpreting in this period were also the most prolific sources of initiative activity.[31] Oregon was one of several states in which voters sought to regulate fair-trial rights in a different manner from judges. The 1986 Oregon Victims' Rights Initiative modified several rules of criminal procedure, increased the number of prosecutorial peremptory challenges, and generally enhanced the rights of victims in the trial process.[32] Similarly, voters in Oregon and Michigan relied on the initiative to respond to judicial interpretations of the right to privacy. Michigan voters used the initiative to ban state-funded abortions in 1987,[33] and in Oregon, similar propositions were defeated in 1978 and 1986, as were a pair of 1990 propositions that would have prohibited virtually all abortions and required parental notification. Citizens also relied on the initiative to respond to judicial interpretations of the guarantee against cruel and unusual punishment, such as when Oregon voters tried to reinstate capital punishment in 1978 and then succeeded in 1984.[34] Finally, although judicial decisions with respect to obscenity and busing were not the subject of initiatives in any of these four states, they generated a significant amount of initiative activity in other states during this period.[35]

What truly distinguished citizen behavior in the judicialist regime from that of previous eras was the way that these initiatives and referendums were received by judges and academics. Whereas direct democratic institutions had once been viewed as a means through which citizens could legitimately express their views, they were now viewed with suspicion and were considered to be more likely to oppress than to secure rights.

To be sure, the populist spirit was not entirely extinguished. Several judges actually argued that initiatives were more likely than legislative statutes to represent the popular will. Michigan Justice Harry Kelly noted in a 1956 opinion that "[t]he initiative and referendum are recognized as instruments of democratic government, widely used and of great value."[36] U.S. Supreme Court Justice Hugo Black, perhaps the most ardent judicial supporter of direct democracy during this period, argued in similar fashion that "[p]rovisions for referendums demonstrate devotion to democracy, not to bias, discrimination, or prejudice."[37] He contended that initiatives were entitled to more deference than legislation, "[b]ecause here, it's moving in the direction of letting the people of the State— the voters of the State—establish their policy, which is as near to a democracy as you can get."[38]

Somewhat more prevalent was the belief that initiatives and statutes should be treated in the same manner. Oregon Justice Arthur Hay argued "that in the construction of statutes there is no essential difference between those enacted by the initiative and referendum and those enacted in the usual way."[39] He believed that, "On the whole, in view of the jealous regard of the people for the initiative process and of the opportunities which exist for the voters to acquaint themselves with the background and merits of a proposed initiative measure, we are of the opinion that, in the construction of such measures, the courts should indulge the same presumption as to the knowledge of historical facts on the part of the people, as they indulge with reference to acts passed by the legislature."[40]

The dominant view in this era, however, was that initiatives were generally threatening to rights and should be treated with less deference than legislative statutes. Law professors, in particular, displayed during this period what Lynn Baker described as a "nearly unanimous distrust" of direct democracy.[41] Professor Preble Stolz, for instance, argued, "The '90s will be a dismal decade for law reform unless something can be done to rid us of government by the initiative." He thought that "the California Supreme Court was nationally regarded as a leader in law reform," but the "success of the initiative process . . . has had a disastrous influence on law reform in California." He believed that initiatives concerning criminal justice had "effectively destroyed the capacity of the state Supreme Court to be inventive in that area," and even more importantly, they tended to "crowd out other matters that might be on the court's agenda."[42] Likewise, Professor Calvin Massey feared for the fate of rights "at the hands of an aroused California electorate indifferent to the integrity of the California Constitution and determined to reduce the constitutional right of some disfavored minority."[43] Accordingly, law professors routinely counseled judges to "be prepared to control individuals or groups attempting to use ballot propositions improperly."[44]

This opposition to direct democratic institutions influenced judicial behavior in several ways. Judges occasionally exercised preelection review of initiative measures and thereby prevented some propositions from even appearing on the ballot.[45] Thus in 1990 the Massachusetts Supreme Court refused to permit the citizens to hold a referendum on a gay-rights statute that the Massachusetts General Court had enacted in its 1989 session. Justice Paul Liacos concluded that because the statute pertained to religious matters, it fell outside the bounds of constitutionally permissible referendums.[46]

Judges also overturned initiatives once they had been approved and taken effect. Thus after Oregon voters approved an initiated statute in 1978 to permit capital punishment,[47] it was overturned by the Oregon Supreme Court.[48] Even after Oregon voters returned to the ballot box to approve a constitutional initiative to reinstate capital punishment, some commentators continued to urge the court to maintain its opposition to the popular will, although in this case the court permitted the amendment to stand.[49] Nor was the Oregon experience atypical. A number of other courts were also active in overturning initiatives during this period. In fact: "Between 1960 and 1980, only two successful California initiatives were not declared unconstitutional in whole or in part by state or federal courts."[50]

Finally, the constitutional amendment and revision process offered an additional avenue through which citizens could participate in the protection of rights. Prior to the middle of the twentieth century, citizens had enacted constitutional amendments primarily for the purpose of restraining legislatures, and only occasionally to restrict judges. In the judicialist era, although citizens still made occasional use of the constitutional amendment process for the purpose of restraining legislatures, they increasingly began to enact amendments to respond to and overturn judicial decisions.[51]

As a result, constitutional convention debates were increasingly dominated during this period by considerations of what the courts had done. Thus on a number of occasions convention delegates refrained from acting, out of deference to the courts. When a question was broached at the Michigan Convention of 1961–1962 whether to retain a search-and-seizure provision in light of recent U.S. Supreme Court decisions, delegate Marjorie McGowan argued that "[t]his is a matter for the courts," and a majority of the convention delegates agreed.[52] Similarly, the Virginia Commission on Constitutional Revision concluded in 1969 that it was "wiser to leave it to the courts to decide, in the context of concrete cases, to what extent a right of association is implicit in other constitutional rights and how that right is to be applied to specific factual situations."[53]

To the extent that conventions did propose to amend or revise the constitution, this was usually for the purpose of ratifying decisions that had already been made by the courts. The Virginia Revision Commission introduced several proposed changes in the Virginia Declaration of Rights by noting: "[C]ertain rights which by judicial decisions have been held implicit in the present Bill of Rights, e.g., the right to a speedy trial and the right of peaceable assembly, are made explicit."[54] Similarly, in the course of the debate over these proposed amendments in the Virginia General Assembly, delegate James Thomson noted: "In fairness to the House, the basic reason for the amendments that have been included in George Mason's Bill of Rights ought to be stated. They all stem from court decisions dealing with clauses that were formerly in the Legislative Article that were transferred into the Bill of Rights. The Court had treated them differently because they were in the Legislative Article and said if they were meant to be given the interpretation that was being advocated in those cases they should have been included in the Bill of Rights."[55]

A number of other amendments were enacted for the purpose of overturning or restricting the effect of judicial decisions. Not surprisingly, the same decisions that generated popular initiatives in this period—namely, search and seizure, school desegregation, and capital punishment—also produced a significant number of constitutional amendments. Thus in 1952 the Michigan legislature approved, and the people ratified, an amendment that excepted drugs from the sweep of the judicially imposed exclusionary rule.[56] In 1956 Virginia held a limited convention in order to overturn a state court decision that prohibited the transfer of public funds to private schools.[57] Then in 1976 the citizens of Massachusetts responded to a series of judicial busing decrees by ratifying a constitutional amendment stipulating that "no student shall be assigned to a public school on the basis of race, color, national origin or creed."[58]

The use of constitutional amendments to respond to judicial rulings was not unprecedented. In particular, citizens in the early twentieth century had occasionally approved amendments for the purpose of overturning judicial decisions. What truly distinguished constitutional activity in the modern period was the ultimate fate of these amendments. Whereas constitutional amendments had always prevailed over judicial decisions in previous eras, there was no longer any such guarantee in the judicialist era.

The prevailing attitude toward constitutional amendments was perhaps best illustrated by the response of the Massachusetts Supreme Court to a constitutional amendment that sought to prevent the courts from invalidating the death penalty. The amendment, which was proposed by the legislature and ratified by the voters in 1982, stated: "No provision of the Constitution . . . shall be construed as prohibiting the imposition of the punishment of death. The general court may, for the purpose of protecting the general welfare of the citizens, authorize the imposition of the punishment of death by the courts of law having jurisdiction of crimes subject to the punishment of death."[59] In 1984, however, the Massachusetts Supreme Court ruled that the amendment did not preclude "consideration of the statutory *implementation* of the death penalty."[60] Justice Paul Liacos concluded, "Nothing in the arguments for and against the amendment circulated to the voters concerned the total insulation of death penalty legislation from constitutional review."[61] In the view of a majority of the court, the most recent death-penalty statute offended another provision of the Massachusetts Constitution, the right to a trial by jury.[62]

It was left to the dissenters to point out the full effect of the decision. Justice Joseph Nolan argued: "The court's interpretation . . . contravenes the desires of the citizens of Massachusetts and the court's duty to construe laws, when possible, so as to avoid the conclusion that they are unconstitutional." He believed that "the people made it clear that the capital punishment statute must escape invalidation by any article of the Massachusetts Constitution," and he was unable to "comprehend how the phrase, '[n]o provision of the Constitution . . . shall be construed as prohibiting the imposition of the punishment of death,' could be interpreted to mean other than that the court cannot invalidate the statute under the State Constitution."[63]

These arguments were advanced to no avail, however, against a majority of justices who were determined to prevent the imposition of the legislative and popular will. In previous eras, there was little doubt that a constitutional amendment would eventually prevail over a judicial decision. But this was a judicialist age in all respects. Legislative statutes, popular initiatives, and even constitutional amendments would have to yield on occasion to the judicial will.

CONCLUSION

This regime is characterized as a judicialist regime primarily because each institution was infused with a judicialist, rather than a republican or populist, ethos. But it is also possible to distinguish this regime from its predecessors by identifying the constitutional provisions that served as the principal guarantors of rights, the institution that was entrusted with primary responsibility for protecting rights, and the means by which rights were ordinarily secured.

Bills of rights were looked upon as the chief security for liberties during this period. Although this is virtually uncontested in the modern era, the reliance on bills of rights represented a dramatic departure from the republican regime, which placed its faith in constitutional provisions that allocated powers and responsibilities to representative institutions, as well as from the populist regime, which placed its faith in provisions that limited the powers of representative institutions.

The judiciary was entrusted with primary responsibility for securing rights. Although the reliance on courts is also unexceptionable in the contemporary era, it too represented a significant departure from previous eras—both from the republican regime, which understood that legislators were best positioned to secure rights, and from the populist regime, which relied on the collective citizenry. According to the judicialist regime, the public voice would be more consonant with the public good if pronounced by judges than if pronounced by the people themselves or their elected representatives.

Finally, constitutional decision making was thought to provide the most effective protection for individual rights. In previous regimes, security for rights was associated with popular participation in drafting the laws, either indirectly, as in the republican regime, or directly, as in the populist regime. By contrast, the judicialist regime held that rights were best secured when the people had as little agency as possible in their protection, and that this could best be achieved by relying on constitutional decisions that precluded legislative or popular interference.

9

Judicialist Institutions as Keepers
of the People's Liberties

The most remarkable aspect of the judicialist regime is the virtual absence of any reflection on its effectiveness. To be sure, law reviews are filled with critiques of particular justices, courts, and opinions. With slightly more digging one can uncover critiques of judicial competence in entire areas of the law. But there are few analyses of the success of the entire enterprise of entrusting judges with the protection of rights.

This lack of reflection is surprising for several reasons. One might expect that the extensive criticism of particular judicial decisions would lead to more sustained reflection about the general fitness of courts to protect rights. But as Robert Nagel has written, "serious criticism of the courts' actual performance" is often expressed in tandem with "the widespread belief that judges are personally and institutionally competent." In general, "commentators pay almost no attention to the possibility, certainly suggested by the barrage of criticism, that both judges and adjudication are unsuited for the broad task being urged upon them."[1] The relative absence of critical inquiry is also surprising in light of the fact that it is only recently that courts have come to be seen as the best keepers of liberties. Throughout much of American history, the dominant understanding has been precisely the opposite, and as late as 1943, Henry Steele Commager could still maintain that legislators were on balance better keepers of the people's liberties than judges.[2] One might well expect that the novelty of the modern view would inspire at least some reflection about whether the current preference for courts is an ephemeral product of twentieth-century circumstances or a more enduring judgment.

To the extent that scholars have engaged in such reflection, the resulting studies have generally fallen short of qualifying as institutional analyses. In the first place, we have generally failed to distinguish the effects of institutions from the effects of federalism. It is not uncommon to find instances in which federal courts have protected certain rights more effectively than have state legislatures, and on the strength of this observation to conclude that judges are generally superior to legislators. But it is possible that the greater effectiveness of federal judges in protecting rights in these cases owes more to their federal than to their judicial character.[3]

In addition, we have not always distinguished the role of institutions from the role of public opinion. It is not difficult to find instances in which certain rights have been protected more effectively in the late twentieth century, when courts are primarily responsible for their protection, than they were in the early nineteenth century, when legislatures were entrusted with their protection, and to conclude from this that courts are superior to legislatures. But as Michael Klarman noted, "little effort has been devoted to identifying and elaborating the background historical forces that rendered possible the postwar revolution in civil rights and civil liberties jurisprudence."[4] As a result, it is important to leave open the possibility that the improved record of rights protection in the modern age is due to the more mature conception of rights that exists today rather than to the fact that courts are now responsible for their protection.

Furthermore, we have not always distinguished the role of institutions from the role of different standards of evaluation. There is a natural tendency to assume that the manner in which rights are currently secured, at a time when courts are responsible for their protection, is inevitably superior to the manner in which rights were previously secured, and therefore to conclude that judges are superior to legislators. But as Nagel has argued, the conclusion that courts have succeeded in protecting rights better than legislatures "papers over important difficulties in defining 'success.' "[5] It may be the case that courts have merely protected certain rights in a different manner from legislatures rather than that they have provided a superior level of protection.

Finally, we have not always distinguished between the broad claim that courts protect rights better than legislatures and the particular claim that courts protect certain rights more effectively under certain circumstances. Even after controlling for different levels of government, changes in popular conceptions of rights, and varying standards of evaluation, it is still possible that courts will be shown to protect certain rights more effectively than legislatures. But the fact that courts provide better security for rights in certain cases "does not justify a routine or pervasive judicial program of protections of the kind that now exists."[6] It is important to leave open the possibility that judges may not necessarily be superior to legislators in all cases, but they may be particularly well suited to protecting certain rights in certain situations.[7]

What is needed, therefore, is an institutional analysis of the judicial record of rights protection between 1940 and 1990. Once we take account of the shortcomings in existing studies, it becomes possible to structure the analysis in such a way as to yield a set of more more nuanced conclusions about the capacity of judges to secure rights. In particular, it is helpful to concentrate on state institutions, to compare the records of state courts and state legislatures, to identify cases in which courts have actually secured a higher level of protection for rights, and to examine a broad range of rights and circumstances.

FREEDOM OF WORSHIP

The meaning of religious liberty was contested in several ways in the latter half of the twentieth century. Questions arose as to whether public funds could support parochial schools, and to what extent; whether religious materials could be introduced into public schools and other public places; and finally, whether individuals could be exempt from general laws on account of their religious beliefs. For all the controversy generated by these questions, however, there were surprisingly few occasions on which the courts provided a markedly higher level of protection for religious liberty than did legislatures. In most cases, judicial activity was confined to upholding and applying rights that had been secured by legislative statutes. To be sure, in several areas, courts and legislatures regulated rights in a slightly different manner, but it is not clear that the judicial interpretation was preferable to the legislative interpretation, and in some cases the legislature appeared to provide the higher level of protection.

Courts consistently interpreted the ban on religious establishment in a different manner from legislatures. For one thing, courts prohibited the appropriation of public funds for religious schools.[8] For years, legislatures had regulated this right; some interpreted the religious establishment clauses of their bills of rights to permit public aid for school transportation, textbooks, and assorted supplies, and others determined that only certain forms of assistance, such as transportation aid, were appropriate.[9] But in the 1960s and early 1970s, the supreme courts of Oregon, Michigan, and Massachusetts assumed responsibility for protecting the right and ruled that several of these forms of assistance, most notably textbook aid, were constitutionally invalid.[10]

Courts also banned the introduction of religious materials into schools and other public places.[11] Throughout the nineteenth century, legislatures had retained responsibility for drawing appropriate distinctions in this area. They had enacted statutes to prohibit schools from using sectarian books, to forbid teachers to comment on religious materials, and to provide student exemptions from any religious activities that discomforted them. In the 1960s and 1970s, however, judges determined that religious liberty could be protected only by prohibiting prayers, meditation, and moments of silence altogether, such as when the Massachusetts Supreme Court overturned a series of school prayer and meditation statutes.[12] Judges also proscribed religious-oriented materials in other public places, such as when the Oregon Supreme Court ruled that a concrete cross could not be erected on the public property of the city of Eugene.[13]

In evaluating the judicial record in these religious establishment cases, it is clear that in certain states and on certain questions, courts enunciated a different understanding from that of legislatures. It would be difficult, however, to determine which of these positions—the separationist position generally advanced by judges, or the accommodationist position usually maintained by legislators—is a superior interpretation of the guarantee of religious liberty. One would be especially hard-pressed to give a decided edge to either the judiciary or the legislature in view of the ongoing debate among legal scholars and the judges themselves as to which interpretation is preferable.[14] At the least, the question remains open as to whether legislators or judges secured rights more effectively in these cases.

When we turn to religious free-exercise cases, we find that the judicial and legislative records are quite similar and that there is little reason to prefer one institutional forum to the other. For the most part, judges merely upheld and applied statutory guarantees in particular circumstances. Thus the Massachusetts Supreme Court sustained a zoning statute that required that special accommodation be given to churches and religious organizations,[15] and the Michigan Supreme Court upheld a law that permitted Sabbatarians to be exempt from employment on Saturdays.[16]

To be sure, judges occasionally required more expansive exemptions than legislatures. For instance, the Massachusetts Supreme Court held that the legislature must provide exemptions from school immunization requirements not only for members of recognized churches but for all persons who conscientiously object to such practices on religious grounds. Similarly, the Michigan Supreme Court required employers not only to refrain from discriminating on the basis of religious beliefs but also to actively accommodate Sabbatarians in scheduling time slots. Additionally, although the Massachusetts Supreme Court declined to grant a religious exemption from marijuana laws, the Oregon Supreme Court was willing to make an exception to laws prohibiting the ingestion of peyote.[17]

Many exemptions, though, were granted by legislatures. Legislative statutes were the vehicle for exempting students from general immunization laws[18] and from other school activities.[19] Legislatures also exempted Sabbatarians from Sunday-closing laws, as long as they agreed to rest on another day.[20] They also exempted religious organizations from general antidiscrimination laws[21] and medical personnel from being required to perform abortions.[22]

In some of these cases, it should be noted, legislatures were quite solicitous of the interests of minority religions. For instance, as part of a law regulating the slaughter of animals, the Massachusetts General Court stipulated that nothing in the act "shall prohibit, abridge, or in any way hinder the religious freedom of any person or group, and, in order to protect freedom of religion, ritual slaughter and the handling or other preparation of livestock for ritual slaughter shall be exempt from the provisions."[23] Moreover, in some of these cases, legislative exemptions were granted only after the judiciary had failed to do so, such as when the Massachusetts General Court recognized an exemption for Jewish shopkeepers from Sunday-closing laws after the state supreme court declined to do so.[24]

It is apparent from the sheer number of these exemptions that legislatures were often quite competent to redress the grievances of religious groups whose members were few in number and whose beliefs met with little favor in the general populace. This became even more clear in the wake of the U.S. Supreme Court's decision in the 1990 case *Oregon v. Smith,* when attention began to be focused on the respective records of courts and legislatures in securing the right to free exercise of religion. According to James Ryan: "[T]he evidence demonstrates that faith in the courts in this area is misplaced, and that religious groups and individuals fared better in the legislature than in the courts before the *Smith* decision. Indeed, perhaps the most lasting and helpful legacy of the case will be that it finally dispelled the mistaken notion that courts were the leading institutional protectors of religious liberty."[25]

FREEDOM OF EXPRESSION

Wartime concerns over free-speech rights were in large part responsible for the creation of the judicialist regime, and it is no surprise that free-speech issues generated a fair amount of controversy throughout the era. Disputes arose over whether individuals had a right to decline to take loyalty oaths, to refuse to testify at legislative hearings, to assemble peaceably, to disseminate controversial political or religious views, to distribute obscene or indecent materials, and to be accorded special journalistic privileges.[26] The judicial record on these issues is a mixed one. In one group of cases, judges provided a markedly different as well as an undeniably superior level of protection. In another set of cases, judges protected rights in a different but not necessarily superior manner. In a final group of cases, the courts actually provided an inferior level of protection.[27]

Courts provided a decidedly better level of protection for the free-speech rights of political dissenters in times of political excitement. In the first place, judges secured the right of individuals to be exempt from loyalty oaths. In the 1930s, and then again in the 1950s, fears of communism led state legislatures to enact loyalty-oath laws that applied to public employees, teachers, and members of a variety of professions.[28] Although a number of courts declined to overturn these loyalty oaths,[29] judges were on the whole more likely than legislators to secure this right.[30] Thus in 1966 the Oregon Supreme Court invalidated a statute that required all public school teachers to subscribe to a loyalty oath,[31] and in 1967 the Massachusetts Supreme Court sided with an MIT math professor in his challenge of a law that required oaths by teachers in private institutions as well.[32]

Courts also secured more effective protection, in similar circumstances, for the privilege against self-incrimination. In the 1950s fears of communism generated a number of legislative hearings that were designed to ferret out communist sympathizers from the ranks of the teaching, law, and medical professions.[33] In several cases, state courts ruled that these hearings violated an individual's privilege against self-incrimination. Thus the Massachusetts Supreme Court held in 1951 that a trial judge could not ask a defendant whether he was a communist,[34] and in 1955 that a teacher could not be discharged for refusing to answer questions concerning his membership in the Communist Party.[35]

Courts also provided a superior level of protection for the free-speech rights of politically unpopular groups. Perhaps the most controversial group during this period was the Jehovah's Witnesses, whose members fared much better in the courts than in legislatures. The Massachusetts Supreme Court, in particular, invalidated a number of laws and ordinances that restricted the Witnesses' ability to distribute their pamphlets.[36] Labor unions were another highly unpopular group in a number of these states, and they occasionally fared better in the judicial chambers than in the assembly halls. For instance, in Virginia and Michigan, courts secured the right to picket in the face of hostile legislatures.[37] Finally, courts were generally more protective of the right of political dissenters to assemble peaceably. When members of the Socialist Party were effectively prevented by a city ordinance from speaking in the Boston Common, the Massachusetts Supreme Court ruled that the ordinance offended constitutional guarantees.[38] Similarly, when African Americans in Danville, Virginia, were prevented from demonstrating by a city parade ordinance, the Virginia Supreme Court held the requirement unconstitutional.[39]

Courts in these cases protected rights in a way that was both different from and superior to legislatures, but it is not so easy to render a judgment in the case of the right to distribute obscene or indecent materials. Courts were certainly active in overturning legislative regulations in this area. Both the Massachusetts and the Oregon supreme courts voided movie-licensing ordinances.[40] Several courts also overturned general prohibitions on obscene materials,[41] as well as bans on specific books and movies.[42] Finally, courts delivered decisions overturning a variety of other laws regulating obscenity and indecency, including an Oregon Supreme Court decision that struck down a ban on the public and reckless use of obscene language,[43] a Massachusetts Supreme Court ruling that invalidated a ban on nude dancing,[44] and a Massachusetts ruling that overturned a law under which a man had been prosecuted for taking seminude photographs of his fifteen-year-old stepdaughter.[45]

Although it is undeniable that courts regulated obscenity and indecency in a different manner from legislatures, reasonable persons can disagree as to whether these decisions constituted an overall advance for liberty. Thomas Emerson concluded that, "Taken as a whole, the Court's decisions [in the area of obscenity] have resulted in some notable gains for the system of freedom of expression."[46] But Harry Clor is one of several scholars who have expressed doubts about the success of the judicial enterprise in regulating this right,[47] and he has been joined by several state justices.[48] At the least, the question remains open as to whether courts actually provided a superior level of protection in this area.

In one final area of freedom of expression, courts provided an inferior level of protection. From the 1960s through the 1980s, judges were frequently importuned to recognize journalists' right to decline to divulge their sources, but they consistently refused to establish such a right, on either constitutional or common-law grounds.[49] Accordingly: "The failure of the common law to recognize a news reporter's privilege has led journalists to seek statutory relief."[50] Legislators turned out to be generally quite receptive to these arguments, and certainly more receptive than judges. In fact, over half the states enacted statutes that secured this right.[51] Moreover, when courts construed these statutes narrowly, as they did on several occasions, some legislatures enacted broader statutes to overturn these decisions and to make it clear that they intended to create a broad claim of immunity.[52]

THE GUARANTEE OF A FAIR TRIAL

Legislatures did not enact any statutes during this period that actually violated an individual's right to a fair trial. Most of the controversies centered around the best way to expand existing guarantees. Public officials deliberated over whether to provide indigent defendants with court-appointed lawyers and free trial transcripts and how best to guarantee the privilege against self-incrimination, prevent coerced confessions, provide public and speedy trials, and prevent improper searches and seizures.[53]

Because these rights were elevated to constitutional status through a series of federal and state court decisions, there is a tendency to conclude that judges provided a superior level of protection than did legislators. This assumes, however, that rights can be protected only through judicial constitutional decisions. In fact, most of these rights had already been secured through statutes or interpretations of the common law. The Oregon Supreme Court provided some indication of the extent of these statutory protections in a 1943 opinion:

> The statutes of this state, like those of all the states in the Union, contain many provisions designed to safeguard the rights of a person accused of crime. Upon being arrested he must without delay be taken before a magistrate (s.26-1515, 26-1521, 26-1519, O.C.L.A). The magistrate must immediately inform him of the charge against him and his rights to the aid of counsel (s.26-1547); he must be allowed a reasonable time to send for counsel (s.26-1548); the magistrate must then proceed to examine the case (s.26-1549); the witnesses must be examined in the presence of the defendant, and may be cross-examined in his behalf or against him (s.26-1555); the magistrate must inform the defendant that it is his right to make a statement in relation to the charge against him, but that he is at liberty to waive making a statement, and that his waiver cannot be used against him at the trial (s.26-1556); upon the conclusion of the examination the magistrate, if he finds that

there is sufficient cause to believe the defendant guilty, must make a written order holding the defendant to answer the same, which order must designate the crime (s.26-1570); and make out a commitment accordingly, and the defendant must be delivered into the proper custody together with the commitment (s.26-1571).[54]

When we turn to compare the legislative and judicial records of protecting fair-trial rights, we find that in one group of cases, judicial decisions merely elevated to constitutional status rights that had previously been secured by other means. In a second group of cases, judicial decisions secured rights somewhat more quickly than legislation, but not in a significantly different manner. Finally, in one area, judicial decisions provided a decidedly different type of protection from legislation, but it is unclear whether they secured the right in a superior manner.

In the first place, judicial decisions that constitutionalized the privilege against self-incrimination generally confirmed a right that had already been established on a statutory and common-law footing. For nearly a century, legislatures had prevented induced or coerced confessions and provided that defendants could refuse to testify and not be tainted by that choice. Where legislatures had not acted, judges had interpreted common-law principles to require the exclusion of involuntary confessions. As the Oregon Supreme Court noted in a 1965 case, "The Oregon decisions excluding involuntary confessions have based the exclusion upon common-law rules of evidence, codified into an Oregon statute."[55]

The rights to a speedy trial and to a public trial were also placed on constitutional grounds by judicial decisions in the 1960s, but neither was thereby secured for the first time. Legislatures had already guaranteed the right to a speedy trial in a variety of ways. Massachusetts and Michigan ordered defendants to be let out on bail if they were not tried within a certain period, and Oregon and Virginia ordered them to be forever discharged.[56] In adjudicating claims that the right had been violated, judges had rested their decisions nearly exclusively on statutory grounds. As Oregon Justice Hall Lusk wrote in one 1959 case, "We do not reach the constitutional question, as we are of the opinion that, under the statute properly construed, the motion to dismiss the indictment should have been allowed."[57] The right to a public trial was secured in Virginia and Massachusetts in similar fashion.[58]

In a second group of cases, the judicial and legislative records are slightly but not significantly different. When courts constitutionalized the right to counsel in the 1960s, they expanded on the current legislative understanding, but not by a dramatic margin. For a number of years, legislatures assumed responsibility for securing the right to counsel for indigent defendants.[59] They steadily increased the crimes for which counsel was provided, first guaranteeing counsel in capital crimes, then in certain felony cases, and finally in misdemeanor cases when the judge deemed it appropriate.[60] They then provided these defendants with more effective representation, by gradually increasing the amount of compensation for court-appointed attorneys.[61] They also provided counsel at increasingly early stages of the trial process, such as at lineups and arraignments.[62] Finally, they occasionally assisted indigent defendants by providing them with free transcripts for pursuing appeals.

In cases in which legislatures had not secured the right, judges relied on their rule-making powers to ensure that counsel was appointed in appropriate circumstances. Thus Oregon Justice George Rossman noted in one 1960 case, "The fact that we do not believe that Art. I, s. 11, Oregon Constitution, confers power to appoint counsel does not mean that courts lack power to appoint counsel for the poor."[63] In similar fashion, Michigan Justice Theodore Souris noted in a 1967 case: "[E]ven before *Gideon,* this Court required, by rule adopted in 1947, that in every felony prosecution the accused be advised of his right to have the assistance of counsel and, if financially unable to employ counsel, that counsel be appointed for him upon his request. Whatever the nature of the right, constitutional or rule, [the defendant], accused of a felony, was entitled to be represented."[64]

Consequently, when the courts elevated the right to counsel to constitutional status in the 1960s, they did not secure the right for the first time. Constitutional decisions had the effect of mandating counsel for a greater number of crimes (such as for violations of municipal ordinances)[65] and at a greater number of stages of the trial process (such as during probation revocation hearings).[66] But overall the courts did not regulate this right in a significantly different fashion from legislatures.

In one final area—the guarantee against improper search and seizure—the courts provided a significantly different but not necessarily superior level of protection. Prior to the 1960s, most state legislatures sought to prevent unreasonable searches through a series of statutory rules. They were concerned with limiting the purposes for which search warrants could be obtained,[67] providing detailed requirements for obtaining a warrant,[68] and prohibiting certain types of searches altogether.[69] But perhaps the most important aspect of this approach was the means by which legislators chose to enforce these provisions. They concluded that the best way to prevent improper searches was to hold public officials liable for violating these guarantees. The view was that the right was best enforced by arranging incentives in such a way that the personal interest of the public official in avoiding liability coincided with the public interest in preventing improper searches.

When courts constitutionalized this right in the 1960s, the principal effect was to alter the manner in which the right was guaranteed. Acting at first at the direction of the U.S. Supreme Court and then on their own initiative, state courts implemented the exclusionary rule as the primary means of securing the right.[70] In 1980 Virginia Justice George Cochran had occasion to compare the two approaches. The new approach, he noted, held that "evidence obtained in violation of the Fourth

Amendment proscription of unreasonable searches and seizures may not be used against an accused." This was quite different from the traditional approach, he noted, which relied on a statute that "made it a misdemeanor for any law enforcement officer to search without a warrant. An offending officer was liable to the victim in compensatory and punitive damages and, upon a second conviction, forfeited his office."[71]

It cannot be denied that the judicial approach to securing this right differed significantly from the legislative approach. The evidence is less conclusive on the question of whether judges actually secured the right more effectively. In 1970 Dallin Oaks conducted one of the most extensive surveys of the evidence but was still unable to provide a definitive answer: "The data contains little support for the proposition that the exclusionary rule discourages illegal searches and seizures, but it falls short of establishing that it does not."[72] In subsequent years, scholars have conducted additional studies, analyzed the methodology of previous studies, and measured the effectiveness of alternative means of securing the right.[73] But "[t]o date, no empirical researcher has been able to determine with any certainty whether the rule has a deterrent effect."[74] At the least, the question remains open whether the judicial or the legislative interpretation provided greater security for the right.

THE RIGHT TO EQUAL PROTECTION UNDER THE LAW

The conventional understanding that courts protect civil rights better than legislatures is generally confirmed. It is important, however, to be more specific about the particular conditions under which this holds true. In certain states and during certain eras, judges did in fact secure civil rights better than did legislators. In most cases, however, there was little difference between the legislative and judicial record, and the majority of civil rights in this period was secured through statutes rather than through constitutional decisions.

The Right to Nondiscrimination on Account of Race

At particular points in the judicialist era, the supreme courts of Oregon, Virginia, and Massachusetts each provided a higher level of protection than did the legislatures for the right to nondiscrimination on account of race. The Oregon Supreme Court secured the rights of Asian Americans on several occasions immediately following the Second World War. In 1947 the court overturned a law that had the effect of denying a barber's license to a Filipino man, and in 1949 the justices overturned a statute that restricted the right of aliens to own land.[75] In Virginia the state supreme court secured the rights of African Americans against oppressive legislation on several occasions in the 1950s and 1960s.[76] In 1959, in the wake of the U.S. Supreme Court's decision in *Brown v. Board of*

Education, the Virginia Supreme Court secured the right to attend integrated schools by overturning a statute designed to "prevent the enrollment and instruction of white and colored children in the same public schools."[77] In 1963 the court secured the right to equal treatment in public accommodations when it overturned a pair of statutes that mandated segregated seating at the Richmond Symphony and at Richmond's Parker Field baseball stadium.[78] Finally, in Massachusetts, the state supreme court provided a slightly higher level of protection for the rights of blacks in the early 1970s, but the institutional differences are less dramatic in this instance. The Massachusetts General Court actually took the first step toward securing the right to attend integrated schools in 1965, when it enacted a statute that sought to eliminate "racial imbalance in the public schools."[79] The act, which was upheld by the state supreme court, required all school committees to identify any instances of racial imbalance and to devise plans for remedying them.[80] In subsequent years, however, the legislature sought to modify this law in several ways, first by providing that no student could be transported to a school outside of his or her district without the consent of his or her parents, and then by prohibiting any student assignments on the basis of race. In both cases, the Massachusetts Supreme Court held that the statutes were constitutionally infirm.[81]

Apart from these decisions, which were delivered during periods of political or social excitement, legislation was the ordinary means by which civil rights were secured and extended.[82] The legislatures of Michigan and Massachusetts had enacted civil rights statutes in the nineteenth century, and they continued to amend these laws to respond to the public desire for more extensive guarantees and stricter penalties for violating them. Oregon and Virginia implemented these guarantees for the first time during this period. Statutes were enacted in all these states in order to prohibit discrimination in employment.[83] Legislatures also banned discrimination in public accommodations.[84] Finally, legislatures prohibited discrimination in housing, private organizations, loans, and educational institutions, among other areas.[85] For the most part, the judicial role was limited to upholding these statutes or enforcing them in various circumstances.[86]

The Right to Nondiscrimination on Account of Sex

Women sought to secure the right to nondiscrimination in several ways during this period. In the first place, they desired equal treatment with regard to employment, political participation, and the receipt of governmental benefits. At the same time, they demanded legal recognition and accommodation of their special circumstances, such as pregnancy and maternity.[87] Each of these goals was pursued and obtained almost entirely through the legislative process. To be sure, courts contributed in certain respects to the recognition of these rights, but they did not provide a markedly superior level of protection.[88]

It was through legislation that women secured the right to nondiscrimination in salary and employment, such as when the Massachusetts General Court acted in 1945 to prohibit wage differentials based on sex,[89] and then in 1965 to prohibit sex discrimination in employment.[90] Likewise, legislation was the means by which women secured the right to participate fully in public life, such as when the Virginia General Assembly in 1952 permitted women to serve on grand juries.[91] Finally, legislatures occasionally secured women's rights by taking account of their different circumstances, such as when the Oregon Legislative Assembly prohibited employment discrimination on the basis of pregnancy.[92] In some of these cases, moreover, legislatures secured these rights only after courts had declined to do so. For instance, after the U.S. Supreme Court in 1948 refused to recognize a woman's right to serve as a bartender,[93] the Michigan Legislature secured the right by enacting the appropriate statute.[94]

It is not that the courts were inactive in regulating women's rights, but there were few cases in which they secured an important advance for women against an intransigent legislature.[95] That is, to the extent that courts invalidated laws, they were not so much overruling legislative determinations as they were overcoming legislative inertia,[96] for instance, when the Oregon Supreme Court overturned an outdated law that extended certain benefits to men but not to similarly situated women.[97] In addition, in the few cases in which courts overturned laws that represented the considered judgment of the legislature, the rights were generally insignificant. It is unclear, for instance, how much weight to accord to a Massachusetts Supreme Court decision that proclaimed a right for high school boys to participate on girls' athletic teams.[98]

The Right to Nondiscrimination on Account of Sexual Orientation, Age, and Disability

Gays and lesbians sought to secure a variety of rights during this period, but they were primarily concerned with repealing antisodomy laws and obtaining the right to nondiscrimination in employment, housing, and accommodations. To be sure, these efforts inspired a great deal of controversy and were unsuccessful in many states. In general, though, legislatures have been at least as receptive to these arguments as have the courts, if not more so.

With respect to the right to engage in consensual sodomy, the only one of these states to secure that right is Oregon, where it was achieved through the legislative repeal of an antisodomy statute.[99] This experience, it should be noted, is typical of states across the country. Where the right has been secured, as it has been in nearly half the states over the last thirty-five years, legislative statutes have been the usual vehicle.[100] State courts "have been reluctant to take the decision to decriminalize sodomy away from the legislature,"[101] and in fact, judges have consistently declined to recognize the right through constitutional decisions.[102] Kentucky is the only state in which the right has been secured through a judicial decision, as a result of a state supreme court ruling in 1993 that overturned an antisodomy law on the ground that it offended the state constitutional right to privacy.[103]

Homosexuals have been less successful in their efforts to eliminate discrimination in housing, employment, and public accommodations, but again, legislation has been the primary means by which these rights have been secured. Massachusetts is the only one of the states in our sample that has secured this right, when the Massachusetts General Court in 1989 enacted a statute that provided "that the sexual orientation of a person is an invalid basis for discrimination in areas of housing, employment and the granting of credit," among other areas.[104] Wisconsin was the only other state that explicitly established the right to equal treatment without regard to sexual orientation, and there the right was also secured through a legislative statute.[105]

With respect, finally, to the rights to nondiscrimination on account of age or disability, these too have been secured primarily through legislation. The 1950s and 1960s produced a series of statutes that prevented age discrimination in employment.[106] Then, in the mid-1970s, legislatures enacted a number of statutes to prohibit employment discrimination on the basis of physical disability.[107] These laws were later extended to apply to housing, public accommodations, and other forums as well.[108]

THE RIGHT TO VOTE

By the mid-twentieth century, the suffrage had been formally extended to virtually all citizens, and most voting restrictions had been repealed. Still to be secured, though, was the suffrage for eighteen-year-olds and transients, as well as the right to cast an absentee ballot. Citizens also remained vigilant against legislative failures to secure an equitable apportionment, as well as against legislators' efforts to limit the suffrage in order to reduce their electoral insecurity. Each of these rights was generally secured through statutes, constitutional amendments, or initiatives, but in several cases they were obtained through judicial decisions.

Courts secured the right to an equal vote in the face of legislative intransigence on several occasions. For the most part, reapportionment was handled through the legislatures, but the Michigan Supreme Court intervened after the 1960, 1970, and 1980 rounds of redistricting to secure an equitable apportionment. As Michigan Justice Thomas Kavanagh explained in a case following the 1960 census: "Some of the veterans of the legislature, along with their predecessors, failed regularly to execute the constitutional oath each had taken to redistrict and reapportion under original section 4 of the fifth article of the Michigan Constitution (1908). They and they alone are responsible for justiciable presentation and consideration of the issue before this court."[109] The court had another occasion to revisit the work of the legislature after the 1970 census, and now

Chief Justice Kavanagh again explained the reason for judicial activity. He noted that in the intervening years, the people had set up a commission to carry out the task of redistricting. But the court concluded: "The activities of the political parties during the 1964 Commission on Legislative Apportionment, and the political shenanigans of both political parties making up the Commission this year, as brought out in oral argument before this Court, convinced a majority of the Court that it would be futile to remand this cause to the Commission for further proceedings. We, having no reasonable alternative, must carry out the constitutional mandate placed upon us by the people of this state."[110] The 1980 census brought yet another judicial decision and a further explanation of the court's involvement. The court noted that the issue "goes to the heart of the political process in a constitutional democracy. . . . A constitutional democracy cannot exist . . . without a legislature that represents the people, freely and popularly elected in accordance with a process upon which they have agreed."[111]

Judges provided a higher level of protection for voting rights in one other area, one that pitted the legislators' interest in maintaining their offices against the right of college students to vote. At issue were statutes that effectively denied students the ability to vote at their college residences. When the Michigan Supreme Court heard a challenge to one such law in 1971, the justices commented on the probable reason for its enactment. "A purported fear of the states involved is that the students would have a significant political impact if they were granted the elective franchise,"[112] a fear that was particularly acute at the height of the Vietnam War. The court struck down the law and concluded: "We agree that it is no longer constitutionally permissible to exclude students from the franchise because of the fear of the way they may vote."[113]

CONCLUSION

Admittedly, this study falls short of being comprehensive. It would be helpful to examine an even greater variety of rights and to do even more to separate the effects of legislative and judicial institutions from the effects of federalism. Nevertheless, the data lead to several conclusions about the capacity of courts to protect rights.

In the first place, courts provided a decidedly higher level of protection for civil rights and liberties in crisis times. Because judges were relatively insulated from social and political passions, they were better positioned than legislators to protect the rights of disfavored minorities during these periods. Thus the courts provided better protection for Jehovah's Witnesses and other political protesters in the 1940s, for Asian Americans in Oregon in the late 1940s, for African Americans in Virginia in the 1950s and 1960s, and for persons seeking to invoke the privilege against self-incrimination in a number of states during the period of heightened fear of communism in the 1950s and 1960s. In these cases, judicial chambers provided a superior forum than legislative assemblies for undertaking the requisite deliberation and providing adequate security for rights.

Judges also provided a significantly higher level of protection for certain voting rights, such as the right to an equal apportionment and the extension of the suffrage. Just as the initiative and referendum provided citizens with a means of bypassing legislators and securing these rights, judges were personally unaffected by reapportionment and by certain extensions of the suffrage and therefore well positioned to regulate these rights.

In another group of cases, of which the right to counsel would be one example, courts provided a marginally higher level of protection than legislatures. Throughout the twentieth century, legislatures had been steadily providing counsel in an increasing number of cases and at an increasing number of stages in the trial process. When the courts began in the 1960s to extend this right to even more cases and more stages, they thereby accelerated the process by which the right was secured but did not provide a dramatically higher level of protection.

In another group of cases, which includes the vast majority of rights, there was little difference between the judicial and legislative records. Legislatures and courts were equal partners in securing the privilege against self-incrimination, the right to a public and speedy trial, and the right to nondiscrimination on the basis of gender, sexual orientation, age, and disability. In these instances, judicial involvement was confined to upholding and applying rights that were initially secured through legislation.

An additional group of cases encompasses rights that were protected differently in the courts but not necessarily in a more effective fashion. The ban on religious establishment is one example of a right that received dramatically different interpretations in the judicial and legislative branches, but where reasonable persons have disagreed as to which interpretation is superior. Likewise, courts and legislatures reached different conclusions on whether freedom of expression is best secured by permitting the distribution of obscene materials, but it is not evident that one interpretation is clearly superior. Finally, with respect to the guarantee against improper searches and seizures, legislators frequently concluded that the right was best guaranteed by devising institutional arrangements and incentives in such a way as to prevent improper searches. In contrast, judges routinely concluded that the best way to secure the right was to exclude improperly seized evidence from trials. Although social science has not yet resolved the question of whether the legislative or the judicial approach is superior, a significant body of evidence suggests that the exclusionary rule has not demonstrated any marked improvement over the reliance on civil and financial penalties. In each of these cases, it appears that there are various ways to secure certain rights, and there is no overriding reason to prefer the judiciary over the legislature as a forum for deliberating about and selecting among these approaches.

In one final group of cases, the courts actually provided a slightly inferior level of protection for rights, on account of their insulation from public concerns or their inattentiveness to the effects of their decisions. The courts were fre-quently unwilling, for instance, to secure journalists' right to maintain the secrecy of their sources, and even when this right was secured through legisla-tion, judges sought to limit its reach. Likewise, legislators were occasionally more zealous than judges in granting religious exemptions from general laws, such as animal-slaughter and Sunday-closing laws.

In the end, it appears that courts provided a decidedly higher level of protec-tion than did existing institutions primarily during periods of social or political agitation. In particular, it is undeniable that courts provided a superior forum for deliberating about civil rights and liberties in crisis times. In one sense, of course, to conclude that courts can protect rights more effectively than legislatures is hardly a novel finding. Viewed from another perspective, though, this contrasts dramatically with the conventional understanding. In most areas, this study sug-gests, there is no significant difference between legislative and judicial capacity, and in several areas, legislatures actually provide a higher level of protection.

Conclusion

Conventional accounts of American political development identify three regime moments. Institutions of rights protection are thought to have been established at the founding. The enactment of the Civil War Amendments then shifted responsibility for rights protection from the states to the federal government. Finally, the passage of New Deal legislation redefined and expanded the spectrum of rights that governments are responsible for protecting. The results of this study demonstrate the need to supplement this interpretation. Alongside these changes in the level and scope of governmental responsibility for rights protection, one can also identify regime moments associated with changes in the institutions through which rights are protected. In particular, it becomes possible to point to a republican regime moment in the late eighteenth and early nineteenth centuries, a populist regime moment at the turn of the twentieth century, and a judicialist regime moment in the middle of the twentieth century.

Rather than being content with identifying these regimes, I have also sought to explain their origins, to describe the way in which public officials ordinarily secured rights in each period, and to evaluate the effectiveness of each of the various institutions.

We have seen that these regimes were in part the product of social and economic developments that forced a reassessment of existing political forms. They can also be attributed to the efforts of individuals who sought to implement institutional reforms. But the direction and shape of these reforms cannot be explained solely, or even primarily, by reference to these social and economic developments or individual efforts. Rather, these regime changes were animated by transformations in the realm of ideas, and in particular by distinctive conceptions of how best to represent public opinion, provide for deliberation, and secure popular compliance. At each of these regime moments, leaders of intellectual opinion determined that contemporary principles of governance were ill suited to address current demands. After considering various alternative arrangements, they reconstituted political institutions on a different foundation.

The republican regime therefore emerged out of the founding of state and national institutions in the late eighteenth and early nineteenth centuries. Republicanism understood that legislators were best capable of representing the public voice, representative assemblies were the ideal forum for deliberating about rights, and statutes were the best means of securing compliance with legal guarantees. Consequently, public officials during this period rejected the idea that rights could best be secured either through direct democratic institutions or through judicial institutions that were relatively immune from popular influence.

This understanding was then challenged by a populist regime that emerged out of deliberations in state constitutional conventions in the first two decades of the twentieth century. Populism was rooted in a belief that representative institutions were dominated by particular interests and therefore were incapable of representing the public will. Accordingly, populism understood that the public voice could best be expressed through direct democratic institutions, deliberation would ideally take place among the general public, and individuals would be most likely to comply with laws that they had initiated and approved.

Finally, in the middle of the twentieth century, a judicialist regime emerged out of a series of colloquies among federal and state judges and the faculty of the nation's law schools. Judicialism originated in a belief that representative institutions were overly susceptible to momentary ill humors and therefore were generally incapable of deliberating in the public interest. Judges were presumed to be best qualified to pronounce the public voice, the courtroom and judicial chambers were thought to provide the ideal forum for deliberation, and judicial decisions were uniquely capable of commanding popular compliance and support.

I have also shown that these regimes produced not only a distinctive set of institutional arrangements but also a particular mode of institutional behavior. There were any number of instances during these periods when legislators, judges, convention delegates, or citizens preferred a policy on its merits but refrained from taking action because to do so would have violated regime principles. Public officials were guided, therefore, not only by an understanding of their powers and their interests but also by a consideration of the proper role and behavior of their institutions. Even when these norms did not actually prevent departures from regime principles, they marked certain behavior as deviant and forced individuals to defend these actions.

Republicanism therefore understood that legislators were primarily responsible for securing rights, but it also influenced the behavior of other public officials. Although judges possessed the authority to overturn laws that violated provisions of bills of rights, they generally declined to exercise this power on the view that the protection of rights was the proper domain of the legislature. Likewise, delegates to constitutional conventions were often in a position to enact constitutional amendments that would remove rights from the legislative purview, but they ordinarily refrained from doing so in the belief that this would improperly restrain the operation of the political process.

In similar fashion, populism introduced the initiative and referendum as a means by which the people could secure rights directly, but it also influenced the behavior of a number of public officials. Convention delegates who had previously refrained from constitutional legislating now overcame this reluctance and began to protect rights by enacting constitutional provisions. Legislators still possessed the power to secure rights by enacting statutes, but in an increasing number of cases they declined to do so out of deference to direct democratic institutions. Finally, although judges occasionally assumed responsibility for protecting certain rights in this period, they also began to defer the resolution of many issues to popular institutions.

Judicialism, which was implemented almost entirely through changes in behavioral norms, influenced the actions of each of the major governing institutions. Judges, who had once consciously refrained from deciding cases on constitutional grounds in order to preserve opportunities for legislative participation, now relied almost exclusively on constitutional decisions in order to prevent them from being modified by legislative action. Legislators, although they still had the power to secure rights by enacting statutes, increasingly declined to exercise this power out of deference to the courts. Similarly, although citizens retained the formal power to regulate rights through the initiative process, they were increasingly prevented from doing so by the prevailing climate of intellectual opinion and the force of judicial decisions.

Finally, I have shown that the record of rights protection in each of these regimes can further our understanding of the capacity of various institutions to serve as guardians of rights. As we have seen, the principal theoretical debate over the last two centuries concerns the viability and desirability of entrusting rights protection to republican institutions. Throughout the nineteenth century, representative institutions were thought to be generally capable of protecting rights, but this view has been challenged in the twentieth century by those who would bypass these institutions and rely on either the collective citizenry or the judiciary. The data collected in this study permit an assessment of these claims and lead to several conclusions.

It turns out that representative institutions generally achieved a commendable level of rights protection: they prevented encroachments on existing rights, permitted the recognition of newly discovered rights, and provided a forum for deliberating over rights whose status has been contested. To be sure, these institutions occasionally fell short of securing adequate protection for rights, but these failures were confined to a particular set of cases. Legislators were frequently incapable of regulating the suffrage in a reasonable manner because they were interested in maintaining their offices. In addition, they did not always succeed in resisting momentary passions and were therefore occasionally incapable of securing civil rights and liberties in crisis times.

The principal occasions on which populist institutions provided a higher level of protection for rights than representative institutions were cases when legislators' self-interest prevented them from deliberating reasonably about rights. On the whole, however, direct democratic institutions did not secure a degree of protection for rights that was markedly higher than that achieved through representative institutions. Moreover, in periods of political and social agitation, these institutions were shown to be insufficiently deliberative and to provide inadequate security for rights.

The principal occasions on which judicialist institutions secured rights in a markedly superior manner to representative institutions were periods of social and political ferment, at which time judges, on account of their greater insulation from momentary ill humors, proved to be better positioned than legislators to protect civil rights and liberties. In general, though, there was little difference between the way that rights were protected through judicial decisions and through legislative statutes. Courts and legislatures were either partners in the protection of rights, or courts secured a level of protection that was only marginally higher or lower or slightly more or less accelerated than that achieved by legislatures. Moreover, on other occasions, judges were prevented from providing adequate security for rights because of their insulation from popular opinion or their inattentiveness to the practical effects of their decisions.

To advance these conclusions about the capacity of legislators, citizens, and judges to serve as guardians of rights is, in one sense, to exhaust the role of political science. From another perspective, though, political science can be thought to have a broader purpose. It might be concerned not only with identifying the consequences of arranging institutions in particular ways or of pursuing certain modes of institutional behavior but also with providing guidance to the officials who are responsible for maintaining these institutions. Accordingly, we would be remiss if we did not consider the implications of these findings for the individuals who are entrusted with the protection of rights.

Generally, this analysis suggests that an ideal regime of rights protection would combine the advantages of each of these institutions. Rather than viewing the protection of rights as the peculiar responsibility of any single institution, it might be considered the province of a variety of institutions.

In particular, it appears that legislators in the past assumed and lived up to their responsibility for securing rights, and it would be appropriate in the present to fortify their resolve to continue to perform this role. Although elected representatives are currently disfavored as agents of rights protection, to the point that representatives themselves are not convinced that the protection of rights falls within their domain, it was once thought that there were numerous advantages to resolving these questions through representative institutions. A reacquaintance with this tradition and an awareness of its virtues might go some way toward demonstrating that legislators, no less than other officials, are properly charged with and, in most cases, quite capable of keeping the people's liberties.

Citizens could also glean some lessons about the consequences of securing various kinds of rights through direct democratic institutions. The people might be led, in particular, to engage in further reflection about the occasions when direct democratic institutions are likely to secure rights and when they are prone to infringe on rights. Rather than viewing initiatives and referendums as either invariably hostile to the protection of rights or inherently preferable to representative institutions, this analysis suggests that direct democratic institutions can contribute to the protection of rights in a limited set of cases. As a result, citizens might do well to rely on these institutions primarily in circumstances when elected representatives are rendered incapable, by virtue of the strength of their own interests, of acting in the general welfare.

Finally, judges, who have become accustomed to relying on constitutional decision making as the primary, and even the exclusive, vehicle for protecting rights, might gain a renewed appreciation for the virtues of other institutional mechanisms for securing rights. In particular, they might be led to engage in more extensive deliberation about the circumstances when rights are likely to be best secured through statutory or common-law decisions or through constitutional decisions. Rather than routinely grounding their decisions in interpretations of constitutional provisions, judges might conclude that constitutional decision making is best employed on occasions when representative officials are prevented, by the force of momentary passions, from securing the public interest.

For political scientists to raise and seek answers to these questions is not a novel enterprise. It hearkens back to the inquiries into "Who Are the Best Keepers of the People's Liberties" that were conducted by James Madison and other members of the founding generation. Over the past two centuries, people have increasingly concluded that these questions are no longer worth asking, or at least that they have long since been resolved on the side of judicial enforcement of bills of rights. But this study has exhumed a variety of other ways in which rights have been protected, including a republican regime that possessed anchor as well as sail. In the end, something more than a reburial may be in order.

Notes

PREFACE

1. James Madison, "Who Are the Best Keepers of the People's Liberties?" *National Gazette* (December 20, 1792), in *The Papers of James Madison,* ed. Robert A. Rutland et al., 17 vols. (Chicago and Charlottesville: University of Chicago Press and University Press of Virginia, 1962–1983), 14:426.

2. Robert F. Nagel, *Constitutional Cultures: The Mentality and Consequences of Judicial Review* (Los Angeles: University of California Press, 1989), 2.

3. Ronald Dworkin, *Law's Empire* (Cambridge: Belknap Press, 1986), 356, 449 n.2. I am indebted for this reference to Daniel Lazare, *The Frozen Republic: How the Constitution is Paralyzing Democracy* (New York: Harcourt, Brace, and Co., 1996), 215.

4. Jesse H. Choper, *Judicial Review and the National Political Process: A Functional Reconsideration of the Role of the Supreme Court* (Chicago: University of Chicago Press, 1980), 65–66. Choper actually did go on to conduct a brief analysis (pp. 83–128) and then to complete an expanded study in Choper, "Consequences of Supreme Court Decisions Upholding Individual Constitutional Rights," *Michigan Law Review* 83 (1984): 1.

5. A regime refers to "the matrix of institutional relationships and fundamental values that are usually taken as the constitutional baseline in normal political life." Bruce Ackerman, *We the People: Foundations* (Cambridge: Belknap Press, 1991), 59. For similar conceptions of a regime, see David Easton, "An Approach to the Analysis of Political Systems," *World Politics* 9 (1956–1957): 391–393; Eldon J. Eisenach, *The Lost Promise of Progressivism* (Lawrence: University Press of Kansas, 1994), 19.

1. THE THEORY AND DESIGN OF REPUBLICAN INSTITUTIONS

1. Adrienne Koch, ed., *Madison's Notes on Debates in the Federal Convention of 1787* (New York: Norton, 1987), 230.

2. *West Virginia Board of Education v. Barnette,* 319 U.S. 624, 638 (1943).

3. Connecticut, Georgia, and Massachusetts did not ratify the first ten amendments until the 150th anniversary of their adoption. David E. Kyvig, *Explicit and Authentic Amending Acts: Amending the U.S. Constitution, 1776–1995* (Lawrence: University Press of Kansas, 1996), 109.

4. Eleven states ratified constitutions between 1776 and 1789, and seven of these states (Massachusetts, Maryland, New Hampshire, Pennsylvania, North Carolina, Vermont, and Virginia) approved separate declarations of rights. The drafting of these initial state constitutions is recounted in Willi Paul Adams, *The First American Constitutions: Republican Ideology and the Making of the State Constitutions in the Revolutionary Era,* trans. Rita Kimber and Robert Kimber (Chapel Hill: University of North Carolina Press, 1980), 63–98.

5. James Madison to Thomas Jefferson, May 27, 1789, in *The Papers of James Madison,* ed. Robert Rutland et al., 17 vols. (Chicago and Charlottesville: University of Chicago Press and University Press of Virginia, 1962–1983), 11: 297–299; and James Wilson, "Address to the Citizens of Philadelphia," October 7, 1787, in *Pennsylvania and the Federal Constitution, 1787–1788,* ed. John Bach McMaster and Frederick D. Stone (Philadelphia: Historical Society of Pennsylvania, 1888), 143–149.

6. Alexander Hamilton, "Federalist No. 84," in *The Federalist Papers,* ed. Clinton Rossiter (New York: Mentor, 1961), 510–520.

7. Accounts of the adoption of the federal Bill of Rights are contained in Kenneth R. Bowling, "'A Tub to the Whale': The Founding Fathers and the Adoption of the Federal Bill of Rights," *Journal of the Early Republic* 8 (1988): 223; Paul Finkelman, "James Madison and the Bill of Rights: A Reluctant Paternity," *Supreme Court Review* (1990): 301; Jack N. Rakove, "Parchment Barriers and the Politics of Rights," in *A Culture of Rights: The Bill of Rights in Philosophy, Politics, and Law—1791 and 1991,* ed. Michael J. Lacey and Knud Haakonssen (New York: Cambridge University Press, 1991), 98–143; Robert A. Goldwin, *From Parchment to Power: How James Madison Used the Bill of Rights to Save the Constitution* (Washington, DC: American Enterprise Institute Press, 1997).

8. For a discussion of the original understanding of the way in which rights would be protected, see Herbert J. Storing, "The Constitution and the Bill of Rights," in *Essays on the Constitution of the United States,* ed. M. Judd Harmon (Port Washington, NY: Kennikat Press, 1978); Lane V. Sunderland, *Popular Government and the Supreme Court: Securing the Public Good and Private Rights* (Lawrence: University Press of Kansas, 1996), 32–90.

9. Jack N. Rakove, *Original Meanings: Politics and Ideas in the Making of the Constitution* (New York: Alfred A. Knopf, 1996), 336.

The contrary position—that the members of the founding generation thought that bills of rights would be secured through judicial enforcement—is frequently advanced but ill supported. Virtually the only evidence for this proposition is a letter from Jefferson to Madison, in which he held that one argument in favor of a declaration of rights was the "legal check which it puts into the hands of the judiciary" (*Papers of James Madison,* 12: 13), as well as Madison's speech in the First Congress while introducing the bill of rights, where he noted that the judiciary would come to consider itself "in a peculiar manner the guardians of those rights" (*Papers of James Madison,* 12: 207). The only other statement of this kind of which I am aware is a comment from an anti-Federalist writer who argued during the Pennsylvania ratification debates that there would be no way to limit congressional power under the new constitution, "unless we had a bill of rights to which we might appeal, and under which we might contend against any assumption of undue power and appeal to the judicial branch of the government to protect us by their judgements" ("An Old Whig," in *The Complete Anti-Federalist,* ed. Herbert J. Storing, 7 vols. [Chicago: University of Chicago Press, 1981], 3.3.12).

There is a reason, however, why the first two quotations, especially the one from Madison, are so ubiquitous in the literature. To my knowledge, there is not a single other instance in which Madison argued that the judiciary would be expected to interpret the bill of rights nor in which any other participant in the drafting and ratification of the bill of rights thought that a bill of rights would serve this purpose.

10. *The Michigan Constitutional Conventions of 1835–1836: Debates and Proceedings,* ed. Harold M. Dorr (Ann Arbor: University of Michigan Press, 1940), 276.

11. *The Oregon Constitution and Proceedings and Debates of the Constitutional Convention of 1857,* ed. Charles H. Carey (Salem: State Printing Office, 1926), 314.

12. Ibid., 100.

13. *Report of the Proceedings and Debates in the Convention to Revise the Constitution of the State of Michigan, 1850* (Lansing: R. W. Ingals, 1850), 236.

14. The inaugural Michigan Constitution of 1835 contained a bill of rights, but it was eliminated in the Constitution of 1850, only to reappear in the Constitution of 1908. The Virginia Declaration of Rights of 1776, the Massachusetts Declaration of Rights of 1780, and the Oregon Bill of Rights of 1857 were retained throughout the century.

15. The best accounts of the purposes of the initial state bills of rights are found in Donald S. Lutz, *Popular Consent and Popular Control: Whig Political Theory in the Early State Constitutions* (Baton Rouge: Louisiana State University Press, 1980), 59–69; Robert C. Palmer, "Liberties as Constitutional Provisions: 1776–1791," in William E. Nelson and Robert C. Palmer, *Liberty and Community: Constitution and Rights in the Early American Republic* (Williamsburg, VA: Institute of Bill of Rights Law, 1987), 61–86; Mark W. Kruman, *Between Authority and Liberty: State Constitution Making in Revolutionary America* (Chapel Hill: University of North Carolina Press, 1997), 37–49.

16. Virginia Declaration of Rights (1776), s. 1, in Frances Newton Thorpe, comp. and ed., *The Federal and State Constitutions, Colonial Charters, and Other Organic Laws of the States, Territories and Colonies of the United States of America,* 7 vols. (Washington, DC: U.S. Government Printing Office, 1909), 7:3813.

17. Oregon Constitution (1857), Art. I, s. 2, in ibid., 5: 2998.

18. Michigan Constitution (1835), Art. I, s. 7, 10, 11, 12, in ibid., 4:1931.

19. *The Oregon Constitution and Proceedings and Debates of the Constitutional Convention of 1857,* 103.

20. Thomas M. Cooley, *A Treatise on the Constitutional Limitations Which Rest upon the Legislative Power of the States of the American Union* (1868; repr. New York: Da Capo Press, 1972), 176.

21. Michigan Constitution (1835), Art. I, s. 17, in Thorpe, *Federal and State Constitutions,* 4:1932.

22. Massachusetts Constitution (1780), Art. 12, in ibid., 3:1891.

23. Cooley, *Treatise on Constitutional Limitations,* 176.

24. Ibid., 177.

25. Virginia Declaration of Rights (1776), s. 12, in Thorpe, *Federal and State Constitutions,* 7:3814.

26. Oregon Constitution (1857), Art. I, s. 15, in ibid., 5:2999.

27. *The Oregon Constitution and Proceedings and Debates of the Constitutional Convention of 1857,* 101–102.

28. Massachusetts Constitution (1780), Art. 19, in ibid., 3:1892.

29. Massachusetts Constitution (1780), Art. 22, in ibid., 3:1892.

30. Oregon Constitution (1857), Art. I, s. 22, in ibid., 5:2999.

31. Oregon Constitution (1857), Art. I, s. 23, in ibid., 5:2999. See also Virginia Declaration of Rights (1776), s. 7, in ibid., 7:3813.

32. Massachusetts Constitution (1780), Art. 18, in ibid., 3:1892.

33. Massachusetts Constitution (1780), Art. 7, in ibid., 3:1890.

34. Virginia Declaration of Rights (1776), s. 16, in ibid., 7:3814.

35. Massachusetts Constitution (1780), Art. 2, in ibid., 3:1889.

36. James Kent, *Commentaries on American Law,* 4 vols. (1827; repr. New York: Da Capo Press, 1971), 2:8.

37. Gordon S. Wood, *The Creation of the American Republic: 1776–1789* (Chapel Hill: University of North Carolina Press, 1969), 452–453.

38. Ibid., 455–462.

39. Michigan Constitution (1850), Art. IV, s. 12, in Thorpe, *Federal and State Constitutions,* 4:1947.

40. Oregon Constitution (1857), Art. IV, s. 20, in ibid., 5:3004.

41. Oregon Constitution (1857), Art. IV, s. 22, in ibid.

42. Oregon Constitution (1857), Art. IV, s. 21, in ibid. For similar provisions in other state constitutions, see Michigan Constitution (1850), Art. IV, s. 20, 25, in ibid., 4:1948, 1949; Virginia Constitution (1851), Art. IV, s. 16, in ibid., 7:3840.

43. Jackson Turner Main, *The Sovereign States, 1775–1783* (New York: Franklin Watts, 1973), 152, quoted in Robert F. Williams, "State Constitutional Limits on Legislative Procedure: Legislative Compliance and Judicial Enforcement," *Publius: The Journal of Federalism* 17 (winter 1987): 91, 94 n.13.

44. Virginia Constitution (1870), Art. XII, in Thorpe, *Federal and State Constitutions,* 7:3898.

45. Massachusetts Constitution (1780), c. VI, Art. X, in ibid., 3:1911.

46. Michigan Constitution (1850), Art. XX, s. 2, in ibid., 4: 1969.

47. Robert J. Martineau, "The Mandatory Referendum on Calling a State Constitutional Convention: Enforcing the People's Right to Reform Their Government," *Ohio State Law Journal* 31 (1970): 421.

48. Virginia Constitution (1829), Art. III, s. 4, in Thorpe, *Federal and State Constitutions,* 7:3823; Oregon Constitution (1857), Art. IV, s. 5-6, in ibid., 5:3003; Michigan Constitution (1835), Art. IV, s. 3, in ibid., 4:1933.

49. Virginia Constitution (1851), Art. IV, s. 5-6, in ibid., 7:3837–3838.

50. Akhil Reed Amar, "The Bill of Rights as a Constitution," *Yale Law Journal* 100 (1991): 1131.

2. REPUBLICAN INSTITUTIONS AND THE PROTECTION OF RIGHTS

1. Francis Robert Aumann, *The Changing American Legal System: Some Selected Phases* (Columbus: Ohio State University Press, 1940), 154–194; Arthur N.

Holcombe, *State Government in the United States,* 2d ed. (New York: Macmillan, 1926), 109–126.

2. *Rice v. Foster,* 4 Del. (4 Harr.) 479, 485–486 (1847).

3. *Report of the Proceedings and Debates in the Convention to Revise the Constitution of the State of Michigan, 1850* (Lansing: R. W. Ingals, 1850), 213.

4. *Sears v. Cottrell,* 5 Mich. 251, 255 (1858).

5. Alexis de Tocqueville, *Democracy in America,* ed. J. P. Mayer, trans. George Lawrence (New York: Harper and Row, 1966), 241.

6. James Bryce, *The American Commonwealth,* 2 vols. (New York: Macmillan, 1888) 2:475.

7. *Virginia Acts of Assembly, 1785,* c. 34, s. 3.

8. *Commonwealth v. Adcock,* 49 Va. (8 Gratt.) 661, 676 (1851).

9. *Virginia Acts of Assembly, 1783,* c. 158.

10. *Acts and Resolves of Massachusetts, 1855,* c. 410; *Acts and Resolves of Massachusetts, 1862,* c. 57.

11. *Virginia Acts of Assembly, 1798–1799,* c. 9.

12. *Commonwealth v. Blanding,* 20 Mass. 304, 311 (1825).

13. *Acts and Revolves of Massachusetts, 1827,* c. 107.

14. For a discussion of the early development of judicial review in the states, see James Bradley Thayer, *Cases in Constitutional Law,* 4 vols. (Cambridge, MA: John Wilson and Son, 1894), 1:55–83; Brinton Coxe, *An Essay on Judicial Power and Unconstitutional Legislation* (Philadelphia: Kay and Brother, 1893), 219–269.

15. *Commonwealth v. Caton,* 8 Va. (4 Call) 5, 21 (1782).

16. *Holden v. James,* 11 Mass. 396 (1814). The Massachusetts Supreme Judicial Court had earlier declared an act passed by the Georgia legislature to be unconstitutional, on the ground that it violated the U.S. Constitution (*Derby v. Blake,* 226 Mass. 618 [1917]).

17. *Goddin v. Crump,* 35 Va. (8 Leigh) 120, 154 (1837).

18. The nineteenth-century conception of the judicial role in the political system has been explored through biographies of particular justices and through examinations of legal development in various states. Studies of particular justices include G. Edward White, *The American Judicial Tradition: Profiles of Leading American Judges,* exp. ed. (New York: Oxford University Press, 1988), 35–63, 109–128; Leonard W. Levy, *The Law of the Commonwealth and Chief Justice Shaw* (Cambridge: Harvard University Press, 1957); Alan R. Jones, *The Constitutional Conservatism of Thomas McIntyre Cooley: A Study in the History of Ideas* (New York: Garland Press, 1987); David M. Gold, *The Shaping of Nineteenth-Century Law: John Appleton and Responsible Individualism* (New York: Greenwood Press, 1990); John T. Horton, *James Kent: A Study in Conservatism, 1763–1847* (New York: Da Capo Press, 1969); John Phillip Reid, *Chief Justice: The Judicial World of Charles Doe* (Cambridge: Harvard University Press, 1967). Studies of particular states include Margaret V. Nelson, *A Study of Judicial Review in Virginia, 1789–1928* (New York: Columbia University Press, 1947); William E. Nelson, *Americanization of the Common Law: The Impact of Legal Change on Massachusetts Society, 1760–1830* (Cambridge: Harvard University Press, 1975).

19. To be sure, there were significant differences in the way that judges behaved at different times during the nineteenth century. For one thing, state judges exercised judicial

review relatively infrequently in the first part of the nineteenth century, and not until after the Civil War did they begin to overturn legislation on a routine basis (Charles Grove Haines, *The American Doctrine of Judicial Supremacy* [New York: Russell and Russell, 1932]). Additionally, at the beginning of the century, judicial review was considered to be a device for protecting the people from their governors, but by the second half of the century it had come to be regarded as a means of protecting the people from themselves (William E. Nelson, "Changing Conceptions of Judicial Review: The Evolution of Constitutional Theory in the States, 1790–1860," *University of Pennsylvania Law Review* 120 [1972]: 1166). It has also been shown that judicial opinions prior to 1850 were informed by an instrumental conception of law, which was subsequently replaced by a formalist view of law (Morton J. Horwitz, *The Transformation of American Law, 1780–1960* [Cambridge: Harvard University Press, 1977]). Finally, it has been argued that the first half of the nineteenth century was characterized by a jurisprudence of the head, whereas the latter half of the century saw the emergence of a jurisprudence of the heart (Peter Karsten, *Heart versus Head: Judge-Made Law in Nineteenth-Century America* [Chapel Hill: University of North Carolina Press, 1997]). These differences notwithstanding, when early- and late-nineteenth-century judges reflected on the respective roles of legislators and judges in protecting rights, they arrived at conclusions that were sufficiently similar and at the same time sufficiently distinct from the conclusions of twentieth-century judges, that it is possible to speak of a norm of nineteenth-century judicial behavior.

20. *The People v. Gallagher,* 4 Mich. 244, 266–267 (1856).

21. Ibid., 248.

22. Ibid., 255.

23. To be sure, the New York Court of Appeals (*Wynehamer v. The People*, 13 N.Y. 378 [1856]) and the Indiana Supreme Court (*Beebe v. The State*, 6 Ind. 501 [1855]) departed from this norm and overturned their states' prohibitory liquor laws. But as William J. Novak noted, "*Wynehamer* and *Beebe* remained anomalous" throughout the nineteenth century (Novak, *The People's Welfare: Law and Regulation in Nineteenth-Century America* [Chapel Hill: University of North Carolina Press, 1996], 187).

The justices on the Indiana Supreme Court conducted an extended discussion of the role of the judiciary in securing rights. Justice Samuel Perkins, writing for the majority, argued that the judiciary was properly charged with safeguarding the provisions in the bill of rights, which "were inserted in the constitution to protect the minority from the oppression of the majority, and all from the usurpation of the legislature" (6 Ind. 501, 521). Justice William Stuart responded, however, that the protection of rights "does not fall exclusively within our jurisdiction. With the rights themselves the people have also prudently retained in their own hands the means of redress. They are ever ready to vindicate them at the ballot box or by revolution, as the case may require. Among our people revolution has attained perfection. The evils or errors which afflict the body politic are intelligently investigated and traced to their source. The remedy is simple and effectual. A constitutional convention of eminent citizens is the substitute for the armed mob of other countries. If the powers hitherto delegated are too great consistently with the private rights of the citizen, they are quietly abridged. If insufficient to afford protection, they are enlarged and molded to meet the circumstances. So that revolution should begin with the people, and not with the Courts" (ibid., 526–527).

In similar fashion, Justice William Wright of the New York Court of Appeals noted in an opinion delivered a decade after *Wynehamer:* "No one, heretofore, has questioned, on constitutional grounds, the validity of such an enactment, or called upon the judiciary to declare it void, and, perhaps, would not at this time, except as emboldened by the inconsiderate *dicta* of some of the judges in the case of *Wynehamer v. The People.*" He argued: "Men are not to violate legislative enactments, and expect from courts immunity and protection instead of punishment. . . . It is the exercise of a judicial function, of the most delicate nature, to declare an act of the legislature void, and it is not to be expected that courts will assume it unless the case be plainly and clearly in derogation of constitutional limitations; nor is it to be expected that they will be zealous or astute to find grounds to thwart or defeat the legislative will, or resort to subtle or strained constructions to bring a statute into conflict with the organic law. . . . Errors or mistakes in legislation are not to be referred to the judiciary for correction, or its aid invoked, by men chafing under the restraints of particular statutes, to nullify the legislative power" (*Metropolitan Board of Excise v. Barrie,* 34 N.Y. 657, 668–669 [1866]).

24. See, for example, the comments of Virginia Court of Appeals Justice Alexander Rives: "No doubt, therefore, exists that the Assembly duly considered and decided for themselves this constitutional question, and that the passage of the law is to be taken as their judgment that there is nothing in it in conflict with the constitution of the United States or the constitution of this State. This fact truly admonishes us to the greater caution in our deliberations and the closer scrutiny in our reasonings; but it cannot exonerate us from the duty of following our convictions where, by the constitution, public interests and private rights are made to abide our independent judgments in the last resort" (*Taylor v. Stearns,* 59 Va. [18 Gratt.] 244, 270 [1868]). See also Nelson, "Changing Conceptions of Judicial Review," 1178–1185.

25. *Ratcliffe v. Anderson,* 72 Va. (31 Gratt.) 105, 107 (1878).

26. *Case of Supervisors of Election,* 114 Mass. 247, 250, 251 (1873).

27. Robert F. Williams, "State Constitutional Limits on Legislative Procedure: Legislative Compliance and Judicial Enforcement," *Publius: The Journal of Federalism* 17 (winter 1987): 91.

28. Thomas M. Cooley, *A Treatise on the Constitutional Limitations Which Rest upon the Legislative Power of the States of the American Union* (1868; repr. New York: Da Capo Press, 1972), 139.

29. *Attorney General v. Rice,* 64 Mich. 385, 388–389 (1887).

30. See Millard H. Ruud, "No Law Shall Embrace More Than One Subject," *Minnesota Law Review* 42 (1958): 389.

31. *Simpson v. Bailey,* 3 Or. 515, 517 (1869).

32. *People v. Mahaney,* 13 Mich. 481, 495 (1865).

33. Ibid.

34. *The People v. Beadle,* 60 Mich. 22, 25 (1886).

35. *In re Snyder,* 108 Mich. 48, 48 (1895).

36. Charles Chauncey Binney, *Restriction upon Local and Special Legislation in State Constitutions* (Philadelphia: Kay Brothers, 1894).

37. *Teft v. Teft,* 3 Mich. 67, 69 (1853). See Howard Gillman, *The Constitution Besieged: The Rise and Demise of Lochner Era Police Powers Jurisprudence* (Durham, NC: Duke University Press, 1993), 49–60.

38. *Chaddock v. Day,* 75 Mich. 527, 531–532 (1889).

39. Judith S. Kaye, "Foreword: The Common Law and State Constitutional Law as Full Partners in the Protection of Individual Rights," *Rutgers Law Journal* 23 (1992): 727, 728. See also Robert Force, "State 'Bills of Rights': A Case of Neglect and the Need for a Renaissance," *Valparaiso Law Review* 3 (1969): 125; G. Alan Tarr, "The Past and Future of the New Judicial Federalism," *Publius: The Journal of Federalism* 24 (spring 1994): 63.

40. *Commonwealth v. Smith*, 9 Mass. 106 (1812).

41. *Commonwealth v. Harlow*, 110 Mass. 411 (1872); *Commonwealth v. Scott*, 123 Mass. 239 (1877).

42. *The People v. Murray*, 89 Mich. 276 (1891).

43. *The People v. Jenness*, 5 Mich. 305, 319 (1858) (emphasis supplied).

44. *Vaughan v. The Commonwealth*, 58 Va. (17 Gratt.) 576, 580 (1867).

45. *Chahoon v. The Commonwealth*, 61 Va. (20 Gratt.) 733, 782 (1871).

46. *Commonwealth v. Blackington*, 41 Mass. 352, 356 (1837).

47. *Jones v. Robbins*, 74 Mass. 329, 340 (1857).

48. *Commonwealth v. Blackington*, 41 Mass. 352, 356.

49. *Opinion of the Justices*, 80 Mass. 614, 620 (1859).

50. *Ruffin v. The Commonwealth*, 62 Va. (21 Gratt.) 790, 794 (1871).

51. See Suzanna Sherry, "The Founders' Unwritten Constitution," *University of Chicago Law Review* 54 (1987): 1127, 1175.

52. *Jones v. The Commonwealth*, 5 Va. (1 Call) 557, 559 (1799).

53. *Fisher v. McGirr*, 67 Mass. 1, 28 (1854).

54. *Hibbard v. The People*, 4 Mich 125 (1856).

55. *Emery's Case*, 107 Mass. 172 (1871).

56. *Cullen v. Commonwealth*, 65 Va. (24 Gratt.) 624 (1873).

57. *Emery's Case*, 107 Mass. 172, 185.

58. *Jones v. Robbins*, 74 Mass. 329 (1857); *Nolan's Case*, 122 Mass. 330 (1877).

59. *Kinneen v. Wells*, 144 Mass. 497 (1887).

60. *Swart v. Kimball*, 43 Mich. 443, 445 (1880).

61. *Louthan v. Commonwealth*, 79 Va. 196 (1884).

62. Cooley, *Treatise on Limitations*, 168.

63. James Madison, "Federalist No. 63," in *The Federalist Papers*, ed. Clinton Rossiter (New York: Mentor, 1961), 387.

64. *The Oregon Constitution and Proceedings and Debates of the Constitutional Convention of 1857*, ed. Charles H. Carey (Salem: State Printing Office, 1926), 330.

65. *The People v. Collins*, 3 Mich. 343 (1854).

66. *Opinion of the Justices to the House of Representatives*, 160 Mass. 586 (1894).

67. Ibid., 595.

68. *People v. Collins*, 3 Mich. 343, 416.

69. *Opinion of the Justices*, 160 Mass. 586, 588–589.

70. Ibid., 589.

71. *People v. Collins*, 3 Mich. 343, 416–417.

72. Ibid., 367.

73. Ibid., 417.

74. Ibid., 368.

75. *Report of the Proceedings and Debates in the Convention to Revise the Constitution of the State of Michigan, 1850*, 186.

76. Ibid., 744.

77. Ibid., 96.

78. Ibid., 89–90.

79. Ibid., 745.

80. *Journal, Acts, and Proceedings of a General Convention of the State of Virginia, Assembled at Richmond, on Monday, the Fourteenth Day of October, Eighteen Hundred and Fifty* (Richmond: W. Culley, 1850), 60.

81. *Journal of Debates and Proceedings in the Convention of Delegates, Chosen to Revise the Constitution of Massachusetts, Begun and Holden in Boston, Nov. 15, 1820 and Continued by Adjournment to Jan. 9, 1821* (Boston: Daily Advertiser, 1853), 463.

82. Ibid., 542.

83. Ibid., 380.

84. Ibid., 419.

85. Ibid., 420.

86. Ibid., 447.

87. Ibid., 424–425.

88. Ibid., 587–588.

89. James Willard Hurst, *The Growth of American Law: The Law Makers* (Boston: Little, Brown, 1950), 246.

90. See Chilton Williamson, *American Suffrage: From Property to Democracy, 1760–1860* (Princeton, NJ: Princeton University Press, 1960), 182–207, 223–241, 260–271; Ward E. Y. Elliott, *The Rise of Guardian Democracy: The Supreme Court's Role in Voting Rights Disputes, 1845–1969* (Cambridge: Harvard University Press, 1974), 37–44; John Bach McMaster, *The Acquisition of Political, Social, and Industrial Rights of Man in America* (New York: Frederick Ungar, 1961), 77–123; James A. Henretta, "Foreword: Rethinking the State Constitutional Tradition," *Rutgers Law Journal* 22 (1991): 826–831.

91. *The Oregon Constitution and Proceedings and Debates of the Constitutional Convention of 1857,* 129.

92. Byron R. Abernethy, *Constitutional Limitations on the Legislature* (Lawrence: University of Kansas Governmental Research Center, 1959), 11–15; Hurst, *Growth of American Law*, 232–234, 237–246.

93. *Journal, Acts, and Proceedings, of a General Convention of the Commonwealth of Virginia, Assembled in Richmond, 1829* (Richmond: T. Ritchie, 1829), 523.

3. REPUBLICAN INSTITUTIONS AS KEEPERS OF THE PEOPLE'S LIBERTIES

1. Robert A. Rutland, "How the Constitution Protects Our Rights: A Look at the Seminal Years," in *How Does the Constitution Secure Rights?* ed. Robert A. Goldwin and William A. Schambra (Washington, DC: American Enterprise Institute for Public Policy Research, 1985), 12.

2. Donald S. Lutz, "Political Participation in Eighteenth-Century America," in *Toward a Usable Past: Liberty Under State Constitutions,* ed. Paul Finkelman and Stephen E. Gottlieb (Athens: University of Georgia Press, 1991), 31.

3. Lawrence M. Friedman, "State Constitutions and Criminal Justice in the Late Nineteenth Century," in ibid., 278.

4. Suzanna Sherry, "The Early Virginia Tradition of Extratextual Interpretation," in ibid., 157.

5. Ellen A. Peters, "Common Law Antecedents of Constitutional Law in Connecticut," in ibid., 191.

6. Friedman, "State Constitutions and Criminal Justice," 275.

7. Ibid. David J. Bodenhamer has argued, along the same lines: "When discussing rights of the accused, it is tempting to draw a direct line of descent from the colonial period to contemporary America. The language of rights is similar, but not its substance. Due process of law held a sharply different meaning for the seventeenth and eighteenth centuries than it does for the twentieth" (Bodenhamer, *Fair Trial: Rights of the Accused in American History* [New York: Oxford University Press, 1992], 28).

8. For petitions in favor of disestablishment, see *Virginia Legislative Petitions: Bibliography, Calendar, and Abstracts from Original Sources: 6 May 1776–21 June 1782*, comp. Randolph W. Church (Richmond: Virginia State Library, 1984), 31, 38, 43, 46, 47, 48, 49, 55, 65. For petitions supporting the existing establishment, see pp. 52, 65.

9. *Virginia Acts of Assembly, October, 1776,* c. 2.

10. Hamilton J. Eckenrode, *Separation of Church and State in Virginia* (1910; repr. New York: Da Capo Press, 1971), 53.

11. Ibid.

12. Quoted in Charles F. James, *Documentary History of the Struggle for Religious Liberty in Virginia* (1899; repr. New York: Da Capo Press, 1971), 80.

13. Quoted in ibid., 135.

14. *Virginia Acts of Assembly, October, 1785,* c. 34. See Merrill D. Peterson and Robert C. Vaughan, eds., *The Virginia Statute for Religious Freedom: Its Evolution and Consequences in American History* (New York: Cambridge University Press, 1988).

15. *Virginia Acts of Assembly, 1798–1799,* c. 9.

16. *Turpin v. Locket,* 10 Va. (6 Call) 113 (1804).

17. *Virginia Acts of Assembly, 1802,* c. 5.

18. Quoted in Margaret V. Nelson, *A Study of Judicial Review in Virginia: 1789–1928* (New York: Columbia University Press, 1947), 48. See also Eckenrode, *Separation of Church and State in Virginia,* 148–150.

19. *Turpin v. Lockett,* 10 Va. 113, 187.

20. For a discussion of the legislative role in disestablishment in Virginia, see G. MacLaren Brydon, "The Antiecclesiastical Laws of Virginia," *Virginia Magazine of History and Biography* 64 (1956): 259.

21. John D. Cushing, "Notes on Disestablishment in Massachusetts, 1780–1833," *William and Mary Quarterly* 26 (1969): 169, 182.

22. Jacob C. Meyer, *Church and State in Massachusetts from 1744 to 1833* (Cleveland: Western Reserve University, 1930), 59.

23. Ibid., 107.

24. Massachusetts Constitution (1780), Art. III, in Frances Newton Thorpe, comp. and ed., *The Federal and State Constitutions, Colonial Charters, and Other Organic Laws of the States, Territories and Colonies of the United States of America,* 7 vols. (Washington, DC: U.S. Government Printing Office), 3:1890.

25. Cushing, "Disestablishment in Massachusetts," 173.

26. *Massachusetts Acts of 1797,* c. 23.

27. *Massachusetts Acts of 1799*, c. 87.

28. *Barnes v. First Parish in Falmouth*, 6 Mass. 401, 418 (1810).

29. Ibid., 408.

30. Ibid., 405–406.

31. *Massachusetts Acts of 1811*, c. 6.

32. Cushing, "Disestablishment in Massachusetts," 186.

33. Meyer, *Church and State in Massachusetts*, 157–158.

34. *Adams v. Howe*, 14 Mass. 340, 348 (1817).

35. Ibid., 345.

36. *Massachusetts Acts of 1823*, c. 106.

37. John T. Noonan, "Quota of Imps," in Peterson and Vaughan, *Virginia Statute on Religious Freedom*, 191. For a discussion of the political battles that led to disestablishment in other states during this period, see Anson Phelps Stokes, *Church and State in the United States*, 3 vols. (New York: Harper and Brothers, 1950), 1: 358–446.

38. *Massachusetts Acts of 1775–1776*, c. 1; *Virginia Acts of Assembly, October, 1777*, c. 1; *Michigan Territory Laws, 1825*, "An Act to Organize the Militia."

39. *Massachusetts Acts of 1775–1776*, c. 1.

40. *Massachusetts Acts of May, 1793*, c. 1, s. 3.

41. *Michigan Territory Laws, 1825*, "An Act to Organize the Militia."

42. *Virginia Acts of Assembly, October, 1777*, c. 1.

43. *Massachusetts Acts of 1809*, c. 108. Likewise, Virginia in 1783 determined that an objector should produce a "testimonial" that "he is really and bona fide one of the people called quakers" (*Virginia Acts of Assembly, 1783*, c. 22).

44. *Massachusetts Acts of January, 1781*, c. 21, p. 42.

45. *Virginia Acts of Assembly, October, 1777*, c. 1.

46. *Virginia Acts of Assembly, 1861–62*, c. 25.

47. *Commonwealth v. Fletcher*, 12 Mass. 441, 442 (1815).

48. *Lees v. Childs*, 17 Mass. 351, 354 (1821).

49. In one area, religious oaths for officeholders, the right was secured through constitutional action. The Massachusetts Constitution of 1780 provided that all state officials were required to declare their belief in the Christian religion, renounce and abjure any allegiance to every other foreign power, and to declare that no foreign person, prince, or prelate should have "any jurisdiction, superiority, preeminence, authority, dispensing or other power, in any matter, civil, ecclesiastical or spiritual within this Commonwealth." Once public opinion had evolved to the point that it was seen as appropriate to repeal the second part of the clause, which excluded Catholics from serving in office, as well as the first part of the clause, which affected all non-Christians, these changes could be achieved only through constitutional action, which was taken in the Massachusetts Convention of 1820 (Robert Lord and John Sexton, *History of the Archdiocese of Boston*, 3 vols. [New York: Sheed and Ward, 1944], 1: 774–780).

50. *Virginia Acts of Assembly, May, 1779*, c. 7; *Michigan Compiled Laws, 1857*, s. 4334, 4335; *Statutes Passed by the Legislative Assembly of the Territory of Oregon, 1850*, p. 182.

51. *Massachusetts Acts of January, 1798*, c. 3.

52. *Massachusetts Acts of 1810*, c. 127.

53. *Commonwealth v. Smith*, 9 Mass. 107, 112 (1812).

54. *Massachusetts Acts of 1824*, c. 91.

55. *The Portable Thomas Jefferson*, ed. Merrill Peterson (New York: Penguin Books, 1975), 210.

56. *Perry v. The Commonwealth*, 44 Va. (3 Gratt.) 632, 638 (1846).

57. In 1779 the Virginia General Assembly directed that individuals reluctant to take the required oath could still be "deemed as competent a witness" (*Virginia Acts of Assembly, May, 1779*, c. 7). The Massachusetts General Court passed such an act in 1825 (*Massachusetts Acts of 1824*, c. 91). The Michigan Legislature stipulated in 1842 that "[n]o person shall be deemed incompetent as a witness . . . on account of his opinions on the subject of religion" (*Public Acts of Michigan, 1842*, no. 18). The Oregon Territorial Legislature provided in 1853 that no person could be "disqualified from being a witness on account of the want of religious belief" (*Oregon Territory Laws, 1853*, p. 111).

58. In 1842 the Michigan Legislature provided that no witness could be "questioned in relation to his opinions" on the matter of religion (*Michigan Laws of 1842*, no. 18). Accordingly, the Michigan Supreme Court applied the statute in an 1858 case to prohibit a subject from being questioned at any point on her religious views. "We think, therefore, it was clearly the intention of the legislature to prevent the first step, and every subsequent step, in all inquiries of this kind" (*The People v. Jenness*, 5 Mich. 318, 319 [1858]). When called to decide this question, the Virginia Court of Appeals noted that although the common law had permitted such questions, this had been "wholly abrogated by our Bill of Rights, and the act for securing religious freedom" (*Perry v. The Commonwealth*, 44 Va. 632, 611). In similar fashion, the Massachusetts court noted that one was "not to be questioned as to his religious belief" (*Commonwealth v. Smith*, 68 Mass. 516, 516 [1854]).

59. *Thurston v. Whitney*, 56 Mass. 104, 110 (1848).

60. Lord and Sexton, *History of the Archdiocese of Boston*, 2: 583–584.

61. *Virginia Acts of Assembly, 1839*, c. 12, s. 7; *Virginia Acts of Assembly, 1849–50*, c. 192, s. 9. See Sadie Bell, *The Church, the State, and Education in Virginia* (Philadelphia: Science Press, 1930), 344–365.

62. *Michigan Compiled Laws, 1897*, par. 4676.

63. Samuel T. Spear, "The Bible and the Public School," *Princeton Review* 54 (1878): 361.

64. *Massachusetts Acts of 1827*, c. 143, s. 7.

65. *Massachusetts Acts of 1855*, c. 410.

66. Lord and Sexton, *The Archdiocese of Boston*, 2: 589–600.

67. Ibid., 601.

68. *Massachusetts Acts of 1862*, c. 57.

69. Quoted in Lord and Sexton, *The Archdiocese of Boston*, 2: 604–605.

70. *Massachusetts Acts of 1880*, c. 176.

71. *Virginia Acts of Assembly, 1846–47*, c. 33, s. 5. See Bell, *The Church, the State, and Education in Virginia*, 356–357.

72. Bell, *The Church, the State, and Education in Virginia*, 426.

73. *Spiller v. Woburn*, 94 Mass. 127, 127 (1866).

74. Ibid., 129–130.

75. *Pfeiffer v. Board of Education of Detroit*, 118 Mich. 560, 562, 569 (1898). Although this aspect of the right to worship was secured in these states through legislation rather than adjudication, it should be noted that in several other states around the

country, Ohio and Wisconsin in particular, this right was secured through constitutional decisions delivered by state supreme courts. See Samuel W. Brown, *The Secularization of American Education as Shown by State Legislation, State Constitutional Provisions, and State Supreme Court Decisions* (New York: Columbia University, 1912), 144–146.

76. Lord and Sexton, *The Archdiocese of Boston*, 2:586.

77. Quoted in ibid., 2:586–587.

78. Ibid., 3:129–130.

79. *Massachusetts Acts of 1889*, c. 464. See Sister Raymond McLaughlin, *A History of State Legislation Affecting Private Elementary and Secondary Schools in the United States, 1870–1945* (Washington, DC: Catholic University of America Press, 1946), 69–72.

80. Lord and Sexton, *The Archdiocese of Boston*, 3:132.

81. *American State Papers Bearing on Sunday Legislation*, ed. William Addison Blakely (Washington, DC: Religious Liberty Association, 1911), 328–329.

82. Ibid., 335.

83. *Massachusetts General Statutes of 1860*, c. 84, s. 9. See also *Michigan Compiled Laws of 1857*, par. 1580; *Virginia Code of 1908*, s. 3800.

84. *Public Acts of Michigan, 1861*, no. 117.

85. *Public Acts of Michigan, 1893*, no. 148.

86. *The People v. Bellet*, 99 Mich. 151, 155 (1894).

87. *Commonwealth v. Has*, 122 Mass. 40, 41 (1877).

88. *Commonwealth v. Starr*, 144 Mass. 359 (1887).

89. Lord and Sexton, *The Archdiocese of Boston*, 1:564–566.

90. In Virginia, exemptions were made for Quakers and Mennonites (*Virginia Acts of Assembly, October, 1780*, c. 16) and for all Christian dissenters (*Virginia Acts of Assembly, October, 1784*, c. 76). In Massachusetts, exemptions were made for Quakers (*Massachusetts Acts of 1834*, c. 177, s. 6) and for Jews (*Massachusetts Acts of 1893*, c. 361). In Michigan, exemptions were made for Quakers and for all other dissenters (*Michigan Compiled Laws of 1857*, c. 107, s. 17). In Oregon, exemptions were made in 1845 for all denominations (*Oregon Territory Laws, 1843–1849*, p. 36).

91. *Virginia Acts of Assembly, October, 1784*, c. 76, s. 3. For a discussion of the memorials, see Church, *Virginia Legislative Petitions*, 323; James, *Documentary History of the Struggle for Religious Liberty in Virginia*, 118–120.

92. Lord and Sexton, *The Archdiocese of Boston*, 3:71.

93. *Public Acts of Michigan, 1859*, no. 185.

94. *Massachusetts Acts of 1875*, c. 126.

95. *Massachusetts Acts of 1879*, c. 158.

96. See generally Leonard W. Levy, *Blasphemy: Verbal Offense Against the Sacred* (New York: Alfred A. Knopf, 1993).

97. *Massachusetts Acts of April, 1782*, c. 9.

98. *Commonwealth v. Kneeland*, 37 Mass. 206 (1838).

99. Leonard W. Levy, ed. *Blasphemy in Massachusetts: Freedom of Conscience and the Abner Kneeland Case* (New York: Da Capo Press, 1973).

100. See Leonard W. Levy, *Legacy of Suppression: Freedom of Speech and Press in Early American History* (Cambridge: Belknap Press, 1960); Leonard W. Levy, *Emergence of a Free Press* (New York: Oxford University Press, 1985).

101. Levy, *Emergence of a Free Press*, 3.

102. For a review of the issues that did arise in the nineteenth century, see Margaret A. Blanchard, "Filling in the Void: Speech and Press in State Courts Prior to *Gitlow*," in *The First Amendment Reconsidered: New Perspectives on the Meaning of Speech and Press*, ed. Bill F. Chamberlin and Charlene J. Brown (New York: Longman, 1982); David M. Rabban, *Free Speech in Its Forgotten Years* (New York: Cambridge University Press, 1997).

103. *Virginia Acts of Assembly, 1798–1799*, c. 11.

104. Clement Eaton, "Censorship of the Southern Mails," *American Historical Review* 48 (1942): 266, 267.

105. *Virginia Acts of Assembly, 1835–36*, c. 66, s. 3. See generally Russell B. Nye, *Fettered Freedom: Civil Liberties and the Slavery Controversy, 1830–1860* (Lansing: University of Michigan State Press, 1963).

106. For an account of this episode, see William E. Nelson, *Americanization of the Common Law: The Impact of Legal Change on Massachusetts Society, 1760–1830* (Cambridge: Harvard University Press, 1975), 94–95; Norman L. Rosenberg, *Protecting the Best Men: An Interpretive History of the Law of Libel* (Chapel Hill: University of North Carolina Press, 1986), 115–116, 118–120.

107. *Commonwealth v. Clap*, 4 Mass. 163 (1808).

108. *Commonwealth v. Blanding*, 20 Mass. 304, 311 (1825).

109. Ibid., 312.

110. *Massachusetts Acts of 1827*, c. 107.

111. *Oregon Code of Criminal Procedure, 1864*, c. 22, s. 708.

112. Jay A. Sigler, *Double Jeopardy: The Development of a Legal and Social Policy* (Ithaca, NY: Cornell University Press, 1969), 77.

113. *Massachusetts Revised Statutes*, c. 123, s. 4, 5.

114. *Virginia Acts of Assembly, 1847–48*, c. 120, t. 1, c. 11, s. 10, 11.

115. *Michigan Compiled Laws, 1871*, c. 242, s. 7505.

116. *Oregon Code of Criminal Procedure, 1864*, c. 12, s. 138, 139, 140.

117. Sigler, *Double Jeopardy*, 80.

118. *Oregon Code of Criminal Procedure, 1864*, c. 22, s. 214.

119. *Michigan Public Acts, 1875*, No. 99.

120. *Edwards v. The People*, 39 Mich. 760, 761 (1878).

121. *The People v. Thomas*, 9 Mich. 314, 320–321 (1861).

122. Leonard W. Levy, "The Right Against Self-Incrimination: History and Judicial History," *Political Science Quarterly* 84 (1969): 1, 18; David M. Gold, *The Shaping of Nineteenth-Century Law: John Appleton and Responsible Individualism* (New York: Greenwood Press, 1990), 57–71.

123. *Public Acts of Michigan, 1861*, No. 125, s. 2.

124. *Massachusetts Acts of 1866*, c. 260; *Massachusetts Acts of 1870*, c. 393, s. 1.

125. *Virginia Acts of Assembly, 1871–72*, c. 350.

126. *Virginia Acts of Assembly, 1881–82*, c. 228.

127. *Virginia Acts of Assembly, 1885–86*, c. 39.

128. See *Ferguson v. Georgia*, 365 U.S. 570, 577 (1960), for a list of the dates of enactment of these statutes.

129. Joel Bodansky, "The Abolition of the Party-Witness Disqualification: An Historical Survey," *Kentucky Law Journal* 70 (1981): 91.

130. *Virginia Acts of Assembly, 1885–86*, c. 39.

131. *Massachusetts Acts of 1866*, c. 260; *Massachusetts Acts of 1870*, c. 393, s. 1.

132. *Commonwealth v. Scott*, 123 Mass. 239, 240–241 (1877).

133. *People v. Williams*, 225 Mich. 133, 137 (1923).

134. *Oregon Code of Criminal Procedure, 1864*, c. 37, s. 379, 380, 381.

135. *Massachusetts Acts of 1820*, c. 14, s. 8.

136. *Massachusetts Acts of 1877*, c. 184.

137. William M. Beaney, *The Right to Counsel in American Courts* (Ann Arbor: University of Michigan Press, 1955), 84–85.

138. *Bacon v. Wayne*, 1 Mich. 461 (1850).

139. *Public Acts of Michigan, 1857*, no. 109. The Massachusetts General Court enacted a similar law in 1893 (*Massachusetts Acts of 1893*, c. 394).

140. *Conant v. Burnham*, 133 Mass. 503, 506 (1882).

141. Beaney, *Right to Counsel*, 84. For a list of the state statutes on the subject, see pp. 84–87.

142. *Howell's (Michigan) Statutes, 1846*, s. 7244.

143. *The People v. Murray*, 89 Mich. 276, 286 (1891).

144. *Virginia Acts of Assembly, 1814*, c. 74, s. 10.

145. *Virginia Acts of Assembly, 1847–48*, c. 20, s. 12. The law was further amended in 1871 (*Virginia Acts of Assembly, 1871–72*, c. 236).

146. *Brown v. Epps*, 91 Va. 726, 733 (1895).

147. Akhil Reed Amar, *The Constitution and Criminal Procedure: First Principles* (New Haven, CT: Yale University Press, 1997), 11.

148. Telford Taylor, *Two Studies in Constitutional Interpretation* (Columbus: Ohio State University Press, 1969), 41.

149. See, for example, *Massachusetts Revised Statutes of 1835*, c. 142, s. 3.

150. *Virginia Acts of Assembly, 1847–48*, c. 25, s. 3.

151. *Oregon Code of Criminal Procedure, 1864*, c. 41, s. 472, 473.

152. Bradford P. Wilson, *Enforcing the Fourth Amendment* (New York: Garland Press, 1986), 14–16, 31–33.

153. Amar, *The Constitution and Criminal Procedure*, 21.

154. *Commonwealth v. Dana*, 43 Mass. 329, 337 (1841).

155. *Fischer v. McGirr*, 67 Mass. 1, 29–31 (1854).

156. *Hibbard v. The People*, 4 Mich. 125, 128 (1856).

157. *Massachusetts Acts of 1855*, c. 215; *Public Acts of Michigan, 1857*, no. 172.

158. *Massachusetts Acts of 1869*, c. 415, s. 44, 45, 46.

159. *Commonwealth v. Intoxicating Liquors*, 109 Mass. 371, 372 (1872).

160. *The Michigan Constitutional Conventions of 1835–36: Debates and Proceedings*, ed. Harold M. Dorr (Ann Arbor: University of Michigan Press, 1940), 157, 158–159.

161. The precise extent to which the initial constitutions secured these conventional rights differed dramatically from state to state. Prior to the Civil War, Virginia did not even secure all persons in their natural rights, as demonstrated by the continued enslavement of African Americans. Oregon did not initially recognize a right for African Americans, Chinese, or mulattos to vote; nor did it recognize a right for immigrant blacks or mulattos to own land or bring suit, nor the right of Chinese immigrants to either hold land or work in mines. Michigan declined to provide for Negro suffrage.

162. Lawrence M. Friedman, *Total Justice* (New York: Russell Sage Foundation, 1985), 107–121.

163. Quoted in J. Morgan Kousser, "'The Supremacy of Equal Rights': The Struggle Against Racial Discrimination in Antebellum Massachusetts and the Foundations of the Fourteenth Amendment," *Northwestern Law Review* 82 (1988): 941, 953 n. 61.

164. *Massachusetts Acts of 1843,* c. 5.

165. *Public Acts of Michigan, 1883,* no. 23. In Virginia and Oregon, the right was not secured until the middle of the twentieth century. For a list of the states that secured this right through statute, see Cyrus E. Phillips IV, "Miscegenation: The Courts and the Constitution," *William and Mary Law Review* 8 (1966): 133 n.2.

166. Legislative deliberation also led some states to deny the right. For instance, in an 1870 law that established the state public school system, Virginia stipulated that blacks and whites should be educated separately (*Virginia Acts of Assembly, 1869–1870,* c. 259, s. 47).

167. Kousser, "Supremacy of Equal Rights," 960–962.

168. Quoted in ibid., 967.

169. Leonard W. Levy and Douglas L. Jones, eds., *Jim Crow in Boston: The Origin of the Separate but Equal Doctrine* (New York: Da Capo Press, 1974), 206.

170. *Roberts v. Boston,* 59 Mass. 198, 206–207 (1849).

171. Ibid., 207, 209.

172. Kousser, "Supremacy of Equal Rights," 989.

173. *Massachusetts Acts of 1855,* c. 256.

174. Levy and Jones, *Jim Crow in Boston,* 272.

175. Ibid., 278–279.

176. *Public Acts of Michigan, 1842,* no. 70, s. 1.

177. *The People v. Board of Education of Detroit,* 18 Mich. 400, 411 (1869).

178. *Public Acts of Michigan, 1867,* no. 34, s. 28.

179. *People v. Board of Education,* 18 Mich. 400, 409.

180. They did succeed, however, in persuading all Massachusetts railroads to voluntarily end segregated railcars in 1844 (Kousser, "Supremacy of Equal Rights," 954–957).

181. *Day v. Owen,* 5 Mich. 520 (1858).

182. *Massachusetts Acts of 1865,* c. 277.

183. *Massachusetts Acts of 1866,* c. 252.

184. *Massachusetts Acts of 1885,* c. 316.

185. *Massachusetts Acts of 1893,* c. 436.

186. *Massachusetts Acts of 1895,* c. 461. See Richard Bardolph, ed., *The Civil Rights Record: Black Americans and the Law, 1849–1970* (New York: Thomas Y. Crowell, 1970), 129.

187. *Massachusetts Acts of 1896,* pp. 659–660.

188. *Public Acts of Michigan, 1885,* no. 130.

189. Francis H. Fox, "Discrimination and Antidiscrimination in Massachusetts Law," *Boston University Law Review* 44 (1964): 30, 77, 78.

190. *Massachusetts Acts of 1844,* c. 268, s. 5. Mississippi enacted the first such law in 1839. See Norma Basch, *In the Eyes of the Law: Women, Marriage, and Property in Nineteenth-Century New York* (Ithaca, NY: Cornell University Press, 1982), 136–161.

191. *Oregon Laws, 1880,* p. 6.

192. *Oregon Laws, 1885 (Special Session)*, p. 5; *Michigan Compiled Laws, 1897*, s. 1121.

193. *Lelia J. Robinson's Case*, 131 Mass. 376, 384 (1881).

194. *Massachusetts Acts of 1882*, c. 139. See Douglas Lamar Jones, "*Lelia J. Robinson's Case* and the Entry of Women into the Legal Profession in Massachusetts," in *The History of the Law in Massachusetts: The Supreme Judicial Court, 1692–1992*, ed. Russell Osgood (Boston: Supreme Judicial Court Historical Society, 1992), 241–274.

195. *Massachusetts Acts of 1883*, c. 252.

196. *Massachusetts Acts of 1874*, c. 389.

197. *Oregon General Laws, 1893*, S.B. 78.

198. *Opinion of the Justices*, 115 Mass. 602 (1874).

199. *State v. Stevens*, 29 Or. 464, 473 (1896). The Michigan Supreme Court determined, on the basis of similar reasoning, that women could not serve as prosecuting attorneys, although in this case the court did not overturn a statute; rather, it declined to extend the right in the absence of enabling legislation (*Attorney General v. Abbott*, 121 Mich. 540 [1899]).

200. *Public Acts of Michigan, 1867*, no. 110, s. 1 (see *Belles v. Burr*, 76 Mich. 1, 9 [1889]); *Massachusetts Acts of 1879*, c. 223. See Robert J. Dinkin, *Before Equal Suffrage: Women in Partisan Politics from Colonial Times to 1920* (Westport, CT: Greenwood Press, 1995), 101–102; Eleanor Flexner, *Century of Struggle: The Women's Rights Movement in the United States* (Cambridge, MA: Belknap Press, 1959), 180–181.

201. *Public Acts of Michigan, 1893*, no. 138

202. *Coffin v. Election Commissioners*, 97 Mich. 188 (1893).

203. *Public Acts of Michigan, 1841*, no. 54.

204. *Virginia Acts of Assembly, 1867 (Extra Session)*, c. 118, ch. ccxi, s. 1.

205. *Massachusetts Acts of 1859*, c. 266; *Massachusetts Acts of 1862*, c. 184; *Massachusetts Acts of 1869*, c. 463.

206. *Oregon Laws of 1872*, p. 10.

207. *Oregon Laws of 1891*, p. 42; *Massachusetts Acts of 1852*, c. 154.

4. THE THEORY AND DESIGN OF POPULIST INSTITUTIONS

1. The choice of the term *populism* requires some explanation. It does not refer to the Populist movement that emerged in the last several decades of the nineteenth century. Rather, it refers to the strain of the Progressive movement that sought to implement more democratic institutions in the first two decades of the twentieth century. Although in one sense a case can be made for labeling this the progressive regime, in the end it is more helpful to characterize it as the populist regime, because this provides a more accurate description of the intellectual impetus behind these reforms.

2. General accounts of the social and economic changes in the Progressive era include Richard Hofstadter, *The Age of Reform: From Bryan to FDR* (New York: Alfred A. Knopf, 1955); Robert H. Wiebe, *The Search for Order: 1877–1920* (New York: Hill and Wang, 1967); Eldon J. Eisenach, *The Lost Promise of Progressivism* (Lawrence: University Press of Kansas, 1994).

3. J. Allen Smith, *The Spirit of American Government* (New York: Macmillan, 1907), 291.

4. Walter Weyl, *The New Democracy: An Essay on Certain Political and Economic Tendencies in the United States* (New York: Macmillan, 1912), 162.

5. James Q. Dealey, *The Growth of American State Constitutions from 1776 Until the End of the Year 1914* (New York: Ginn and Co., 1915), 126.

6. Arthur N. Holcombe, *State Government in the United States* (New York: Macmillan, 1916), 435.

7. *Debates in the Massachusetts Constitutional Convention, 1917–18* (Boston: Wright and Potter Printing Co., 1919), 2:45. See also Sylvester Baxter, "Legislative Degeneracy in Massachusetts," *Arena* 2 (September 1890): 503.

8. *Proceedings and Debates of the Constitutional Convention of the State of Michigan, 1907–1908* (Lansing: Wynkoop, Hallenbeck, Crawford Co., 1908), 592.

9. Emmet O'Neal, "Distrust of State Legislatures—The Cause; the Remedy," *North American Review* 199 (May 1914): 684, 685, 693.

10. Charles Beard and Birl Schultz, eds., *Documents on the State-Wide Initiative, Referendum and Recall* (New York: Macmillan, 1912), 9.

11. James Q. Dealey, *Our State Constitutions* (Philadelphia: American Academy of Political and Social Science, 1907), 1.

12. See George W. Alger, "The Courts and Legislative Freedom," *Atlantic Monthly* 111 (March 1913): 345; Gilbert E. Roe, *Our Judicial Oligarchy* (New York: B. W. Huebsch, 1912); William G. Ross, *A Muted Fury: Populists, Progressives, and Labor Unions Confront the Courts, 1890–1937* (Princeton, NJ: Princeton University Press, 1994), 23–69.

13. William E. Forbath, *Law and the Shaping of the Modern Labor Movement* (Cambridge: Harvard University Press, 1991), 37–97.

14. *Massachusetts Convention of 1917–1918*, 1:478–479, 480.

15. Louis B. Boudin, "Government by Judiciary," *Political Science Quarterly* 26 (1911): 238, 264.

16. Frederick Judson, "The Future of Representative Government," *American Political Science Review* 2 (1908): 185, 192.

17. Benjamin Parke De Witt, *The Progressive Movement: A Non-partisan, Comprehensive Discussion of Current Tendencies in American Politics* (New York: Macmillan, 1915), 15–24.

18. Woodrow Wilson, "Letter to Heath Dabney," and "An Interview," in *The Papers of Woodrow Wilson*, ed. Arthur S. Link (Princeton, NJ: Princeton University Press, 1966–1992), 23:451, 369.

19. *Proceedings and Debates of the Constitutional Convention of the State of Ohio, 1912* (Columbus: F. J. Heer Printing Co., 1912), 1: 378, 379.

20. *Equity* 14 (October 1912): 123, 124.

21. *Ohio Convention of 1912*, 1: 544.

22. Quoted in ibid., 2: 1132.

23. Smith, *Spirit of American Government*, 296.

24. Weyl, *New Democracy*, 13. For discussions of these efforts to reform national institutions, see James W. Ceaser, *Presidential Selection: Theory and Development* (Princeton, NJ: Princeton University Press, 1979); Jeffrey K. Tulis, *The Rhetorical Presidency* (Princeton, NJ: Princeton University Press, 1987); Stephen Skowronek, *Building a New American State: The Expansion of National Administrative Capabilities, 1877–1920* (New York: Cambridge University Press, 1982).

25. Smith, *Spirit of American Government,* 357.

26. Ibid., 353–355.

27. Amasa M. Eaton, "Recent State Constitutions," *Harvard Law Review* 6 (1892): 109.

28. Ibid., 121.

29. See, for instance, the extended debate in the Virginia Convention of 1901–1902 over whether to limit the legislature to quadrennial sessions (*Report of the Proceedings and Debates of the Constitutional Convention, State of Virginia, 1901–1902* [Richmond: Hermitage Press, 1906], 1:459–615).

30. See, for instance, *Massachusetts Convention of 1917–1918,* 1:453–454.

31. See William L. Ransom, *Majority Rule and the Judiciary: An Examination of Current Proposals for Constitutional Change Affecting the Relations of Courts to Legislation* (New York: Scribner's Sons, 1912); Roe, *Our Judicial Oligarchy,* 189–226; Ross, *Muted Fury,* 110–154, 193–232; John G. Palfrey, "The Constitution and the Courts," *Harvard Law Review* 26 (1913): 507.

32. *Massachusetts Convention of 1917–1918,* 1: 462.

33. Ibid., 1: 464.

34. See George M. Mowry, *The California Progressives* (Los Angeles: University of California Press, 1951); Richard Coke Lower, *A Bloc of One: The Political Career of Hiram W. Johnson* (Palo Alto, CA: Stanford University Press, 1993); Tom Sitton, *John Randolph Haynes: California Progressive* (Palo Alto, CA: Stanford University Press, 1992).

35. Tony Howard Evans, "Oregon Progressive Reform, 1902–1914" (Ph.D. dissertation, University of California, Berkeley, 1966), 58; David Schuman, "The Origin of State Constitutional Direct Democracy: William Simon U'Ren and 'The Oregon System,'" *Temple Law Review* 67 (1994): 947, 950.

36. William S. U'Ren, "Report of Single Tax Conference," quoted in James D. Barnett, *The Operation of the Initiative, Referendum, and Recall in Oregon* (New York: Macmillan, 1915), 4 n.1.

37. David D. Schmidt, *Citizen Lawmakers: The Ballot Initiative Revolution* (Philadelphia: Temple University Press, 1989), 261–266.

38. Barnett, *Operation of the Initiative, Referendum, and Recall in Oregon,* 17; William S. U'Ren, "The Operation of the Initiative and Referendum in Oregon," *Arena* 32 (1904): 128; R. T. Paine, "Lincoln's Ideal Carried Out in Oregon," *Arena* 40 (1908): 283; Joseph Stephens, "U'Ren the Law Giver: The Legislative Blacksmith of Oregon and the Tools He Has Fashioned for Democracy," *American Magazine* 65 (1908): 527; Burton J. Hendrick, "The Initiative and Referendum and How Oregon Got Them," *McClure's* 37 (July 1911): 234.

39. *Michigan Convention of 1907–1908,* 554.

40. Ibid., 322.

41. Helen Combs Genung, "The Initiative and Referendum in Michigan" (master's thesis, Wayne State University, 1940), 21–24.

42. *Massachusetts Convention of 1917–1918,* 1:4.

43. *Virginia Convention of 1901–1902,* 1:152.

44. Schmidt, *Citizen Lawmakers,* 271.

45. Wythe Holt, "Constitutional Revision in Virginia, 1902 and 1928: Some Lessons

on Roadblocks to Institutional Reform," in *State Constitutional Revision*, ed. A. E. Dick Howard (Charlottesville: Virginia Law Review Association, 1968), 96.

46. Eisenach, *The Lost Promise of Progressivism*, 19.

47. *Massachusetts Convention of 1917–1918*, 2:235–236 (emphasis supplied).

48. *Michigan Convention of 1907–1908*, 572.

49. *Massachusetts Convention of 1917–1918*, 2:140.

50. Ibid., 38.

51. Ibid., 421.

52. Ibid., 3:377, 379.

53. Ibid., 2:947.

54. Ibid., 76.

55. *Michigan Convention of 1907–1908*, 566.

56. Jonathan Bourne, Jr., "Initiative, Referendum, and Recall," *Atlantic Monthly* 109 (January 1912): 122, 123.

57. *Massachusetts Convention of 1917–1918*, 2:655–656.

58. *Michigan Convention of 1907–1908*, 613.

59. *Massachusetts Convention of 1917–1918*, 2:610–611.

60. Ibid., 407.

61. Ibid., 796.

62. Ibid., 26.

63. Ibid., 532.

64. Ibid., 167, quoting John Randolph Haynes.

65. Ibid., 268.

66. *Michigan Convention of 1907–1908*, 597.

67. Ibid., 674.

68. Herbert Croly, *Progressive Democracy* (New York: Macmillan, 1914), 264–265.

69. *Michigan Convention of 1907–1908*, 591.

70. Ibid., 603.

71. Quoted in *Massachusetts Convention of 1917–1918*, 2:839.

72. "Minority Report on the Initiative and Referendum," ibid., 2:12.

73. *Michigan Convention of 1907–1908*, 548.

74. *Massachusetts Convention of 1917–1918*, 2:12.

75. Ibid., 55.

76. *Michigan Convention of 1907–1908*, 558.

77. Elihu Root, "Experiments in Government and the Essentials of the Constitution," in Elihu Root, *Addresses on Government and Citizenship* (Cambridge: Harvard University Press, 1916), 95.

78. Bourne, "Initiative, Referendum, and Recall," 127.

79. *Michigan Convention of 1907–1908*, 603.

80. *Massachusetts Convention of 1917–1918*, 3:967.

81. Ibid., 2:27.

82. Ibid.

83. *Ohio Convention of 1912*, 2:1883

84. Ibid.

85. Ibid.

86. Ibid.

5. POPULIST INSTITUTIONS AND THE PROTECTION OF RIGHTS

1. Herbert Croly, *Progressive Democracy* (New York: Macmillan, 1914), 254–255.

2. Quoted in James D. Barnett, *Operation of the Initiative, Referendum, and Recall in Oregon* (New York: Macmillan, 1915), 168.

3. *Massachusetts Laws of 1921,* c. 438.

4. *Massachusetts Laws of 1923,* pp. 610–613.

5. *Oregon Laws, 1911,* c. 3.

6. *Oregon Laws, 1913,* p. 7.

7. James Q. Dealey, *The Growth of American State Constitutions* (New York: Ginn and Co., 1915), 269.

8. *Proceedings and Debates of the Constitutional Convention of the State of Michigan, 1907–1908* (Lansing: Wynkoop, Hallenbeck, Crawford Co., 1908), 83.

9. Ibid., 390.

10. *Report on the Proceedings and Debates of the Constitutional Convention, State of Virginia, 1901–1902* (Richmond: Hermitage Press, 1906), 2:2248.

11. Frances Newton Thorpe, "Recent Constitution-Making in the United States," *Annals of the American Academy of Political and Social Sciences* 2 (1891): 145, 161.

12. Ellis Oberholtzer, "Law-Making by Popular Vote," *Annals of the American Academy of Political and Social Sciences* 2 (1891): 324, 333.

13. Ellis Oberholtzer, *The Referendum in America* (New York: Scribner's Sons, 1911), 96, 97.

14. Charles Beard and Birl Schultz, eds., *Documents on the State-Wide Initiative, Referendum, and Recall* (New York: Macmillan 1912), 4.

15. Arthur N. Holcombe, *State Government in the United States,* 2d ed. (New York: Macmillan, 1926), 475, 476. See also John Alexander Jameson, *A Treatise on Constitutional Conventions,* 4th ed. (Chicago: Callaghan and Co., 1887), 561; James Bryce, *The American Commonwealth* (New York: Macmillan, 1888), 1:475.

16. *Michigan Convention of 1907–1908,* 398.

17. *Debates in the Massachusetts Constitutional Convention, 1917–1918* (Boston: Wright and Potter, 1919), 3:543–618, 674–740. It should be noted that in some cases these measures were proposed for the purpose of restricting courts rather than legislatures. According to Walter Dodd: "A large and important series of provisions now found in state constitutions has been inserted into these constitutions, not for the purpose of limiting state legislative power, but for the direct and express purpose of relieving state legislative power from broad constitutional restrictions as construed by the courts" (Dodd, *State Government* [New York: Century Co., 1922], 144).

18. See *Michigan Convention of 1907–1908,* 154–155; *Massachusetts Convention of 1917–1918,* 1:44–230; *Virginia Convention of 1901–1902,* 796–818.

19. The Massachusetts Convention amended the constitution to prohibit the appropriation of public funds to any private "college, infirmary, hospital, institution, or educational, charitable, or religious undertaking" (*Massachusetts Convention of 1917–1918,* 1:49). Virginia prohibited appropriations to any "church, or sectarian society, association, or institution of any kind whatever, which is entirely or partly, directly or indirectly, controlled by any church or sectarian society" (*Virginia Convention of 1901–1902,* 1:818).

20. *Massachusetts Convention of 1917–1918,* 1:133.

21. Ibid., 109.

22. Ibid., 79.

23. *Virginia Convention of 1901–1902*, 1:801.

24. Dealey, *Growth of American State Constitutions*, 182.

25. Frank Parsons, *The City for the People* (Philadelphia: C. F. Taylor, 1901), 375–376.

26. Allen H. Eaton, *The Oregon System: The Story of Direct Legislation in Oregon* (Chicago: McClurg and Co., 1912), 116–117.

27. Gilbert Hedges, *Where the People Rule* (San Francisco: Bender-Moss, 1914), 113.

28. *Kalich v. Knapp*, 73 Or. 558, 582 (1914).

29. *Massachusetts Acts of 1911*, c. 328; *Massachusetts Acts of 1928*, c. 234.

30. *Massachusetts Acts of 1904*, c. 363; *Massachusetts Acts of 1935*, c. 193.

31. *Durham Bros. v. Woodson*, 155 Va. 93, 101 (1930).

32. *Virginia Acts of Assembly, 1920*, c. 345.

33. See *Massachusetts Acts of 1900*, c. 378; *Massachusetts Acts of 1908*, c. 645; *Massachusetts Acts of 1911*, c. 484; *Massachusetts Acts of 1917*, c. 294.

34. Samuel Warren and Louis D. Brandeis, "The Right to Privacy," *Harvard Law Review* 4 (1890): 193.

35. *Atkinson v. Doherty*, 121 Mich. 372, 375 (1899).

36. Ibid., 383–384.

37. *Virginia Acts of Assembly, 1904*, c. 66. See William L. Prosser, *Handbook of the Law of Torts*, 4th ed. (St. Paul: West Publishing Co., 1971), 802–805.

38. *Feek v. Township Board*, 82 Mich. 393, 418, 417 (1890).

39. Ibid., 394–416.

40. *Virginia Acts of Assembly, 1914*, c. 15; *Virginia Acts of Assembly, 1916*, c. 146.

41. *Feek v. Township*, 82 Mich. 393, 415.

42. *Massachusetts Convention of 1917–1918*, 2:888, quoting the Commission to Compile Information and Data.

43. *Massachusetts Acts of 1913*, c. 822.

44. *Massachusetts Acts of 1923*, c. 460.

45. *Massachusetts Convention of 1917–1918*, 2:886.

46. Ibid., 887.

47. Eaton, *The Oregon System*, 116.

48. Barnett, *Operation of the Initiative, Referendum, and Recall in Oregon*, 169.

49. *People v. Quider*, 183 Mich. 82, 85 (1914).

50. *Ideal Tea Company v. Salem*, 77 Or. 182, 189 (1915). See generally Lyman H. Cloe and Sumner Marcus, "Special and Local Legislation," *Kentucky Law Journal* 24 (1936): 351.

51. *Attorney General v. Lacy*, 180 Mich. 329, 337, 338 (1914).

52. *Commonwealth v. Karvonen*, 219 Mass. 30, 32 (1914).

53. *Farmer v. Christian*, 154 Va. 48, 57 (1930).

54. Howard Gillman, *The Constitution Besieged: The Rise and Demise of Lochner Era Police Powers Jurisprudence* (Durham, NC: Duke University Press, 1993), 10.

55. Dodd, *State Government*, 136.

56. *Butts v. Commonwealth*, 145 Va. 800, 806 (1926).

57. *State v. Butchek,* 121 Or. 141, 153 (1927).

58. *Hall v. Commonwealth,* 138 Va. 727, 733 (1924).

59. Ibid., 733–734.

60. Ibid., 740–741.

61. *Durham Bros. v. Woodson,* 155 Va. 93, 101 (1930). Although this was the normal mode of decision making in these cases, there were some notable exceptions. The Michigan court, for one, fashioned several constitutional rules for deciding search-and-seizure cases (*People v. Marxhausen,* 204 Mich. 559 [1919]; *People v. De La Mater,* 213 Mich. 167 [1921]). In addition, the Oregon Supreme Court suggested in dicta in one case that the exclusionary rule that had been adopted by the U.S. Supreme Court for federal cases should "be adopted and followed by the courts of this state" (*State v. Laundy,* 103 Or. 443, 494 [1922]).

62. *Commonwealth v. Gardner,* 300 Mass. 372, 377 (1938).

63. *Commonwealth v. Perry,* 155 Mass. 117 (1891).

64. *Massachusetts Convention of 1917–1918,* 2:122. See also John G. Palfrey, "The Constitution and the Courts," *Harvard Law Review* 26 (1913): 507, 518 n.42.

65. Melvin I. Urofsky, "State Courts and Protective Legislation During the Progressive Era: A Reevaluation," *Journal of American History* 72 (1985): 63, 64. See also Elizabeth Brandeis, "Labor Legislation," in *History of Labour in the United States,* ed. John R. Commons, 4 vols. (New York: Macmillan, 1918–1935), 3:554; William G. Ross, *A Muted Fury: Populists, Progressives, and Labor Unions Confront the Courts, 1890–1937* (Princeton, NJ: Princeton University Press, 1994), 16–17. But for an argument that the received wisdom still has some merit and that state legislatures were, in fact, restrained to a significant extent by judicial decisions during this period, see Paul Kens, "The Source of a Myth: Police Powers of the States and Laissez Faire Constitutionalism," *American Journal of Legal History* 35 (1991): 70; Theda Skocpol, *Protecting Soldiers and Mothers: The Political Origins of Social Policy in the United States* (Cambridge, MA: Belknap Press, 1992), 259–261.

66. See Charles Warren, "The Progressiveness of the United States Supreme Court," *Columbia Law Review* 13 (April 1913): 294; Alan R. Jones, "Thomas Cooley and 'Laissez-Faire Constitutionalism': A Reconsideration," *Journal of American History* 53 (1967): 751; Charles W. McCurdy, "Justice Field and the Jurisprudence of Government-Business Relations: Some Parameters of Laissez-Faire Constitutionalism, 1863–1897," *Journal of American History* 61 (1975): 970; John E. Semonche, *Charting the Future: The Supreme Court Responds to a Changing Society, 1890–1920* (Westport, CT: Greenwood Press, 1978), 424.

67. *Commonwealth v. Boston and Maine Railroad,* 222 Mass. 206, 208 (1915).

68. Urofsky, "State Courts and Protective Legislation," 79.

69. Seymour Thompson, *American Law Review* 26 (May–June 1892): 404, 405, quoted in Arnold M. Paul, *Conservative Crisis and the Rule of Law: Attitudes of Bar and Bench, 1887–1895* (Ithaca, NY: Cornell University Press, 1960), 49.

70. Herbert Darling, "Legislative Control over Contracts of Employment: The Weavers' Fines Bill," *Harvard Law Review* 6 (May 1892): 85, 96, quoted in Paul, *Conservative Crisis,* 51.

71. With respect to the New York Supreme Court's invalidation of a workmen's compensation law in the 1911 case of *Ives v. South Buffalo,* which was one of the more

prominent liberty-of-contract decisions during this period, Ernst Freund noted that "in a questionnaire sent to some of the most prominent legal minds in the country, he received two replies that favored the Court and seventeen that disagreed" (quoted in Hace S. Tishler, *Self-Reliance and Social Security, 1870–1917* [Port Washington, NY: Kennikat Press, 1971], 121).

72. See James Bradley Thayer, "The Origin and Scope of the American Doctrine of Constitutional Law," *Harvard Law Review* 7 (1893): 129; Roscoe Pound, "Liberty of Contract," *Yale Law Journal* 18 (1909): 454; Felix Frankfurter, "Hours of Labor and Realism in Constitutional Law," *Harvard Law Review* 29 (1916): 353.

73. Dodd, *State Government*, 154.

74. William Allen White, *The Old Order Changeth: A View of American Democracy* (New York: Macmillan, 1910), 90.

75. George W. Alger, "The Courts and Legislative Freedom," *Atlantic Monthly* 111 (March 1913): 345, 352–353.

6. POPULIST INSTITUTIONS AS KEEPERS OF THE PEOPLE'S LIBERTIES

1. Early analyses include Robert E. Cushman, "Recent Experience with the Initiative and Referendum," *American Political Science Review* 10 (1916): 532; Allen H. Eaton, *The Oregon System: The Story of Direct Legislation in Oregon* (Chicago: McClurg and Co., 1912). Middle-age evaluations include James K. Pollock, *The Initiative and the Referendum in Michigan* (Ann Arbor: University of Michigan Press, 1940); V. O. Key and Winston W. Crouch, *The Initiative and Referendum in California* (Berkeley: University of California Press, 1939). The literature in recent years is voluminous. Several of the more important works are Janice C. May, "The Constitutional Initiative: A Threat to Rights?" in *Human Rights in the States,* ed. Stanley H. Friedelbaum (New York: Greenwood Press, 1988); Julian N. Eule, "Judicial Review of Direct Democracy," *Yale Law Journal* 99 (1990): 1503; Robin Charlow, "Judicial Review, Equal Protection, and the Problem with Plebiscites," *Cornell Law Review* 79 (1994): 527.

2. Single-state analyses include David Y. Thomas, "The Initiative and Referendum in Arkansas Come of Age," *American Political Science Review* 27 (1933): 66; Legislative Reference Office, *The Initiative and Referendum in Colorado* (Denver: State Legislative Reference Office, 1939); Barbara F. Grossman, "The Initiative and Referendum Process: The Michigan Experience," *Wayne Law Review* 28 (1981): 77; Hugh A. Bone and Robert C. Benedict, "Perspectives on Direct Legislation: Washington State's Experience 1914-1973," *Western Political Quarterly* 28 (1975): 330. Significant multistate studies include Betty H. Zisk, *Money, Media, and the Grass Roots* (Newbury Park, CA: Sage Publications, 1987); David B. Magleby, *Direct Legislation: Voting on Ballot Propositions in the United States* (Baltimore: Johns Hopkins University Press, 1984); David D. Schmidt, *Citizen Lawmakers: The Ballot Initiative Revolution* (Philadelphia: Temple University Press, 1989); Thomas E. Cronin, *Direct Democracy: The Politics of Initiative, Referendum, and Recall* (Cambridge: Harvard University Press, 1989).

3. Empirical analyses are somewhat sparse, but several important compendiums of initiatives are Virginia Graham, *A Compilation of Statewide Initiative Proposals Appearing on Ballots Through 1976* (Washington, DC: Congressional Research Service, 1976);

Laura Tallian, *Direct Democracy* (Los Angeles: People's Lobby, 1977). I have relied on Graham's compilation throughout the chapter. Notable public-choice analyses are Lynn Baker, "Direct Democracy and Discrimination: A Public Choice Perspective," *Chicago–Kent Law Review* 67 (1991): 705; Clayton P. Gillette, "Plebiscites, Participation, and Collective Action in Local Government Law," *Michigan Law Review* 86 (1988): 930.

4. Arthur N. Holcombe, *State Government in the United States,* 2d ed. (New York: Macmillan, 1926), 511.

5. Pollock, *Initiative and Referendum in Michigan,* 65. See Max Radin, "Popular Legislation in California," *Minnesota Law Review* 23 (1939): 559; Winston W. Crouch, "The Constitutional Initiative in Operation," *American Political Science Review* 33 (1939): 634.

6. Referendums forced a temporary halt in appropriations to the state university, and the citizens adopted a pair of apparently irreconcilable initiatives that restricted certain forms of fishing. See Ellis Oberholtzer, *The Referendum in America: Together with Some Chapters on the Initiative and Recall* (New York: Charles Scribner's Sons, 1911), 505–506; Samuel W. McCall, "Representative as Against Direct Democracy," *Atlantic Monhtly* 108 (1911): 454, 457–458; Frederick V. Holman, "The Unfavorable Results of Direct Legislation in Oregon," in *Initiative, Referendum, and Recall,* ed. William B. Munro (New York: Appleton, 1912).

7. George Haynes, "People's Rule in Oregon, 1910," *Political Science Quarterly* 26 (1911): 32, 62.

8. Derrick A. Bell, "The Referendum: Democracy's Barrier to Racial Equality," *Washington Law Review* 54 (1978): 1, 23.

9. Priscilla Gunn, "Initiatives and Referendums: Direct Democracy and Minority Interests," *Urban Law Annual* 22 (1981): 135, 158.

10. James J. Seeley, "The Public Referendum and Minority Group Legislation: Post-script to *Reitman v. Mulkey,*" *Cornell Law Review* 55 (1970): 881, 902. See also Michael G. Colantuono, "The Revision of American State Constitutions: Legislative Power, Popular Sovereignty, and Constitutional Change," *California Law Review* 75 (1987): 1473, 1511.

11. Charlow, "Judicial Review, Equal Protection, and the Problem with Plebiscites," 541. See also Hans A. Linde, "When Initiative Lawmaking Is Not Republican Government: The Campaign Against Homosexuality," *Oregon Law Review* 72 (1993): 19; David B. Magleby, "Direct Legislation in the States," in *Referendums Around the World,* ed. David Butler and Austin Ranney (New York: Macmillan, 1994), 241; Barbara S. Gamble, "Putting Civil Rights to a Popular Vote," *American Journal of Political Science* 41 (1997): 245.

12. See Baker, "Direct Democracy and Discrimination," 776.

13. Ronald Allen, "National Initiative Proposal," *Nebraska Law Review* 58 (1979): 966, 1021.

14. David Butler and Austin Ranney, "Practice," in Butler and Ranney, *Referendums Around the World,* 20.

15. May, "The Constitutional Initiative," 168.

16. Alexander G. Gray, Jr., and Thomas R. Kiley, "The Initiative and Referendum in Massachusetts," *New England Law Review* 26 (1991): 27, 108.

17. Richard Briffault, "Distrust of Democracy (Book Review)," *Texas Law Review* 63 (1985): 1347, 1366.

18. Allen, "National Initiative Proposal," 1010.

19. Louis J. Sirico, "The Constitutionality of the Initiative and Referendum," *Iowa Law Review* 65 (1980): 637, 641.

20. Eule, "Judicial Review of Direct Democracy," 1552.

21. Holcombe, *State Government,* 520. In fact, a review of the operation of direct democracy in Switzerland indicates that this has become their primary purpose. "[I]t is a mistake to focus exclusively on victory at the polls. For sponsors of many Swiss initiatives, winning a popular vote is not necessary; and it may not even be an objective. Rather, initiatives are submitted with the intent of offering their withdrawal in bargaining for desired policy changes" (Kris W. Kobach, "Switzerland," in Butler and Ranney, *Referendums Around the World,* 146).

22. Between 1900 and 1970, populist institutions were used primarily to secure rights in a different manner from the legislature. As will become clear in a later chapter, after that time, these institutions began to be used more often to secure rights in response to judicial decisions.

23. This point is made in Briffault, "Distrust of Democracy," 1364; Allen, "National Initiative Proposal," 1026 n.304.

24. Henry M. Campbell, "The Initiative and Referendum," *Michigan Law Review* 10 (1912): 427, 430. For similar concerns, see *Debates in the Massachusetts Constitutional Convention, 1917–1918* (Boston: Wright and Potter, 1919), 2:655–656.

25. *Massachusetts Acts of 1919,* c. 295. See generally Edward George Hartmann, *The Movement to Americanize the Immigrant* (New York: Columbia University Press, 1948), 237–253; John Higham, *Strangers in the Land: Patterns of Nativism: 1860–1925* (New Brunswick, NJ: Rutgers University Press, 1955).

26. Sister Raymond McLaughlin, *A History of State Legislation Affecting Private Elementary and Secondary Schools in the United States, 1870–1945* (Washington, DC: Catholic University of America Press, 1946), 84–85.

27. Hartmann, *Movement to Americanize the Immigrant,* 253.

28. David B. Tyack, "The Pitfalls of Pluralism: The Background of the Pierce Case," *American Historical Review* 74 (1968): 74, 75.

29. *Michigan Public Acts of 1921,* no. 302.

30. McLaughlin, *History of State Legislation,* 87.

31. Tyack, "Pitfalls of Pluralism," 74–98; James Burns, *A History of Catholic Education in the United States* (New York: Benziger Brothers, 1937), 167; "Oregon's Outlawing of Catholic Schools," *Literary Digest* 76 (January 6, 1923): 34–35; Waldo Roberts, "The Ku-Kluxing of Oregon," *The Outlook* 133 (March 14, 1923): 490; William G. Ross, *Forging New Freedoms: Nativism, Education, and the Constitution, 1917–1927* (Lincoln: University of Nebraska Press, 1994), 148–173.

32. McLaughlin, *History of State Legislation,* 112.

33. *Oregon Laws, 1923,* c. 1. The law was not scheduled to take effect until 1926, but administrators of both a Catholic and a military school filed suit to challenge its validity. A federal district court in 1924 enjoined the operation of the law, and in 1925 the U.S. Supreme Court ruled that the initiative constituted an invalid interference with "the liberty of parents and guardians to direct the upbringing and education of children under their control" (*Pierce v. Society of Seven Sisters,* 268 U.S. 510, 535 [1925]).

34. Initiatives were also also passed during this period in Arkansas to prevent the teaching of evolution, in 1928, and to require Bible reading in the public schools, in 1930.

35. *Michigan Laws, 1970,* no. 100, c. 2, s. 56.

36. *Michigan Laws, 1970,* p. 692. One other initiative that regulated religious free-dom was a 1948 North Dakota measure that prohibited public school teachers from wear-ing religious dress.

37. *Oregon Laws, 1917,* c. 1.

38. *Massachusetts Acts of 1928,* pp. 587–593.

39. *Laws of North Dakota, 1921,* p. 253.

40. *Laws of North Dakota, 1935,* p. 499.

41. *Laws of Washington, 1967,* c. 1.

42. *Oregon Laws, 1939,* c. 2. The measure was invalidated by a ruling of the Oregon Supreme Court in 1940, which relied on a set of recently decided U.S. Supreme Court cases that held such regulations to be impermissible violations of free-speech rights (*American Federation of Labor v. Bain,* 165 Or. 183, 212 [1940]).

43. *Massachusetts Acts of 1947,* pp. 837–843.

44. Jerome Hellerstein, "Picketing Legislation and the Courts," *North Carolina Law Review* 10 (1931): 158.

45. Tony Howard Evans, "Oregon Progressive Reform, 1902–1916" (Ph.D. disserta-tion, University of California, Berkeley, 1966), 273–274.

46. *Statutes of California, 1939,* p. cxl.

47. *Massachusetts Acts of 1949,* pp. 849–855; *Massachusetts Acts of 1949,* pp. 856–862.

48. Zechariah Chafee, Jr., *Free Speech in the United States* (Cambridge: Harvard University Press, 1941), 575–597.

49. *Laws of North Dakota, 1921,* pp. 253–254.

50. For example, Oregon's criminal syndicalism law was enacted by the legislature in 1930 and invalidated by the U.S. Supreme Court in *De Jonge v. Oregon,* 299 U.S. 353 (1936).

51. Evans, "Oregon Progressive Reform," 273–274.

52. *Statutes of California, 1963,* p. cxxix.

53. Margaret A. Blanchard, "Filling in the Void: Speech and Press in State Courts Prior to *Gitlow,*" in *The First Amendment Reconsidered: New Perspectives on Freedom of Speech and Press,* ed. Bill F. Chamberlin and Charlene J. Brown (New York: Long-man, 1982), 27–28; Note, "Censorship of Motion Pictures," *Yale Law Journal* 49 (1939): 87.

54. *Massachusetts Acts of 1921,* c. 438.

55. Sidney Grant and S. E. Angoff, "Massachusetts and Censorship," *Boston University Law Review* 10 (1930): 36, 43.

56. *Massachusetts Acts of 1923,* pp. 610–613.

57. Richard D. Younger, *The People's Panel: The Grand Jury in the United States, 1634–1941* (Providence: Brown University Press, 1963), 134–154.

58. *Oregon General Laws, 1899,* H.B. 15.

59. *State v. Tucker,* 36 Or. 291, 302 (1900).

60. Ibid., 303.

61. *Public Laws of Oregon, 1909,* p. 12.

62. Roscoe Pound, "Legal Interrogation of Persons Accused or Suspected of Crime," *Journal of Criminal Law and Criminology* 24 (1934): 1014, 1015.

63. Ibid., 1016; see also Paul Kauper, "Judicial Examination of the Accused—A Remedy for the Third Degree," *Michigan Law Review* 30 (1931): 1224.

64. Pound, "Legal Interrogation," 1017.

65. *Statutes of California, 1935,* p. xcv.

66. Ibid., pp. xcv, xcvi.

67. *Laws of Arizona, 1915,* "Initiated Measures," p. 12.

68. Raymond L. Buell, "The Development of Anti-Japanese Agitation in the United States II," *Political Science Quarterly* 38 (1923): 57, 70–71. See, generally, Charles McClain, ed., *Japanese Immigrants and American Law: The Alien Land Laws and Other Issues* (New York: Garland Press, 1994).

69. Dudley O. McGovney, "The Anti-Japanese Land Laws of California and Ten Other States," *California Law Review* 35 (1947): 7, 26. This initiative was challenged in the courts on several occasions and survived virtually intact (ibid., 34–35).

70. This was subsequently overturned by a decision of the California Supreme Court (Buell, "Development of Anti-Japanese Agitation," 70, 74).

71. *Guinn and Beal v. U.S.,* 238 U.S. 347 (1915).

72. Schmidt, *Citizen Lawmakers,* 259–260.

73. See Walter F. Dodd, *The Revision and Amendment of State Constitutions* (Baltimore: Johns Hopkins University Press, 1910), 67; Charles S. Lobingier, *The People's Law, or Popular Participation in Law Making* (New York: Macmillan, 1909), 301–325.

74. *Statutes of California, 1947,* p. cxlvi.

75. *Statutes of California, 1965,* p. A-131.

76. Raymond E. Wolfinger and Fred I. Greenstein, "The Repeal of Fair Housing in California: An Analysis of Referendum Voting," *American Political Science Review* 62 (1968): 753, 767.

77. Ibid., 768.

78. It was later declared unconstitutional by the U.S. Supreme Court in *Reitman v. Mulkey,* 387 U.S. 369 (1967).

79. Delos Wilcox, *Government by All the People* (New York: Macmillan, 1912), 117–118.

80. Ibid., 118.

81. *Oregon Laws, 1909,* c. 3.

82. Eaton, *The Oregon System,* 107. In similar fashion, Massachusetts voters relied on the initiative in 1974 to limit campaign expenditures, require disclosure of donations, and establish a Corrupt Practices Commission (*Massachusetts Acts of 1975,* pp. 1417–1424). Alaska (1974), California (1974), Florida (1976), Missouri (1974), and Washington (1972) also used the initiative to enact campaign disclosure laws, as did Montana (1912) to limit campaign expenditures.

83. William Allen White, *The Old Order Changeth: A View of American Democracy* (New York: Macmillan, 1910), 78.

84. Evans, "Oregon Progressive Reform," 109.

85. Eaton, *The Oregon System,* 30, 61.

86. Wilcox, *Government by All the People,* 161–162.

87. James D. Barnett, *The Operation of the Initiative, Referendum, and Recall in Oregon* (New York: Macmillan, 1915), 167.

88. *Oregon Laws, 1953,* c. 1, which overturned *Oregon Laws of 1949,* c. 373.

89. *Michigan Public Laws, 1972*, p. 1155, which repealed *Michigan Public Laws, 1967*, no. 6.

90. Initiatives to relocate the state capital were approved in Oklahoma in 1912 and Alaska in 1976, and rejected in North Dakota in 1932.

91. *Oregon Laws of 1909*, pp. 9–10. Voters in Arkansas (1912), Colorado (1912), and Montana (1976), also approved recall measures, and Colorado voters also applied the recall to judicial decisions.

92. *Michigan Public Laws, 1939*, pp. 910–911.

93. *Oregon Laws, 1905*, c. 1.

94. *Oregon Laws, 1909*, c. 2. In 1912 Montana and Oklahoma also used the initiative to transfer this power from the legislature to the citizens.

95. *Oregon Laws, 1905*, c. 1.

96. *Oregon Laws, 1911*, c. 5.

97. The law altered the order of the party conventions and primaries and regulated the selection of primary and convention delegates (*Massachusetts Acts of 1933*, pp. 785–791).

98. Eaton, *The Oregon System*, 58–59.

99. *Michigan Public Laws, 1961*, pp. 764–765.

100. *Massachusetts Acts of 1969*, pp. 1041–1047. In this instance, however, the Massachusetts Supreme Court ruled that this was as impermissible use of the initiative procedure (*Cohen v. Attorney General*, 357 Mass. 564 [1970]).

101. Evans, "Oregon Progressive Reform," 295–296. Similar initiatives were defeated in Arizona in 1916, Missouri in 1944, and Oklahoma in 1914.

102. Alaska voters approved an advisory initiative in 1976 that sought to accomplish the same goal.

103. *Massachusetts Acts of 1975*, pp. 1393–1400.

104. *Massachusetts Acts of 1938*, pp. 765–771. Biennial sessions were also introduced through initiated amendments in Nevada in 1960 and Montana in 1974. In 1912 Arkansas voters relied on the initiative to impose a sixty-day limit on legislative sessions.

105. For the most part, the representative process accurately represented popular opinion on the question of women's suffrage. In states where a majority of the public *opposed* women's suffrage, either the legislature or the people rejected a suffrage amendment. Thus, in Massachusetts and Michigan in the late nineteenth century, the legislatures for many years declined to recommend women's suffrage amendments, and when amendments were placed on the ballot they were rejected at the polls. In states where a majority of the public *supported* women's suffrage, legislators approved the amendment and the people ratified it, as was the case in Michigan in 1918. See generally Susan B. Anthony, Elizabeth C. Stanton, Melinda J. Gage, and Ida H. Harper, eds., *The History of Woman Suffrage*, 6 vols. (New York: Arno Press, 1969), vols. 4 and 5.

106. Carrie Chapman Catt and Nettie Rogers Shuler, *Woman Suffrage and Politics: The Inner Story of the Suffrage Movement* (New York: Charles Scribner's Sons, 1923), 132–159.

107. Ibid., 110–111, 124–125, 179–186. Irregularities were so widespread in the Michigan women's suffrage election of 1912, for instance, that Governor Chase Osborn was moved to announce: "If the liquor interests defeat the amendment by fraud, proved or suspected, the people of Michigan will retaliate in my opinion by adopting statewide

prohibition; the question seems to be largely one as to whether the liquor interests own and control and run Michigan" (quoted ibid., 181).

108. Women's suffrage amendments were also defeated at the polls in Oklahoma in 1910, Missouri in 1914, Nebraska in 1914, and Ohio in 1914.

109. *Oregon Laws, 1913*, p. 7. Arizona voters also approved a women's suffrage initiative in the same year.

110. Wilcox, *Government by All the People*, 127.

111. *Oregon Laws, 1911*, p. 9. Abolishing the poll tax had such strong appeal among the public that in Oregon advocates of the single tax took advantage of this support by combining the single-tax and poll-tax measures into one ballot proposition, which was approved in the 1910 election. Upon realizing that they had been fooled, the voters turned around in the next election and removed the single-tax measure, but kept the ban on the poll tax (*Oregon Laws, 1913*, p. 7). See Eaton, *The Oregon System*, 134–136.

112. The voters of California in 1914, Washington in 1922, and Arkansas in 1964 each removed the poll tax through the initiative.

113. Gordon E. Baker, *Rural Versus Urban Political Power: The Nature and Consequences of Unbalanced Representation* (Garden City, NY: Doubleday, 1955), 13.

114. See, generally, Hugh A. Bone, "States Attempting to Comply with Reapportionment Requirements," *Law and Contemporary Problems* 17 (1952): 387, 409–412; Charles M. Hardin, "Issues in Legislative Reapportionment," *Review of Politics* 27 (1965): 147; Gordon E. Baker, *State Constitutions: Reapportionment* (New York: National Municipal League, 1960) 47–50; Robert G. Dixon, *Democratic Representation: Reapportionment in Law and Politics* (New York: Oxford University Press, 1968), 235–237, 400–402.

115. The citizens of California (1948, 1960, and 1962), Colorado (1962), Missouri (1922), Oklahoma (1956), and Washington (1962) also voted down specific reapportionment plans in this period. However, in Arizona (1932), Colorado (1932 and 1962), and Washington (1930 and 1956), voters approved initiated measures.

116. Waldo Schumacher, "Reapportionment in Oregon," *Western Political Quarterly* 3 (1950): 428.

117. Gordon E. Baker, "Reapportionment by Initiative in Oregon," *Western Political Quarterly* 13 (1960): 508, 518.

118. *Oregon Laws, 1953*, pp. 8–12.

119. Schmidt, *Citizen Lawmakers*, 265.

120. *Public Laws of Michigan, 1953*, pp. 438–439. This 1952 plan was challenged on the ground that it still maintained unconstitutional differences in voting power, but it was upheld by the Michigan Supreme Court in *Scholle v. Secretary of State*, 360 Mich. 1 (1960).

Voters in Michigan in 1930, Oklahoma in 1960 and 1962, and North Dakota in 1973 rejected propositions to establish a commission or to empower the secretary of state to conduct reapportionment, but California voters in 1926 and Arkansas voters in 1936 ratified such an initiative amendment.

121. *Baker v. Carr*, 369 U.S. 186, 193 n.14 (1962).

122. Ibid., 258–259. The Court took note of the absence of the initiative procedure in subsequent decisions involving Alabama, Delaware, Maryland, New York, and Virginia. See Robert B. McKay, *Reapportionment: The Law and Politics of Equal Representation* (New York: Twentieth Century Fund, 1965), 127–128. Significantly, though, the Court

also ruled in the case of Colorado that the use of the initiative did not necessarily render an apportionment plan immune from judicial review (*Lucas v. Colorado General Assembly*, 377 U.S. 713, 736 [1964]).

123. Quoted in Bone, "States Attempting to Comply with Reapportionment Requirements," 412.

124. Quoted in McKay, *Reapportionment*, 186 n.87. See also Baker, *Rural Versus Urban Political Power*, 63–64.

125. Theda Skocpol, *Protecting Soldiers and Mothers: The Political Origins of Social Policy in the United States* (Cambridge, MA: Belknap Press, 1992), 236.

126. *Massachusetts Acts of 1842*, c. 60.

127. Elizabeth Brandeis, "Labor Legislation," in *History of Labour in the United States*, ed. John R. Commons, 4 vols. (New York: Macmillan, 1918–1935), chap. 2. In 1914, Arkansas became the only state to adopt a child-labor law through the initiative.

128. Ibid., chap. 3.

129. Ibid., chap. 5.

130. *Oregon Laws, 1913*, c. 1; *Session Laws of Colorado, 1913*, pp. 688–691.

131. Skocpol, *Protecting Soldiers and Mothers*, 211.

132. Lawrence M. Friedman, *Total Justice* (New York: Russell Sage Foundation, 1985); Roy Lubove, *The Struggle for Social Security: 1900–1935* (Cambridge: Harvard University Press, 1968), 49–50.

133. Melvin I. Urofsky, "State Courts and Protective Legislation During the Progressive Era: A Reevaluation," *Journal of American History* 72 (1985): 63, 86.

134. Brandeis, "Labor Legislation," chap. 6.

135. Hace S. Tishler, *Self-Reliance and Social Security: 1870–1917* (Port Washington, NY: Kennikat Press, 1971), 109.

136. Robert Asher, "Workmen's Compensation in the United States, 1880–1935" (Ph.D. dissertation, University of Minnesota, 1971), 129–159, 229–261.

137. Tishler, *Self-Reliance and Social Security*, 114.

138. Evans, "Oregon Progressive Reform," 78–79.

139. Ibid., 218.

140. *Oregon Laws, 1911*, c. 3. Likewise, Colorado in 1936 and Arkansas in 1938 and 1956 amended their workmen's compensation laws to better guarantee the right to safe working conditions. Similar initiatives were presented to the voters but failed to secure a popular majority in Arizona in 1916, Montana in 1914, and Ohio in 1955.

141. Evans, "Oregon Progressive Reform," 230–231; Eaton, *The Oregon System*, 73. These gains were then preserved in a referendum held in 1914.

142. Mark H. Leff, "Consensus for Reform: The Mothers-Pension-Movement in the Progressive Era," *Social Service Review* 47 (1973): 389.

143. Edna Mae Bullock, ed., *Selected Articles on Mothers' Pensions* (New York: H. W. Wilson and Co., 1915), 1.

144. Skocpol, *Protecting Soldiers and Mothers*, 425–426; Tishler, *Self-Reliance and Social Security*, 144–156.

145. *Session Laws of Colorado, 1913*, pp. 694–696. One writer noted in 1914: "The opposition to the law in Denver was so bitter that it has not yet subsided. The reactionary and corporation daily papers in Denver were crowded with anonymous articles bitterly attacking it. The principal objections were that it would bankrupt the county: that it would

encourage an influx of pauper parents into the state: that it gave the judges of the courts too much authority over county funds: that it would cost Denver $100,000 to build an expensive workhouse: that the children were to be 'farmed out' and horribly maltreated" (Bullock, *Mothers' Pensions,* 22).

146. *Laws of Arizona, 1915,* "Initiated Measures," pp. 10–11. Because the Arizona measure not only provided pensions but also abolished the existing system of poor relief, however, the Arizona Supreme Court held that it violated the dual-subject rule and was therefore unconstitutional (*Board of Control v. Buckstegge,* 18 Ariz. 277 [1916]).

147. Lubove, *Struggle for Social Security,* 135.

148. Several states enacted pensions for certain groups of disabled persons during this time, and this too was occasionally accomplished through the initiative. Colorado, for instance, enacted annuities for the blind by an initiative approved in 1918.

149. Lubove, *Struggle for Social Security,* 136.

150. Colorado (1936), Ohio (1933), North Dakota (1938), and Oklahoma (1936) approved old-age pension measures, whereas Nevada (1936) and Washington (1936) rejected them.

151. Abraham Holtzman, *The Townsend Movement: A Political Study* (New York: Bookman Associates, 1963), 35–36.

152. Ibid., 193.

153. Ibid., 196.

154. *Oregon Laws, 1939,* c. 1.

155. Holtzman, *Townsend Movement,* 196–198.

156. *Massachusetts Acts of 1947,* pp. 827–836.

157. *Massachusetts Acts of 1951,* pp. 936–942.

158. *Oregon Laws, 1949,* c. 1. Rounding out the list of states that approved pension plans or pension increases through the initiative during this period were California in 1948, Idaho in 1942, Nevada in 1944, and Washington in 1948; Arizona rejected them in 1944 and 1950.

159. *Massachusetts Acts of 1949,* pp. 842–848.

160. Arizona (1946 and 1948), Arkansas (1944), California (1944 and 1958), Colorado (1958), Idaho (1958), Massachusetts (1948), Nebraska (1946), Nevada (1952, 1954, and 1956), Ohio (1958), Oklahoma (1964), and Washington (1956 and 1958).

161. See, generally, Paul Sultan, *Right-to-Work Laws: A Study in Conflict* (Los Angeles: University of California, 1958), 21–30; Gilbert Gall, *The Politics of Right to Work: The Labor Federations as Special Interests, 1943–1979* (New York: Greenwood Press, 1988), 18–19.

162. Gall, *Politics of Right to Work,* 20.

163. *Acts of Arkansas, 1945,* p. 770; *Laws of Nebraska, 1947,* pp. 46–47; *Laws of Arizona, 1945–1946,* p. 399.

164. *Laws of Nevada, 1953,* c. 1.

165. Propositions were defeated in California (1944 and 1958), Colorado (1958), Idaho (1958), Ohio (1958), Oklahoma (1964), and Washington (1956 and 1968).

166. Alabama (1954), Georgia (1947), Indiana (1957), Iowa (1947), Mississippi (1954), North Carolina (1947), North Dakota (1948), South Carolina (1954), Texas (1947), and Utah (1955).

167. Florida (1944) and South Dakota (1946).

7. THE THEORY AND DESIGN OF JUDICIALIST INSTITUTIONS

1. Osmond K. Fraenkel, *Our Civil Liberties* (New York: Viking, 1944), 21.

2. Paul L. Murphy, *World War I and the Origin of Civil Liberties in the United States* (New York: W. W. Norton, 1979), 71–132; Zechariah Chafee, Jr., *Freedom of Speech* (New York: Harcourt, Brace, and Howe, 1920), 42–46, 110–113, 399–405.

3. Leon V. Whipple, *The Story of Civil Liberty in the United States* (New York: Vanguard Press, 1927), vi. See also *American Civil Liberties Union Annual Reports* (New York: Arno Press, 1970), vols. 1 and 2; Morton Keller, "Powers and Rights: Two Centuries of American Constitutionalism," *Journal of American History* 74 (1987): 675, 688.

4. The Civil War produced some of the same types of laws and controversies but did not lead to the same kind of reevaluation of the institutional arrangements for protecting civil liberties. See James G. Randall, *Constitutional Problems Under Lincoln* (New York: D. Appleton and Company, 1926); Harold M. Hyman, *Era of the Oath: Northern Loyalty Tests During the Civil War and Reconstruction* (Philadelphia: University of Pennsylvania Press, 1954).

5. Whipple, *Story of Civil Liberty,* v.

6. Zechariah Chafee, Jr., "Freedom of Speech," *New Republic* 17 (November 16, 1918): 66; Chafee, "Freedom of Speech in War Time," *Harvard Law Review* 32 (1919): 932; Chafee, *Freedom of Speech;* James P. Hall, "Free Speech in War Time," *Columbia Law Review* 21 (1921): 526.

7. Donald O. Johnson, *The Challenge to American Freedoms: World War I and the Rise of the American Civil Liberties Union* (Lexington: University of Kentucky Press, 1963).

8. Quoted in Murphy, *World War I and the Origin of Civil Liberties,* 154 n.35.

9. Ibid., 249.

10. Johnson, *Challenge to American Freedoms,* 196–197.

11. Whipple, *Story of Civil Liberty,* 327.

12. Murphy, *Origin of Civil Liberties,* 134–178.

13. Ibid., 240–243; Robert M. Cover, "The Left, the Right, and the First Amendment: 1918–1928," *Maryland Law Review* 40 (1981): 349; David M. Rabban, "The Emergence of Modern First Amendment Doctrine," *University of Chicago Law Review* 50 (1983): 1205.

14. Oliver Wendell Holmes, Jr., "The Path of the Law," *Harvard Law Review* 10 (1897): 457, 461.

15. Jerome Frank, "What Courts Do in Fact," *Illinois Law Review* 26 (1932): 645, 662.

16. Karl N. Llewellyn, "Some Realism About Realism–Responding to Dean Pound," *Harvard Law Review* 44 (1931): 1222, 1236.

17. William W. Fisher III, "The Development of Modern American Legal Theory and the Judicial Interpretation of the Bill of Rights," in *A Culture of Rights: The Bill of Rights in Philosophy, Politics, and Law—1791 and 1991,* ed. Michael J. Lacey and Knud Haakonssen (New York: Cambridge University Press, 1991).

18. Holmes, "The Path of the Law," 477.

19. Hans A. Linde, "Judges, Critics, and the Realist Tradition," *Yale Law Journal* 82 (1972): 227.

20. Quoted in ibid.

21. Harold J. Laski, "The Obsolescence of Federalism," *New Republic* 98 (May 3, 1939): 367.

22. George C. S. Benson, *The New Centralization: A Study of Intergovernmental Relationships in the United States* (New York: Farrar and Rhinehart, 1941), 157.

23. John Kincaid, "Foreword: The New Federalism Context of the New Judicial Federalism," *Rutgers Law Journal* 26 (1995): 913, 935.

24. William H. Riker, *Federalism: Origin, Operation, Significance* (Boston: Little, Brown, 1964), 155.

25. Monrad G. Paulsen, "State Constitutions, State Courts and First Amendment Freedoms," *Vanderbilt Law Review* 4 (1951): 620, 642.

26. The lack of assurance that the Congress possessed a national police power, even under Section 5 of the Fourteenth Amendment, contributed in at least one case to the willingness of the U.S. Supreme Court to assume responsibility for the protection of rights. Justice Robert H. Jackson was persuaded to join the majority opinion in *Brown v. Board of Education* in part because "he gradually came to subscribe to the argument, pressed by one of Warren's clerks, that Congress lacked the authority under the Fourteenth Amendment to desegregate schools" (Eugene W. Hickok and Garry L. McDowell, *Justice v. Law: Courts and Politics in American Society* [New York: Free Press, 1993], 200).

27. Ernst Freund, *Standards of American Legislation: An Estimate of Restrictive and Constructive Factors* (Chicago: University of Chicago Press, 1917), 180.

28. John E. Nowak, "Essay on the Bill of Rights: The 'Sixty Something' Anniversary of the Bill of Rights," *University of Illinois Law Review* (1992): 445, 456–461.

29. Michael G. Kammen, *A Machine That Would Go of Itself: The Constitution in American Culture* (New York: Alfred A. Knopf, 1986), 338–339.

30. *U.S. v. Carolene Products,* 304 U.S. 144 (1938).

31. Louis Lusky, "Footnote Redux: A *Carolene Products* Reminiscence," *Columbia Law Review* 82 (1982): 1093.

32. *U.S. v. Carolene Products,* 304 U.S. 144, 152 n.4.

33. Ibid.

34. Owen M. Fiss, "The Supreme Court 1978 Term: Foreword—The Forms of Justice," *Harvard Law Review* 93 (1979): 1, 6.

35. Erwin Chemerinsky, "The Supreme Court 1988 Term: Foreword—The Vanishing Constitution," *Harvard Law Review* 103 (1989): 43, 68.

36. *West Virginia Board of Education v. Barnette,* 319 U.S. 624 (1943).

37. *Minersville School District v. Gobitis,* 310 U.S. 586, 597–598, 600 (1940).

38. *West Virginia v. Barnette,* 319 U.S. 624, 638.

39. Laurence H. Tribe, *American Constitutional Law,* 2d ed. (Mineola, NY: Foundation Press, 1988), 1310–1311.

40. Lawrence G. Sager, "Fair Measure: The Legal Status of Underenforced Constitutional Norms," *Harvard Law Review* 91 (1978): 1212, 1220.

41. Chemerinsky, "Vanishing Constitution," 47.

42. Eugene V. Rostow, "The Democratic Character of Judicial Review," *Harvard Law Review* 66 (1952): 193, 197.

43. *Lovell v. Griffin,* 303 U.S. 444 (1938); *Hague v. CIO,* 307 U.S. 496 (1939); *Schneider v. State,* 308 U.S. 147 (1939); *Thornhill v. Alabama,* 310 U.S. 88 (1940); *Carlson v. California,* 310 U.S. 106 (1940); *Cantwell v. Connecticut,* 310 U.S. 296 (1940).

44. *Book Tower Garage v. Local No. 415,* 295 Mich. 580, 586 (1940).

45. *Commonwealth v. Anderson,* 308 Mass. 370, 372–373 (1941).

46. *Commonwealth v. Pascone,* 308 Mass. 591, 594 (1941).

47. *McConkey v. Fredericksburg,* 179 Va. 556, 559 (1942).

48. Ibid., 560.

49. *Edwards v. Commonwealth,* 191 Va. 272, 277 (1950).

50. *People v. Lechner,* 307 Mich. 358, 360–361 (1943).

51. *People v. Simon,* 324 Mich. 450, 455 (1949).

52. Ibid., 456.

53. David Fellman, "The Nationalization of Civil Liberties," in *Essays on the Constitution of the United States,* ed. M. Judd Harmon (Port Washington, NY: Kennikat Press, 1978).

54. *State v. Neely,* 239 Or. 487, 493–494 (1965).

55. Ibid., 492.

56. *Commonwealth v. Spofford,* 343 Mass. 703, 707 (1962).

57. *Minielly v. State,* 242 Or. 490, 507 (1966).

58. Herbert P. Wilkins, "Judicial Treatment of the Massachusetts Declaration of Rights in Relation to Cognate Provisions of the United States Constitution," *Suffolk Law Review* 14 (1980): 887, 901 (emphasis supplied).

59. *Barber v. Gladden,* 210 Or. 46, 54 (1957).

60. *Commonwealth v. Jacobs,* 333 Mass. 204, 206 (1955).

61. Ibid.

62. *People v. Pennington,* 383 Mich. 611, 618–619 (1970). For even more hostile comments from state judges, see Bradley C. Canon, "Organizational Contumacy in the Transmission of Judicial Policies: The *Mapp, Escobedo, Miranda,* and *Gault* Cases," *Villanova Law Review* 20 (1974): 50. Additional studies of state court compliance with federal decisions include G. Alan Tarr, *Judicial Impact and State Supreme Courts* (Lexington, MA: Lexington Books, 1977); Jerry K. Beatty, "State Court Evasion of the United States Supreme Court Mandates During the Last Decade of the Warren Court," *Valparaiso University Law Review* 6 (1972): 260.

63. *People v. Pennington,* 383 Mich. 611, 619–620.

64. The first articles to take note of this development were Project Report, "Toward an Activist Role for State Bills of Rights," *Harvard Civil Rights–Civil Liberties Law Review* 8 (1973): 271; Donald E. Wilkes, "The New Federalism in Criminal Procedure," *Kentucky Law Journal* 62 (1974): 421; A. E. Dick Howard, "State Courts and Constitutional Rights in the Day of the Burger Court," *Virginia Law Review* 62 (1976): 873. Several particularly helpful articles are Robert F. Williams, "In the Supreme Court's Shadow: Legitimacy of State Court Rejection of Supreme Court Reasoning and Result," *South Carolina Law Review* 35 (1984): 353; Hans Linde, "First Things First: Rediscovering the States' Bills of Rights," *University of Baltimore Law Review* 9 (1980): 377.

65. One of the few scholars to emphasize this continuity is Earl M. Maltz, "The Dark Side of State Court Activism," *Texas Law Review* 63 (1985): 995.

66. G. Alan Tarr, "The Past and Future of the New Judicial Federalism," *Publius: The Journal of Federalism* 24 (spring 1994): 63, 72.

67. Hans A. Linde, "Without Due Process: Unconstitutional Law in Oregon," *Oregon Law Review* 49 (1970): 125.

68. William J. Brennan, Jr., "State Constitutions and the Protection of Individual Rights," *Harvard Law Review* 90 (1977): 489.

69. *Portland v. Welch,* 229 Or. 308 (1961).

70. *Dickman v. School District,* 232 Or. 238 (1962).

71. *State v. Spencer,* 289 Or. 225 (1980) (free speech); *Sterling v. Cupp,* 290 Or. 611 (1981) (right to privacy); *State v. Quinn,* 290 Or. 383 (1981) (death penalty); *State v. Caraher,* 293 Or. 741 (1982) (search and seizure). See Linde, "First Things First," 393–396; John H. Buttler, "Oregon's Constitutional Renaissance: Federalism Revisited," *Vermont Law Review* 13 (1988): 107.

72. *Commonwealth v. O'Neal,* 369 Mass. 242 (1975).

73. *Commonwealth v. Sees,* 374 Mass. 532 (1978).

74. *Moe v. Secretary,* 382 Mass. 629 (1981).

75. *Commonwealth v. Upton,* 394 Mass. 363 (1984), and *Commonwealth v. Bishop,* 402 Mass. 449 (1988). See, generally, Wilkins, "Judicial Treatment of the Massachusetts Declaration of Rights."

76. *People v. White,* 390 Mich. 245 (1973) (double jeopardy); *People v. Beavers,* 393 Mich. 554 (1975) (search and seizure).

77. *People v. Nash,* 418 Mich. 196, 214–215 (1983).

78. See James A. Gardner, "The Failed Discourse of State Constitutionalism," *Michigan Law Review* 90 (1992): 761, 780, 786.

79. Commission on Constitutional Revision, *The Constitution of Virginia* (Charlottesville: Michie Publishing Co., 1969), 86.

80. *Richmond Newspapers v. Commonwealth,* 222 Va. 574, 588 (1981).

81. John Kincaid, "The New Judicial Federalism," *Journal of State Government* 61 (1988): 163, 168.

82. *State v. Biggs,* 198 Or. 413, 430 (1953).

83. *Suffolk v. Watson,* 381 Mass. 648, 662 (1980).

84. *Commonwealth v. O'Neal,* 369 Mass. 242, 271 (1975).

85. See, for instance, Justice James Brand of Oregon, who argued: "So long as the doctrine of separation of powers remains basic in our system, the ultimate power and duty of the courts to construe the constitution must rest with the courts alone. That power should not be lightly whittled away by any rule which recognizes the power of the legislature to authoritatively construe the constitution" (*State v. Kuhnhausen,* 201 Or. 478, 517 [1954]). A per curiam decision of the Michigan Supreme Court argued, likewise: "Interpretation of the State Constitution is the exclusive function of the judicial branch. Construction of the Constitution is the province of the courts and this Court's construction of a State constitutional provision is binding on all departments of government, including the legislature" (*Richardson v. Secretary of State,* 381 Mich. 304, 309 [1968]).

86. Ralph Lerner, *The Thinking Revolutionary: Principle and Practice in the New Republic* (Ithaca, NY: Cornell University Press, 1987), 124.

87. Ronald Dworkin, *Taking Rights Seriously* (Cambridge: Harvard University Press, 1977), 141.

88. Robert Kramer, "Foreword," *Law and Contemporary Problems* 17 (1952): 253.

89. Ibid.

90. Jesse H. Choper, *Judicial Review and the National Political Process: A Functional*

Reconsideration of the Role of the Supreme Court (Chicago: University of Chicago Press, 1980), 65.

91. Richard D. Parker, "The Past of Constitutional Theory—And Its Future," *Ohio State Law Journal* 42 (1981): 223, 249.

92. Choper, *Judicial Review and the National Political Process*, 79–80. See also Laurence H. Tribe, "The Puzzling Persistence of Process-Based Constitutional Theories," *Yale Law Journal* 89 (1980): 1063; Mark V. Tushnet, "Darkness on the Edge of Town: The Contributions of John Hart Ely to Constitutional Theory," *Yale Law Journal* 89 (1980): 1037; Bruce Ackerman, "Beyond *Carolene Products*," *Harvard Law Review* 98 (1985): 713.

93. Chemerinsky, "Vanishing Constitution," 97–98.

94. Choper, *Judicial Review and the National Political Process,* 68.

95. John Hart Ely, *Democracy and Distrust: A Theory of Judicial Review* (Cambridge: Harvard University Press, 1980), 100–101.

96. Henry Steele Commager, *Majority Rule and Minority Rights* (New York: Oxford University Press, 1943), 80. It should be noted, however, that midway through the judicialist era, Commager reversed course and joined the defenders of the judicialist regime. See Robert F. Nagel, *Constitutional Cultures: The Mentality and Consequences of Judicial Review* (Los Angeles: University of California Press, 1989), 33.

97. See Learned Hand, *The Bill of Rights* (Cambridge: Harvard University Press, 1958), 71–74.

98. Nagel, *Constitutional Cultures,* 4.

99. *Commonwealth v. O'Neal,* 369 Mass. 242, 271–272 (1975).

100. C. Herman Pritchett, "The Development of Judicial Research," in *Frontiers of Judicial Research,* ed. Joel B. Grossman and Joseph Tanenhaus (New York: John H. Wiley and Sons, 1969), 31, quoted in Louis Fisher, *Constitutional Dialogues: Interpretation as Political Process* (Princeton, NJ: Princeton University Press, 1988), 9–10.

101. Dworkin, *Taking Rights Seriously,* 147. Dworkin is the chief advocate of this view of rights that has come to dominate the legal profession, but see also David A. J. Richards, *Foundations of American Constitutionalism* (New York: Oxford University Press, 1989), and, to an extent, Michael J. Perry, *The Constitution, the Courts, and Human Rights* (New Haven, CT: Yale University Press, 1982).

102. Ronald Dworkin, "The Forum of Principle," *New York University Law Review* 56 (1981): 469, 517.

103. Charles L. Black, Jr., *The People and the Court: Judicial Review in a Democracy* (New York: Macmillan, 1960), 177.

104. Chemerinsky, "Vanishing Constitution," 97.

105. Abram Chayes, "The Role of the Judge in Public Law Litigation," *Harvard Law Review* 89 (1976): 1281, 1307–1309.

106. Fiss, "Forms of Justice," 10.

107. Paul Brest, "Congress as Constitutional Decisionmaker and Its Power to Counter Judicial Doctrine," *Georgia Law Review* 21 (1986): 57, 98. See also Paul Brest, "The Conscientious Legislator's Guide to Constitutional Interpretation," *Stanford Law Review* 27 (1975): 585, 588; Abner J. Mikva, "How Well Does Congress Support and Defend the Constitution?" *North Carolina Law Review* 61 (1983): 587, 590; Abner J. Mikva and Joseph R. Lundy, "The 91st Congress and the Constitution," *University of Chicago Law Review* 38 (1971): 449, 499.

108. J. Skelly Wright, "The Role of the Supreme Court in a Democratic Society—Judicial Activism or Restraint?" *Cornell Law Review* 54 (1968): 1, 12.

109. Black, *The People and the Court,* 177–178.

110. Commager, *Majority Rule and Minority Rights,* 44.

111. Donald G. Morgan, *Congress and the Constitution: A Study of Responsibility* (Cambridge: Harvard University Press, 1966).

112. Louis Fisher, "Constitutional Interpretation by Members of Congress," *North Carolina Law Review* 63 (1985): 707, 744.

113. Commager, *Majority Rule and Minority Rights,* 44.

114. Donald L. Horowitz, *The Courts and Social Policy* (Washington, DC: Brookings Institution, 1977), 23, 25, 34.

115. Linde, "Judges, Critics, and the Realist Tradition," 229.

116. Ibid.

117. Ibid., 237.

118. Ibid., 238, quoting Alexander Bickel.

119. See, for instance, Michigan Justice Talbot Smith's remarks in a dissenting opinion: "We keep the mightiest armory known to man, the sovereign conscience. It is our duty to give voice to its demands as well as to implement it with our decrees. As Rostow put it: 'The work of the court can have, and when wisely exercised does have, the effect not of inhibiting but of releasing and encouraging the dominantly democratic forces of American life. The historic reason for this paradox is that American life in all its aspects is an attempt to express and to fulfill a far-reaching moral code. . . . The prestige and authority of the supreme court derive from the fact that it is accepted as the ultimate interpreter of the American code in many of its most important applications'" (*Scholle v. Secretary of State,* 360 Mich. 1, 80 [1960]).

120. Erwin Chemerinsky, *Interpreting the Constitution* (New York: Praeger, 1987), 91.

121. Christopher L. Eisgruber, "Is the Supreme Court an Educative Institution?" *New York University Law Review* 67 (1992): 961, 1004. In similar fashion, Thomas Emerson argued: "[T]he Court should not underestimate the authority and prestige it has achieved over the years. Representing the 'conscience of the community,' it has come to possess a very real power to keep alive and vital the higher values and goals toward which our society imperfectly strives" (Thomas I. Emerson, *The System of Freedom of Expression* [New York: Random House, 1970], 14).

122. Lerner, *The Thinking Revolutionary,* 91–136.

123. Rostow, "The Democratic Character of Judicial Review," 208. In this view, the judicial opinion "is a piece of rhetoric and of literature, intended to educate and persuade. In the clearest possible way, it represents the conception of the judges speaking directly to the people, as participants in an endless public conversation on the nature and purposes of law, in all its applications. It recognizes the special responsibility of judges, appointed for a time as delegates of the people, charged with the duty of doing justice to the men before them, as spokesmen for the people of their common or customary conception of law" (Rostow, "The Court and its Critics," *South Texas Law Review* 4 [1959]: 160, 163).

124. Eisgruber, "Is the Supreme Court an Educative Institution?" 1009.

125. Alexander M. Bickel, *The Least Dangerous Branch: The Supreme Court at the Bar of Politics* (Indianapolis: Bobbs-Merrill, 1962), 239.

126. Hand, *The Bill of Rights,* 71.

127. One important exception is Archibald Cox, *The Role of the Supreme Court in American Government* (New York: Oxford University Press, 1976), 103–106.

8. JUDICIALIST INSTITUTIONS AND THE PROTECTION OF RIGHTS

1. See Alexander M. Bickel, "The Supreme Court 1960 Term—Foreword: The Passive Virtues," *Harvard Law Review* 75 (1961): 40; Guido Calabresi, *A Common Law for the Age of Statutes* (Cambridge: Harvard University Press, 1982), 9–11.

2. *Flanary v. Commonwealth,* 184 Va. 204, 212 (1945).

3. *Shenandoah Publishing v. Fanning,* 235 Va. 253, 256, 258 (1988).

4. *State v. Mains,* 295 Or. 640, 645 (1983).

5. *Lloyd v. Whiffen,* 307 Or. 674, 679–680 (1989).

6. Ibid., 680 n.4.

7. *Williams v. Commonwealth.* 350 Mass. 732, 736 (1966). See Herbert P. Wilkins, "Judicial Treatment of the Massachusetts Declaration of Rights in Relation to Cognate Provisions of the United States Constitution," *Suffolk Law Review* 14 (1980): 887, 888 n.7.

8. *State v. Delaney,* 221 Or. 620, 641 (1960).

9. Laurence H. Tribe, *American Constitutional Law,* 2d. ed. (Mineola, NY: Foundation Press, 1988), 1310.

10. Note, "Developments in the Law—The Interpretation of State Constitutional Rights," *Harvard Law Review* 95 (1982): 1324, 1353.

11. Peter P. Miller, "Freedom of Expression Under State Constitutions," *Stanford Law Review* 20 (1968): 318, 323.

12. Project Report, "Toward an Activist Role for State Bills of Rights," *Harvard Civil Rights–Civil Liberties* 8 (1973): 271, 311.

13. *Commonwealth v. Ford,* 394 Mass. 421, 431 (1985).

14. *Hart v. Commonwealth,* 221 Va. 283, 287 (1980).

15. *Hewitt v. SAIF,* 294 Or. 33, 41–42 (1982).

16. Ibid., 58–59.

17. Hans A. Linde, "E Pluribus—Constitutional Theory in State Courts," *Georgia Law Review* 18 (1984): 165, 169.

18. Legislative protection of rights was encouraged during this period by Cass Sunstein, *The Partial Constitution* (Cambridge: Harvard University Press, 1993), 9, 13; Ira C. Lupu, "Statutes Revolving in Constitutional Law Orbits," *Virginia Law Review* 79 (1993): 1, 83; Louis Fisher, "The Curious Belief in Judicial Supremacy," *Suffolk Law Review* 25 (1991): 85; Lawrence Marshall, "Divesting the Courts: Breaking the Judicial Monopoly on Constitutional Interpretation," *Chicago–Kent Law Review* 66 (1990): 481.

19. William J. Keefe, "The Functions and Powers of the State Legislature," in *State Legislatures in American Politics*, ed. Alexander Heard (Englewood Cliffs, NJ: Prentice-Hall, 1966), 61, 64.

20. *State v. Childs,* 252 Or. 91, 101 (1968).

21. *Virginia Acts of Assembly, 1972,* S.J.R. no. 71.

22. *Virginia Acts of Assembly, 1973,* c. 316.

23. Tribe, *American Constitutional Law,* 1311.

24. *Commonwealth v. O'Neal,* 367 Mass. 440, 449 (1975).

25. *Commonwealth v, O'Neal,* 369 Mass. 242 (1975).

26. *Massachusetts Acts, 1979,* c. 488.

27. *Suffolk v. Watson,* 381 Mass. 648 (1980).

28. *Kent v. Commissioner of Education,* 380 Mass. 235 (1980).

29. House no. 54, quoted in *Opinion of the Justices,* 387 Mass. 1201, 1202 (1982).

30. Ibid., 1205–1206 (emphasis supplied).

31. Janice C. May, "The Constitutional Initiative: A Threat to Rights?" in *Human Rights in the States,* ed. Stanley H. Friedelbaum (New York: Greenwood Press, 1988), 175–177; James M. Fischer, "Ballot Propositions: The Challenge of Direct Democracy to State Constitutional Jurisprudence," *Hastings Law Quarterly* 11 (1984): 43, 78–79; John F. Cooper and Thomas C. Marks, Jr., "An Expansive State Constitutional Provision: Does It Sow the Seeds of Its Own Destruction?" *State Constitutional Commentaries and Notes* 1 (winter 1990): 1.

32. *Oregon Laws, 1987,* c. 2.

33. *Michigan Public Acts, 1987,* p. 1759.

34. *Oregon Laws, 1979,* c. 2; *Oregon Laws, 1985,* c. 3. The death penalty was a frequent subject of initiatives during this period, as measures were also approved in California in 1972 and 1978, Colorado in 1974, and Washington in 1975.

35. Initiatives in California in 1972, Colorado in 1974, and Washington in 1977 sought to limit busing. Initiatives in Montana in 1978 and Washington in 1977 tried to restrict the circulation of obscene materials.

36. *Stadle v. Township of Battle Creek,* 346 Mich. 64, 69 (1956), quoting *McQuillin Municipal Corporations.*

37. *James v. Valtierra,* 402 U.S. 137, 141 (1971).

38. Philip B. Kurland and Gerhard Casper, eds., *64 Landmark Briefs and Arguments of the Supreme Court of the United States: Constitutional Law* (Washington, DC: University Publications of America, 1975), 668, quoted in Julian Eule, "Judicial Review of Direct Democracy," *Yale Law Journal* 99 (1990): 1503, 1506.

39. *Anthony v. Veatch,* 189 Or. 462, 496–497 (1950).

40. Ibid., 498.

41. Lynn Baker, "Direct Democracy and Discrimination: A Public Choice Perspective," *Chicago–Kent Law Review* 67 (1991): 707, 776.

42. Preble Stolz, "Say Good-Bye to Hiram Johnson's Ghost," *California Lawyer* 10 (January 1990): 44.

43. Calvin R. Massey, "The 'Underlying Principle' of the Independence of the California Constitution," *State Constitutional Commentaries and Notes* 2 (winter 1991): 1, 4.

44. Fischer, "Ballot Propositions," 89. See also Gerald F. Uelmen, "California's Crime Victims Reform Act: Limiting State Constitutional Rights of Criminal Defendants," *State Constitutional Commentaries and Notes* 1 (summer 1990): 5; Hans A. Linde, "When Is Initiative Lawmaking Not 'Republican Government'?" *Hastings Constitutional Law Quarterly* 17 (1989): 159; Hans A. Linde, "When Initiative Lawmaking Is Not Republican Government: The Campaign Against Homosexuality," *Oregon Law Review* 72 (1993): 19.

45. David B. Magleby and James D. Gordon III, "Pre-Election Judicial Review of Initiatives and Referendums," *Notre Dame Lawyer* 64 (1989): 298.

46. *Collins v. Secretary,* 407 Mass. 837 (1990).

47. *Oregon Laws, 1979,* c. 2.

48. *State v. Quinn,* 290 Or. 383 (1981).

49. Katherine Waldo, "The 1984 Oregon Death Penalty Initiatives: A State Constitutional Analysis," *Willamette Law Review* 22 (1986): 285, 293.

50. David B. Magleby, "Let the Voters Decide? An Assessment of the Initiative and Referendum Process," *University of Colorado Law Review* 66 (1995): 13, 40. See also David D. Schmidt, *Citizen Lawmakers: The Ballot Initiative Revolution* (Philadelphia: Temple University Press, 1989), 287–294; Fischer, "Ballot Propositions," 82.

51. General treatments of constitutional amendment and revision activity in this period include John P. Wheeler, ed., *Salient Issues of Constitutional Revision* (New York: National Municipal League, 1961); Charles R. Adrian, "Trends in State Constitutions," *Harvard Journal on Legislation* 5 (1966): 311; W. Brooke Graves, "State Constitutional Law: A Twenty-five Year Summary," *William and Mary Law Review* 8 (1966): 1; Robert B. Dishman, *State Constitutions: The Shape of the Document* (New York: National Municipal League, 1960); Albert L. Sturm, *Thirty Years of State Constitution-Making: 1938–1968* (New York: National Municipal League, 1970).

52. *Acts and Proceedings of the Michigan Convention of 1962* (Lansing: State Printer, 1964), 3006.

53. Commission on Constitutional Revision, *The Virginia Constitution* (Charlottesville: Michie Publishing Co., 1969), 98.

54. Ibid., 15.

55. *Proceedings and Debates of the Virginia House of Delegates Pertaining to Amendment of the Constitution, Extra Session 1969, Regular Session 1970* (Richmond: State Printer, 1971), 493.

56. *Michigan Laws of 1952,* p. 479.

57. A. E. Dick Howard, *Commentaries on the Constitution of Virginia,* 2 vols. (Charlottesville: University Press of Virginia, 1974), 1:21.

58. Massachusetts Constitution (Amendment no. 111).

59. Massachusetts Constitution (Amendment no. 116).

60. *Commonwealth v. Colon-Cruz,* 393 Mass. 150, 173 (1984) (Hennessey, J., concurring).

61. Ibid., 161.

62. Ibid., 163.

63. Ibid., 181–182.

9. JUDICIALIST INSTITUTIONS AS KEEPERS OF THE PEOPLE'S LIBERTIES

1. Robert F. Nagel, *Constitutional Cultures: The Mentality and Consequences of Judicial Review* (Los Angeles: University of California Press, 1989), 35.

2. Henry Steele Commager, *Majority Rule and Minority Rights* (New York: Oxford University Press, 1943).

3. Grant McConnell, *Private Power and American Democracy* (New York: Alfred A. Knopf, 1966), 91–118.

4. Michael J. Klarman, "Rethinking the Civil Rights and Civil Liberties Revolutions," *Virginia Law Review* 82 (1996): 1, 32.

5. Nagel, *Constitutional Cultures,* 57.

6. Ibid., 58.

7. Ibid.

8. G. Alan Tarr, "Church and State in the States," *Washington Law Review* 64 (1989): 73, 95–99.

9. Jesse H. Choper, "The Establishment Clause and Aid to Parochial Schools," *California Law Review* 56 (1968): 260; Judith C. Areen, "Public Aid to Nonpublic Schools: A Breach in the Sacred Wall?" *Case Western Reserve Law Review* 22 (1971): 230, 230–233.

10. *Dickman v. School District,* 232 Or. 238 (1962); *Constitutionality of 1974 PA 242,* 394 Mich. 41 (1975); *Bloom v. School Committee of Springfield,* 376 Mass. 35 (1978). Most of these states continued to fund transportation for parochial students. See *Michigan Laws, 1976,* no. 451, part 16, s. 1217; *Massachusetts Acts, 1983,* c. 663.

11. Tarr, "Church and State in the States," 99–103.

12. *Commissioner of Education v. Leyden,* 358 Mass. 776 (1971); *Kent v. Commissioner of Education,* 380 Mass. 235 (1980); *Opinion of the Justices,* 387 Mass. 1201 (1982).

13. Tarr, "Church and State in the States," 103–106; *Lowe v. City of Eugene,* 254 Or. 518 (1969). Seven years later, the court revisited the issue and noted that "[t]he cross has never been removed," but the circumstances of the case had changed significantly. In light of the new circumstances, the court let the cross stand (*Eugene Sand and Gravel v. City of Eugene,* 276 Or. 1007, 1009 [1976]).

14. Several of the major positions in this debate are expressed in Douglas Laycock, "Equal Access and Moments of Silence: The Equal Status of Religious Speech by Private Speakers," *Northwestern Law Review* 81 (1986): 1; Michael W. McConnell, "Religious Freedom at a Crossroads," *University of Chicago Law Review* 59 (1992): 115; Leonard W. Levy, *The Establishment Clause: Religion and the First Amendment* (New York: Macmillan, 1986); Ira C. Lupu, "The Trouble with Accommodation," *George Washington Law Review* 60 (1992): 743; "Symposium: Religion and the Public Schools After *Lee v. Weisman,*" *Case Western Reserve Law Review* 43 (1993): 699.

15. *Sisters of the Holy Cross v. Brookline,* 347 Mass. 486 (1964).

16. *Marks Furs v. City of Detroit,* 365 Mich. 108 (1961).

17. *Dalli v. Board of Education,* 358 Mass. 753 (1971); *Civil Rights Department v. GMC,* 412 Mich. 610 (1982); *Commonwealth v. Nissenbaum,* 404 Mass. 575 (1989); *Smith v. Employment Division,* 301 Or. 209 (1986).

18. *Massachusetts Acts of 1971,* c. 285; *Michigan Laws of 1960,* c. 12; *Virginia Acts of Assembly, 1974,* c. 160.

19. *Michigan Laws of 1976,* no. 451, part 15, s. 1170; *Oregon Laws, 1957,* c. 409.

20. *Virginia Acts of Assembly, 1960,* c. 465.

21. *Massachusetts Acts of 1989,* c. 516; *Michigan Laws of 1976,* no. 453, art. 4, s. 403.

22. *Massachusetts Acts of 1973,* c. 521; *Massachusetts Acts of 1979,* c. 216; *Massachusetts Acts of 1981,* c. 285; *Virginia Acts of Assembly, 1974,* c. 679.

23. *Massachusetts Acts of 1960,* c. 444, s. 139G.

24. *Massachusetts Acts of 1964,* c. 216. In 1957 the Massachusetts Supreme Court had rejected the argument of a Jewish shopkeeper that he should be permitted to open his supermarket on Sundays (*Commonwealth v. Chernock,* 336 Mass. 384 [1958]).

25. James E. Ryan, "*Smith* and the Religious Freedom Restoration Act: An Iconoclastic Assessment," *Virginia Law Review* 78 (1992): 1407, 1413.

26. Thomas I. Emerson, *The System of Freedom of Expression* (New York: Random House, 1970); Thomas I. Emerson, David Haber, and Norman Dorsen, *Political and Civil Rights in the United States*, 2 vols., 3d ed. (Boston: Little, Brown, 1967), 1:1–735.

27. For a general analysis of judicial treatment of free-speech issues, see Nagel, *Constitutional Cultures*, 27–59.

28. Walter Gellhorn, ed., *The States and Subversion* (Ithaca, NY: Cornell University Press, 1952); Harold M. Hyman, *To Try Men's Souls: Loyalty Tests in American History* (Los Angeles: University of California Press, 1959), 316–348; Ralph S. Brown, *Loyalty and Security: Employment Tests in the United States* (New Haven, CT: Yale University Press, 1958), 92–163; Note, "Loyalty Oaths," *Yale Law Journal* 77 (1968): 739.

29. For instance, the Michigan Supreme Court upheld a loyalty oath for teachers in 1935 and maintained this position in subsequent years (*Sauder v. School District*, 271 Mich. 413 [1935]; Gellhorn, *The States and Subversion*, 196–206).

30. Arval A. Morris, "Academic Freedom and Loyalty Oaths," *Law and Contemporary Problems* 28 (1963): 487; Alan M. Sager, "The Impact of Supreme Court Loyalty Oath Decisions," *American University Law Review* 22 (1972): 39, 74.

31. *Brush v. State Board of Higher Education*, 245 Or. 373 (1966).

32. *Pedlosky v. M.I.T.*, 352 Mass. 127 (1967).

33. O. John Rogge, "Compelling the Testimony of Political Deviants," *Michigan Law Review* 55 (1956): 163.

34. *Jones v. Commonwealth*, 327 Mass. 491 (1951).

35. *Opinion of the Justices*, 332 Mass. 763 (1955). But the court upheld a law that permitted the dismissal of a public school teacher who asserted his privilege against self-incrimination at a U.S. Senate subcommittee hearing (*Faxon v. School Committee of Boston*, 331 Mass. 531 [1954]).

36. *Commonwealth v. Pascone*, 308 Mass. 591 (1941); *Kenyon v. Chicopee*, 320 Mass. 528 (1946). In the late 1940s and 1950s the courts also increased communicative opportunities for magazine distributors and public speakers (*Robert v. City of Norfolk*, 188 Va. 413 [1948]; *Commonwealth v. Jacobs*, 333 Mass. 204 [1955]).

37. *Book Tower Garage v. Local No. 415*, 295 Mich. 580 (1940); *Edwards v. Commonwealth*, 191 Va. 272 (1950).

38. *Commonwealth v. Gilfedder*, 321 Mass. 335 (1947).

39. *York v. City of Danville*, 207 Va. 665 (1967).

40. *Brattle Films v. Commissioner of Public Safety*, 333 Mass. 58 (1955); *City of Portland v. Welch*, 229 Or. 308 (1961).

41. *Goldstein v. Commonwealth*, 200 Va. 25 (1958). For a contemporary discussion, see William Lockhart and Robert McClure, "Censorship of Obscenity: The Developing Constitutional Standards," *Minnesota Law Review* 45 (1960): 5.

42. *Attorney General v. "Tropic of Cancer,"* 345 Mass. 11 (1962). See, generally, Note, "Community Standards, Class Actions, and Obscenity Under *Miller v. California*," *Harvard Law Review* 88 (1975): 1838, 1847–1848 n.51.

43. *State v. Spencer*, 289 Or. 225 (1980).

44. *Commonwealth v. Sees*, 374 Mass. 532 (1978).

45. *Commonwealth v. Oakes,* 401 Mass. 602 (1988) (reversed by the U.S. Supreme Court).

46. Emerson, *System of Freedom of Expression,* 485.

47. Harry M. Clor, *Obscenity and Public Morality: Censorship in a Liberal Society* (Chicago: University of Chicago Press, 1969).

48. See, for instance, the comments of the justices of the Massachusetts Supreme Court in *Commonwealth v. Horton,* 365 Mass. 164, 178 (1974).

49. *State v. Buchanan,* 250 Or. 244, 250–251 (1968); *In the Matter of Roche,* 381 Mass. 624, 639–640 (1980). See, generally, Jeffrey Schreck, "Journalist's Privilege: *In Re Farber* and the New Jersey Shield Laws," *Rutgers Law Review* 32 (1979): 545, 547–548.

50. Schreck, "Journalist's Privilege," 548.

51. Ibid., 549 n.20. See also Note, "The Right of a Newsman to Refrain from Divulging the Sources of His Information," *Virginia Law Review* 36 (1950): 61; Steven Peifer, "State Newsman's Privilege Statutes: A Critical Analysis," *Notre Dame Lawyer* 49 (1973): 150.

52. Schreck, "Journalist's Privilege," 550.

53. For a comprehensive discussion of these fair-trial rights, see Stuart S. Nagel, ed., *The Rights of the Accused in Law and Action* (Beverly Hills: Sage Publications, 1972); David Fellman, *The Defendant's Rights Today* (Madison: University of Wisconsin Press, 1976).

54. *State v. Lillie,* 172 Or. 194, 201–202 (1943).

55. *State v. Neely,* 239 Or. 487, 493–494 (1965).

56. For a list of state statutes guaranteeing the right to a speedy trial, see Note, "Convicts—The Right to a Speedy Trial and the New Detainer Statutes," *Rutgers Law Review* 18 (1964): 828, 869–874.

57. *State v. Crosby,* 217 Or. 393, 397 (1959).

58. Note, "The Right to a Public Trial in Criminal Cases," *New York University Law Review* 41 (1966): 1138, 1140. See *Commonwealth v. Blondin,* 324 Mass. 564, 569 (1949); *Virginia Acts of Assembly, 1971 (Special Session),* c. 28.

59. For a comprehensive list of state statutes guaranteeing the right to counsel, see William M. Beaney, *The Right to Counsel in American Courts* (Ann Arbor: University of Michigan Press, 1955), 84–87.

60. See, for instance, *Oregon Laws, 1941,* c. 456; *Oregon Laws, 1961,* c. 696.

61. *Virginia Acts, 1946,* c. 72; *Virginia Acts, 1950,* c. 266; *Virginia Acts, 1960,* c. 236; *Virginia Acts, 1964,* c. 651.

62. See, for instance, *Michigan Laws, 1965,* c. 251; *Oregon Laws, 1967,* c. 475.

63. *State v. Delaney,* 221 Or. 620, 639 (1960).

64. *People v. Parshay,* 379 Mich. 7, 11–12 (1967).

65. *Stevenson v. Holzman,* 254 Or. 94 (1969).

66. *Gebhardt v. Gladden,* 243 Or. 145 (1966).

67. *Virginia Acts, 1950,* c. 102; *Virginia Acts, 1956,* c. 416.

68. *Massachusetts Acts, 1964,* c. 557; *Virginia Acts, 1968,* c. 572; *Michigan Acts, 1966,* No. 189; *Michigan Acts, 1988,* no. 80.

69. *Massachusetts Acts, 1959,* c. 449.

70. Barry Latzer, *State Constitutions and Criminal Justice* (New York: Greenwood Press, 1991), 31–50. Michigan and Oregon had already adopted the exclusionary rule on constitutional grounds prior to this era. In the 1960s, all four state courts began to enforce

the rule at the direction of the U.S. Supreme Court. Then, in the 1970s and 1980s, the Michigan, Massachusetts, and Oregon supreme courts implemented versions of the exclusionary rule that were even more stringent than the federal rule.

71. *Hart v. Commonwealth,* 221 Va. 283, 287 (1980).

72. Dallin H. Oaks, "Studying the Exclusionary Rule in Search and Seizure," *University of Chicago Law Review* 37 (1970): 665, 667.

73. Several of the more important articles include James Spiotto, "Search and Seizure: An Empirical Study of the Exclusionary Rule and Its Alternatives," *Journal of Legal Studies* 2 (1973): 243; Bradley C. Canon, "The Exclusionary Rule: Have Critics Proven That It Doesn't Deter Police?" *Judicature* 62 (1979): 398; Akhil Reed Amar, "Fourth Amendment First Principles," *Harvard Law Review* 107 (1994): 757.

74. William A. Schroeder, "Deterring Fourth Amendment Violations: Alternatives to the Exclusionary Rule," *Georgetown Law Journal* 69 (1981): 1361, 1379.

75. *State v. Ellis,* 181 Or. 615 (1947); *Namba v. McCourt and Neuner,* 185 Or. 579 (1949).

76. For a discussion of the reaction of southern state legislatures to *Brown,* see Richard Bardolph, ed., *The Civil Rights Record: Black Americans and the Law, 1849–1970* (New York: Thomas Y. Crowell, 1970), 373–394.

77. *Harrison v. Day,* 200 Va. 439, 442 (1959).

78. *Brown v. City of Richmond,* 204 Va. 471 (1963).

79. *Massachusetts Acts, 1965,* c. 641.

80. *School Committee of Boston v. Board of Education,* 352 Mass. 693 (1967).

81. *Opinion of the Justices,* 363 Mass. 899 (1973); *Opinion of the Justices,* 365 Mass. 648 (1974).

82. For a list of state statutes in this period, see Bardolph, *Civil Rights Record,* 366–372; Jack Greenberg, *Race Relations and American Law* (New York: Columbia University Press, 1959), 372–400.

83. *Massachusetts Acts of 1946,* c. 368; *Michigan Acts, 1955,* No. 251; *Oregon Laws, 1947,* c. 508; *Virginia Acts, 1975,* c. 626.

84. *Massachusetts Acts, 1948,* c. 51; *Massachusetts Acts, 1957,* c. 426; *Massachusetts Acts, 1959,* c. 239; *Michigan Acts, 1952,* no. 101; *Oregon Laws, 1957,* c. 724; *Oregon Laws, 1961,* c. 247, s. 1; *Oregon Laws, 1969,* c. 618, s. 6.

85. *Massachusetts Acts, 1949,* c. 726; *Massachusetts Acts, 1960,* c. 163; *Michigan Acts, 1968,* no. 112; *Michigan Acts, 1974,* no. 246; *Oregon Laws, 1953,* c. 495.

86. *Massachusetts Commission Against Discrimination v. Colangelo,* 344 Mass. 387 (1962) (upholding a housing discrimination law); *Highland Park v. F.E.P.C.,* 364 Mich. 508 (1961) (upholding a fair employment practices act).

87. For a discussion of the multiple goals of the women's movement in this era, see Ruth Bader Ginsburg, "Gender and the Constitution," *University of Cincinnati Law Review* 44 (1975): 1; Mary E. Becker, "Prince Charming: Abstract Equality," *Supreme Court Review* (1987): 201.

88. For examples of the conventional view that courts played an important role in this area, see Winifred L. Hepperle and Laura L. Crites, *Women in the Courts* (Williamsburg, VA: National Center for State Courts, 1978); Margaret A. Berger, *Litigation on Behalf of Women* (New York: Ford Foundation, 1980); Susan Gluck Mezey, *In Pursuit of Equality: Women, Public Policy, and the Federal Courts* (New York: St. Martin's Press, 1992).

89. *Massachusetts Acts, 1945,* c. 584, 727; *Massachusetts Acts, 1947,* c. 565; *Massachusetts Acts, 1951,* c. 180.

90. *Massachusetts Acts, 1965,* c. 397.

91. *Virginia Acts, 1952,* c. 54.

92. *Oregon Laws, 1977,* c. 330.

93. *Goesart v. Cleary,* 335 U.S. 464 (1948).

94. *Michigan Acts, 1949,* no. 82.

95. This holds true even if we expand our sample to include Congress and the U.S. Supreme Court. Although discussions of the women's rights movement historically focus on the role of U.S. Supreme Court decisions in the 1970s, the major gains for women's rights were actually secured through congressional statutes that were enacted in the 1960s. See Jesse H. Choper, "Consequences of Supreme Court Decisions Upholding Individual Constitutional Rights," *Michigan Law Review* 83 (1984): 1, 200; Gerald N. Rosenberg, *The Hollow Hope: Can Courts Bring About Social Change?* (Chicago: University of Chicago Press, 1991), 205–206; Klarman, "Rethinking the Civil Rights and Civil Liberties Revolutions," 9.

96. For a discussion of the use of judicial decisions to overcome legislative inertia, see Richard Neely, *How Courts Govern America* (New Haven, CT: Yale University Press, 1981), 15; Guido Calabresi, *A Common Law for the Age of Statutes* (Cambridge: Harvard University Press, 1982), 6–7.

97. *Hewitt v. State Accident Insurance Fund Corporation,* 294 Or. 33 (1982).

98. *Attorney General v. MIAA,* 378 Mass. 342 (1979).

99. *Oregon Laws, 1971,* c. 743, s. 432.

100. Rhonda R. Rivera, "Our Straight-Laced Judges: The Legal Position of Homosexual Persons in the United States," *Hastings Law Journal* 30 (1979): 799, 950–951; Nan Feyler, "The Use of the State Constitutional Right to Privacy to Defeat State Sodomy Laws," *New York University Review of Law and Social Change* 14 (1986): 973, 979.

101. "Recent Case—Kentucky Supreme Court Finds That Criminalization of Homosexual Sodomy Violates State Constitutional Guarantee of Privacy and Equal Protection," *Harvard Law Review* 106 (1993): 1370, 1373 n.27.

102. Stephanie Grauerholz, "Colorado's Amendment 2 Defeated: The Emergence of a Fundamental Right to Participate in the Political Process," *DePaul Law Review* 44 (1995): 841, 859.

103. *Commonwealth v. Wasson,* 842 S.W.2d 487 (Ky. 1992). The supreme courts of both New York and Pennsylvania overturned their states' antisodomy laws, but it is not clear that they intended to recognize the right to engage in homosexual sodomy.

104. *Massachusetts Acts, 1989,* c. 516.

105. Note, "Developments in the Law—Sexual Orientation and the Law," *Harvard Law Review* 102 (1989): 1508, 1667.

106. *Oregon Laws, 1959,* c. 547; *Massachusetts Acts, 1950,* c. 697.

107. *Michigan Acts, 1976,* no. 220; *Virginia Acts, 1975,* c. 457.

108. *Massachusetts Acts, 1975,* c. 338; *Virginia Acts, 1984,* c. 685.

109. *Scholle v. Secretary of State,* 367 Mich. 176, 181–182 (1962) (on remand).

110. *In re Apportionment of Legislature,* 387 Mich. 442, 450 (1972).

111. *In re Apportionment,* 413 Mich. 96, 136 (1982).

112. *Wilkins v. Ann Arbor City Clerk,* 385 Mich. 670, 691 (1971).

113. Ibid., 693.

Bibliography

CONSTITUTIONAL CONVENTION RECORDS

Acts and Proceedings of the Michigan Convention of 1962. Lansing: State Printer, 1964.

Commission on Constitutional Revision. *The Virginia Constitution.* Charlottesville: Michie Publishing Co., 1969.

Debates and Proceedings of the Constitutional Convention of the State of Michigan, 1867. Lansing: John A. Kerr and Co., 1907.

Debates in the Massachusetts Constitutional Convention, 1917–1918. Boston: Wright and Potter, 1919.

Journal, Acts, and Proceedings, of a General Convention of the Commonwealth of Virginia, Assembled in Richmond, 1829. Richmond: T. Ritchie, 1829.

Journal, Acts, and Proceedings of a General Convention of the State of Virginia, Assembled at Richmond, on Monday, the Fourteenth Day of October, Eighteen Hundred and Fifty. Richmond: W. Culley, 1850.

Journal of the Convention for Framing a Constitution of Government for the State of Massachusetts Bay. Boston: Dutton and Wentworth, 1832.

Journal of Debates and Proceedings in the Convention of Delegates, Chosen to Revise the Constitution of Massachusetts, Begun and Holden in Boston, Nov. 15, 1820 and Continued by Adjournment to Jan. 9, 1821. Boston: Daily Advertiser, 1853.

Michigan Constitutional Conventions of 1835–1836: Debates and Proceedings. Ed. Harold M. Dorr. Ann Arbor: University of Michigan Press, 1940.

Oregon Constitution and Proceedings and Debates of the Constitutional Convention of 1857. Ed. Charles H. Carey. Salem: State Printing Office, 1926.

Poore, Benjamin Perley, ed. *Federal and State Constitutions, Colonial Charters, and Other Organic Laws of the United States.* 2 vols. Washington, DC: U.S. Government Printing Office, 1878.

Proceedings and Debates of the Constitutional Convention of the State of Michigan, 1907–1908. Lansing: Wynkoop, Hallenbeck, Crawford Co., 1908.

Proceedings and Debates of the Constitutional Convention of the State of Ohio, 1912. Columbus: F. J. Heer Printing Co., 1912.

Proceedings and Debates of the Senate of Virginia Pertaining to Amendments of the Constitution, Extra Session 1969, Regular Session 1970 (Richmond: State Printer, 1971).

Proceedings and Debates of the Virginia House of Delegates Pertaining to Amendment of the Constitution, Extra Session 1969, Regular Session 1970 (Richmond: State Printer, 1971).

Proceedings and Debates of the Virginia State Convention of 1829–1830. Richmond: S. Shepherd and Co., 1830.

Proceedings of the Convention of Delegates Held at the Capitol in the City of Williamsburg in the Colony of Virginia, 1776. Williamsburg: Alexander Purdie, 1776.

Record of the Michigan Constitutional Convention, 1961. Lansing: State Printer, 1962.

Report of the Debates and Proceedings of the State Convention Assembled May 4th, 1853 to Revise and Amend the Constitution of the Commonwealth of Massachusetts. Boston: White and Potter, 1853.

Report of the Proceedings and Debates of the Constitutional Convention, State of Virginia, Held in the City of Richmond, June, 1901, to June 26, 1902. Richmond: Hermitage Press, 1906.

Report of the Proceedings and Debates in the Convention to Revise the Constitution of the State of Michigan, 1850. Lansing: R. W. Ingals, 1850.

Thorpe, Frances Newton, comp. and ed. *Federal and State Constitutions, Colonial Charters, and Other Organic Laws of the States, Territories and Colonies of the United States of America.* 7 vols. Washington, DC: U.S. Government Printing Office, 1909.

BOOKS AND ARTICLES

Abernethy, Byron R. *Constitutional Limitations on the Legislature.* Lawrence: University of Kansas Governmental Research Center, 1959.

Abrahamson, Shirley S. "Criminal Law and State Constitutions: The Emergence of State Constitutional Law." *Texas Law Review* 63 (1985): 1141–1193.

Ackerman, Bruce. "Beyond *Carolene Products.*" *Harvard Law Journal* 98 (1985): 713–746.

———. *We the People: Foundations.* Cambridge, MA: Belknap Press, 1991.

Adams, Willi Paul. *The First American Constitutions: Republican Ideology and the Making of the State Constitutions in the Revolutionary Era.* Trans. Rita Kimber and Robert Kimber. Chapel Hill: University of North Carolina Press, 1980.

Adrian, Charles R. "Trends in State Constitutions." *Harvard Journal on Legislation* 5 (1966): 311–341.

Agresto, John. *The Supreme Court and Constitutional Democracy.* Ithaca, NY: Cornell University Press, 1984.

Alger, George W. "The Courts and Legislative Freedom." *Atlantic Monthly* 111 (March 1913): 345–353.

Allen, Ronald. "National Initiative Proposal." *Nebraska Law Review* 58 (1979): 965–1052.

Amar, Akhil Reed. "The Bill of Rights as a Constitution." *Yale Law Journal* 100 (1991): 1131–1210.

———. "Fourth Amendment First Principles." *Harvard Law Review* 107 (1994): 757–819.

———. *The Constitution and Criminal Procedure: First Principles.* New Haven, CT: Yale University Press, 1997.

Anthony, Susan B., Elizabeth C. Stanton, Melinda J. Gage, and Ida H. Harper, eds. *The History of Woman Suffrage.* 6 vols. New York: Arno Press, 1969.

Antieau, Chester J., Phillip M. Carroll, and Thomas C. Burke. *Religion Under the State Constitutions.* Brooklyn, NY: Central Book Co., 1965.

Areen, Judith C. "Public Aid to Nonpublic Schools: A Breach in the Sacred Wall?" *Case Western Reserve Law Review* 22 (1971): 230–255.

Asher, Robert. "Workmen's Compensation in the United States, 1880-1935." Ph.D. dissertation, University of Minnesota, 1971.

Aumann, Francis Robert. *The Changing American Legal System: Some Selected Phases.* Columbus: Ohio State University Press, 1940.

Bailey, Raymond C. *Popular Influence upon Public Policy: Petitioning in Eighteenth-Century Virginia.* New York: Greenwood Press, 1979.

Baker, Gordon E. *Rural Versus Urban Political Power: The Nature and Consequences of Unbalanced Representation.* Garden City, NY: Doubleday, 1955.

———. "Reapportionment by Initiative in Oregon." *Western Political Quarterly* 13 (1960): 508–519.

———. *State Constitutions: Reapportionment.* New York: National Municipal League, 1960.

Baker, Lynn. "Direct Democracy and Discrimination: A Public Choice Perspective." *Chicago–Kent Law Review* 67 (1991): 705–776.

Barber, Sotirios A. *On What the Constitution Means.* Baltimore: Johns Hopkins University Press, 1984.

Barclay, Thomas. "The Reapportionment Struggle in California in 1948." *Western Political Quarterly* 4 (1951): 313–324.

Bardolph, Richard, ed. *The Civil Rights Record: Black Americans and the Law, 1849–1970.* New York: Thomas Y. Crowell, 1970.

Barnett, James D. *The Operation of the Initiative, Referendum, and Recall in Oregon.* New York: Macmillan, 1915.

Basch, Norma. *In the Eyes of the Law: Women, Marriage, and Property in Nineteenth-Century New York.* Ithaca, NY: Cornell University Press, 1982.

Baxter, Sylvester. "Legislative Degeneracy in Massachusetts." *Arena* 2 (1890): 503–506.

Beaney, William M. *The Right to Counsel in American Courts.* Ann Arbor: University of Michigan Press, 1955.

Beard, Charles, and Birl Schultz, eds. *Documents on the State-wide Initiative, Referendum and Recall.* New York: Macmillan, 1912.

Beatty, Jerry K. "State Court Evasion of the United States Supreme Court Mandates During the Last Decade of the Warren Court." *Valparaiso University Law Review* 6 (1972): 260–285.

Becker, Mary E. "Prince Charming: Abstract Equality." *Supreme Court Review* (1987): 201–247.

Bell, Derrick A. "The Referendum: Democracy's Barrier to Racial Equality." *Washington Law Review* 54 (1978): 1–29.

Bell, Sadie. *The Church, the State, and Education in Virginia.* Philadelphia: Science Press, 1930.

Belz, Herman. "The Constitution in the Gilded Age: The Beginnings of Constitutional Realism in American Scholarship." *American Journal of Legal History* 13 (1969): 110–125.

Benson, George C. S. *The New Centralization: A Study of Intergovernmental Relationships in the United States.* New York: Farrar and Rhinehart, 1941.

Berger, Margaret A. *Litigation on Behalf of Women.* New York: Ford Foundation, 1980.

Bessette, Joseph M. *The Mild Voice of Reason: Deliberative Democracy and American National Government.* Chicago: University of Chicago Press, 1994.

Bickel, Alexander M. "The Supreme Court 1960 Term—Foreword: The Passive Virtues." *Harvard Law Review* 75 (1961): 40–79.

———. *The Least Dangerous Branch: The Supreme Court at the Bar of Politics.* Indianapolis: Bobbs-Merrill, 1962.

———. *The Supreme Court and the Idea of Progress.* New York: Harper and Row, 1970.

———. *The Morality of Consent.* New Haven, CT: Yale University Press, 1975.

Binney, Charles Chauncey. *Restrictions upon Local and Special Legislation in State Constitutions.* Philadelphia: Kay and Brothers, 1894.

Black, Charles L., Jr. *The People and the Court: Judicial Review in a Democracy.* New York: Macmillan, 1960.

Blakely, William Addison, ed. *American State Papers Bearing on Sunday Legislation.* Washington, DC: Religious Liberty Association, 1911.

Blanchard, Margaret A. *Revolutionary Sparks: Freedom of Expression in Modern America.* New York: Oxford University Press, 1992.

Bodansky, Joel. "The Abolition of the Party-Witness Disqualification: An Historical Survey." *Kentucky Law Journal* 70 (1981): 91–130.

Bodenhamer, David J. *Fair Trial: Rights of the Accused in American History.* New York: Oxford University Press, 1992.

Bone, Hugh A. "States Attempting to Comply with Reapportionment Requirements." *Law and Contemporary Problems* 17 (1952): 387–416.

Bone, Hugh A., and Robert C. Benedict. "Perspectives on Direct Legislation: Washington State's Experience 1914–1973." *Western Political Quarterly* 28 (1975): 330–351.

Boudin, Louis B. "Government by Judiciary." *Political Science Quarterly* 26 (1911): 238–270.

Bourne, Jonathan, Jr. "Initiative, Referendum, and Recall," *Atlantic Monthly* 109 (January 1912): 122–131.

Bowling, Kenneth R. " 'A Tub to the Whale': The Founding Fathers and the Adoption of the Federal Bill of Rights." *Journal of the Early Republic* 8 (1988): 223–251.

Boyle, James A. *The Initiative and Referendum: Its Folly, Fallacies, and Failure.* Columbus, OH: A. H. Smythe, 1912.

Brenaman, Jacob. *A History of Virginia Conventions.* Richmond, VA: J. L. Hill, 1902.

Brennan, William J., Jr. "The Bill of Rights and the States." *New York University Law Review* 36 (1961): 761–778.

———. "State Constitutions and the Protection of Individual Rights." *Harvard Law Review* 90 (1977): 489–504.

———. "The Bill of Rights and the States: The Revival of State Constitutions as Guardians of Individual Rights." *New York University Law Review* 61 (1986): 535–553.

Brest, Paul. "The Conscientious Legislator's Guide to Constitutional Interpretation." *Stanford Law Review* 27 (1975): 585–601.

———. "Congress as Constitutional Decisionmaker and Its Power to Counter Judicial Doctrine." *Georgia Law Review* 21 (1986): 57–105.

Briffault, Richard. "Distrust of Democracy (Book Review)." *Texas Law Review* 63 (1985): 1347–1375.

Brown, Ralph S. *Loyalty and Security: Employment Tests in the United States.* New Haven, CT: Yale University Press, 1958.

Brown, Samuel W. *The Secularization of American Education as Shown by State Legislation, State Constitutional Provisions, and State Supreme Court Decisions.* New York: Columbia University, 1912.

Bruce, Dickson D., Jr. *The Rhetoric of Conservatism: The Virginia Convention of 1829–30 and the Conservative Tradition in the South.* San Marino, CA: Huntington Library, 1982.

Bryce, James. *The American Commonwealth.* 2 vols. New York: Macmillan, 1888.

Brydon, G. MacLaren. "The Antiecclesiastical Laws of Virginia." *Virginia Magazine of History and Biography* 64 (1956): 259–285.

Buckley, Thomas E. *Church and State in Revolutionary Virginia, 1776–1787.* Charlottesville: University Press of Virginia, 1977.

Buell, Raymond L. "The Development of Anti-Japanese Agitation in the United States." *Political Science Quarterly* 37 (1922): 605–638.

———. "The Development of Anti-Japanese Agitation in the United States II." *Political Science Quarterly* 38 (1923): 57–81.

Bullock, Edna Mae, ed. *Selected Articles on Mothers' Pensions.* New York: H. W. Wilson and Co., 1915.

Burns, James. *A History of Catholic Education in the United States.* New York: Benziger Brothers, 1937.

Butler, David, and Austin Ranney, eds. *Referendums: A Comparative Study of Practice and Theory.* Washington, DC: American Enterprise Institute for Public Policy Research, 1978.

———. *Referendums Around the World.* New York: Macmillan, 1994.

Buttler, John H. "Oregon's Constitutional Renaissance: Federalism Revisited." *Vermont Law Review* 13 (1988): 107–125.

Bye, Raymond. *Capital Punishment in the United States.* Menasha, WI: Collegiate Press, 1919.

Calabresi, Guido. *A Common Law for the Age of Statutes.* Cambridge: Harvard University Press, 1982.

Campbell, Henry M. "The Initiative and Referendum." *Michigan Law Review* 10 (1912): 427–436.

Canon, Bradley C. "Is the Exclusionary Rule in Failing Health? Some New Data and a Plea Against a Precipitous Conclusion." *Kentucky Law Journal* 62 (1974): 681–730.

————. "Organizational Contumacy in the Transmission of Judicial Policies: The *Mapp, Escobedo, Miranda,* and *Gault* Cases." *Villanova Law Review* 20 (1974): 50–79.

————. "The Exclusionary Rule: Have Critics Proven That It Doesn't Deter Police?" *Judicature* 62 (1979): 398–403.

Catt, Carrie Chapman, and Nettie Rogers Shuler. *Woman Suffrage and Politics: The Inner Story of the Suffrage Movement.* New York: Charles Scribner's Sons, 1923.

Ceaser, James W. *Presidential Selection: Theory and Development.* Princeton, NJ: Princeton University Press, 1979.

Chafee, Zechariah, Jr. "Freedom of Speech." *New Republic* 17 (November 16, 1918): 66–69.

————. "Freedom of Speech in War Time." *Harvard Law Review* 32 (1919): 932–973.

————. *Freedom of Speech.* New York: Harcourt, Brace and Howe, 1920.

————. *Free Speech in the United States.* Cambridge: Harvard University Press, 1941.

Chamberlin, Bill F., and Charlene J. Brown, eds. *The First Amendment Reconsidered: New Perspectives of the Meaning of Freedom of Speech and Press.* New York: Longman, 1982.

Charlow, Robin. "Judicial Review, Equal Protection, and the Problem with Plebiscites." *Cornell Law Review* 79 (1994): 527–630.

Chayes, Abram. "The Role of the Judge in Public Law Litigation." *Harvard Law Review* 89 (1976): 1281–1316.

Chemerinsky, Erwin. *Interpreting the Constitution.* New York: Praeger, 1987.

————. "The Supreme Court 1988 Term: Foreword—The Vanishing Constitution." *Harvard Law Review* 103 (1989): 43–104.

Cherrington, Ernest H. *The Evolution of Prohibition in the United States of America.* Westerville, OH: American Issue Press, 1920.

Choper, Jesse H. "The Establishment Clause and Aid to Parochial Schools." *California Law Review* 56 (1968): 260–341.

————. *Judicial Review and the National Political Process: A Functional Reconsideration of the Role of the Supreme Court.* Chicago: University of Chicago Press, 1980.

————. "Consequences of Supreme Court Decisions Upholding Individual Constitutional Rights." *Michigan Law Review* 83 (1984): 1–212.

Church, Randolph W., comp. *Virginia Legislative Petitions: Bibliography, Calendar, and Abstracts from Original Sources: 6 May 1776–21 June 1782.* Richmond: Virginia State Library, 1984.

Clinton, Robert Lowry. *Marbury v. Madison and Judicial Review.* Lawrence: University Press of Kansas, 1989.

Cloe, Lyman H., and Sumner Marcus. "Special and Local Legislation." *Kentucky Law Journal* 24 (1936): 351–386.

Clor, Harry M. *Obscenity and Public Morality: Censorship in a Liberal Society.* Chicago: University of Chicago Press, 1969.

Colantuono, Michael G. "The Revision of American State Constitutions: Legislative Power, Popular Sovereignty, and Constitutional Change." *California Law Review* 75 (1987): 1473–1512.

Collins, Ronald K. L. "Reliance on State Constitutions—Away from a Reactionary Approach." *Hastings Constitutional Law Quarterly* 9 (1981): 1–19.

Commager, Henry Steele. *Majority Rule and Minority Rights.* New York: Oxford University Press, 1943.

————. *Freedom, Loyalty, Dissent.* New York: Oxford University Press, 1954.

Commons, John R., ed. *History of Labour in the United States.* 4 vols. New York: Macmillan, 1918–1935.

Cooley, Thomas M. *The General Principles of Constitutional Law in the United States of America.* Boston: Little, Brown, 1880.

———. "Comparative Merits of Written and Prescriptive Constitutions." *Harvard Law Review* 2 (1889): 341–357.

———. *A Treatise on the Constitutional Limitations Which Rest upon the Legislative Power of the States of the American Union.* 1868. Repr. New York: Da Capo Press, 1972.

Cooper, John F., and Thomas C. Marks, Jr. "An Expansive State Constitutional Provision: Does It Sow the Seeds of Its Own Destruction?" *State Constitutional Commentaries and Notes* 1 (winter 1990): 1–3.

Cornwell, Elmer E., Jay S. Goodman, and Wayne R. Swanson. *Constitutional Conventions: The Politics of Revision.* New York: National Municipal League, 1974.

———. *State Constitutional Conventions: The Politics of the Revision Process in Seven States.* New York: Praeger, 1975.

Corwin, Edward S. "The Doctrine of Due Process Before the Civil War." *Harvard Law Review* 24 (1911): 366–385.

Countryman, Vern. "Why a State Bill of Rights?" *Washington Law Review* 45 (1970): 453–496.

Cover, Robert M. "The Left, the Right, and the First Amendment: 1918–1928." *Maryland Law Review* 40 (1981): 349–388.

———. "The Origins of Judicial Activism in the Protection of Minorities." *Yale Law Journal* 91 (1982): 1287–1316.

Cox, Archibald. *The Role of the Supreme Court in American Government.* New York: Oxford University Press, 1976.

Coxe, Brinton. *An Essay on Judicial Power and Unconstitutional Legislation, Being a Commentary on Parts of the Constitution of the United States.* Philadelphia: Kay and Brother, 1893.

Croly, Herbert. *Progressive Democracy.* New York: Macmillan, 1914.

Cronin, Thomas E. *Direct Democracy: The Politics of Initiative, Referendum, and Recall.* Cambridge: Harvard University Press, 1989.

Crouch, Winston W. "The Constitutional Initiative in Operation." *American Political Science Review* 33 (1939): 634–645.

Crunden, Robert M. *Ministers of Reform: The Progressives' Achievement in American Civilization: 1889–1920.* New York: Basic Books, 1982.

Culver, Raymond B. *Horace Mann and Religion in the Massachusetts Public Schools.* New Haven, CT: Yale University Press, 1929.

Curry, Thomas J. *The First Freedoms: Church and State in America to the Passage of the First Amendment.* New York: Oxford University Press, 1986.

Cushing, John D. "The Cushing Court and the Abolition of Slavery in Massachusetts: More Notes on the 'Quock Walker Case.'" *American Journal of Legal History* 5 (1961): 118–144.

———. "Notes on Disestablishment in Massachusetts, 1780–1833." *William and Mary Quarterly* 26 (1969): 169–190.

Cushman, Robert E. "Recent Experience with the Initiative and Referendum." *American Political Science Review* 10 (1916): 532–539.

————. "Civil Liberty After the War." *American Political Science Review* 38 (1944): 1–20.

Danbom, David B. *"The World of Hope": Progressives and the Struggle for an Ethical Public Life*. Philadelphia: Temple University Press, 1987.

Darling, Herbert. "Legislative Control over Contracts of Employment: The Weavers' Fines Bill." *Harvard Law Review* 6 (May 1892): 85–97.

Davis, David Brion. "The Movement to Abolish Capital Punishment in America, 1787–1861." *American Historical Review* 63 (1958): 23–46.

Dealey, James Q. *Our State Constitutions*. Philadelphia: American Academy of Political and Social Science. 1907.

————. *The Growth of American State Constitutions from 1776 to the End of the Year 1914*. New York: Ginn and Co., 1915. Repr. New York: Da Capo Press, 1972.

De Grazia, Alfred. *Public and Republic: Political Representation in America*. New York: Alfred A. Knopf, 1951.

De Witt, Benjamin Parke. *The Progressive Movement: A Non-partisan, Comprehensive Discussion of Current Tendencies in American Politics*. New York: Macmillan, 1915.

Dinkin, Robert J. *Before Equal Suffrage: Women in Partisan Politics from Colonial Times to 1920*. Westport, CT: Greenwood Press, 1995.

Dishman, Robert B. *State Constitutions: The Shape of the Document*. New York: National Municipal League, 1960.

Diver, Colin S. "The Judge as Powerbroker: Superintending Change in Political Institutions." *Virginia Law Review* 65 (1978): 43–106.

Dixon, Robert G. *Democratic Representation: Reapportionment in Law and Politics*. New York: Oxford University Press, 1968.

Dodd, Walter F. *The Revision and Amendment of State Constitutions*. Baltimore: Johns Hopkins University Press, 1910.

————. "Social Legislation and the Courts." *Political Science Quarterly* 28 (1913): 1–17.

————. *State Government*. New York: Century Co., 1922.

Dole, Charles F. *The Spirit of Democracy*. New York: Thomas Y. Crowell and Co., 1906.

Douglass, Elisha P. *Rebels and Democrats: The Struggle for Equal Political Rights and Majority Rule During the American Revolution*. Chapel Hill: University of North Carolina Press, 1955.

Dworkin, Ronald. *Taking Rights Seriously*. Cambridge: Harvard University Press, 1977.

————. "The Forum of Principle." *New York University Law Review* 56 (1981): 469–518.

————. *A Matter of Principle*. Cambridge: Harvard University Press, 1985.

————. *Law's Empire*. Cambridge, MA: Belknap Press, 1986.

Easton, David. "An Approach to the Analysis of Political Systems." *World Politics* 9 (1956–1957): 383–400.

Eaton, Allen H. *The Oregon System: The Story of Direct Legislation in Oregon*. Chicago: McClurg and Co., 1912.

Eaton, Amasa M. "Recent State Constitutions." *Harvard Law Review* 6 (1892): 53–72, 109–124.

Eaton, Clement. *Freedom of Thought in the Old South*. Durham, NC: Duke University Press, 1940.

————. "Censorship of the Southern Mails." *American Historical Review* 48 (1942): 266–280.

Eckenrode, Hamilton J. *Separation of Church and State in Virginia.* 1910. Repr. New York: Da Capo Press, 1971.

Eisenach, Eldon J. *The Lost Promise of Progressivism.* Lawrence: University Press of Kansas, 1994.

Eisgruber, Christopher L. "Is the Supreme Court an Educative Institution?" *New York University Law Review* 67 (1992): 961–1032.

Elliott, Jonathan. *The Debates in the Several State Conventions on the Adoption of the Federal Constitution.* 5 vols. Philadelphia: Lippincott, 1937.

Elliott, Ward E. Y. *The Rise of Guardian Democracy: The Supreme Court's Role in Voting Rights Disputes, 1845-1969.* Cambridge: Harvard University Press, 1974.

Ely, John Hart. *Democracy and Distrust: A Theory of Judicial Review.* Cambridge: Harvard University Press, 1980.

Emerson, Thomas I. *The System of Freedom of Expression.* New York: Random House, 1970.

Emerson, Thomas I., David Haber, and Norman Dorsen. *Political and Civil Rights in the United States.* 2 vols. 3d ed. Boston: Little, Brown, 1967.

Eule, Julian N. "Judicial Review of Direct Democracy." *Yale Law Journal* 99 (1990): 1503–1590.

Evans, Tony Howard. "Oregon Progressive Reform, 1902–1914." Ph.D. dissertation, University of California, Berkeley, 1966.

Fellman, David. *The Defendant's Rights Today.* Madison: University of Wisconsin Press, 1976.

Feyler, Nan. "The Use of the State Constitutional Right to Privacy to Defeat State Sodomy Laws." *New York University Review of Law and Social Change* 14 (1986): 973–994.

Finkelman, Paul. "James Madison and the Bill of Rights: A Reluctant Paternity." *Supreme Court Review* (1990): 301–347.

Finkelman, Paul, and Stephen E. Gottlieb, eds. *Toward a Usable Past: Liberty Under State Constitutions.* Athens: University of Georgia Press, 1991.

Fino, Susan P. *The Role of State Supreme Courts in the New Judicial Federalism.* New York: Greenwood Press, 1987.

———. *The Michigan State Constitution: A Reference Guide.* Westport, CT: Greenwood Press, 1996.

Fischer, James M. "Ballot Propositions: The Challenge of Direct Democracy to State Constitutional Jurisprudence." *Hastings Law Quarterly* 11 (1984): 43–89.

Fisher, Louis. "Constitutional Interpretation by Members of Congress." *North Carolina Law Review* 63 (1985): 707–747.

———. *Constitutional Dialogues: Interpretation as Political Process.* Princeton, NJ: Princeton University Press, 1988.

———. "The Curious Belief in Judicial Supremacy." *Suffolk Law Review* 25 (1991): 85–116.

Fiss, Owen M. "The Supreme Court 1978 Term: Foreword—The Forms of Justice." *Harvard Law Review* 93 (1979): 1–58.

Flexner, Eleanor. *Century of Struggle: The Women's Rights Movement in the United States.* Cambridge, MA: Belknap Press, 1959.

Forbath, William E. *Law and the Shaping of the Modern Labor Movement.* Cambridge: Harvard University Press, 1991.

Force, Robert. "State 'Bills of Rights': A Case of Neglect and the Need for a Renaissance." *Valparaiso Law Review* 3 (1969): 125–182.

Ford, Henry Jones. *The Rise and Growth of American Politics: A Sketch of Constitutional Development.* New York: Macmillan, 1898.

Fordham, Jefferson B. *The State Legislative Institution.* Philadelphia: University of Pennsylvania Press, 1959.

Fountaine, Cynthia L. "Lousy Lawmaking: Questioning the Desirability and Constitutionality of Legislating by Initiative." *Southern California Law Review* 61 (1988): 733–776.

Fox, Francis H. "Discrimination and Antidiscrimination in Massachusetts Law." *Boston University Law Review* 44 (1964): 30–78.

Fraenkel, Osmond K. *Our Civil Liberties.* New York: Viking, 1944.

Frank, Jerome. "What Courts Do in Fact." *Illinois Law Review* 26 (1932): 645–666.

Frankfurter, Felix. "Hours of Labor and Realism in Constitutional Law." *Harvard Law Review* 29 (1916): 353–373.

Freund, Ernst. *Standards of American Legislation: An Estimate of Restrictive and Constructive Factors.* Chicago: University of Chicago Press, 1917.

Friedelbaum, Stanley H., ed. *Human Rights in the States: New Directions in Constitutional Policymaking.* New York: Greenwood Press, 1988.

Friedman, Lawrence M. *A History of American Law.* New York: Simon and Schuster, 1973.

———. *Total Justice.* New York: Russell Sage Foundation, 1985.

———. "State Constitutions in Historical Perspective." *Annals of the American Academy of Political and Social Sciences* 496 (1988): 33–42.

Fritz, Christian G. "The American Constitutional Tradition Revisited: Preliminary Observations on State Constitution-Making in the Nineteenth-Century West." *Rutgers Law Journal* 25 (1994): 945–998.

Gall, Gilbert. *The Politics of Right to Work: The Labor Federations as Special Interests, 1943–1979.* New York: Greenwood Press, 1988.

Gamble, Barbara S. "Putting Civil Rights to a Popular Vote." *American Journal of Political Science* 41 (1997): 245–269.

Gardner, James A. "The Failed Discourse of State Constitutionalism." *Michigan Law Review* 90 (1992): 761–837.

Gellhorn, Walter, ed. *The States and Subversion.* Ithaca, NY: Cornell University Press, 1952.

Genung, Helen C. "The Initiative and Referendum in Michigan." Master's thesis, Wayne State University, 1940.

Gillette, Clayton P. "Plebiscites, Participation, and Collective Action in Local Government Law." *Michigan Law Review* 86 (1988): 930–988.

Gillman, Howard. *The Constitution Besieged: The Rise and Demise of Lochner Era Police Powers Jurisprudence.* Durham, NC: Duke University Press, 1993.

Ginsburg, Ruth Bader. "Gender and the Constitution." *University of Cincinnati Law Review* 44 (1975): 1–42.

Gold, David M. *The Shaping of Nineteenth-Century Law: John Appleton and Responsible Individualism.* New York: Greenwood Press, 1990.

Goldings, Morris M. "Massachusetts Amends: A Decade of State Constitutional Revision." *Harvard Journal on Legislation* 5 (1966): 373–393.

Goldwin, Robert A. *From Parchment to Power: How James Madison Used the Bill of Rights to Save the Constitution.* Washington, DC: American Enterprise Institute Press, 1997.

Goldwin, Robert A., and Art Kaufman, eds. *How Does the Constitution Protect Religious Freedom?* Washington, DC: American Enterprise Institute for Public Policy Research, 1987.

Goldwin, Robert A., and William A. Schambra, eds. *How Does the Constitution Secure Rights?* Washington, DC: American Enterprise Institute for Public Policy Research, 1985.

———. *The Constitution, the Courts, and the Quest for Justice.* Washington, DC: American Enterprise Institute for Public Policy Research, 1989.

Graham, Virginia. *A Compilation of Statewide Initiative Proposals Appearing on Ballots Through 1976.* Washington, DC: Congressional Research Service, 1976.

Grant, Sydney, and S. E. Angoff. "Massachusetts and Censorship." *Boston University Law Review* 10 (1930): 36–60.

Grauerholz, Stephanie. "Colorado's Amendment 2 Defeated: The Emergence of a Fundamental Right to Participate in the Political Process." *DePaul Law Review* 44 (1995): 841–915.

Graves, W. Brooke. "State Constitutional Law: A Twenty-five Year Summary." *William and Mary Law Review* 8 (1966): 1–42.

Gray, Alexander G., Jr., and Thomas R. Kiley. "The Initiative and Referendum in Massachusetts." *New England Law Review* 26 (1991): 27–109.

Green, Fletcher M. *Constitutional Development in the South Atlantic States: 1776–1860.* Chapel Hill: University of North Carolina Press, 1930.

Greenberg. Jack. *Race Relations and American Law.* New York: Columbia University Press, 1959.

Grossman, Barbara F. "The Initiative and Referendum Process: The Michigan Experience." *Wayne Law Review* 28 (1981): 77–136.

Gunn, Priscilla. "Initiatives and Referendums: Direct Democracy and Minority Interests." *Urban Law Annual* 22 (1981): 135–159.

Gunther, Gerald. "In Defense of the 'Passive Virtues': A Comment on Principle and Expediency in Judicial Review." *Columbia Law Review* 64 (1964): 1–25.

Haines, Charles Grove. *The American Doctrine of Judicial Supremacy.* New York: Russell and Russell, 1932.

Hall, James P. "Free Speech in War Time." *Columbia Law Review* 21 (1921): 526–537.

Hall, Kermit L. *The Magic Mirror: Law in American History.* New York: Oxford University Press, 1989.

Hall, Kermit L., Harold M. Hyman, and Leon V. Sigal, eds. *The Constitutional Convention as an Amending Device.* Washington, DC: American Historical Association and American Political Science Association, 1981.

Hampel, Robert L. *Temperance and Prohibition in Massachusetts, 1813–1852.* Ann Arbor, MI: UMI Research Press, 1982.

Hand, Learned. *The Spirit of Liberty: Papers and Addresses.* New York: Alfred A. Knopf, 1952.

———. *The Bill of Rights.* Cambridge: Harvard University Press, 1958.

Handlin, Oscar, and Mary Handlin. *The Popular Sources of Popular Authority: Documents on the Massachusetts Constitution of 1780.* Cambridge, MA: Belknap Press, 1966.

Handy, Robert T. *Undermined Establishment: Church-State Relations in America, 1880–1920.* Princeton, NJ: Princeton University Press, 1991.

Hardin, Charles M. "Issues in Legislative Reapportionment." *Review of Politics* 27 (1965): 147–172.

Harmon, M. Judd, ed. *Essays on the Constitution of the United States.* Port Washington, NY: Kennikat Press, 1978.

Hart, Albert Bushnell. *Actual Government as Applied Under American Conditions.* New York: Longmans, Green, and Co., 1903.

Hart, James P. "The Bill of Rights: Safeguard of Individual Liberty." *Texas Law Review* 35 (1957): 919–925.

Hartmann, Edward George. *The Movement to Americanize the Immigrant.* New York: Columbia University Press, 1948.

Hartog, Hendrik, ed. *Law in the American Revolution and the Revolution in the Law: A Collection of Review Essays on American Legal History.* New York: New York University Press, 1981.

Haynes, George. "People's Rule in Oregon, 1910." *Political Science Quarterly* 26 (1911): 32–62.

Heard, Alexander, ed. *State Legislatures in American Politics.* Englewood Cliffs, NJ: Prentice-Hall, 1966.

Hedges, Gilbert. *Where the People Rule.* San Francisco: Bender-Moss, 1914.

Hellerstein, Jerome. "Picketing Legislation and the Courts." *North Carolina Law Review* 10 (1931): 158–188.

Hendrick, Burton J. "The Initiative and Referendum and How Oregon Got Them." *McClure's* 37 (July 1911): 235–248.

———. "Law-Making by the Voters: How the People of Oregon, Working Under the Initiative and Referendum, Have Become Their Own Political Bosses." *McClure's* 37 (September 1911): 435–450.

———. "Woodrow Wilson, Political Leader." *McClure's* 38 (December 1911): 217–231.

Henretta, James A. "Foreword: Rethinking the State Constitutional Tradition." *Rutgers Law Journal* 22 (1991): 819–839.

Hepperle, Winifred L., and Laura L. Crites. *Women in the Courts.* Williamsburg, VA: National Center for State Courts, 1978.

Hickok, Eugene W., and Garry L. McDowell. *Justice v. Law: Courts and Politics in American Society.* New York: Free Press, 1993.

Higham, John. *Strangers in the Land: Patterns of American Nativism: 1860–1925.* New Brunswick, NJ: Rutgers University Press, 1955.

Hitchcock, Henry. *American State Constitutions: A Study of Their Growth.* New York: G. P. Putnam's Sons, 1887.

Hofstadter, Richard. *The Age of Reform: From Bryan to FDR.* New York: Alfred A. Knopf, 1955.

Holcombe, Arthur N. *State Government in the United States.* New York: Macmillan, 1916.

———. *State Government in the United States,* 2d ed. New York: Macmillan, 1926.

———. *State Government in the United States.* 3d ed. New York: Macmillan, 1931.

Holmes, Oliver Wendell, Jr. "The Path of the Law." *Harvard Law Review* 10 (1897): 457–478.

Holtzman, Abraham. *The Townsend Movement: A Political Study.* New York: Bookman Associates, 1963.

Horowitz, Donald L. *The Courts and Social Policy.* Washington, DC: Brookings Institution, 1977.

Horton, John T. *James Kent: A Study in Conservatism, 1763–1847.* New York: Da Capo Press, 1969.

Horwitz, Morton J. *The Transformation of American Law, 1780–1860.* Cambridge: Harvard University Press, 1977.

————. *The Transformation of American Law 1870–1960: The Crisis of Legal Orthodoxy.* New York: Oxford University Press, 1992.

Howard, A. E. Dick. *Commentaries on the Constitution of Virginia.* 2 vols. Charlottesville: University Press of Virginia, 1974.

————. *Road from Runnymede: Magna Carta and Constitutionalism in America.* Charlottesville: University Press of Virginia, 1968.

————. "State Courts and Constitutional Rights in the Day of the Burger Court." *Virginia Law Review* 62 (1976): 873–944.

————, ed. *State Constitutional Revision.* Charlottesville: Virginia Law Review Association, 1968.

Hurst, James Willard. *The Growth of American Law: The Law Makers.* Boston: Little, Brown, 1950.

————. *Law and the Conditions of Freedom in the Nineteenth-Century United States.* Madison: University of Wisconsin Press, 1956.

Hyman, Harold M. *Era of the Oath: Northern Loyalty Tests During the Civil War and Reconstruction.* Philadelphia: University of Pennsylvania Press, 1954.

————. *To Try Men's Souls: Loyalty Tests in American History.* Los Angeles: University of California Press, 1959.

Hyman, Harold M., and William M. Wiecek. *Equal Justice Under Law: Constitutional Development, 1835–1875.* New York: Harper and Row, 1982.

Jacobs, Clyde. *Law Writers and the Courts: The Influence of Thomas M. Cooley, Christopher G. Tiedeman, and John F. Dillon Upon American Constitutional Law.* Los Angeles: University of California Press, 1954.

James, Charles F. *Documentary History of the Struggle for Religious Liberty in Virginia.* 1899. Repr. New York: Da Capo Press, 1971.

Jameson, John Alexander. *The Constitutional Convention: Its History, Powers, and Modes of Proceeding.* 3d ed. Chicago: Callaghan and Co., 1873.

————. *A Treatise on Constitutional Conventions.* 4th ed. Chicago: Callaghan and Co., 1887.

Johnson, Donald O. *The Challenge to American Freedoms: World War I and the Rise of the American Civil Liberties Union.* Lexington: University of Kentucky Press, 1963.

Jones, Alan R. "Thomas Cooley and 'Laissez-Faire Constitutionalism': A Reconsideration." *Journal of American History* 53 (1967): 751–771.

————. *The Constitutional Conservatism of Thomas McIntyre Cooley: A Study in the History of Ideas.* New York: Garland Press, 1987.

Judson, Frederick. "The Future of Representative Government." *American Political Science Review* 2 (1908): 185–203.

Kagan, Robert A., Bliss Cartwright, Lawrence M. Friedman, and Stanton Wheeler. "The Business of State Supreme Courts, 1870–1970." *Stanford Law Review* 30 (1977): 121–156.

Kahn, Paul W. "Interpretation and Authority in State Constitutionalism." *Harvard Law Review* 106 (1993): 1147–1168.

Kammen, Michael G. *A Machine That Would Go of Itself: The Constitution in American Culture.* New York: Alfred A. Knopf, 1986.

Karsten, Peter. *Heart versus Head: Judge-Made Law in Nineteenth-Century America.* Chapel Hill: University of North Carolina Press, 1997.

Kauper, Paul. "Judicial Examination of the Accused—A Remedy for the Third Degree." *Michigan Law Review* 30 (1931): 1224–1255.

Kaye, Judith S. "Foreword: The Common Law and State Constitutional Law as Full Partners in the Protection of Individual Rights." *Rutgers Law Journal* 23 (1992): 727–752.

Keller, Morton. *Affairs of State: Public Life in Late Nineteenth Century America.* Cambridge, MA: Belknap Press, 1977.

———. "Powers and Rights: Two Centuries of American Constitutionalism." *Journal of American History* 74 (1987): 675–694.

———. *Regulating a New Society: Public Policy and Social Change in America, 1900–1933.* Cambridge: Harvard University Press, 1994.

Kens, Paul. "The Source of a Myth: Police Powers of the States and Laissez Faire Constitutionalism." *American Journal of Legal History* 35 (1991): 70–98.

Kent, James. *Commentaries on American Law.* 4 vols. 1827. Repr. New York: Da Capo Press, 1971.

Key, V. O., and Winston W. Crouch. *The Initiative and the Referendum in California.* Los Angeles: University of California Press, 1939.

Kincaid, John. "The New Judicial Federalism." *Journal of State Government* 61 (1988): 163–169.

———. "Foreword: The New Federalism Context of the New Judicial Federalism." *Rutgers Law Journal* 26 (1995): 913–948.

Klarman, Michael J. "Rethinking the Civil Rights and Civil Liberties Revolutions." *Virginia Law Review* 82 (1996): 1–67.

Koch, Adrienne, ed. *Madison's Notes on Debates in the Federal Convention of 1787.* New York: Norton, 1987.

Konvitz, Milton R. *Fundamental Liberties of a Free People: Religion, Speech, Press, Assembly.* Ithaca, NY: Cornell University Press, 1957.

Konvitz, Milton R., and Clinton Rossiter, eds. *Aspects of Liberty: Essays Presented to Robert E. Cushman.* Ithaca, NY: Cornell University Press, 1958.

Kousser, J. Morgan. *Dead End: The Development of Nineteenth-Century Litigation on Racial Discrimination in Schools.* New York: Oxford University Press, 1986.

———. " 'The Supremacy of Equal Rights': The Struggle Against Racial Discrimination in Antebellum Massachusetts and the Foundations of the Fourteenth Amendment." *Northwestern Law Review* 82 (1988): 941–1010.

Kramer, Robert. "Foreword." *Law and Contemporary Problems* 17 (1952): 253–255.

Kruman, Mark W. *Between Authority and Liberty: State Constitution Making in Revolutionary America.* Chapel Hill: University of North Carolina Press, 1997.

Kukla, Jon, ed. *The Bill of Rights: A Lively Heritage.* Richmond: Virginia State Library, 1987.

Kurland, Philip B., and Ralph Lerner, eds. *The Founders' Constitution.* 5 vols. Chicago: University of Chicago Press, 1987.

Kyvig, David E. *Explicit and Authentic Amending Acts: Amending the U.S. Constitution, 1776–1995.* Lawrence: University Press of Kansas, 1996.

Lacey, Michael J., and Knud Haakonssen, eds. *A Culture of Rights: The Bill of Rights in Philosophy, Politics, and Law—1791 and 1991.* New York: Cambridge University Press, 1991.

LaPalombara, Joseph G. *The Initiative and Referendum in Oregon: 1938–1948.* Corvallis: Oregon State College, 1950.

Laski, Harold J. "The Obsolescence of Federalism." *New Republic* 98 (May 3, 1939): 367–369.

Latzer, Barry. *State Constitutions and Criminal Justice.* New York: Greenwood Press, 1991.

Laycock, Douglas. "Equal Access and Moments of Silence: The Equal Status of Religious Speech by Private Speakers." *Northwestern Law Review* 81 (1986): 1–67.

Lazare, Daniel. *The Frozen Republic: How the Constitition Is Paralyzing Democracy.* New York: Harcourt, Brace, and Co., 1996.

Leff, Mark H. "Consensus for Reform: The Mothers-Pension-Movement in the Progressive Era." *Social Service Review* 47 (1973): 397–417.

Legislative Reference Office. *The Initiative and Referendum in Colorado.* Denver: State Legislative Reference Office, 1939.

Lerner, Ralph. *The Thinking Revolutionary: Principle and Practice in the New Republic.* Ithaca, NY: Cornell University Press, 1987.

Levy, Leonard W. *The Law of the Commonwealth and Chief Justice Shaw.* Cambridge: Harvard University Press, 1957.

———. *Legacy of Suppression: Freedom of Speech and Press in Early American History,* Cambridge, MA: Belknap Press, 1960.

———. "The Right Against Self-Incrimination: History and Judicial History." *Political Science Quarterly* 84 (1969): 1–29.

———. *Emergence of a Free Press.* New York: Oxford University Press, 1985.

———. *The Establishment Clause: Religion and the First Amendment.* New York: Macmillan, 1986.

———. *Blasphemy: Verbal Offense Against the Sacred.* New York: Alfred A. Knopf, 1993.

———, ed. *Blasphemy in Massachusetts: Freedom of Conscience and the Abner Kneeland Case.* New York: Da Capo Press, 1973.

Levy, Leonard W., and Douglas L. Jones, eds. *Jim Crow in Boston: The Origin of the Separate but Equal Doctrine.* New York: Da Capo Press, 1974.

Lewis, Anthony. *Gideon's Trumpet.* New York: Random House, 1964.

Licht, Robert A., ed. *Is the Supreme Court the Guardian of the Constitution?* Washington, DC: American Enterprise Institute Press, 1993.

Licht, Robert A., and Robert A. Goldwin, eds. *The Spirit of the Constitution: Five Conversations.* Washington, DC: American Enterprise Institute for Public Policy Research, 1990.

Linde, Hans A. "Without Due Process: Unconstitutional Law in Oregon." *Oregon Law Review* 49 (1970): 125–187.

———. "Judges, Critics, and the Realist Tradition." *Yale Law Journal* 82 (1972): 227–256.

———. "First Things First: Rediscovering the States' Bills of Rights." *University of Baltimore Law Review* 9 (1980): 379–396.

———. "E Pluribus—Constitutional Theory in State Courts." *Georgia Law Review* 18 (1984): 165–200.

———. "When Is Initiative Lawmaking Not 'Republican Government'?" *Hastings Constitutional Law Quarterly* 17 (1989): 159–173.

———. "When Initiative Lawmaking Is Not Republican Government: The Campaign Against Homosexuality." *Oregon Law Review* 72 (1993): 19–45.

Link, Arthur S., ed. *The Papers of Woodrow Wilson*. 67 vols. Princeton, NJ: Princeton University Press, 1966–1992.

Lippmann, Walter. *Public Opinion*. New York: Harcourt, Brace, 1922.

———. *The Phantom Public*. New York: Harcourt, Brace, 1925.

Llewellyn, Karl N. "Some Realism About Realism—Responding to Dean Pound." *Harvard Law Review* 44 (1931): 1222–1264.

Lobingier, Charles S. *The People's Law, or Popular Participation in Law Making from Ancient Folk-Moot to Modern Referendum: A Study in the Evolution of Democracy and Direct Legislation*. New York: Macmillan, 1909.

Lockhart, William, and Robert McClure. "Censorship of Obscenity: The Developing Constitutional Standards." *Minnesota Law Review* 45 (1960): 5–121.

Lord, Robert, and John Sexton. *The History of the Archdiocese of Boston*. 3 vols. New York: Sheed and Ward, 1944.

Lowell, A. Lawrence. *Public Opinion and Popular Government*. New York: Longmans, Green, and Co., 1913.

Lowenstein, Daniel H. "Campaign Spending and Ballot Propositions: Recent Experience, Public Choice Theory, and the First Amendment." *U.C.L.A. Law Review* 29 (1982): 505–641.

Lower, Richard Coke. *A Bloc of One: The Political Career of Hiram W. Johnson*. Palo Alto, CA: Stanford University Press, 1993.

Lubove, Roy. *The Struggle for Social Security: 1900–1935*. Cambridge: Harvard University Press, 1968.

Luce, Robert. *Legislative Procedure: Parliamentary Practices and the Course of Business in the Framing of Statutes*. Boston: Houghton Mifflin, 1922.

———. *Legislative Assemblies: Their Framework, Make-up, Character, Characteristics, Habits, and Manners*. Boston: Houghton Mifflin, 1924.

———. *Legislative Principles: The History and Theory of Lawmaking by Representative Government*. Boston: Houghton Mifflin, 1930.

———. *Legislative Problems: Development, Status, and Trend of the Treatment and Exercise of Law-making Powers*. Boston: Houghton Mifflin, 1935.

Lupu, Ira C. "The Trouble with Accommodation." *George Washington Law Review* 60 (1992): 743–781.

———. "Statutes Revolving in Constitutional Law Orbits." *Virginia Law Review* 79 (1993): 1–89.

Lusky, Louis. "Footnote Redux: A *Carolene Products* Reminiscence." *Columbia Law Review* 82 (1982): 1093–1109.

Lutz, Donald S. *Popular Consent and Popular Control: Whig Political Theory in the Early State Constitutions.* Baton Rouge: Louisiana State University Press, 1980.

———. "The Purposes of American State Constitutions," *Publius: The Journal of Federalism* 12 (winter 1982): 27–44.

———. *The Origins of American Constitutionalism.* Baton Rouge: Louisiana State University Press, 1988.

Magleby, David B. *Direct Legislation: Voting on Ballot Propositions in the United States.* Baltimore: Johns Hopkins University Press, 1984.

———. "Let the Voters Decide? An Assessment of the Initiative and Referendum Process." *University of Colorado Law Review* 66 (1995): 13–46.

Magleby, David B., and James D. Gordon III. "Pre-Election Judicial Review of Initiatives and Referendums." *Notre Dame Law Review* 64 (1989): 298–320.

Maltz, Earl M. "The Dark Side of State Court Activism." *Texas Law Review* 63 (1985): 995–1023.

———. "False Prophet—Justice Brennan and the Theory of State Constitutional Law." *Hastings Constitutional Law Quarterly* 15 (1988): 429–449.

Marshall, Lawrence. "Divesting the Courts: Breaking the Judicial Monopoly on Constitutional Interpretation." *Chicago–Kent Law Review* 66 (1990): 481–505.

Martineau, Robert J. "The Mandatory Referendum on Calling a State Constitutional Convention: Enforcing the People's Right to Reform their Government." *Ohio State Law Journal* 31 (1970): 421–455.

Massey, Calvin R. "The 'Underlying Principle' of the Independence of the California Constitution." *State Constitutional Commentaries and Notes* 2 (winter 1991): 1–4.

Maxwell, Robert. *La Follette and the Rise of the Progressives in Wisconsin.* Madison: State Historical Society of Wisconsin, 1956.

Mazor, Lester J. "Notes on a Bill of Rights in a State Constitution." *Utah Law Review* 10 (1966): 326–350.

McCall, Samuel W. "Representative as Against Direct Democracy." *Atlantic Monthly* 108 (1911): 454–466.

McClain, Charles, ed. *Japanese Immigrants and American Law: The Alien Land Laws and Other Issues.* New York: Garland Press, 1994.

McCloskey, Robert G. *The American Supreme Court.* Chicago: University of Chicago Press, 1960.

———. *The Modern Supreme Court.* Cambridge: Harvard University Press, 1972.

McConnell, Grant. *Private Power and American Democracy.* New York: Alfred A. Knopf, 1966.

McConnell, Michael W. "Religious Freedom at a Crossroads." *University of Chicago Law Review* 59 (1992): 115–194.

McCurdy, Charles W. "Justice Field and the Jurisprudence of Government-Business Relations: Some Parameters of Laissez-Faire Constitutionalism, 1863–1897." *Journal of American History* 61 (1975): 970–1005.

McGovney, Dudley O. "The Anti-Japanese Land Laws of California and Ten Other States." *California Law Review* 35 (1947): 7–60.

McGraw, Bradley, ed. *Developments in State Constitutional Law.* St. Paul: West Publishing, 1985.

McKay, Robert B. *Reapportionment: The Law and Politics of Equal Representation.* New York: Twentieth Century Fund, 1965.

McLaughlin, Sister Raymond. *A History of State Legislation Affecting Private Elementary and Secondary Schools in the United States, 1870–1945.* Washington, DC: Catholic University of America Press, 1946.

McMaster, John Bach. *The Acquisition of Political, Social, and Industrial Rights of Man in America.* New York: Frederick Ungar, 1961.

McMaster, John Bach, and Frederick D. Stone, eds. *Pennsylvania and the Federal Constitution, 1787–1788.* Philadelphia: Historical Society of Pennsylvania, 1888.

Meyer, Jacob C. *Church and State in Massachusetts from 1740 to 1833.* Cleveland: Western Reserve University, 1930.

Mezey, Susan Gluck. *In Pursuit of Equality: Women, Public Policy, and the Federal Courts.* New York: St. Martin's Press, 1992.

Michael, Helen. "The Role of Natural Law in Early American Constitutionalism: Did the Founders Contemplate Judicial Enforcement of 'Unwritten' Individual Rights?" *North Carolina Law Review* 69 (1991): 421–490.

Mikva, Abner J. "How Well Does Congress Support and Defend the Constitution?" *North Carolina Law Review* 61 (1983): 587–611.

Mikva, Abner J., and Joseph R. Lundy. "The 91st Congress and the Constitution." *University of Chicago Law Review* 38 (1971): 449–499.

Miller, Peter P. "Freedom of Expression Under State Constitutions." *Stanford Law Review* 20 (1968): 318–335.

Monaghan, Henry. "The Supreme Court, 1974 Term—Foreword: Constitutional Common Law." *Harvard Law Review* 89 (1975): 1–45.

Morgan, Donald G. *Congress and the Constitution: A Study of Responsibility.* Cambridge, MA: Belknap Press, 1966.

Morris, Arval A. "Academic Freedom and Loyalty Oaths." *Law and Contemporary Problems* 28 (1963): 487–514.

Mowry, George M. *The California Progressives.* Los Angeles: University of California Press, 1951.

Munro, William B. "An Ideal State Constitution." *Annals of the American Academy of Political and Social Science* 181 (1935): 1–10.

———, ed. *Initiative, Referendum, and Recall.* New York: Appleton, 1912.

Murphy, Paul L. *The Constitution in Crisis Times, 1918–1969.* New York: Harper and Row, 1971.

———. *World War I and the Origin of Civil Liberties in the United States.* New York: W. W. Norton, 1979.

Nagel, Robert F. *Constitutional Cultures: The Mentality and Consequences of Judicial Review.* Los Angeles: University of California Press, 1989.

———. *Judicial Power and American Character: Censoring Ourselves in an Anxious Age.* New York: Oxford University Press, 1994.

———, ed. *Intellect and Craft: The Contributions of Justice Hans Linde to American Constitutionalism.* Boulder, CO: Westview Press, 1995.

Nagel, Stuart S., ed. *The Rights of the Accused in Law and Action.* Beverly Hills: Sage Publications, 1972.

National Municipal League. *Model State Constitution.* 6th ed. New York: National Municipal League, 1968.

Neely, Richard. *How Courts Govern America.* New Haven, CT: Yale University Press, 1981.

Nelson, Margaret V. *A Study of Judicial Review in Virginia, 1789–1928.* New York: Columbia University Press, 1947.

Nelson, William E. "Changing Conceptions of Judicial Review: The Evolution of Constitutional Theory in the States, 1790–1860." *University of Pennsylvania Law Review* 120 (1972): 1166–1185.

———. *Americanization of the Common Law: The Impact of Legal Change on Massachusetts Society, 1760–1830.* Cambridge: Harvard University Press, 1975.

Nelson, William E., and Robert C. Palmer. *Liberty and Community: Constitution and Rights in the Early American Republic.* Williamsburg, VA: Institute of Bill of Rights Law, 1987.

Nevins, Allan. *The American States During and After the Revolution, 1775–1789.* New York: Macmillan, 1924.

Nichols, David K. "The Promise of Progressivism: Herbert Croly and the Progressive Rejection of Individual Rights." *Publius: The Journal of Federalism* 17 (spring 1987): 27–39.

Note. "California's Constitutional Amendomania." *Stanford Law Review* 1 (1949): 279–288.

———. "Censorship of Motion Pictures." *Yale Law Journal* 49 (1939): 87–113.

———. "Community Standards, Class Actions, and Obscenity Under *Miller v. California.*" *Harvard Law Review* 88 (1975): 1838–1874.

———. "Convicts—The Right to a Speedy Trial and the New Detainer Statutes." *Rutgers Law Review* 18 (1964): 828–874.

———. "Developments in the Law—The Interpretation of State Constitutional Rights." *Harvard Law Review* 95 (1982): 1324–1502.

———. "Developments in the Law—Sexual Orientation and the Law." *Harvard Law Review* 102 (1989): 1508–1671.

———. "Loyalty Oaths." *Yale Law Journal* 77 (1968): 739–766.

———. "The Right of a Newsman to Refrain from Divulging the Sources of His Information." *Virginia Law Review* 36 (1950): 61–83.

———. "The Right to a Public Trial in Criminal Cases." *New York University Law Review* 41 (1966): 1138–1157.

Novak, William J. *The People's Welfare: Law and Regulation in Nineteenth-Century America.* Chapel Hill: University of North Carolina Press, 1996.

Nowak, John E. "Essay on the Bill of Rights: The 'Sixty Something' Anniversary of the Bill of Rights." *University of Illinois Law Review* (1992): 445–481.

Nye, Russell B. *Fettered Freedom: Civil Liberties and the Slavery Controversy 1830–1860.* Lansing: University of Michigan State Press, 1963.

Oaks, Dallin H. "Studying the Exclusionary Rule in Search and Seizure." *University of Chicago Law Review* 37 (1970): 665–757.

Oberholtzer, Ellis. "Law-Making by Popular Vote." *Annals of the American Academy of Political and Social Sciences* 2 (1891): 324–344.

———. *The Referendum in America: Together with Some Chapters on the Initiative and Recall.* New York: Scribner's Sons, 1911.

Odegard, Peter H. *Pressure Politics: The Story of the Anti-Saloon League.* New York: Columbia University Press, 1928.

O'Neal, Emmet. "Distrust of State Legislatures—The Cause; the Remedy." *North American Review* 199 (1914): 684–699.

Ong, Bruce Nelson. "Constitutionalism and Political Change: James Madison, Thomas Jefferson, and Progressive Reinterpretation." Ph.D. dissertation, University of Virginia, 1985.

Osgood, Russell, ed. *The History of the Law in Massachusetts: The Supreme Judicial Court, 1692–1992.* Boston: Supreme Judicial Court Historical Society, 1992.

Paine, Robert T. "Lincoln's Ideal Carried Out in Oregon." *Arena* 40 (1908): 283–286.

Palfrey, John G. "The Constitution and the Courts." *Harvard Law Review* 26 (1913): 507–530.

Parker, Richard D. "The Past of Constitutional Theory—And Its Future." *Ohio State Law Journal* 42 (1981): 223–259.

———. *"Here the People Rule": A Constitutional Populist Manifesto.* Cambridge: Harvard University Press, 1994.

Parsons, Frank. *The City for the People, or the Municipalization of the City Government and of Local Franchises.* Philadelphia: C. F. Taylor, 1901.

Paul, Arnold M. *Conservative Crisis and the Rule of Law: Attitudes of Bar and Bench, 1887–1895.* Ithaca, NY: Cornell University Press, 1960.

Paulsen, Monrad G. "State Constitutions, State Courts and First Amendment Freedoms." *Vanderbilt Law Review* 4 (1951): 620–642.

Pearson, C. C., and J. Edwin Hendricks. *Liquor and Anti-Liquor in Virginia, 1619–1919.* Durham, NC: Duke University Press, 1967.

Peifer, Steven. "State Newsman's Privilege Statutes: A Critical Analysis." *Notre Dame Lawyer* 49 (1973): 150–161.

Perry, Michael J. *The Constitution, the Courts, and Human Rights.* New Haven, CT: Yale University Press, 1982.

Peters, Ellen A. "State Constitutional Law: Federalism in the Common Law Tradition." *Michigan Law Review* 84 (1986): 583–593.

Peters, Ronald M. *The Massachusetts Constitution of 1780: A Social Compact.* Amherst: University of Massachusetts Press, 1978.

Peterson, Merrill D., ed. *Democracy, Liberty, and Property: The State Constitutional Conventions of the 1820s.* Indianapolis: Bobbs-Merrill, 1966.

———, ed. *The Portable Thomas Jefferson.* New York: Penguin Books, 1975.

Peterson, Merrill D., and Robert C. Vaughan, eds. *The Virginia Statute for Religious Freedom: Its Evolution and Consequences in American History.* New York: Cambridge University Press, 1988.

Phillips, Cyrus E., IV. "Miscegenation: The Courts and the Constitution." *William and Mary Law Review* 8 (1966): 133–142.

Pitkin, Hannah F. *The Concept of Representation.* Los Angeles: University of California Press, 1967.

Pollock, James K. *The Initiative and Referendum in Michigan*. Ann Arbor: University of Michigan Press, 1940.

———. *Making Michigan's New Constitution, 1961–1962*. Ann Arbor: G. Wahr Publishing Company, 1962.

Pollock, Stewart. "State Constitutions as Separate Sources of Fundamental Rights." *Rutgers Law Review* 35 (1983): 707–722.

Pound, Roscoe. "Liberty of Contract." *Yale Law Journal* 18 (1909): 454–487.

———. "Legal Interrogation of Persons Accused or Suspected of Crime." *Journal of Criminal Law and Criminology* 24 (1934): 1014–1018.

Project Report. "Toward an Activist Role for State Bills of Rights." *Harvard Civil Rights–Civil Liberties Law Review* 8 (1973): 271–350.

Prosser, William L. *Handbook of the Law of Torts*. 4th ed. St. Paul: West Publishing Co., 1971.

Quadagno, Jill. *The Transformation of Old Age Security: Class and Politics in the American Welfare State*. Chicago: University of Chicago Press, 1988.

Quadagno, Jill, and Madonna Meyer. "Organized Labor, State Structures, and Social Policy Development: A Case Study of Old-Age Assistance in Ohio, 1916–1940." *Social Problems* 36 (1989): 181–196.

Rabban, David M. "The Emergence of Modern First Amendment Doctrine." *University of Chicago Law Review* 50 (1983): 1205–1355.

———. *Free Speech in Its Forgotten Years*. New York: Cambridge University Press, 1997.

Radin, Max. "Popular Legislation in California." *Minnesota Law Review* 23 (1939): 559–584.

Rakove, Jack N. *Original Meanings: Politics and Ideas in the Making of the Constitution*. New York: Alfred A. Knopf, 1996.

Randall, James G. *Constitutional Problems Under Lincoln*. New York: D. Appleton and Company, 1926.

Ransom, William L. *Majority Rule and the Judiciary: An Examination of Current Proposals for Constitutional Change Affecting the Relation of Courts to Legislation*. New York: Scribner's Sons, 1912.

Reid, John Phillip. *Chief Justice: The Judicial World of Charles Doe*. Cambridge: Harvard University Press, 1967.

———. *The Concept of Liberty in the Age of the American Revolution*. Chicago: University of Chicago Press, 1988.

———. *The Concept of Representation in the Age of the American Revolution*. Chicago: University of Chicago Press, 1989.

Reinsch, Paul S. *American Legislatures and Legislative Methods*. New York: Century Co., 1913.

Richards, David A. J. *Foundations of American Constitutionalism*. New York: Oxford University Press, 1989.

Riker, William H. *Federalism: Origin, Operation, Significance*. Boston: Little, Brown, 1964.

Rivera, Rhonda R. "Our Straight-Laced Judges: The Legal Position of Homosexual Persons in the United States." *Hastings Law Journal* 30 (1979): 799–955.

Roberts, Waldo. "The Ku-Kluxing of Oregon." *The Outlook* 133 (March 14, 1923): 490–491.

Roche, John P. *The Quest for the Dream: The Development of Civil Rights and Human Relations in Modern America.* New York: Macmillan, 1963.

Roe, Gilbert E. *Our Judicial Oligarchy.* New York: B. W. Huebsch, 1912.

Rogge, O. John. "Compelling the Testimony of Political Deviants." *Michigan Law Review* 55 (1956): 163–200.

Root, Elihu. *Addresses on Government and Citizenship.* Cambridge: Harvard University Press, 1916.

Rosenberg, Gerald N. *The Hollow Hope: Can Courts Bring About Social Change?* Chicago: University of Chicago Press, 1991.

Rosenberg, Norman L. *Protecting the Best Men: An Interpretive History of the Law of Libel.* Chapel Hill: University of North Carolina Press, 1986.

Rosenthal, James M. "Massachusetts Acts and Resolves Declared Unconstitutional by the Supreme Judicial Court of Massachusetts." *Massachusetts Law Quarterly* 1 (1916): 301–318.

Ross, William G. *Forging New Freedoms: Nativism, Education, and the Constitution, 1917–1927.* Lincoln: University of Nebraska Press, 1994.

———. *A Muted Fury: Populists, Progressives, and Labor Unions Confront the Courts, 1890–1937.* Princeton, NJ: Princeton University Press, 1994.

Rossiter, Clinton, ed. *The Federalist Papers.* New York: Mentor, 1961.

Rostow, Eugene V. "The Democratic Character of Judicial Review." *Harvard Law Review* 66 (1952): 193–224.

———. "The Court and Its Critics." *South Texas Law Review* 4 (1959): 160–178.

———. *The Sovereign Prerogative: The Supreme Court and the Quest for Law.* New Haven, CT: Yale University Press, 1962.

Rutland, Robert A. *The Birth of the Bill of Rights.* Madison, WI: Madison House, 1992.

Rutland, Robert A., William M. E. Rachal, and William Thomas Hutchinson. *The Papers of James Madison.* 17 vols. Chicago and Charlottesville: University of Chicago Press and University Press of Virginia, 1962–1983.

Ruud, Millard H. "No Law Shall Embrace More Than One Subject." *Minnesota Law Review* 42 (1958): 389–452.

Ryan, James E. "*Smith* and the Religious Freedom Restoration Act: An Iconoclastic Assessment." *Virginia Law Review* 78 (1992): 1407–1457.

Sager, Alan M. "The Impact of Supreme Court Loyalty Oath Decisions." *American University Law Review* 22 (1972): 39–78.

Sager, Lawrence G. "Fair Measure: The Legal Status of Underenforced Constitutional Norms." *Harvard Law Review* 91 (1978): 1212–1264.

Schaefer, Walter V. "Federalism and State Criminal Procedure." *Harvard Law Review* 70 (1956): 1–26.

Schmidt, David D. *Citizen Lawmakers: The Ballot Initiative Revolution.* Philadelphia: Temple University Press, 1989.

Schreck, Jeffrey. "Journalist's Privilege: *In Re Farber* and the New Jersey Shield Laws." *Rutgers Law Review* 32 (1979): 545–576.

Schroeder, William A. "Deterring Fourth Amendment Violations: Alternatives to the Exclusionary Rule." *Georgetown Law Journal* 69 (1981): 1361–1426.

Schumacher, Waldo. "Reapportionment in Oregon." *Western Political Quarterly* 3 (1950): 428–434.

Schuman, David. "The Origin of State Constitutional Direct Democracy: William Simon U'Ren and 'The Oregon System.'" *Temple Law Review* 67 (1994): 947–963.

Schwartz, Bernard. *The Great Rights of Mankind: A History of the American Bill of Rights.* New York: Oxford University Press, 1977.

Seager, Henry R. *Labor and Other Economic Essays.* Ed. Charles A. Gulick. New York: Harper and Bros., 1931.

Seeley, James J. "The Public Referendum and Minority Group Legislation: Postscript to *Reitman v. Mulkey.*" *Cornell Law Review* 55 (1970): 881–910.

Semonche, John E. *Charting the Future: The Supreme Court Responds to a Changing Society, 1890–1920.* Westport, CT: Greenwood Press, 1978.

Sherry, Suzanna. "The Founders' Unwritten Constitution." *University of Chicago Law Review* 54 (1987): 1127–1177.

———. "Natural Law in the States." *University of Cincinnati Law Review* 61 (1992): 171–222.

———. "Foreword: State Constitutional Law: Doing the Right Thing." *Rutgers Law Journal* 25 (1994): 935–944.

Sigler, Jay A. *Double Jeopardy: The Development of a Legal and Social Policy.* Ithaca, NY: Cornell University Press, 1969.

Sirico, Louis J. "The Constitutionality of the Initiative and Referendum." *Iowa Law Review* 65 (1980): 637–677.

Sitton, Tom. *John Randolph Haynes: California Progressive.* Palo Alto, CA: Stanford University Press, 1992.

Skocpol, Theda. *Protecting Soldiers and Mothers: The Political Origins of Social Policy in the United States.* Cambridge, MA: Belknap Press, 1992.

Skowronek, Stephen. *Building a New American State: The Expansion of National Administrative Capabilities, 1877–1920.* New York: Cambridge University Press, 1982.

Slonim, Mark, and James H. Lowe. "Judicial Review of Laws Enacted by Popular Vote." *Washington Law Review* 55 (1979): 175–209.

Smith, J. Allen. *The Spirit of American Government.* New York: Macmillan, 1907.

Snowiss, Sylvia. *Judicial Review and the Law of the Constitution.* New Haven, CT: Yale University Press, 1990.

Spear, Samuel T. "The Bible and the Public School." *Princeton Review* 54 (1878): 361–394.

Spiotto, James. "Search and Seizure: An Empirical Study of the Exclusionary Rule and Its Alternatives." *Journal of Legal Studies* 2 (1973): 243–278.

Stephens, Joseph. "U'Ren the Law Giver: The Legislative Blacksmith of Oregon and the Tools He Has Fashioned for Democracy." *American Magazine* 65 (1908): 527–540.

Stimson, Shannon C. *The American Revolution in the Law: Anglo-American Jurisprudence Before John Marshall.* Princeton, NJ: Princeton University Press, 1990.

Stokes, Anson Phelps. *Church and State in the United States.* 3 vols. New York: Harper and Brothers, 1950.

Stolz, Preble. "Say Good-Bye to Hiram Johnson's Ghost." *California Lawyer* 10 (January 1990): 44.

Stoner, James R. *Common Law and Liberal Theory: Coke, Hobbes, and the Origins of American Constitutionalism.* Lawrence: University Press of Kansas, 1992.

Storing, Herbert J. *The Complete Anti-Federalist.* 7 vols. Chicago: University of Chicago Press, 1981.

Story, Joseph. *Commentaries on the Constitution of the United States.* 2 vols. Boston: Hilliard, Gray, and Company, 1833.

Sturm, Albert L. *Constitution-Making in Michigan, 1961–1962.* Ann Arbor: Institute of Public Administration, 1963.

———. *Thirty Years of State Constitution-Making: 1938–1968.* New York: National Municipal League, 1970.

———. "The Development of American State Constitutions." *Publius: The Journal of Federalism* 12 (winter 1982): 57–98.

Sullivan, J. W. *Direct Legislation by the Citizenship Through the Initiative and Referendum.* New York: True Nationalist Publishing, 1893.

Sultan, Paul. *Right-to-Work Laws: A Study in Conflict.* Los Angeles: University of California, 1958.

Sunderland, Lane V. *Popular Government and the Supreme Court: Securing the Public Good and Private Rights.* Lawrence: University Press of Kansas, 1996.

Sunstein, Cass. "Three Civil Rights Fallacies." *California Law Review* 79 (1991): 751–774.

———. *The Partial Constitution.* Cambridge: Harvard University Press, 1993.

Swisher, Carl Brent. *American Constitutional Development.* Boston: Houghton Mifflin, 1943.

———. *The Growth of Constitutional Power in the United States.* Chicago: University of Chicago Press, 1946.

"Symposium: The Emergence of State Constitutional Law." *Texas Law Review* 63 (1985): 959–1318.

"Symposium: Governing by Initiative." *University of Colorado Law Review* 66 (1995): 13–158.

"Symposium: Perspectives on the Authoritativeness of Supreme Court Decisions." *Tulane Law Review* 61 (1987): 977–1095.

"Symposium: Religion and the Public Schools After *Lee v. Weisman.*" *Case Western Reserve Law Review* 43 (1993): 699–1020.

"Symposium on the Revolution in State Constitutional Law." *Vermont Law Review* 13 (1988): 11–372.

"Symposium on State Constitutional Law." *Washington Law Review* 64 (1989): 1–226.

Tallian, Laura. *Direct Democracy.* Los Angeles: People's Lobby, 1977.

Tarr, G. Alan. *Judicial Impact and State Supreme Courts.* Lexington, MA: Lexington Books, 1977.

———. "Church and State in the States." *Washington Law Review* 64 (1989): 73–110.

———. "The Past and Future of the New Judicial Federalism." *Publius: The Journal of Federalism* 24 (spring 1994): 63–79.

———, ed. *Constitutional Politics in the States: Contemporary Controversies and Historical Patterns.* New York: Greenwood Press, 1996.

Tarr, G. Alan, and Ellis Katz, eds. *Federalism and Rights.* Lanham, MD: Rowman and Littlefield, 1996.

Tarr, G. Alan, and Mary Cornelia Aldis Porter. *State Supreme Courts in State and Nation.* New Haven, CT: Yale University Press, 1988.

————, eds. *State Supreme Courts: Policymakers in the Federal System.* Westport, CT: Greenwood Press, 1982.

Taylor, Telford. *Two Studies in Constitutional Interpretation.* Columbus: Ohio State University Press, 1969.

Thayer, James Bradley. "The Origin and Scope of the American Doctrine of Constitutional Law." *Harvard Law Review* 7 (1893): 129–156.

————. *Cases in Constitutional Law.* 4 vols. Cambridge: John Wilson and Son, 1894.

Thomas, David Y. "The Initiative and Referendum in Arkansas Come of Age." *American Political Science Review* 27 (1933): 66–75.

Thorpe, Frances Newton. "Recent Constitution-Making in the United States." *Annals of the American Academy of Political and Social Sciences* 2 (1891): 145–201.

Tiedeman, Christopher G. *A Treatise on the Limitations of Police Power in the United States.* St. Louis: F. H. Thomas, 1886.

Tishler, Hace S. *Self-Reliance and Social Security, 1870–1917.* Port Washington, NY: Kennikat Press, 1971.

Tocqueville, Alexis de. *Democracy in America.* Ed. J. P. Mayer. Trans. George Lawrence. New York: Harper and Row, 1966.

Tomlins, Christopher L. *The State and the Unions: Labor Relations, Law, and the Organized Labor Movement in America, 1880–1960.* New York: Cambridge University Press, 1985.

Tribe, Laurence H. "The Puzzling Persistence of Process-Based Constitutional Theories." *Yale Law Journal* 89 (1980): 1063–1080.

————. *American Constitutional Law.* 2d ed. Mineola, NY: Foundation Press, 1988.

Tucker, Henry St. George. *Commentaries on the Laws of Virginia.* Winchester, VA: Winchester Virginian, 1831.

————. *Lectures on Constitutional Law.* Richmond, VA: Shepherd and Colin, 1843.

Tulis, Jeffrey K. *The Rhetorical Presidency.* Princeton, NJ: Princeton University Press, 1987.

Tushnet, Mark V. "Darkness on the Edge of Town: The Contributions of John Hart Ely to Constitutional Theory." *Yale Law Journal* 89 (1980): 1037–1062.

Twiss, Benjamin R. *Lawyers and the Constitution: How Laissez Faire Came to the Supreme Court.* Princeton, NJ: Princeton University Press, 1942.

Tyack, David B. "The Pitfalls of Pluralism: The Background of the Pierce Case." *American Historical Review* 74 (1968): 74–98.

Uelmen, Gerald F. "California's Crime Victims Reform Act: Limiting State Constitutional Rights of Criminal Defendants." *State Constitutional Commentaries and Notes* 1 (summer 1990): 5–9.

U'Ren, William S. "The Operation of the Initiative and Referendum in Oregon." *Arena* 32 (1904): 128–131.

Urofsky, Melvin I. "State Courts and Protective Legislation During the Progressive Era: A Reevaluation." *Journal of American History* 72 (1985): 63–91.

Von Hayek, Friedrich. *The Constitution of Liberty.* Chicago: University of Chicago Press, 1960.

Wade, Michael S. *The Bitter Issue: The Right to Work Law in Arizona.* Tucson: Arizona Historical Society, 1976.

Waldo, Katherine. "The 1984 Oregon Death Penalty Initiatives: A State Constitutional Analysis." *Willamette Law Review* 22 (1986): 285–353.

Warren, Charles. "The Progressiveness of the United States Supreme Court." *Columbia Law Review* 13 (April 1913): 294–313.

Warren, Samuel, and Louis D. Brandeis. "The Right to Privacy." *Harvard Law Review* 4 (1890): 193–220.

Webster, William C. "Comparative Study of the State Constitutions of the American Revolution." *Annals of the American Academy of Political and Social Sciences* 9 (1897): 380–420.

Weyl, Walter. *The New Democracy: An Essay on Certain Political and Economic Tendencies in the United States.* New York: Macmillan, 1912.

Wheeler, John P., ed. *Salient Issues of Constitutional Revision.* New York: National Municipal League, 1961.

Whipple, Leon V. *The Story of Civil Liberty in the United States.* New York: Vanguard Press, 1927.

White, G. Edward. *The American Judicial Tradition: Profiles of Leading American Judges.* Exp. ed. New York: Oxford University Press, 1988.

White, William Allen. *The Old Order Changeth: A View of American Democracy.* New York: Macmillan, 1910.

Wiebe, Robert H. *The Search for Order: 1877–1920.* New York: Hill and Wang, 1967.

Wilcox, Delos. *Government by All the People.* New York: Macmillan, 1912.

Wilkes, Donald E. "The New Federalism in Criminal Procedure." *Kentucky Law Journal* 62 (1974): 421–451.

Wilkins, Herbert P. "Judicial Treatment of the Massachusetts Declaration of Rights in Relation to Cognate Provisions of the United States Constitution." *Suffolk Law Review* 14 (1980): 887–930.

Williams, Robert F. "State Constitutional Law Processes." *William and Mary Law Review* 24 (1983): 169–228.

———. "In the Supreme Court's Shadow: Legitimacy of State Court Rejection of Supreme Court Reasoning and Result." *South Carolina Law Review* 35 (1984): 353–404.

———. "State Constitutional Limits on Legislative Procedure: Legislative Compliance and Judicial Enforcement." *Publius: The Journal of Federalism* 17 (winter 1987): 91–114.

———. "The State Constitutions of the Founding Decade: Pennsylvania's Radical 1776 Constitution and Its Influences on American Constitutionalism." *Temple Law Review* 62 (1989): 541–585.

———, ed. *Cases and Materials on State Constitutional Law.* Washington, DC: Advisory Commission on Intergovernmental Relations, 1993.

Williamson, Chilton. *American Suffrage: From Property to Democracy, 1760–1860.* Princeton, NJ: Princeton University Press, 1960.

Wilson, Bradford P. *Enforcing the Fourth Amendment.* New York: Garland Press, 1986.

Wolfe, Christopher. *The Rise of Modern Judicial Review: From Constitutional Interpretation to Judge-Made Law.* New York: Basic Books, 1986.

Wolfinger, Raymond E., and Fred I. Greenstein. "The Repeal of Fair Housing in California: An Analysis of Referendum Voting." *American Political Science Review* 62 (1968): 753–769.

Wood, Gordon S. *The Creation of the American Republic, 1776–1789*. Chapel Hill: University of North Carolina Press, 1969.
———. "Foreword: State Constitution-Making in the American Revolution." *Rutgers Law Journal* 24 (1993): 911–926.
Wright, Benjamin F. *The Growth of American Constitutional Law*. New York: Holt, Rhinehart, 1942.
Wright, J. Skelly. "The Role of the Supreme Court in a Democratic Society—Judicial Activism or Restraint?" *Cornell Law Review* 54 (1968): 1–28.
Younger, Richard D. *The People's Panel: The Grand Jury in the United States, 1634–1941*. Providence: Brown University Press, 1963.
Zimmerman, Joseph F. *Participatory Democracy: Populism Revived*. New York: Praeger, 1986.
Zisk, Betty H. *Money, Media, and the Grass Roots: State Ballot Issues and the Electoral Process*. Newbury Park, CA: Sage Publications, 1987.

CASES

Adams v. Howe, 14 Mass. 340 (1817).
American Federation of Labor v. Bain, 165 Or. 183 (1940).
Anthony v. Veatch, 189 Or. 462 (1950).
Atkinson v. Doherty, 121 Mich. 372 (1899).
Attorney General v. Abbott, 121 Mich. 540 (1899).
Attorney General v. Lacy, 180 Mich. 329 (1914).
Attorney General v. MIAA, 378 Mass. 342 (1979).
Attorney General v. Rice, 64 Mich. 385 (1887).
Attorney General v. "Tropic of Cancer," 345 Mass. 11 (1962).
Bacon v. Wayne, 1 Mich. 461 (1850).
Baker v. Carr, 369 U.S. 186 (1962).
Barber v. Gladden, 210 Or. 46 (1957).
Barnes v. First Parish in Falmouth, 6 Mass. 401 (1810).
Beebe v. The State, 6 Ind. 501 (1855).
Belles v. Burr, 76 Mich. 1 (1889).
Bloom v. School Committee of Springfield, 376 Mass. 35 (1978).
Board of Control v. Buckstegge, 18 Ariz. 277 (1916).
Book Tower Garage v. Local No. 415, 295 Mich. 580 (1940).
Brattle Films v. Commissioner of Public Safety, 333 Mass. 58 (1955).
Brown v. City of Richmond, 204 Va. 471 (1963).
Brown v. Epps, 91 Va. 726 (1895).
Brush v. State Board of Higher Education, 245 Or. 373 (1966).
Butts v. Commonwealth, 145 Va. 800 (1926).
Cantwell v. Connecticut, 310 U.S. 296 (1940).
Carlson v. California, 310 U.S. 106 (1940).
Case of Supervisors of Election, 114 Mass. 247 (1873).
Chaddock v. Day, 75 Mich. 527 (1889).

Chahoon v. The Commonwealth, 61 Va. (20 Gratt.) 733 (1871).
Civil Rights Department v. GMC, 412 Mich. 610 (1982).
Coffin v. Election Commissioners, 97 Mich. 188 (1893).
Cohen v. Attorney General, 357 U.S. 564 (1970).
Collins v. Secretary, 407 Mass. 837 (1990).
Commissioner of Education v. Leyden, 358 Mass. 776 (1971).
Commonwealth v. Adcock, 49 Va. (8 Gratt.) 661 (1851).
Commonwealth v. Anderson, 308 Mass. 370 (1941).
Commonwealth v. Bishop, 402 Mass. 449 (1988).
Commonwealth v. Blackington, 41 Mass. 352 (1837).
Commonwealth v. Blanding, 20 Mass. 304 (1825).
Commonwealth v. Blondin, 324 Mass. 564 (1949).
Commonwealth v. Boston and Maine Railroad, 222 Mass. 206 (1915).
Commonwealth v. Caton, 8 Va. (4 Call.) 5 (1782).
Commonwealth v. Chernock, 336 Mass. 384 (1958).
Commonwealth v. Clap, 4 Mass. 163 (1808).
Commonwealth v. Colon-Cruz, 393 Mass. 150 (1984).
Commonwealth v. Dana, 43 Mass. 329 (1841).
Commonwealth v. Fletcher, 12 Mass. 441 (1815).
Commonwealth v. Ford, 394 Mass. 421 (1985).
Commonwealth v. Gardner, 300 Mass. 372 (1938).
Commonwealth v. Gilfedder, 321 Mass. 335 (1947).
Commonwealth v. Harlow, 110 Mass. 411 (1872).
Commonwealth v. Has, 122 Mass. 40 (1877).
Commonwealth v. Horton, 365 Mass. 164 (1974).
Commonwealth v. Intoxicating Liquors, 109 Mass. 371 (1872).
Commonwealth v. Jacobs, 333 Mass. 204 (1955).
Commonwealth v. Karvonen, 219 Mass. 30 (1914).
Commonwealth v. Kneeland, 37 Mass. 206 (1838).
Commonwealth v. Nissenbaum, 404 Mass. 575 (1989).
Commonwealth v. Oakes, 401 Mass. 602 (1988).
Commonwealth v. O'Neal, 367 Mass. 440 (1975).
Commonwealth v. O'Neal, 369 Mass. 242 (1975).
Commonwealth v. Pascone, 308 Mass. 591 (1941).
Commonwealth v. Perry, 155 Mass. 117 (1891).
Commonwealth v. Scott, 123 Mass. 239 (1877).
Commonwealth v. Sees, 374 Mass. 532 (1978).
Commonwealth v. Smith, 9 Mass. 106 (1812).
Commonwealth v. Smith, 68 Mass. 516 (1854).
Commonwealth v. Spofford, 343 Mass. 703 (1962).
Commonwealth v. Starr, 144 Mass. 359 (1887).
Commonwealth v. Upton, 394 Mass. 363 (1984).
Commonwealth v. Wasson, 842 S.W.2d 487 (Ky. 1992).
Conant v. Burnham, 133 Mass. 503 (1882).
Constitutionality of 1974 PA 242, 394 Mich. 41 (1975).
Cullen v. Commonwealth, 65 Va. (24 Gratt.) 624 (1873).

Dalli v. Board of Education, 358 Mass. 753 (1971).

Day v. Owen, 5 Mich. 520 (1858).

De Jonge v. Oregon, 299 U.S. 353 (1936).

Derby v. Blake, 226 Mass. 618 (1917).

Dickman v. School District, 232 Or. 238 (1962).

Durham Bros. v. Woodson, 155 Va. 93 (1930).

Edwards v. Commonwealth, 191 Va. 272 (1950).

Edwards v. The People, 39 Mich. 760 (1878).

Emery's Case, 107 Mass. 172 (1871).

Eugene Sand and Gravel v. City of Eugene, 276 Or. 1007 (1976).

Farmer v. Christian, 154 Va. 48 (1930).

Faxon v. School Committee of Boston, 331 Mass. 531 (1954).

Feek v. Township Board, 82 Mich. 393 (1890).

Ferguson v. Georgia, 365 U.S. 570 (1960).

Fisher v. McGirr, 67 Mass. 1 (1854).

Flanary v. Commonwealth, 184 Va. 204 (1945).

Gebhardt v. Gladden, 243 Or. 145 (1966).

Goddin v. Crump, 35 Va. (8 Leigh). 120 (1837).

Goesart v. Cleary, 335 U.S. 464 (1948).

Goldstein v. Commonwealth, 200 Va. 25 (1958).

Guinn and Beal *v. U.S.,* 238 U.S. 347 (1915).

Hague v, CIO, 307 U.S. 496 (1939).

Hall v. Commonwealth, 138 Va. 727 (1924).

Harrison v. Day, 200 Va. 439 (1959).

Hart v. Commonwealth, 221 Va. 283 (1980).

Hewitt v. State Accident Insurance Fund Corporation, 294 Or. 33 (1982).

Hibbard v. The People, 4 Mich 125 (1856).

Highland Park v. F.E.P.C., 364 Mich. 508 (1961).

Holden v. James, 11 Mass. 396 (1814).

Ideal Tea Company v. Salem, 77 Or. 182 (1915).

In re Apportionment, 413 Mich. 96 (1982).

In re Apportionment of Legislature, 387 Mich. 442 (1972).

In re Snyder, 108 Mich. 48 (1895).

In the Matter of Roche, 381 Mass. 624 (1980).

Ives v. South Buffalo Railway Co., 201 N.Y. 217 (1911).

James v. Valtierra, 402 U.S. 137 (1971).

Jones v. Commonwealth, 327 Mass. 491 (1951).

Jones v. The Commonwealth, 5 Va. (1 Call) 557 (1799).

Jones v. Robbins, 74 Mass. 329 (1857).

Kalich v. Knapp, 73 Or. 558 (1914).

Kent v. Commissioner of Education, 380 Mass. 235 (1980).

Kenyon v. Chicopee, 320 Mass. 528 (1946).

Kinneen v. Wells, 144 Mass. 497 (1887).

Lees v. Childs, 17 Mass. 351 (1821).

Lelia J. Robinson's Case, 131 Mass. 376 (1881).

Lloyd v. Whiffen, 307 Or. 674 (1989).

Louthan v. Commonwealth, 79 Va. 196 (1884).

Lovell v. Griffin, 303 U.S. 444 (1938).

Lowe v. City of Eugene, 254 Or. 518 (1969).

Lucas v. Colorado General Assembly, 377 U.S. 713 (1964).

Marks Furs v. City of Detroit, 365 Mich. 108 (1961).

Massachusetts Commission Against Discrimination v. Colangelo, 344 Mass. 387 (1962).

McConkey v. Fredericksburg, 179 Va. 556 (1942).

Metropolitan Board of Excise v. Barrie, 34 N.Y. 657 (1866).

Minersville School District v. Gobitis, 310 U.S. 586 (1940).

Minielly v. State, 242 Or. 490 (1966).

Moe v. Secretary, 382 Mass. 629 (1981).

Namba v. McCourt and Neuner, 185 Or. 579 (1949).

Nolan's Case, 122 Mass. 330 (1877).

Opinion of the Justices, 80 Mass. 614 (1859).

Opinion of the Justices, 115 Mass. 602 (1874).

Opinion of the Justices, 160 Mass. 586 (1894).

Opinion of the Justices, 332 Mass. 763 (1955).

Opinion of the Justices, 363 Mass. 899 (1973).

Opinion of the Justices, 365 Mass. 648 (1974).

Opinion of the Justices, 387 Mass. 1201 (1982).

Pedlosky v. M.I.T., 352 Mass. 127 (1967).

People v. Beadle, 60 Mich. 22 (1886).

People v. Beavers, 393 Mich. 554 (1975).

People v. Bellet, 99 Mich. 151 (1894).

People v. Board of Education of Detroit, 18 Mich. 400 (1869).

People v. Collins, 3 Mich. 343 (1854).

People v. De La Mater, 213 Mich. 167 (1921).

People v. Gallagher, 4 Mich. 244 (1856).

People v. Jenness, 5 Mich. 305 (1858).

People v. Lechner, 307 Mich. 358 (1943).

People v. Mahaney, 13 Mich. 481 (1865).

People v. Marxhausen, 204 Mich 559 (1918).

People v. Murray, 89 Mich. 276 (1891).

People v. Nash, 418 Mich. 196 (1983).

People v. Parshay, 379 Mich. 7 (1967).

People v. Pennington, 383 Mich. 611 (1970).

People v. Quider, 183 Mich. 82 (1914).

People v. Simon, 324 Mich. 450 (1949).

People v. Thomas, 9 Mich. 314 (1861).

People v. White, 390 Mich. 245 (1973).

People v. Williams, 225 Mich. 133 (1923).

Perry v. The Commonwealth, 44 Va. (3 Gratt.) 632 (1846).

Pfeiffer v. Board of Education of Detroit, 118 Mich. 560 (1898).

Pierce v. Society of Seven Sisters, 268 U.S. 510 (1925).

Portland v. Welch, 229 Or. 308 (1961).

Ratcliffe v. Anderson, 72 Va. (31 Gratt.) 105 (1878).

Reitman v. Mulkey, 387 U.S. 369 (1967).

Rice v. Foster, 4 Del (4 Harr.) 479 (1847).

Richardson v. Secretary of State, 381 Mich. 304 (1968).

Richmond Newspapers v. Commonwealth, 222 Va. 574 (1981).

Ritchie v. The People, 155 Ill. 98 (1895).

Roberts v. Boston, 59 Mass. 198 (1849).

Ruffin v. The Commonwealth, 62 Va. (21 Gratt.) 790 (1871).

Sauder v. School District, 271 Mich. 413 (1935).

Schneider v. State, 308 U.S. 147 (1939).

Scholle v. Secretary of State, 360 Mich. 1 (1960).

Scholle v. Secretary of State, 367 Mich. 176 (1962).

School Committee of Boston v. Board of Education, 352 Mass. 693 (1967).

Sears v. Cottrell, 5 Mich. 251 (1858).

Shenandoah Publishing v. Fanning, 235 Va. 253 (1988).

Simpson v. Bailey, 3 Or. 515 (1869).

Sisters of the Holy Cross v. Brookline, 347 Mass. 486 (1964).

Smith v. Employment Division, 301 Or. 209 (1986).

Spiller v. Woburn, 94 Mass. 127 (1866).

Stadle v. Township of Battle Creek, 346 Mich. 64 (1956).

State v. Biggs, 198 Or. 413 (1953).

State v. Buchanan, 250 Or. 244 (1968).

State v. Butchek, 121 Or. 141 (1927).

State v. Caraher, 293 Or. 741 (1982).

State v. Childs, 252 Or. 91 (1968).

State v. Crosby, 217 Or. 393 (1959).

State v. Delaney, 221 Or. 620 (1960).

State v. Ellis, 181 Or. 615 (1947).

State v. Kuhnhausen, 201 Or. 478 (1954).

State v. Laundy, 103 Or. 443 (1922).

State v. Lillie, 172 Or. 194 (1943).

State v. Mains, 295 Or. 640 (1983).

State v. Neely, 239 Or. 487 (1965).

State v. Quinn, 290 Or. 383 (1981).

State v. Spencer, 289 Or. 225 (1980).

State v. Stevens, 29 Or. 464 (1896).

State v. Tucker, 36 Or. 291 (1900).

Sterling v. Cupp, 290 Or. 611 (1981).

Stevenson v. Holzman, 254 Or. 94 (1969).

Suffolk v. Watson, 381 Mass. 648 (1980).

Swart v. Kimball, 43 Mich. 443 (1880).

Taylor v. Stearns, 59 Va. (18 Gratt.) 244 (1868).

Teft v. Teft, 3 Mich. 67 (1853).

Thornhill v. Alabama, 310 U.S. 88 (1940).

Thurston v. Whitney, 56 Mass. 104 (1848).

Turpin v. Locket, 10 Va. (6 Call.) 113 (1804).

U.S. v. Carolene Products, 304 U.S. 144 (1938).

Vaughan v. The Commonwealth, 58 Va. (17 Gratt.) 576 (1867).
West Virginia Board of Education v. Barnette, 319 U.S. 624 (1943).
Wilkins v. Ann Arbor City Clerk, 385 Mich. 670 (1971).
Williams v. Commonwealth, 350 Mass. 732 (1966).
Wynehamer v. The People, 13 N.Y. 378 (1856).
York v. City of Danville, 207 Va. 665 (1967)

Index